EXPLORER

TOTALITY AND BEYOND

THE SEARCH FOR THE ORIGIN OF LIFE — AND BEYOND

$E=mc^2$

Ssjoooo and Zoosh through Robert Shapiro

OTHER BOOKS BY ROBERT SHAPIRO

EXPLORER RACE SERIES

1. The Explorer Race
2. ETs and the Explorer Race
3. The Explorer Race: Origins and the Next 50 Years
4. The Explorer Race: Creators and Friends
5. The Explorer Race: Particle Personalities
6. The Explorer Race and Beyond
7. The Explorer Race: Council of Creators
8. The Explorer Race and Isis
9. The Explorer Race and Jesus
10. The Explorer Race: Earth History and Lost Civilizations
11. The Explorer Race: ET Visitors Speak Vol. 1
12. The Explorer Race: Techniques for Generating Safety
13. The Explorer Race: Animal Souls Speak
14. The Explorer Race: Astrology: Planet Personalities and Signs Speak
15. The Explorer Race: ET Visitors Speak Vol. 2
16. The Explorer Race: Plant Souls Speak
17. The Explorer Race: Time and the Transition to Natural Time
18. The Explorer Race: ETs on Earth Vol. 1
19. The Explorer Race: Walk-Ins
20. The Explorer Race: Totality and Beyond
21. The Explorer Race: ETs on Earth Vol. 2

SHAMANIC SECRETS SERIES

A. Shamanic Secrets for Material Mastery
B. Shamanic Secrets for Physical Mastery
C. Shamanic Secrets for Spiritual Mastery

SHINING THE LIGHT SERIES

Shining the Light I: The Battle Begins!
Shining the Light II: The Battle Continues
Shining the Light III: Humanity Gets a Second Chance
Shining the Light IV: Humanity's Greatest Challenge
Shining the Light V: Humanity Is Going to Make It!
Shining the Light VI: The End of What Was
Shining the Light VII: The First Alignment: World Peace

ULTIMATE UFO SERIES

Andromeda
The Zetas: History, Hybrids, and Human Contacts

SECRETS OF FEMININE SCIENCE SERIES

Transformation

SHIRT POCKET BOOKS SERIES

Benevolent Magic & Living Prayer
Touching Sedona
Feeling Sedona's ET Energies

EXPLORER RACE SERIES

TOTALITY AND BEYOND

THE SEARCH FOR THE ORIGIN OF LIFE — AND BEYOND

Ssjoooo and Zoosh through Robert Shapiro

LIGHT Technology
PUBLISHING

For more information about special discounts for bulk purchases, please contact Light Technology Publishing Special Sales at 1-800-450-0985 or publishing@LightTechnology.net.

Cover art: Alan Gutierrez
Cover design: Rudy Ramos

ISBN-13: 978-1-891824-75-3

Published and printed in the United States of America by

PO Box 3540
Flagstaff, AZ 86003
1-800-450-0985 • 928-526-1345
www.LightTechnology.com

Dedication

Now this book is meant for all those beings who wondered about their source

where they're from – no,

why they are here – not that,

what capacity within them made it possible for them to exist at all.

Contents

Preface...xvii

CHAPTER 1
The Thirteen Envision the Worlds Within Worlds................................ 1
One of Thirteen
June 13, 2000
    The Importance of Feeling 2
    The Vision...3
    The Thirteen and the Explorer Race 3

CHAPTER 2
The Need... 7
One of Thirteen
June 14, 2000
    The Creation of Space 8
    Creating the Vision 9
    The Seeds and the Root...10
    Exploring the Boundaries...11
    Support for the Explorer Race 13
    Violence Is an Effort to Understand...15
    Acknowledging the Creation without Integrating the Parts............17
    The Source of Nurturance 21
    Influence versus Interference..23

CHAPTER 3

The Loop of Time 27

One of Thirteen

June 15, 2000

    Growth Is Sequence Moving Forward 28

    The Loop of Time Was Inserted 28

    Growth and Feeling Are United 29

    Physicality, Feeling, and Growth Are One 31

    The Physical Body Is the Musical Instrument of Growth 33

    The Loop of Time Was Necessary 34

    Society Is Moving Backward 35

    Listen to Your Physical Body 36

    Growth Is Increased Capacity 37

    Stimulate Growth to Move Forward Again.....................................38

    Growth to Fully Move into the Fourth Dimension.........................40

    The Options Are Endless 42

    Embracing Mentality Slows Society's Growth 44

    Growth Attracts Beings from Other Planets...................................45

CHAPTER 4

An Unending Parade of Existence 49

Ssjoooo

July 10, 2000

    All Are One 50

    All Beings Are Creators 52

    Personal Creation Brings Genuine, Universal Love........................56

    Every Action Affects Everyone 58

    Look to Children as Your Teachers 59

    You Are Obligated to Love Yourself..60

    You're Here to Learn Smaller Things 62

    Loving Yourself Radiates Outward..63

    Creating What Came Before 64

    Creation Requires Cooperation...65

    The Thirteen and the Explorer Race 67

    You're All Here to Help One Another..70

CHAPTER 5
Disentanglement 73
Ssjoooo
July 12, 2000
    Disentanglement Exercise 74
    The Heart-Heat Exercise...79
    Connection Exercise 82
    Disentangling and Identifying Connections Were Once Routine ...83
    Disentangle from Lessons You Are Born With 85
    Be Committed to Clearing Your Cellular Memory.........................85
    Negativity Fluctuates with Circumstances....................................87
    Everyone Doesn't Have to Experience Everything 90
    The Unexpressed Need 92
    The Creators of Creators...96

CHAPTER 6
Disentangling Cords of Discomfort...99
The Spirit of Transformation
    Exercise to Connect to Your Personal and Professional Goals.......103
    Some Effects of Disentanglement...104
    Cording at Birth..107
    How We Cord in Childhood...109
    Cording in Adulthood 110
    Disentangling Your Cords..111
    Cord Removal after Physical Death 113
    Cord Connections and Disentanglement....................................115

CHAPTER 7
All Creation Responds to Need 119
Ssjoooo
July 12, 2000
    The Birth of Creating Creations 119
    All Creation Responds to Need 120
    The Directions of Love...122
    Personal Love and the Thirteen 123
    Creator-Like Qualities 124
    Be More Than Your Creator..125

CHAPTER 8
Every Action Has a Reaction: It's Mother Nature's Plan..................133
Ssjoooo
July 13, 2000
   There Is No Barrier in Oneness 133
   The Costs and Benefits of Religion..135
   Predators Are No Accident 137
   Genetic Advances Have Consequences 139
   The Zeta Reticulans: a Case Study in Genetic Experimentation....141
   Little Changes Can Have Big Consequences 142
   The Soul Must Accept the Circumstances of Life.............................144

CHAPTER 9
Love and Care for Others to Embrace the Totality...........................147
Isis
July 14, 2000
   The Rules of Totality Apply to Everyone 148
   Precreation 149

CHAPTER 10
Feel Heat to Learn Oneness..151
Ssjoooo
July 17, 2000
   Creation Seeks Balance..152
   A Journey for the Journey's Sake 154
   Feeling Is the Key to Discovery 157
   All Existence Will Feel Personal 159
   Creations Can Join Together..161
   Nothing Affects You Unless You Want It To 161
   Come from a Place of Love 162
   Vertical Wisdom...166
   Do Not Limit the Heat...168
   Seek Answers through the Heat 169

CHAPTER 11
Expand Your Understanding..171
Ssjoooo
July 18, 2000
    Disentanglement Details 171
    You Grant Permission 173
    How to Make Your List..175
    The Need for Disentanglement on Earth 176
    Allow the Gold-light Beings to Do Their Work 177
    Your Personality Moves from Vehicle to Vehicle to Express Itself...178
    The Mind Constantly Searches for More..............................180
    Retrain Your Mind 183
    The Channel and the Being..185
    Your Perception Is Limited..186
    Disentanglement Re-creates the Past................................188
    Ask Whatever You Want..189

CHAPTER 12
You Planned Your Journey..193
Ssjoooo, Seven of Thirteen, and Zoosh
July 19, 2000
    Be Receptive to the Work 194
    You Plan Your Life 196
    The Density of Your Dimension 198
    Gain Compassion from Understanding the
        Experiences of Others..199
    Learn Felt-Confidence 201
    Feelings Eventually Resolve..203
    You Keep Your Uniqueness..203

CHAPTER 13
The Reservoir of Being..207
Ssjoooo and Zoosh
August 7, 2000
    Seeking Zoosh..208
    The Reservoir of Being..208
    There Is No Boundary..209

Knowledge Expands Spherically 210
You Are Purposely Restricted 212

CHAPTER 14
Take Your Journey..215
Ssjoooo
August 8, 2000
 Everyone Experiences the Point of Light 216
 How to Help Someone Who Cannot Accept Physical Sequence ...220
 The Origins of Those Who Have Never Experienced Sequence 222
 What We Learn from Space-Time Sequencing 224
 You Can Focus on Everything at Once...........................225
 Psychology Will Expand Your Ability to Communicate.................226
 Beings Adapt to One Another 229
 Every Option Is Available..231

CHAPTER 15
You Must Qualify for Physicality......................................235
Zoosh
August 10, 2000
 The Reason to Do the Heart-Heat Exercise 239
 Nothing Is Ever External 242

CHAPTER 16
Beyond..249
Zoosh
August 17, 2000
 The Underlying Joy of Being..249
 The Outer Boundary and Beyond 250
 Beings who Transfer Energy to Earth............................253
 Everyone is Everywhere All the Time.............................254

CHAPTER 17
The Constant Motion of Totality..259
Zoosh
September 11, 2000
 A Call to Channels: Re-create Ancient Cultural Wisdom 260

The Present Is the Point of Origin...................................261
More Is a Constant..262
Stretching from the Totality and Beyond.....................263
The Totality Is Constant but Can Change.....................265
Other Expressions of the Totality..................................266
Moving Outside the Totality...270
Discomfort and Totality..271
The Totality and Growth..273

CHAPTER 18
The Dynamics of the Totality......................................275
Zoosh
September 12, 2000
Feeling Is Omnipresent...275
The Ribbon with Gaps..277
The Canvas of Creation..278
Need Prompts Change..280
Ssjoooo Was Chosen to Act...282
How the Explorer Race Entered the Loop of Time......282
Move Toward Heart Science..286
Preparing Mother Earth for Humankind......................287
The Dangers of Cautionary Tales and Clinging to Pain.........288
The Need for Patience...289

CHAPTER 19
The Constant...293
Ssjoooo
September 14, 2000
Beyond Disentanglement..295
Love Has Physical Substance...297
Joyful Life Is in Constant Motion Around Us..............299
Focus in the Heat to Generate Material Manifestation.........301
The Renewal of Earth Life...302

CHAPTER 20

Body and Soul Connections...307

Ssjoooo 2

September 15, 2000

    The More Is Available to All...307

    The Color of Need 308

    The Nature of Origin...310

    The Ribbon of Time 311

    The Soul and Body Connection...313

    Free Yourself from Conditioning 320

CHAPTER 21

The Journey to the End of the Rainbow...323

Snnn and Zoosh

November 2, 2000

    Existence without Boundaries 324

    Transforming Nonexistence into Preexistence and Existence........325

    Understanding the Reservoir of Being 328

    Taking a New Direction...329

    The Creation of Color and Sound 330

    Embrace the Place Where You Are 331

    The Purpose of the Third Snnn 333

CHAPTER 22

The Mystery Solved...335

Snnn 2 and Zoosh

November 9, 2000

    The Third Leg...336

    Completeness...338

    The Potential for Need 340

    Feeling Snnn 342

    The Origin of the Explorer Race Thread 343

CHAPTER 23

What's Beyond Is Present 347

Ssjoooo

    Connect with the Sun to Cleanse Your Auric Field 348

    The Route to the Higher Self 348

    Connecting to Creators 351

CHAPTER 24

**You Now Have Cords and Connections of Felt Wisdom
to an Ongoing Continuity of Life** 353

Ssjoooo

March 1, 2002

    Formation of the Global Government 354

    Connections Bring Calmness 355

    You Teach One Another 356

    Be Available at Multiple Levels to Serve the Needs of All Beings .. 357

    Creator Training Instead of Re-creation 358

    The Mind Serves the Body 360

    Communicating Physical Energy 361

    More People Fear Life than Fear Death 362

    Responding to a Need 363

    Touching Creates a Temporary Continuum 365

    Children Are Your Most Important Investments 368

About the Author 370

Preface

The book you are about to read attempts to explain and, to a degree, put an order to existence. You might reasonably ask, "What is the purpose?" The purpose is very simply this: In order for you now to be able to function in a world of responsibilities well beyond your own physical life, you need to be able to understand the functionality of creation and the confidence you need to have in simply emerging from seemingly nothing. "Nothing" is not really zero. Nothing is a matrix available to create something. It will always be that, and it has always been that. This book will explain, with some wide variety of points of view at times, those points, and over the next few hundred years, you can consider them as you blend with your total being, creating and re-creating what is now, in order to bring it to a more benevolent state of being.

Ssjoooo
September 18, 2015

Chapter 1

The Thirteen Envision the Worlds Within Worlds

One of Thirteen

June 13, 2000

Let's talk to this new being.

Let us begin.

Welcome!

It is good to be together again. We have, you and I, roamed the worlds before there were worlds. In the time that preceded our being, you and I and others considered how to write the essence of expression. We were assigned to do this by a vision we all had, a vision I now believe came as a result of being in contact with each other. There were thirteen of us, but not always. Sometimes we were seven, sometimes six. But when we all got together as thirteen, the vision immediately presented itself simultaneously to us all, and the vision was worlds within worlds.

It was then that we felt we must do something, not to create these worlds, but to provide the means for the worlds to create themselves. When this began, we then stood, or floated [laughs], at a distance so far in space that it is immeasurable by your current mathematics. We weren't so far away that we couldn't feel each other, and we generated for ourselves the vision that we all felt, which was the same. Once the vision had been generated into space, it grew on its own, not unlike a child grows inside its mother. It took time, and it took nurturing. We all nurtured it, maintaining our positions, and not long after (in terms of our sense of time. It is hard to say in terms of years. I think many billions of years), the vision became solid in multiple dimensions, and it grew from the outside in. The first stage was to grow that way, and then, as it all became sentient (all within the system was sentient) working from the outside in, then it would be the job of those within this creation to re-create it from the inside out. That moment occurred some time ago, and we are now all free to continue our lives. The thirteen have scattered to their various regions of existence and are no longer required to maintain position. I believe this is because the nucleus of that which is called the Explorer Race has become active, and this kind of action prompts creation. Now we are able to leave.

THE IMPORTANCE OF FEELING

I'm having overwhelming feelings and physical sensations that are very powerful since you started talking.

It is in my nature to be able to reflect the source of all beings to themselves. You have been prepared with ideas of who you are and even with visions of who you are, but now you are prepared to receive *feelings* of who you are. When you have feelings, you can then become that in the moment and move beyond the small, the finite, to the infinite while maintaining the finite. In short, it is simultaneous awareness and action. The being that is you of the thirteen is able now to take action while you are able to take action in your life.

This is incredible. Do the other twelve have representatives on this planet?

Yes.

Is Robert your representative?

Yes.

Can you say who the others are?

I do not know the others. They are in other countries. Mostly they are not known. In the case of England, I believe one is a noted author. Other than that, they are largely quiet people, not known. This tells you something important: Because you two are somewhat known, jobs that have to do with informing others of who is known and who is not known and so on might fall to you. If anyone needs to be seen, it will probably be you, Robert, or the author in England. The author in England, I believe, is a foreign national, so that person might also be seen in his or her own country.

Will we learn who these beings are?

There is no great value in that. It is actually of greater value that you do not know each other personally. The matrix of support and nurturance for our worlds that were part of the original vision comes from the thirteen, but I cannot believe that this is a vision entirely ensouled by us; therefore, I have every reason to believe that the vision was given. I have seen another being, so have the other twelve, and this other being is something that exists as a portion of us, but that portion does not activate unless all thirteen of us are together. Then it activates. I believe that this is how "creatorness" works in general, not unlike the two hemispheres of the brain responding well together to make one and the different veins of your body responding well to make one venous system. Combinations of things activate each other.

THE VISION

What level of creation are you talking about? Do you mean everything that is?

Everything that you have mentioned is within this vision. We do not take credit for its creation, only for having the vision and generating it into existence, which then continued to generate from the outside in and when complete was able to regenerate itself in its own vision, its own image of itself, from the inside out.

When will it be complete? You said it started to be active with the Explorer Race, but when will it be complete?

Now that it is under way and is independent of us, it will probably never be complete, because the Explorer Race is intended to be the means by which the capacity for creation is spread. Once the spreading begins, it will move beyond the Explorer Race, and everyone will begin creating his or her own personal vision. It might seem to be chaotic for a very short time, but because you are all part of the same vision, you can ultimately only create something that is compatible.

THE THIRTEEN AND THE EXPLORER RACE

You're the only one [of the thirteen] who is channeling through someone like this? Are you the more conscious one? Why you?

The others are busy [laughs], that's all. It is my job, if I want it, to do things in this way. You two have established the energy link between you as well. Without the energy link, I don't think Robert could do the channeling, because there is more energy than he himself can sustain. But with the link between you two, you can help to support the energy as well.

Well, if it feels this good, let's keep on doing it!

In time, should the other twelve begin to speak more in public, the duty will be shared by other humans. Anybody who partly or even temporarily shares the energy will become, at least for a time, active as a carrier wave for that energy. For a time, probably for at least sixteen hours after you leave here, you will continue to emit that energy.

And that can help other people?

Yes, but you do not have to send it to them. It will just emit. Then because you are working on a daily basis, it will eventually be something you feel almost all the time. When it becomes something that is no longer daily, it will gradually ebb, and you will not feel it for a time.

Now your face looks like Robert's. Before, it expanded and you looked totally different.

I think we will probably have to stop there for today. We are going to continue tomorrow.

This will be the beginning of the book?

This is the beginning. Its purpose and meaning will become known after we are partway into it rather than start out to define. I think it would be best to just relax and be in the energy and enjoy the rest of your day.

Are Zoosh and Isis and the Mother of All Beings and everybody that we have talked to all in the worlds within worlds?

Yes.

Including Jesus.

Yes, there needed to be beings that could keep the focus of this creation on the level at which we envisioned it. So the beings within, as you have mentioned, would maintain that focus even though they themselves have great insights and wisdoms as well. They have much to offer.

But they were created within these worlds within worlds? Or did they come from somewhere else to help?

It is my understanding that they were created within.

Will I be able to remember?

The larger member of yourself has done considerable work to see that you don't. Otherwise, you would not be able to accomplish your goal for this life, which is, from that being's point of view, to understand the smallest so as to value the largest.

Because Robert is open to everything, he has a different goal for his life, or you have a different goal for him?

Yes. For you, details are very important. For him, the larger picture is more of a focus. The details always have to do with the smallest — not meaning insignificant, but simply defining. For example, if you were told a stone has facets, you would wonder how many there are, whereas he would wonder what is around the stone.

I see. But both work.

It is a nice balance. The inner and the outer!

I am looking at the inner to understand the outer more.

To *appreciate* the outer more. The theme for you in other lives, even lives of great significance, has almost always been that you did not appreciate what you were sensing or seeing or feeling. To do that, it would be necessary for you to need to examine things in detail so that you didn't just speed from one place to the next. You would travel slowly, experiencing and noticing the detail and beauty. Before, it was just, "What's the fastest way to get there?"

[Laughs.] It had something to do with the Adventurer?

That's right.

Have all thirteen beings had multiple lives within the Explorer Race?

For one of them, this is the first physical life.

But at this moment, they've all committed to be?

Yes, and that is necessary for us to be able to speak to people through a personal frame of reference rather than being a voice from the distance.

Do the others interact with people?

No, I think that most of them do not interact with people. I don't either, but we have lives in this time and place.

What are Robert and I related to you? Are we vehicles, extrusions, projections? What would you call it?

A means to personal experience.

Are these means to personal experience on the planet all involved somehow in communicating something to the humans or interacting with them?

Naturally, they are all humans themselves, but they are all involved in the project in some way (the project being the Explorer Race) because the Explorer Race is the nucleus that begins the change of creation from the outside in to the inside out. It is that change that allows this mighty vehicle of creation to become its own expression of itself rather than for us to be parents, in a sense. Now it is independent because of what the Explorer Race is doing.

Thank you.

Chapter 2

The Need

One of Thirteen

June 14, 2000

When did you first become aware of who you are?

I have always been aware. There was never any moment that I can recollect that I wasn't.

What's your earliest memory?

When you have always been aware, all memories are connected to all others. When you are at this level, you see, you cannot track it that way. When you are at this level, you do not have memories. Everything that you have ever done, everything that you are doing, everything that you might do, and all of the variations are omnipresent. Therefore, there is no memory, per se, no linear memory. My memory, then, is spherical.

Okay, lets phrase it this way: How did you meet the other twelve that became the thirteen? What were you doing before you met them?

We were always together. We were always in connection even when there was distance between us. We are always in connection, but we rarely came close together, all of us at once.

So what were you doing before you saw the mental vision?

My impression is that the vision came through as a result of a combination of our energies in a specific proximity, and the timing was right for such a venture.

You said it was the first time that all thirteen had been together.

Close, in proximity.

Can you say what your activities, your adventures, and your life situation were before the thirteen came together?

I have always been involved — and as far as I know, the others have as well — in initiating something that others complete. This vision in which we initiated the worlds within worlds is simply another version of what I have done. I am a little awkward saying "I" because the thirteen of us are more along the lines of a "we," parts of the same overall persona.

Okay, say "we."

I will then.

THE CREATION OF SPACE

What were some of the things that you initiated before these worlds within worlds? What were some of your prior experiences?

One of the things we did that I felt was good was to create space, a place where things could be. Before that, there was consciousness, or awareness, but not traversable space.

How does one create space?

It is more of having the consideration of exploring it as value. Once you wish to explore something to see whether it has value or to see whether others find it of value, you only have to be aware of the possibility. Then by working together and using the facets of our personality, we would generate it. It is not magic. It is simply the perception of the desirability of it that allows it to be present or, possibly, allows us to be present in it, meaning there is not a sensation of a creation so much as there is a sensation of our being in the creation. One moment we are conscious, and the next moment we are conscious in space.

It wasn't a vision; it was a concept among you?

Yes.

Do you have form of some type?

Not as you would recognize physical form, no.

But as a spiritual form, are you a point of light or a vast thing or something in between?

No, we can image portions of ourselves as light, but it is rarely necessary to do so. It has, from time to time, been of value when communicating with species who are investigating their origins. When beings investigate their origins, they either go out or in. Either direction will, at some point, bring them into a conscious awareness of us. Sometimes these species are more at ease if they can perceive us, meaning we can be seen, felt, heard, smelled.

But if you looked at one of the other twelve or all of the other twelve ...

If *you* looked at them, you would not see them.

Okay, if you looked at them, would you feel them or see them?

No, I do not need to see them to know that they are there.

Okay, you created space — "created" is not the word you want to use — or you entered space or you became space or you ...

We became aware that space might be a good thing, and then we were in it.

Then you traveled around in it?

No, we didn't need to do that. We didn't feel any desire to do that because we are not spatial in our own right. If you are spatial, the idea of travel from one point to another point is a felt experience, to some extent. But we are not limited to being spatial.

You could touch everything within the space at any time?

That's right. We didn't, but it occurred to us that others might find some pleasure in exploring. It wasn't long after that that the image of worlds within worlds presented itself.

Had you initiated anything else besides space before the worlds within worlds?

Yes, we initiated the precursor of consciousness. The precursor of consciousness is that which identifies. To identify does not require thought or even personality, and it just barely requires recognition, but it does stimulate all those.

So out of your consciousness, you created the precursor to consciousness?

I don't say it that way. I don't think of us as consciousness. Consciousness is one expression of personality, but it is not a foundation in its own right.

Well, you made a statement that you were always conscious, so now it looks like you created something that came before what you were.

I am attempting to communicate but perhaps not doing it very well.

No, you're doing very well, is this the first time you've done this?

I have not spoken to anyone before in your worlds.

In other worlds?

In an outer boundary, I spoke to a race that was attempting to identify itself. I spoke to someone you could call the Navigator.

What about the other twelve — have they communicated?

Not that I'm aware of. The first steps of creation for physical beings such as yourselves always have to do with the precursor to what you know. Let's say you look at an object, and someone tells you what it's made out of. If you were to make an identical object, you would have to look at that object and go back in time to what it's made of. This is a general principle of creation in the physical plane.

So there you were, and you were the only ones. It appears as if you had no one to ask questions of. There was no "up the line"?

We had no questions.

You never wondered who created you?

No.

CREATING THE VISION

Okay, so the worlds within worlds were there as a vision?

It started very small. In terms of spatial reference, all of the worlds within worlds and universes within universes started as something very small, about the size of an average thumbnail but in a sphere, and grew from there. But unlike on your world, where the relative size of the atomic structure would always be the same no matter what size the object, the atomic structure was smaller. So everything was smaller. Initially, there were no beings such as you. There was only the potential of worlds and stars and universes to express themselves, but no individual beings as you understand life.

It was our job, as we took it, to take the image to its next expression, to enliven it from the outside in. Part of that enlivening was that, as the world within worlds began to be more expressive, it needed to grow. And even as it was becoming more conscious, more aware of itself from the outside in, it was growing. Picture that something is growing, and let's say a band of consciousness is moving closer to the center. If growth is happening faster than consciousness is moving toward the center, as it did for a while, then this tells you why it has taken so long for consciousness (in short, awareness) to get to the center.

There was time for the creation to expand as far as it wished to before the Explorer Race showed up in what I call the center of creation. You showed up there not because you are the most important but because your position in the center of creation was valuable when you would do what you intended to do. It's necessary that that accomplishment radiates out spherically and equally in all directions at once. Therefore, your being in the center is necessary.

So this universe is in the center of your worlds within worlds?

The universe you occupy? Yes. And specifically, your world, your planet, is within the center. Now, you have moved from planet to planet, but those planets did not have to be in the center. It only had to be in the center when you were just about there. So you gradually moved from here to there — sometimes some of you here, sometimes some of you there — but when you all needed to be together or at least to express yourselves together, you needed to be in a specific location.

THE SEEDS AND THE ROOT

We were told that there were, I think, two seeds and a root, and that they came from vast, vast, vast distances. Did they come from within your worlds within worlds or from beyond?

They came from the outer boundaries of the worlds within worlds.

But they came from within what you had created?

I don't like to say created. They came from within our vision.

In one of the earlier Explorer Race books channeled through Robert, we were told that there was a vast temple of knowledge with all wisdom, and it broke down into trillions of constituent parts, called seeds. Two of the seeds went on a tremendously long voyage. Then another being from somewhere else joined them, and the three were the basis of the Explorer Race. Is that your perception?

It is as good a description as any, from what I've heard.

But where were all the rest of those who weren't in on it?

This requires a bit of an illustration. To picture the outer boundaries from the outside in, imagine something that looks almost like veins or arteries on the outside of a growing form. Those seeds did not come from beyond that but from that boundary, from the boundary in. With that, they would have all knowledge and all wisdom associated with the entire worlds within worlds, but not beyond that point, though they might extrapolate to some extent.

Okay, but all the rest of them are sitting there waiting for something?

Perhaps they're waiting. Perhaps they're performing a function. Perhaps even the seeds that came were performing a function that is now not being performed.

I see. Do you know what that function is?

Yes. The ability to have a vision and make it happen like that [snaps fingers] is something that those seeds oversaw in the lower dimensions, which is why they've put that ability on hold while you are here.

Because without just two of those seeds they cannot?

That's right. "Lower" does not mean "base" here but "denser," "slower."

Dimension numbers what through what?

Two, three. Looking after those dimensions requires a great deal of extra effort, and because of the potential for mischief, it was believed acceptable for beings of those dimensions to not be able to instantaneously manifest.

Which is why we can't instantaneously manifest and why we have to do it piece by piece by piece?

Yes, and it also gives you a place to train. Without that, you wouldn't have a place to train in this vast creation, as you call it.

EXPLORING THE BOUNDARIES

Well, a vision is a creation, really, isn't it?

It's a creation in its own right. We had the vision, but then it created itself. First we created what we would say is the outside, but then it created itself, with a little guidance on our part, toward the inside, and then you would initiate re-creating it from the inside out. It won't be entirely your responsibility to do it, but you will get it started.

I see. That's one of the purposes, then. Did you function similar to a Council of Creators for the whole vision, as we have a Council of Creators for this part of creation? Did beings come to you and ask for guidance or ask for information?

Only occasionally, when races were looking for their roots, did they ask whether we knew anything or whether we could help them.

And you did?

We would not hinder them. We would guide them as to whether it would be better to go out or to go in to find their roots. Usually we guided them to go within themselves as individuals because more can be understood when using the instrument of yourself than by using only the instruments that you have for perception.

During all this time, did any of the beings on the inside ever poke a hole and go out and start roaming around?

No. Let's say you could travel from the center to the outer boundaries. It would not be possible to go beyond those outer boundaries. There is something like an elastic membrane. You cannot go beyond it, though no one has tried. You cannot go beyond because any sense of yourself would immediately vanish. You would almost immediately feel as if you were fragmented. It would be a terrible feeling, and it would be difficult to reassemble your personality.

But the key is that no one has ever tried.

No one has been motivated to try.

All right. So all these gazillion years that you've been out there holding the vision, you had the key.

No.

What did you do?

After the vision was created and was moving on its own, we continued to do what we do. It's hard to describe to someone in a physical world what we do because it is, essentially, not physical. Nor is it, in your terms, sentient. It is not about thought. It is not about motion. Perhaps, to a lesser degree, it's about function.

It is hard to describe it, but I can give you an example. When you dream and gradually pass through the place between the dream world and your physical life, the matrix that makes up your dreams is very close to what is beyond the boundaries of the dimension that you are in. But the passage between that dream world and the physical world goes through a membrane of separation. That separation allows you to create apart, meaning separate from the totality of the rest of the beings in these worlds. This forces you to learn, to create a training ground at these levels. So it is not the separation itself but the material that makes up the separation that resembles our nature, which maintains parameters of value for others.

The only others that you know of are the ones within the worlds within worlds, right?

No. We have every reason to believe that since we were guided to produce a vision from which others have benefited, there might well be others who will come to see us or will invite us to be present. If we discovered ourselves in space after considering it as a possibility, why wouldn't others discover themselves in our presence after considering us as possibilities? Therefore, since function has something to do with who we are, we expect that to happen at some point: We will either be in their presence and notice it or we will notice them in our presence.

You desire this, but there's never been an opportunity?

I didn't say that we desired it.

But the thought has come up.

We have considered that it is or that it seems to be likely, but it has not happened yet.

If there's going to be an incredible expansion, will the elastic outside of the world be able to expand?

The worlds within worlds? Oh yes. It's very flexible, the inside and the outside. Everything in it is flexible.

So there's plenty of room for potential growth when the Explorer Race becomes the Creator and the expansion comes.

Infinite.

How detailed was this vision? Was it detailed as to what you see now or what we can't see — dimensions, time, beings, violence, everything?

No. It wasn't detailed at all. We just described this shape we saw in space, and after each of us was clear on our description, we noticed it. It was there.

You literally just described it to each other, and it was there.

I am slowing down the process to make it sound like communication that you understand.

There was an instantaneous transmission of this vision among you, and it was there. Was it more like that?

Yes, it was like that. Before the discussion of this shared vision, it was not there. When we observed it from the inside and the outside, it was very simple. It didn't have, as you say, beings or objects or all of this business. It was very simple.

SUPPORT FOR THE EXPLORER RACE

Could you, at any time, go within it? And you did?

Yes, we could, and it is within us in a larger sense. So we could.

When you go within yourself, are you within these worlds within worlds?

No. We don't go within ourselves; we are always in ourselves. And space is in us. And the worlds within worlds are in us. It is not that we are here and something else is there.

So everything is within you, and you look around behind you ...

There is no behind. That's why I say we have spherical awareness. Remember, you're dealing with the limits of spatial reference.

At what point did you start sending down vehicles of expression within these worlds? Was it since the beginning or only since the Explorer Race became sentient?

Very recently. Yes, we could tell that it was ready to take place.

Did you want to experience it or to influence it?

I wanted to influence it in a way that would offer the greatest function for the most people. By "greatest," I mean the most benevolent and with the widest range of possibilities. The author I mentioned is involved in writing material that is quite popular and that stretches the boundaries of people's imaginations. I don't want to identify that person. It's very important to stretch the boundaries of people's imaginations because one of the most difficult problems I've noticed on your world is the transition from life to death. This is very difficult not only because it is compounded by the images given to you by your religions and philosophies and therefore you look for a specific deity, for example, but also because beings, essential personalities such as you, do not instantaneously recognize, through feeling, what is there to benevolently help them. They might follow something that chooses to disguise itself simply because it reminds them of a deity (or something like one) and ignore the feelings of love and warmth from the being that will welcome them back into the fold of knowing.

After what we call death?

Yes, after what you call death, which is really a bridge. And this has been difficult to deal with. That's part of the reason it's important for you all to stretch your imaginations. We encourage people to move beyond concepts of space and time — not necessarily to experience them, because I don't think that is possible for them at this time, but their having some conception of what it might be like would be helpful.

How did you feel — I'm assuming that you only knew benevolence — when you discovered within you this thing we call negativity? Did you try to do something about it?

No, we didn't, because we knew that the creation was generating its own cycles at that point and that it was doing something it needed to do for itself. We didn't like it, but because it was doing something it needed to do and it had a better understanding of its total being — not only in terms of where it had been and what it was doing and where it was going, but also it had an intimate knowledge of itself — we felt that it would not be appropriate for us to interfere even though we wanted to.

I see. Your vision was for the center to become sentient and then expand outward. Did you influence all these beings, such as the Mother of all Beings, Love, Zoosh, or all these beings who have put their existences on the line in support of the Explorer Race? How do you figure in with all of these beings? Do you see it and let it happen? Do you influence it?

The Explorer Race is not our idea. It is part of the need of your worlds within worlds to generate meaning, purpose, and of course, expression.

And expansion?

Expansion is a result of expression.

Did the seeds come of their own volition? Were they called by one of these beings they were talking to in the other books?

Called, as indicated before.

By the need?

Yes.

VIOLENCE IS AN EFFORT TO UNDERSTAND

Do you work with all these beings who are working so hard on this Explorer Race concept and who have pledged, like I said, their existence? Or are they doing this on their own?

We do not. They generate this entirely on their own. It was our job to do what we did, and we largely stay out of it, as you might say.

Is that difficult, in your experience?

No, it was not difficult, but it was unsettling at first when we began to experience strife, as you say, inside of ourselves. That was unsettling. We had to alter the nature of our being to allow for something like this.

The alteration was not permanent but momentary. No, let's put it in your terms: It was a time capsule experience. For a time, we had to alter our capacity, and we did this by essentially putting an envelope, or a little thicker version of our energy, around anything that might be expressing itself as violence.

Now, you have to draw a very fine line between violence and birth. Birth can sometimes be violent in its effect — think of the birth of a star — but we do not identify that as violence. It is a form of creation. Conversely, we do not identify violence that destroys and disrupts as a form of creation. That's the person who is doing the violence. A criminal act is not a psychological thing; it is an attempt to take apart what is not acceptable.

And when the vision is not acceptable to them?

That's right. Expressing violence, aside from being a learned behavior, almost always has to do with a desire to take apart and understand, but it isn't a mental process. That's why you are not experiencing the same energy. Let's say a child is sitting in a mud puddle and thinking, and he or she is slopping a stick into it, which is a typical childlike thing to do. It might simply appear that the child is enjoying the splash, but he or she is also trying to take the water and mud apart to see what lies beneath it. The child is enjoying it for its splash or because it feels cooler than the rest of the atmosphere. So he or she is experiencing on many layers but is also trying to take it apart to see what makes it up.

Okay, but then the criminal who's trying to take apart his enemy or whatever it is that he's trying to kill or...

Or even assault, for that matter.

You don't perceive that as violence?

Yes, we do perceive it as violence. We just recognize that violence is based on the desire to take things apart and understand them even though the being involved might not realize that. The baby does realize that. Very young children would perhaps recognize it as what they're trying to do (though they might not be able to say it), whereas the soldiers or the criminals probably would not recognize it as what they're trying to do. Occasionally, they do. When a criminal or soldier realizes it, he or she very often develops a separate identity, a sort of cold, austere personality that is separate from the violent being. This frequently forms the function of paranoid schizophrenia.

When your cultures truly understand that beings are attempting at every moment to understand the principles and the functions of creation, it will be very easy to treat what is called mental disease. It isn't really mental. It is a physical thing. That's why there is now and will be in the future a great deal of success in treating what was and, in some cases, still is called mental disease with drugs that have a physical effect: These diseases, these inharmonious expressions of personality, are physically based.

Although a relative might say it, the psychologist knows better than to say, "Well, why don't you just change your way of thinking? Then you'll be all right." It's not about thought. You might have thoughts associated with your actions, but it's physical.

Well, some of the other beings who speak through Robert have said that, hopefully, within the next twenty-five to fifty years, the prisons and the insane asylums will be obsolete.

I think before then. I think there's a pretty good chance because even though you're nervous (and perhaps rightly so) about some of the genetic experiments going on, it has already been noted in early animal testing that the alterations of certain genes can make otherwise violent creatures, or those who are violent in certain situations, completely nonviolent.

Some of this has gone on as tests of brain chemistry. But it isn't necessary to get into that. The nervous system and even the pores in human skin have the capacity to alleviate agitation. You could rub a special liquid on the surface of an agitated person's arm, and as long as it covered quite an area (the early liquids will be weak), he or she would calm down.

These liquids are made of what?

We cannot say.

Oh, because we haven't invented it yet?

You haven't brought it that far yet. Genetics will lead to the forms and shapes of molecules as a means to influence behavior. Right now the forms and shapes of molecules are, of course, being experimented with at length, but it's being done largely in pursuit of genetics. To do it on its own to see whether changing the shape of a molecule but not changing the expression could affect behavior is in the future. For example, a molecule of water's shape is changed, but it is still a molecule of water. That different type of water might have an effect on people's social behavior.

Well now, can't you say that normally beings who are violent come here to experience violence? So what's going to happen is that experience is going to be shut off. It's not going to be available for a soul to come here and experience violence, right?

That's right.

Because it won't be allowed here.

It's not that it won't be allowed here, but the motivation or desire to experience violence in some form, even what your Zoosh calls "constructive violence," will no longer be present. Violence is almost always a last resort that has to do with an inability to understand in some other way. To some people, it might seem to be violence for its own sake, but it never starts that way. It might become violence for its own sake after a time, but it always starts as an attempt to understand.

Sometimes it's fear. Fear, anger, rage, and violence make up a cycle, don't they?

They are faces of the same thing. Just because the world is polarized does not mean that the discomforting pole of expression is not seeking to understand.

ACKNOWLEDGING THE CREATION WITHOUT INTEGRATING THE PARTS

Have you watched all of this with interest? Because you didn't know about polarity, you didn't know about many of these things, did you?

We didn't consider them as being parts of ourselves, but as you say, watching or being aware of your creations has stimulated us from time to time to discuss whether we would want to integrate this more fully into the being of our personality. We can't help but to have it integrate somewhat since it's taking place within us, but do we want to embrace it and make it our own? We have not yet agreed on anything like that.

At one point, we had several members who felt that profound love (that is often felt) would be something we ought to experience. We felt that we do experience love, but the profundity of it as it's experienced as I describe here is only profound because you have a basis for comparison. You feel that unconditional love from Creator or after you move through the doorway from life to death. You feel that profound love because you are comparing it to what you have felt before. I do not think that it is any more profound than the love we feel. Some of our members believe that it might be worth experiencing a more intense version of the love, but after some consideration, it was decided to leave things as they are.

So, there are thirteen of you, and you call yourself "we," but there are different opinions among the different personalities?

You might have different thoughts in your mind that sometimes are not in agreement.

Frequently.

This is good because it allows us to experience variety and keeps us from becoming stuck because we are open to the new, which is why when the vision was noticed and shared, we didn't hesitate to have it become factual, as you might say. There wasn't a long discussion on whether we should or shouldn't. The interest in the new was sufficient enough for the image to become its own.

You didn't stop it; you allowed it to create itself.

Very good.

So this is like a profound psychotherapy session. All of this, everything, and all this awesome creation is within you and is a part of you, and you watch all these little pieces. It must be very interesting.

It's very interesting, as you say, because we don't identify it as a portion of ourselves, our personalities. Yet we cannot deny the fact that it's happening within us and that initially it was our vision. We have to accept that it might in some way be related to us, but we do not feel in any way identified with it.

All right, so you have said that you put this envelope of light around everything that was discomforting within the worlds within worlds. You do not experience it directly?

Not directly, no.

Would there be damage to you if you allowed yourself to experience this?

We do not know, but we do not wish to find out after the fact. Also, with the light around it, we can see things and look at things, you might say. We don't have eyes, but we can perceive things through the light that might otherwise be unsettling to look at, such as violence or despair or something like that. It would be very difficult to look at such a thing without wishing to help in some way. And for us, if we wish to help, the help might simply happen.

We are trying to allow you to do this on your own; therefore, when we look through the curtain of light, any personal desires we have in response to what we see are filtered so that our responses do not affect your world.

Well, it's our understanding that soon the level of discomfort we have now will not be there — the maximum will be 2 percent negativity.

It will transform itself in some way, though it is unclear to me how that is going to happen. The only thing I can understand is that it will transform itself into acceleration. I have noticed a similar resonance between what you call negativity and acceleration, or high-speed motion. You understand, of course, that when something is unpleasant, often there is a desire to move away from it. But interestingly enough, the unpleasant energy itself also has a desire to move away. So we believe that the discomfort will somehow be converted at this time. Putting it in your terms, we can say the discomfort will be transformed into acceleration that will allow the transforming moment to quickly reach the outer boundaries of the worlds within worlds but without permeating those worlds with discomfort and without leaving a residual energy in those worlds of what was formerly discomfort. This is my best understanding at the moment.

Which they possibly will perceive as a kind of change or of positive energy or look at themselves differently, be more courageous, and things like that?

It's hard to say because there is so much variety in these worlds. Different civilizations and consciousnesses will experience it different ways. There is a great deal of variety, so I cannot state that any one thing will be a result. But their way of being will certainly be altered.

That's what I was trying to say, but you said it a lot better. So what was the earliest effort by one of the thirteen to send a means of personal expression? You actually send a little piece of soul down to inhabit a human or possibly before human. What was the first desire you had to influence the first projection that you sent down (or however you want to say it)?

Well, we have someone who is ninety-four years old. One of the portions has had a human being present for ninety-four years.

This is just in the past hundred years that you've sent parts of yourself down, never before?

Yes, that's right, never before.

Have you done walk-in experiences over time?

No.

None of the thirteen have?

No. We didn't need to be in your world or in your worlds. When I'm talking about creating a life on Earth, I mean that these lives have some general knowledge that they are different from the rest of the people around them. I'm not necessarily saying that they know who they are, but they know they're different.

If you want to have lives, as you did, but you don't want to be an extension or aware, the only thing you can do is to future base your lives and come back to the time where you wish to begin them in whatever form and go forward from there. That's what you did. You have to look at it as a graph.

All of them have come from the future. They all root in the future and come back in time. Every life you've ever lived here or anywhere in this creation is rooted in the future. It comes back in time to root in whatever present it's in and in whatever form it chooses to express itself. That's the only way, that I'm aware of, that one of the thirteen can live lives without being, in some way, aware of having a projection on Earth, or elsewhere.

A lot of lives, not just for the thirteen, are future anchored in your time now and on your world. I don't want you to think of this as uncommon. A lot of this future anchoring has to do with the connection to Zeta Reticuli. But it runs so deep in your culture where, as has been said before, there is a progression of soul, but to keep from influencing Zeta beings in their time, and conversely, to prevent influence of the beings in your time as this example I'm stating, the being wishing to have a life in your time will future base, meaning it'll go out to a time when it is going to generate its first life, which might be billions of years (for the sake of using years) into the future and then come back to, say, your time, and generate a life. It's just another perception of linear time.

Why wouldn't we just come into this time seeing the need? Why would we have to go into the future and come back?

You didn't have to go into the future. You were going to have a life at some point in the future. Even if it is trillions of years into the future, it doesn't make any difference. Whenever that is, that's what you use your anchor as. Instead of having a past life and lives that go forward from there, you have a future life that lives go backward from there. All you need is an anchor.

Okay, then what happens? Go back to the thirteen, then. Do you feel Robert's experiences? This being who I'm connected to feels my experiences and learns — do you learn someone? Or you don't need to learn someone?

We don't need to learn, but we could. Remember, it has a purpose. The purpose is to influence, to have an effect. We don't need to learn, we just need to motivate the life to have an influence in some specific way. In other words, we set it in motion, but we don't need to maintain checks and balances on it. That would be limiting it.

So are experiences of Robert and his future-oriented past lives parked in you? Or some of these.

I do not need them. But when you or he and others, the others, when you get to that future life from which all other lives are anchored, then you might have recollection of the other lives, but you will not remember all the details. If you did, it would upset that future life. But you will remember that those lives existed.

As one of the thirteen, will you have lives from the next trillion years back to experience what went on in this creation?

If it is my choice to do so, yes. But it is not my choice to influence my personality now with those details.

So do you influence the person? How do you influence? You came here to influence.

We do not influence directly.

How do you do it indirectly? I'm using you as a symbol ...

I understand. As I said in the analogy of the dream versus waking time, you can influence something by putting a portion of yourself or by setting something up that was part of your inspiration, for instance, between a point where one being will go and the next point. So you can change the color and flavor of water by dipping a teabag into it, but it is still water.

So the influence you exert is in dream times, then?

No, I just used that as an example. I said what we do is like that. You have to be careful. When I say things, I mean it, but it's hard to describe to a space-time-oriented consciousness something that is not spatial and not time. Then the only thing I can do is give you an example by which you can say, "I understand what that example means," and then recognize that that is not what I am. But it gives you some idea.

Let me check my understanding. When we go into dreams, are we going, could we say, into the "we-ness" of the consciousness of the thirteen?

No, you are just going into the consciousness that is beyond the second or third dimension. Let's say the average person is going into the place they normally occupy. In your case, you go into the place that you generally occupy based on your future-anchored life because your future anchoring into these worlds within worlds is not a place beyond the worlds within worlds.

It is my intention to reveal new things, to explain to the best of my ability and within your terminology the meaning and purpose of existence and to describe the value of it. People who are having a good time or even some good times don't need an explanation of existence, but people who are not having much fun would perhaps benefit from having a reason why.

Then people living in 50-percent negativity should benefit?

I believe that this is so. Ultimately, I will give homework that will be designed to encourage change that can be used on the component level. "Component" means the tools that one uses to change but not the specific change itself. I'd rather give you the tools, the components, because some of you desire one kind of change while others desire another. If all the tools have certain capacities and incapacities, this will act somewhat as a means to keep mischief from being created.

Does Zoosh know about you?

Oh yes, they all know.

They all know about you as an individual or as a group?

Beings, I believe. I think they know about the thirteen.

THE SOURCE OF NURTURANCE

Who is the Mother of All Beings, and how does she fit into this?

She provides the nurturance that encourages beings to be. If there is no nurturance present, the work of being will predominate as the impact of what being is about. But if a greater level of nurturance is present, then you will identify being as nurturance personified. So aside from other things she might do, that is her basic function, I believe. She's the source of nurturance as you know it. That's the way to put it — "as you know it" — because there are always sources of nurturance but not that you necessarily know.

At this stage?

At, in, and where you are now focused.

Yes, yes, but on another level, does she represent the nurturance of the thirteen? Or is she connected to your nurturance? Or since it's all in you, it must be the part of you that nurtures that she draws on.

I do not think that this is true. You are trying to create a direct connection between all the beings inside the worlds within worlds and us, but there is no direct connection.

Yet they're all within you and were created from you.

That's right. Well, we cannot say that for certain, can we? We can only say that we each, the thirteen, had a vision. Was it a vision that came about as a result of our being within proximity of each other in that exact moment? Or was it from somewhere else? We do not know, nor are we particularly motivated to know. So we haven't looked into it; we're not really interested. We're more interested in the result than in the means.

But eventually, if I poke and pry and push, somebody might turn around and ask?

You can ask. You can always ask.

So those other beings all knew about you. Did they have to do it step by step, from a point where we could understand it, on up the line?

Yes. What is the point of explaining something that makes it sound like you have less responsibility? The more we talk about the responsibility of the individual Explorer Race member on Earth, the more responsibility seems to be present and the more important your day-to-day life seems to become. What would be the point of talking about something that's so vast that you are within, for which you might or might not have, as you like to call it, free will? If we do that, it would be to a great disadvantage. That's why I'm making it very clear that while certain enlightened beings know about us, all beings, such as yourselves, do not necessarily know about us unless you need to. That applies to most human beings.

But the time has come now when you choose to tell most humans that you exist because you've come to help?

Well, not really. We aren't coming to help.

INFLUENCE VERSUS INTERFERENCE

Influence is not related to helping?

Influence might be guiding, but if your goal is something else and someone is guiding you to do something that isn't your goal, you might not consider that help. You might actually consider it interference. It's a value judgment.

So you are putting the information out there for those who choose to find it.

That's right. We are making it available, but we do not claim to be some being from on high who is going to make your life better. If we do that, we overly influence.

And interfere.

Interfere, yes. It is one thing to have the book have energy. The energy will be fairly universal, meaning it will tend to inspire in general. Some people will not feel it too much, but most people will feel it, especially if they put it near them when they are dreaming. Some people want to put it under their pillows, but it would be too uncomfortable. Put it near you when you are dreaming. You might have more interesting dreams that you remember. And some people might simply want to put both their hands down on the pages. Especially if a portion of the book seems to be too wordy or too complicated, you can put your hands on it and then go to sleep. See what happens.

That seems to be how these books get started: I wanted to know something.

That's right. That's often how they get started. The books follow your path of curiosity, for the most part.

So that's why you and the being who is me got together and said, "Here's how we do it," right?

Well, we got together and said, "Let's see what will happen if we do this." We don't want to make it sound too much like a plan. It's not really a plan. It's more like adding something to the mixture to see what results, what comes forth. For instance, if seeds from another planet, not from the planet here, are added to your soil without generating the type of weather that's needed to sprout them, those seeds might blow around on the surface, go into the water, or do many things for thousands of years before they actually sprout. But when they do sprout, they will have an effect of some sort — ideally, a good one. It is intended to have a good one. The intention is to be benevolent.

Yes, well, it's hard not to think spatially.

You are intended to think spatially so that you will remain focused in this world. If you didn't think spatially, then you really couldn't stay here.

Did the other beings who speak through Robert know they were preparing for you?

Not all of them, no. And they didn't all know all the time. Some of them who do know have known only recently and others knew a long time ago.

Zoosh knew a long time ago, for example. Isis didn't. Speaks of Many Truths has only known recently.

Zoosh is not connected to you in any way, though?

He's his own being. All beings within the worlds within worlds are their own beings.

Will there be a time after the expansion when they go to other ... ? Well, you don't know that there's any place to go to then.

I have reason to believe that there is.

There has to be. There's always a beyond.

Well, ultimately, the beyond becomes circular. And when that occurs, it still creates beyond, but it creates it with a different experience on your part. After all, if you could not hear and then you suddenly could, that would vastly change your perception of life.

You know after you talked to me on the phone, I told Zoosh through Robert, "He's the guy who's in the middle of the circle between the beginning and the end." So I think somehow that you are a catalyst for an expansion on some other level. I think this thing is going to go beyond you, beyond the thirteen.

Well, in my experience, there is no end or beginning. There's just a continuance.

Well, if you are here too, could you say that you are the student? You're influencing within right now.

I think there's something you don't realize. You're assuming that the lives that you have functioning on Earth now in the Explorer Race are something that we are directly connected with. We're not. We have given these lives certain bias, certain motivation, and certain intentions, but we are not connected directly, which is why I say that I do not have certain experiences that you take for granted. For example, I do not know what it is like to not know who I am. You could say, "Having a life here, you must understand that," but I do not. I encourage the life to have these motivations, these biases, but then I just allow it to live as it does and without my remaining permanently connected to it.

Okay, you say that everybody in the system is a free being except the ones that you guys created and projected, then?

Free in the sense of being motivated by someone or something other than us. Free from our influence. But the beings who are representatives are motivated by us. This planet is a reward. It's a reward that allows many things; I think Zoosh has gone into that at length. In some cases, it is a reward for service, and in other cases, it is a reward granted before service is provided.

But your answer before actually didn't understand my statement. I didn't mean the beings who are on the planet. I meant that the thirteen of you had to sort of keep holding the vision, you said, until very recently. And now you're free. Now you don't have to do that anymore. Did I understand that right?

We only needed the vision in the beginning when the worlds within worlds were created. We don't really need it now because it is moving on its own.

Chapter 3

The Loop of Time

One of Thirteen

June 15, 2000

Let me show you this illustration. It's something that Zoosh drew to explain the loop of time (see fig. 3.1) Explorer Race Book I. When you said that all of the beings emanating from you who came to the Explorer Race to live among it were anchored in a future time with the Zeta, then is it correct that you allowed everything to go until we turned into the Zeta, being mental with no feelings except calm and peace?

That was a real sequence. I think that I want to avoid the words "probability" and "possibility" because they've been muddied a bit. It was a real sequence that has existed, but now you're attempting to redo it. As you know (or perhaps you don't know), the Zetas were but one of many who found that they were unable to perpetuate their species on their own.

No, that was not made clear to us.

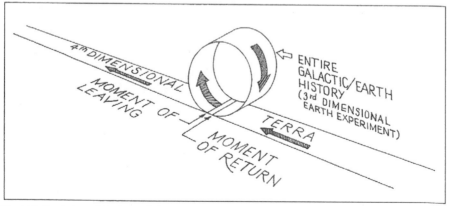

Fig. 3.1. Depiction of the loop of time.

GROWTH IS SEQUENCE MOVING FORWARD

The Zetas were not the only ones. They were just so upset about it that they didn't really stop to ask anybody else whether that was happening for them too. But in fact, even beyond the range of knowledge of the Zetas, many societies on that particular sequence were beginning to stop. It was not because they were doing something wrong — which of course is what they all thought immediately — but because that sequence was not intended to go on indefinitely. It was intended to go on only long enough to show the frailties of such a sequence, meaning that for life in this universe — let's just say in the immediate environs — to perpetuate itself, very fixed boundaries were being put into place. The Zetas were being fixed in the minds of others as good scientists and brilliant engineers and so on, but no one was making any effort whatsoever to encourage the Zetas to become musicians, for example. Now when various cultures travel to different planets and meet other cultures, it is not unusual for them to expose the other cultures to customs — music, for instance — they might not be acquainted with as long as the visitors feel such customs would be of benefit or at least of interest. You know, you can play your music to somebody and say, "This is our culture," and then at the end, you can say, "Would you like to try?" That is typical of societies. People had stopped doing that with the Zetas.

All over this universe, people were being put into fixed roles. If they were librarians, then they were expected to be librarians. No one was really being encouraged to grow in any way. So that sequence was to show that if you build a cycle on principles that are fixed, even those fixed to be the most idyllic, at some point it will begin to cycle back on itself. Cycles might go in a spiral fashion, but if there are very fixed parameters built in — even if, as I say, they are heavenly — there's a good chance it will cycle back on itself because growth is a desire of all beings everywhere. If no growth is possible moving forward in the cycle, then beings will naturally cycle backward and begin processing things they have already completed. Therefore, when races were unable to have offspring, this was a way of saying to themselves, "We have to go backward to make progress because we are unable to go forward with who we are now." So what I am saying is that growth is a factor of sequence moving forward. If there is no growth, sequence is not only stunted but also ultimately stopped, and it reverses itself.

And they just die off.

THE LOOP OF TIME WAS INSERTED

This tells you something important: The loop of time was not unnatural.

Instead of going backward from where they were, one step at a time, the loop was deemed not only valuable in the case of the Explorer Race but also in the case of all other civilizations because the sequence — even in terms of years, for the sake of simplicity — might have taken several million years to go back to the point when the loop in time started. It might have taken longer, and then people would have gone forward. But you understand, they didn't start at the loop of time.

The loop of time, as you noted, was inserted; it wasn't there. This was a solid sequence moving forward, all right? And without growth, it started moving backward. The loop of time was simply inserted in the sequence, coming way back, way back. We're not talking about two sequences; we're talking about the same sequence. So we have something that is growing back on itself. Even now some of the civilizations are still growing back on themselves. The loop of time comes in to install the Explorer Race, and it's going forward with the ultimate intention that the other sequence is moving back, very slowly, looking for growth.

The Zeta sequence or all of them?

Not just the Zeta sequence. All sequences in this universe are moving back very slowly. Then this one is moving forward slowly with the loop of time. It is intended that when the Explorer Race has that moment of expansion, that radiation will come out and catch those moving back in time, not taking them out of their sequence, but once that growth hits them and goes forward from them, they no longer have to go backward in the sequence. They can begin moving forward.

At the point where the loop of time was inserted in the sequence, it went up and then down? Or it was a circle? The up and down doesn't matter, right?

No, it doesn't matter. It's just a means of illustrating it. It's not a physical reality.

GROWTH AND FEELING ARE UNITED

We understood the reason for the loop of time was that our souls as Zetas made a decision to choose the mind instead of the heart. So we went into the loop of time to reexperience various choices, and hopefully, when we came back just before the loop was inserted, we would then make a decision to choose feeling over just the mind — both feeling and mind, not just the mind.

Yes, but you can see that this does not replace that. It builds on it in the sense that growth and feeling are permanently united. This is something that is not understood in your time. When a society begins to overly stress the mental, it can expand within the mental, like in a bubble, but doing so will begin to stunt its growth. And of course, it's seductive to go toward the mental when the physical is chaotic in a polarized society, which it often is, as exemplified by your history. You can see why there is the desire to move toward the mental.

Toward something predictable ...

Yes, something predictable, and to be perfectly clear, something for which it appears there is the potential for control. Of course, growth, by its very nature, is not about control, but that's why it is often confused with trauma or fear, but after you've done it, it becomes less frightening. Maybe you have to do it again, and the next time you know a little bit more about how to do it. Learning how to mountain climb is an example.

Now, it is not an accident that growth and fear are united because growth and feeling are united. And the difficulty your society is experiencing now while trying to spread your culture of mental growth all around the world is that the more your society advocates the process of the mind, the more the mind is assaulted by dramas on Earth. People seem to be doing things for no sensible reason — and not just violence. Young people are climbing the outside of buildings or jumping off bridges with stretchy cords. You must admit that this would appear to be not very logical. But it is, aside from these people's own personal preferences, another way of being told as a society that mental growth is perhaps amusing and certainly interesting, but it is not, in fact, growth.

Of course, you might mentally learn how to do something, such as operate a typewriter, but in fact you are doing something physical. We know that the physical and the feeling are united because feeling stimulates sensations in the physical body. But when those in a society become overly mental — now extrapolating to the Zetas, who became very mental indeed — they become stunted physically. And the physical body is not only affected but also begins to become less capable and have less capacity. The mental society of the Zetas immediately took the strongest of those left and began cloning. That's when cloning started for them. If it were possible for your society to grow or to go forward in your future sequence, cloning would become very desirable to you as well.

Some say that human physical bodies might have been stronger in the past, and there is some truth to that, although they were stronger only in comparison to what they had to do. The body might have had to tolerate gases and noxious fumes in a volcanic world that you do not have to tolerate now because the world you live in, although volcanic occasionally, is not globally so compared to more ancient times on this planet.

So what I'm suggesting is very simple, really: the physical body regulates not only the physical assimilation of growth but also growth in its own right. Think about it. You are always given the basic knowledge you need by observing life. People are born and their physical bodies grow. They become more mature, and they learn how to do things. They learn how to take care of themselves and so on. But the starkly obvious thing is that the physical body grows. That's why this knowledge is vitally important. In a time when mental knowledge — meaning the knowledge of various historical, scientific, and other pursuits — becomes so fascinating, it is very possible to overlook the basic lessons represented by the obvious.

PHYSICALITY, FEELING, AND GROWTH ARE ONE

So physicality, feeling, and growth are one solid unit. The mind is intended to be the observer and to some extent, the librarian. For example, when people on other planets wish to observe Earth from a distance, they will do so either by keying into some mechanical process that they've established or, if they don't need to do that, by keying into the unconscious — either into the cumulative unconscious mind of all beings on Earth or (in the case of a relationship between some being on Earth and a distant being) into the unconscious or even subconscious of an individual on Earth. They will accumulate knowledge (should they desire to) from a distance through the mental body. This tells you that the mental body is important to the individual, but it is not exclusively so. The percentage of the mental self, the portion of the mental body that is actually needed for the individual in his or her lifetime — including the artificial but useful levels of unconscious, subconscious, and so on — is never more than 30 percent.[1] Fifty percent is available and accessible to beings beyond this Earth, including your future and past lives, but it is not limited to that. And the remaining percentage, about 20 percent, has to do with the shared mass consciousness of all beings on Earth.

What if people are born on Earth, as your friend Zoosh says, with one life of spiritual mastery, perhaps more than one, and they come across something that their lives of spiritual mastery or personal experiences have not prepared them for? Where do they get the capacity to deal with that? I'm not talking about something minor but something significant. They will cull that extra 20 percent from the shared mass consciousness. They will go straight to the mass unconscious of your civilizations on Earth to meet that problem or challenge. Perhaps they will not succeed, but at least they will meet it. This is intended.

So if you know that about 30 percent of your mind is intended for your personal use, this raises some other questions: How much of your body do you

---

1. This was as of 2000. It may be different now in 2015 or later.

have? How much of your feelings do you have? How much of your spirit do you have? In the case of your physical body, you have almost 100 percent, but not quite, because some portions of your physical body are constantly being shed — not only from, say, skin cells or hair shedding from the body, as it does in its usual method, but also from liquids and solids passing through your body and taking, as you know, cells and so on from it as well. This is also intended. So there is a constant physical cycling just as there is a mental cycling. To give you a percentage, roughly 95 to 97 percent of your body is available. This tells you something very important: The physical is a lot more important than the mental in terms of your total being.

Now, what about the feeling self? We know that the feeling self interacts with all beings, including those beyond the planet. On the personal level, you have 100 percent accessibility to the feeling self even though there might be simultaneous interaction between you and other feeling beings not only in your immediate environment but also perhaps for some mass circumstance that might take place or some interaction with, say, the weather or the earth that you do not need to consciously know about. Even though that is happening simultaneously, you will still have 100 percent accessibility to your feeling self at all times. If your feeling self has expanded, say, into the mountain, it is possible for you to access the mountain's feeling self as well (more about that later), and that actually is the foundation for the capacity of the Shamanic Secrets books[2] to work.

So we know that you have at least 95 to 97 percent availability of the physical body, and you have 100 percent availability of the feeling body. What about the spirit body? The spirit body is never satisfied with one thing, even if it has multiple levels. So the spirit body of any individual is always interacting with others, doing other things in other places, and so on. The spirit body is not truly comfortable being exclusively personal, so there is always at least 20 percent of the spirit body in your physical body, even at the deepest levels of sleep. In this way, the motivation or the desire of the total being is nurtured by the spirit body within the feeling body in the physical body — not driving it, but nurturing it to accomplish the overall goals of the total being. Now, it is also possible that more of the spirit body, 50 percent and occasionally up to almost 60 percent, maybe 57 percent, might be present. But the spirit body needs to have access to other levels of consciousness, other dimensions. In short, it needs to understand itself within whole systems rather than individual personalities.

2.   Published by Light Technology Publishing. For more information on this series, go to http://www. lighttechnology.com/series/shamanic-secret-series.

This tells you something very important: The spirit body is not a driving force in growth but rather a form of nurturance for growth (support, as it were), and the most regularly accessible means of growth is physical and feeling.

For homework, I'd like you to pay attention to things that you learn, no matter how mental they seem to be, over the next two weeks. I want you to notice as you learn these things — obviously, you will need to pay attention to what you are learning — how your physical body reacts. Make no attempt to control your physical body. (Within reason, of course. Obviously, if you feel the urge to go the bathroom, then go to the bathroom.) Pay attention to your physical body and to your intestines especially, since they closely interact with your solar plexus. Pay attention to how your intestines and your solar plexus and your muscles and tissues react. Of course, it may be necessary to physically move with the thing that you're learning, but if it is a mental activity, take note of what you are feeling, and understand that your feelings respond to what you are doing.

THE PHYSICAL BODY IS THE MUSICAL INSTRUMENT OF GROWTH

You do not understand completely how the physical body works. Your scientists and certainly your physicians and others, such as artists, have always been fascinated with how the physical body works and what it looks like on both the inside and the outside. The physical body is the musical instrument of growth. If you made every effort (and with certain trainings, it would be possible) to limit — not to entirely control, but limit — your physical motion within as you were attempting to learn something mentally, you would find that for the most part, it would be slower to learn.

You might say, "Well, what about fear?" What about it? Fear is intended to stimulate a response within you. For example, if you have fear about learning how to do something physical, that fear is not alone. It stimulates other things in your body — chemical reactions, of course, but you know a lot about chemical reactions, or at least you're pursuing that. What you're not pursuing as a society are the actual physical motions of your physical body. How many times have you heard your physical body gurgling, processing some liquids or air? Very often, the gurgling does not have to do with anything that you have just eaten. The physical body just starts gurgling. You might also feel motion in your physical body if you pay close attention to it. Other times, there is fear for some reason, and then the physical body starts to move. You might say, "I am nervous," and you move your legs or twiddle your fingers. These gestures bear a striking resemblance to playing a musical instrument. On a keyed musical instrument, you press a certain key or combination of keys to make certain tones, and the physical body functions exactly the same way.

Certain motions happen within the physical body. I'm not just talking about the unconscious motions that digest food and cause the heart to beat and all of this but also the actual physical motions that are reactions to fear or enthusiasm or love or even just thinking about something. All of these are keying — let's say "keying," since we're comparing this to, say, a saxophone — responses within your physical body to expand the growth envelope or the mental envelope in that moment. Many times you have had a word or a thought come into your mind, and suddenly it races in many new directions. This is always preceded by something physical.

In your time, there has been confusion about what comes first, which is why you often examine this as a philosophical or humorous question. What comes first? The physical always comes first. If you know that the physical comes first, it raises another question: What about in higher dimensions where physicality is not apparent? It may not be apparent if higher-dimensional beings are unseen when they come to your world, but to those beings, they have substance. They might not feel themselves as solid physical objects, but they will feel themselves in some way. In short, to *be*, to exist, they must have feeling, and they must have some form of *something* that feeling can interact with.

This tells you something very important. If you have difficulty learning something, if it is challenging you and you've been unable to learn it — whether it's physical or mental or spiritual — think about doing it (and it's okay to worry about it for a moment, but I don't want you to excessively worry) and tell yourself, "I can do it like this, or I can do it like that." Try to be constructive. Then notice what your physical body is primarily doing. Are muscles moving in your legs? Are your fingers moving? Allow them to move, and notice what is happening. Very often these physical keys expand your very capacity to accomplish what is so difficult in the moment.

THE LOOP OF TIME WAS NECESSARY

Whose idea was it to create the loop of time?

It wasn't an idea so much as it was a necessity. Societies keep turning back on themselves, reprocessing what they've already processed. If you process something and then you go forward, you've probably found a pretty good solution, but if you go back and reprocess it going the other way, you might jumble things up. When that happens, it invariably puts a strain on all beings everywhere. In short, it puts a strain on your universe. If societies are going backward like that, even slowly, it can very easily create enough tension that the universe itself, as a sentient being in some form, will require a solution. And it cannot force these societies to go forward; it can only create some form of a ripple, as sometimes occurs in time sequences, or some means by which the sequence that is in disrepair or is having problems can be altered without interfering with the societies. This can only mean that whatever is done — either by the universe or by those who function within the universe to do this — must be done far enough (in this case, of the past and the present) into the past that the reverberation or the energy of that thing that is done does not reach into the state of motion of the sequence as it is happening. One cannot interfere directly, but it might be possible to introduce something that has an indirect effect, meaning it is not immediate, but it offers an option.

It does not always happen, this loop of time, but it is certainly not unique. It has happened before. It is a method that allows societies to try something new if they've exhausted everything else, usually when they are in reverse growth. And I do not simply mean a society on a given planet or in a given solar system. If the tendency is for all societies in a universe to be stopped or moving forward only incrementally and the bulk of society is moving backward, then this can be done because it does not create a conflict but rather is a support system.

Okay. Was this need seen from inside the universe or by the friends of the Creator or from your level? At what level was the decision made? At what level was there the inspiration to do something?

I think it was seen by many beings at the same time, and different solutions were proposed among creators. But it was decided that the solution that interfered the least was the loop of time because it offered an option without requiring it, meaning that it allowed more to happen within the same sequence (which any loop might) and more to take place. This doesn't necessarily make it so that it's going to change, but it offers an opportunity for change, should change be desired by the beings in the sequence.

SOCIETY IS MOVING BACKWARD

We were told that the Zetas exist millions of years in our future. So was this loop of time and the Explorer Race set up millions of years in their past?

Yes, but you have to understand that we're talking about time as something that is looked at on a table, meaning that the silverware is here and the napkins are over there. We're not really looking at time as experienced time; we're looking at time here as something more akin to a chart. And with the chart, we can say, well, here are the Zetas, a couple of million years ahead of you in terms of sequence of time. But they are not, in that sense, rigidly attached to maintaining their connection to you.

It doesn't happen right away, but one of the signs that a society is moving backward is that there's a certain amount of chaos. Things that had been reasonably resolved to everyone's satisfaction suddenly come up again, and everyone seems to be totally confused and upset about it, perhaps even more so because they can still recall when things were in balance. "What happened to the balance?" asks everyone. Usually, societies first notice it socially, but after a time, especially in a society like your own, there is some kind of quantifiable measurement, meaning that things take place physically that might not be considered part of your time. For instance, perhaps species are found, such as the fish that was rediscovered recently after it had been considered extinct for thousands of years [coelacanth]. Or there is suddenly more earth activity.

Societies notice that things seem to be moving in an unexpected direction, and scientists begin to say, "Well, these volcanoes haven't erupted in a long time, and this seismic activity hasn't been so strong, (and so on) in a long time. What can it mean?" Of course, individual societies will assume that it means some big change is coming, but it can also be a sign of backward movement. This does not mean, of course, that people are becoming less sophisticated but that people urgently desire and need growth. They are unable to move forward in the sequence because they're either resisting growth or have forgotten how to obtain growth, which is the case for your society and this country: People have forgotten that it is the feeling body and the physical body that sequence growth. Then things become unfortunate and chaotic. Sometimes societies even do radical or strange things such as a mass suicide, as is often noted with segments or groups of one particular religion, or the unofficial mass suicide, war. Often, a war is totally, vastly out of proportion to the original cause and motivation. There is such an urgency to grow that if growth does not take place, death can be seen as preferable to life. Do you realize that growth is that basic of a desire? People do not normally think of growth as being so necessary. They think of food and shelter as necessary, but they have to put growth in there too.

Isn't cancer a sign of that too? One part of the body wants to grow, and the rest doesn't?

Yes. Anything that has to do with a form of growth that is not necessarily good for the body is a sign of this. So it's not always cancer; there might be tumors, but they might not be cancerous.

LISTEN TO YOUR PHYSICAL BODY
Are you saying that, within the loop of time, we're going backward at this moment?

You're going backward, but you're slowing the growth. You can be moving higher in dimension but still be going backward. And that is part of the reason there is so much strife in your society. People are desperate to grow; they are starved for growth, but they are being forced to think more than is healthy for them in the growth cycle.

Since people live in societies and cannot go out and suddenly say to each other, "Stop thinking!" and have that work, it's reasonable to ask what you can do for yourself. Try to become more aware of your physical body's messages, which come in the form of physicality. Take five to ten minutes a day to just sit or lie down and try to focus as much as you can. You can plug your ears or put in earplugs. The quieter it is, the better. The less you need to pay attention to the outside, the better. Try to notice sounds, feelings, and other sensations inside your body. That simple exercise will help you a lot in moving forward because it not only acknowledges the physical body and the feeling body but is also a form of engagement.

When you go somewhere and someone shakes your hand warmly or gives you a hug, you feel engaged in that person's presence. You are important; that person cares about you and wants you to be present. You feel good about that. The same thing can be done with your mental self as you understand yourself to be. You very often think of your mental self as you. You engage your physical body and your feeling body by noticing what you're feeling not only on the outside but also on the inside. This alone, done for five to ten minutes, or even longer if you like, will help you stimulate growth in yourself and to acknowledge to your growth being that you are engaged in the pursuit of growth on an avenue where growth is actually possible, meaning in the physical and in the feeling, rather than where it is not possible, as in the mental. You can acquire information, but that is not growth.

GROWTH IS INCREASED CAPACITY

Say more about growth. Is it learning to dance, learning to do martial arts? Define growth.

Growth is an increased capacity, period. For instance, imagine you do not know how to swim, and you learn how in some nurturing way (which is the best). This is a physical thing, and there are feelings associated with it: It is often exciting, and it is even relaxing. It increases your capacity to experience more. Not only are you a land creature, but you also become, at least in those moments of swimming, a water creature. Growth is an increased capacity.

Can this also be an increased capacity for using machines, driving a car, or flying an airplane?

Yes, it can, but only if you acknowledge the physicality and the "feelingness" of the experience. I'm avoiding the word "emotion" because it is a mental word. Feeling is something tangible. The feeling inside of your body is tangible. It's real, whereas emotion is strictly a mental description of something that is entirely misunderstood by the mind.

So mothers who encourage their children to do basketball and music and dance and theater are helping their children to grow?

Yes, that's right, even though that seems obvious. You also help your children to grow when you teach them how to use a computer, as long as the child is aware of what's going on inside the physical body as well as outside. Yes, your fingers touch the keys, but how is your physical body reacting on the inside? Frightened? Excited? Okay, those are mental descriptions, but what are you feeling physically? This muscle moves in your leg, or your other foot shakes, maybe bouncing like this [moves foot up and down]. It seems as if it's a nervous motion, but it might not be nervous at all. More likely, it is the physical body's means to activate something within the physical that expands the envelope of the growth potential. Be physical. Embrace it, acknowledge it, observe it, and try not to interfere with it. In short, make an effort to cease having so much control. It is not necessary to sit or lie down at attention. These military things are perhaps useful in training a soldier but might not be very helpful if one wishes to grow.

These are new concepts. How can a housewife who has several children and a husband and a house and everything do this? Does she pay attention to her body as she does the housework, to how she feels while she's planting the garden, to how she feels when she's taking the children places?

Yes, but you cannot overdo it, because you must remain in your physical body, meaning that you cannot be constantly conscious of what's going on inside the physical body and still accomplish what you are attempting to accomplish if it requires mental cooperation with the physical body. Maybe you're working in the garden. Notice what's happening in your physical body — not simply that you need to move your leg because it's in an uncomfortable position, but whether your stomach gurgles or you feel a sense of warmth on the inside (not just because it's a hot day). Acknowledge it. You might want to say, "Thank you," because without your physical body, you would obviously not be here. Stay with what you are doing in the activity. Do not be constantly observant. If you are polishing the table or the silverware, take note of your physical body's motion. Try not to restrict your physical body in case you want to move your toes around while you're polishing the silverware. That is useful; your body is *doing* something.

STIMULATE GROWTH TO
MOVE FORWARD AGAIN

At what point chronologically did we cease to grow?

I think that growth came to an end on your world right around 1985. This does not mean that people didn't learn new things mentally, but around 1985 there was an impact from the rest of the universe. It's hard for any society — and in this case, Earth society, not just individual societies — to continue to grow when other societies are going backward. I am not saying shrinking; I want to make that clear. You're not shrinking. You're just moving in the opposite direction, looking for growth. Yet part of the reason for these books — all of these books that we are talking about and other beings who are mentioned in other people's books as well, self-help books, and so on — to come out and have a fantastic impact is there was a mental awareness that self-help (in short, growth) is needed, but the onus was placed on the mind. The mind, as I have said, cannot grow; it can only accumulate. So 1985 is somewhat of an approximation, but it was about then when, en masse, your societies on Earth started looking back for growth rather than forward.

Was this anticipated? Was this a shock? What was your feeling about this?

It was considered inevitable given that the majority of Earth's societies are enamored with the mind. And to some extent, technological automation played a part, since people obviously do not need to work in great numbers in agriculture as they once did. Certainly many people still work in farming but not in great numbers. In short, people were gradually becoming more distanced from doing things on the physical and feeling levels, which obviously nurtured life. So it was very easy to assume that growth was something you did mentally, yet evidence continues to present itself. "No matter how I think" does not mean that I am growing, but it might mean that something gets out of my way so that I can grow, meaning a restricting thought, a binding thought, might get out of the way so that growth is possible. Sometimes when that happens, there is a sudden effect, like a balloon or an elastic effect, and growth takes place.

So you might ask, "How can I grow in a society that is moving back on itself?" The more people try these things, of course, the more likely it is for society to go forward. Remember, you are the Explorer Race. You are expected to not only stimulate your own growth moving forward again but also everybody else's. So it does not behoove you to just accept with resignation that you are moving backward. No, you have a built-in desire to survive even if your mind chooses to let go. Say someone is in a situation in which he or she might die — the person fell in the water and is struggling. It's possible that the soul has already left the body, ready to move on, resigned that death is inevitable. The body, however, will struggle to survive even though the consciousness of the body — not just the mental consciousness, but the consciousness of the body — knows that no matter how it is changed, it is still alive. When the body dies and returns to the earth, the consciousness of the body remains just as conscious. But this is something that is not associated with your personal self. So this raises the question of why, then, does the body struggle so much when the soul has already left with the assumption that it is not possible to survive?

It's built in, meaning that it is intended for you to make every effort to grow, even in the face of impossibility. It is a safety mechanism built into the Explorer Race so that you will not just give up and say, "Okay, that's the end. We're not going to try anymore; that's it. Everybody, bump yourself off." Other societies have done so.

GROWTH TO FULLY MOVE INTO THE FOURTH DIMENSION

All right. Describe growth. What would it look like tomorrow if the entire planet chose growth and proceeded?

It wouldn't look any different at all, but it would *feel* different. You would wake up. For instance, let's say it happens when you wake up. You wake up tomorrow, and everybody on the planet has decided that growth is wonderful. "We're going to go for it physically, recognize it on the feeling level, embrace it, and love it. In short, let's go for growth." If this were to happen, you would wake up with the feeling that you could accomplish anything. Even though it might not be possible for you to jump out of your window and fly, you would have the feeling that you could. When people have these feelings — and you do sometimes have these feelings — it always has to do with embracing growth, usually not only by you but also, in some way, by those in your immediate environment. It is a feeling, and feeling is the key.

Can the Explorer Race books contribute to that?

Yes, because they are intended to help people move beyond the limits that they impose on themselves or that are imposed on them and that they have embraced. The ultimate purpose of the book is to encourage people to become more. All the books are that, even if people move in directions that the books do not encourage but that might stimulate them. The books are intended to stimulate growth.

So what does this do? If we're moving up in dimension by opening to our heart energy, accepting our spirit, can we move into the fourth dimension without growing?

Probably you cannot lock in. You might be able to move into, say, the upper 3.5D without much growth, but beyond that, I don't think so. Growth needs to be embraced, and it is so much easier to embrace growth if it does not *require* that you *change* your mind. Think about it: You might have very rigid beliefs

— religious beliefs, political beliefs, scientific beliefs, or beliefs that come from any number of circumstances — but if you allow your physical body its free expression and you do not condemn it no matter how it looks, then you might conceivably be able to embrace growth while relentlessly holding on to outdated ideas, at least for a time. It is likely that if you embrace growth, your ideas will also expand, but it is not required that they do so, at least not in the immediate sense.

This is a new fact. I'm flabbergasted. I thought we were moving and doing very well.

Why do you take it in the negative? You are suggesting that you're not moving and not doing very well. Why do you say that? Is this a personal statement or one about society?

No, no! Planetary! Nobody's ever said this before, that we quit growing.

But this is how change takes place. If someone tells you that something might be happening, you are likely to look for it, see whether it is happening, take note, and of course, look for a solution. So it is my job to stimulate change. That's my foundational job.

So the loop of time was basically put in from within. It wasn't stimulated from you or others.

No, it was put in from within. It was a need, and some creator or being probably installed it.

I understand that our souls also lived as Zetas, that we have lives along the soul line. So the Zetas are — were — us?

At the moment. But it is a potential for that to change. And that is not necessarily desirable if the Zetas in their own right change, which is their intention. Now, when the Zetas turn into golden beings, of course you'll want to be them.

So this loop of time was put in, and volunteers were called forward to go. What is in this loop of time, the whole universe, or just the local galaxy?

Because of the effect of the Explorer Race, you can see it in different ways. You might say (of course you're comparing something spatial to something time), "What is in _____," and actually, we're talking about a sequence. A sequence does not actually involve any "whats," but I'm using "what" to describe the sequence because a sequence in its own right is basically invisible to your consciousness. So you could say it's the sequence only, which it is, that's in that loop of time or that has had that loop of time made available to it. But because the impact of the potential effect of the loop of time will be so broad, you could say that other sequences beyond this universe are affected. However, I don't think you can say that the loop of time is something that they are actually in.

So everything we can see out there — Andromeda, Arcturus, Sirius, Pleaides, Orion — all the experience of the Explorer Race is in this loop of time but not the Zetas themselves? Can you get out of it? When visitors come here, do they have to access the loop of time?

Let's say they come from some other creation to see what's going on. Do they have to access the loop of time that we're in?

They must if they want to see you in this sequence. If they want to see you before this sequence, before this loop of time started, then they have to go elsewhere. For instance, the Zetas could come to a different time sequence and, let's say, visit themselves as they might have been. But most likely, since they're going to be coming to see what's going on or to observe or experience it, if they come physically, they will want to observe the impact of the loop of time. And they will probably try to measure it if they are intellectual beings. If they are more feeling beings or physical beings or spiritual beings, they'll want to feel it, and they might not have to come to do that. You can feel something almost without limit in terms of distance and time. For example, let's say that you want to experience the feeling of that astronaut jumping off the ladder onto the surface of the Moon. You can remember your own feeling when you watched it on television, or you can imagine yourself in that spacesuit jumping on to the Moon with the thought, "I'm the first one from Earth to do this! That's pretty exciting!" So you can do that at a distance. For that matter, you can imagine what it would have been like to sign the Declaration of Independence: the exultant feeling, the expectancy, the fun, and the importance of it. Using your history, of course.

THE OPTIONS ARE ENDLESS

Again, at what point in what we consider our history did the loop of time start? Was it when the planet was brought here from Sirius or on the first planet before this, the one we blew up? Are all the Explorer Race experiences in Orion included? Is everything that we know of, that we've been told for these books, that we've gone through to get here, in this loop of time?

Let's go forward to the Zetas. Everything has happened, but now everything has a chance to happen differently. So this tells you that if a sequence is to be considered stable, the chances are that it won't have planets blowing up. This brings up a few questions: How long do sequences take to evolve? Are sequences actually taking millions of years to progress? Again, look at time as a chart, just as a piece of paper, as two million years. Here are the Zetas in your future, and then two million years back is you in your present, and sometime back there are all these other events you referred to. But let's say it doesn't take any time at all for a sequence to take place, and time is a means of placement and locality rather than a measurable experience.

I need to introduce that to you so that you don't become fixated on a sequence as being something that happens moment to moment. It doesn't necessarily happen moment to moment; it might all be instantaneous. For example, you have two pots of soup boiling on the stove. To one you add salt or spice, and to the other you don't. The soups are basically the same, but the salted or spiced soup tastes a little bit better. What I am saying is this: Don't be attached to the idea that a sequence actually takes millions of years to establish itself; it might be in the twinkling of an eye. Maybe the loop of time, given that philosophical point of view, hasn't even begun yet, or maybe it has begun but is almost over. It is important to remember that time is a function of placement, not the other way around.

Well, I was just trying to find out at what point we came here. When we look back at our history, how much of it is here on Earth? Or did we get here 500 years ago, 5,000 years ago, 50,000 years ago?

It's very important not to be attached to that. If you're attached to that, do you know what happens? You look for evidence to support that. You go backward. I don't want to encourage too much backward-looking, if possible.

All right. It was my understanding from Zoosh that we were almost at the point of coming back to the point just a moment before we started on the loop of time and that, because of the wisdom we gained in the loop of time, we would decide to be physical, feeling, and mental, not just mental like the Zetas.

Your friend Zoosh will talk to you utilizing the language that you are most comfortable with, but I am attempting to shake it up a little because if I let you maintain that comfort, then it's easy for you to say, "Well, good things are going to happen in twenty-five years," or "Good things are going to happen in fifty years," and to put good things, whatever they are, ahead in the future and just try to live your life without lying down and observing what's going on in your body now.

Growth needs to be embraced, even if you do not have the capacity to measure it on a day-to-day time sequence. How many times has this happened to you and others? You accomplish something and learn something new, and you begin doing the task the new way. Shortly after that, you are either unable or unwilling to remember doing it the old way. That is an example of growth that supersedes time. But you see, you say things must move incrementally forward: In order to have the railroad, you must lay it one track at a time. You will have at least a rail bed at some point, but it doesn't have to be "at some point" for growth.

It can be this instant.

It can be. Your body is moving, your hands are moving, your legs are moving, your internal organs are moving, and you notice it all. You don't try to control it or to figure out what it's doing, and you don't try to interpret it mentally. You just notice it. When you engage that way, your physical body will feel supported, acknowledged, honored, appreciated, and loved. You know that when people feel that way, they almost always feel as if they can do anything.

And that's the tip-off that tells you. That's a landmark telling you that things here are never coincidental. When things seem to be happening at the same time, it is intended to show you something — maybe something about that event or maybe something about life itself and the way it works.

Then negativity was in the Zeta sequence before this loop of time?

Yes. And that makes sense with what you have heard about the formation of the universe. Haven't you had some version of negativity talk to you and indicate that it [the Master of Discomfort] came with Creator or joined Creator shortly thereafter? So that makes sense if you think about it.

There was negativity before this creation, yes, but they used to hide it in corners, like we're trying to hide the atomic waste, you know? Stick it in holes and things.

Yes, when in fact you will find a use for it. You cannot have things that exist and not use them in some way. When too much is not good — too much salt ruins a soup — you use less. But you knew; you and the beings in this universe anticipated it.

EMBRACING MENTALITY SLOWS SOCIETY'S GROWTH

Are you saying, then, that the whole totality, the whole worlds within worlds, has come to a stop?

No, but it's gradually coming to a stop. It's slowing down. No, let's say that differently. The societies that have embraced mentality are slowing down and reversing.

Can we equate mentality with technology?

Not always. There is what I call living technology that becomes a mechanism because it wants to. You join the baseball team because you want to, not because you're forced to. So we cannot equate it directly. And of course, as societies evolve, they are often exposed to such technology. You on Earth have examples of it in your midst — if they are not right under your noses, then somewhere on Earth. There are rock walls that have no apparent explanation as to how they were fit together and things like this, enigmas that might have been assembled by beings from elsewhere or that beings on Earth were instructed on how to assemble or how to encourage the rock to come together.

All right. So the whole worlds within worlds, how do you feel when you look at that? You can look from both inside and outside, right?

I feel like it is as it is intended. Remember that this is intended to be its own thing. Our vision was specifically that. It wasn't a creation as a creator creates; a creator has certain biases or intentions for a given creation, but this was not that. This was something we all envisioned, and then it came to be. And although we give it some support, it's largely self-perpetuating.

But you wouldn't be here now speaking through this channel if you didn't really care, and you're taking the effort to encourage growth so that it doesn't just wind down. You care.

Yes, and so do the others of the thirteen. They all care, although some of them will express differently. They don't all talk through channels.

You don't know at this point the end result of your efforts to influence?

The intention on our part is to not know. Evidenced on our previous experience, we believe that if we know, we can influence. So we do not wish to know; we keep that from ourselves. In this way, we believe (it may not be so, but we believe) that you are more likely to be able to do it on your own.

GROWTH ATTRACTS BEINGS FROM OTHER PLANETS

All right. So how will this play out, then? What are the two options? Let us say we go up in dimensions and we get to 3.75 or something; if we don't grow, we can't go any further, you're saying. So if we get to 3.8 or 3.9, we know we've been growing?

Yes, but it's all somewhat relative. Of course, by the time you're at 3.8 or 3.9, you probably won't even be asking those questions anymore, because you will feel so very different. Growing is valuable; it is not always fun in the experience of it, but because of your increased capacity, it is helpful. Now, think about this: If a whole society, say a planetary society, has more growth (meaning more capacity for growth) than exposure, then their exposure — what they're exposed to to assimilate in order to utilize that growth potential — do you know what always happens? People come from other planets to visit you; they feel pulled. They'll have to come to provide new things to you.

To provide new stimulation for growth.

That's right, because you have the need to grow and the capacity to grow, and you're embracing growth, but there is not sufficient stimulus for you to grow where you are. So either you are drawn to go elsewhere or, in the case of your society in the near future, others from elsewhere will be drawn to you. They won't be able to resist it.

From the 1940s and until the middle of the 1990s, many off-planet societies were drawn to us, but the secret government kept us from interacting with these beings.

Yes, but this is something different. This is something where you had growth, and you let it go, let's say, rather than stating blame. Now you have the potential to reembrace growth. It will happen again.

Up until that time, was growth a constant thing? Or does it come in pulses?

It was decreasing, you understand. It didn't suddenly switch off, but it gradually decreased because you embraced the mind as being the panacea.

So when did that start, then? At the beginning of the industrial age, 1850 or something?

Well, even in the industrial age, the vast bulk of the population (at least in your European history) was not embracing the mental. Certainly in some cases in other countries, there was more exposure to that, but utilizing your understanding of history, the universal (as you describe universal) opportunity for education did not really come along until the nineteen hundreds, when children were expected to go to school instead of being out in the fields helping. Now, children being expected to either be out in the fields helping the parents to grow crops or in the factories in the Industrial Revolution helping the parents to make a living, this changed in the nineteen hundreds. In your more Western societies, children are influenced by European history. The children are expected and even demanded or commanded, perhaps, to be in the educational system. So you can use that as an idea of when the embracing of the mental came along. You might say that it happened before then by some who embraced the mental. You can even go back to the beginning of Buddhism and say that the mental was embraced then and that the example was set, and so on, but this did not affect large masses of the population. So I'm not talking about when it started but rather when it became most influential.

I have a hard time understanding that working in the fields is more growth producing than going to school or college.

It isn't more growth producing, unless you are at ease with your physical body, meaning you feel something. If you want to move, you move. So working in the fields today isn't any more stimulating to growth unless you are what I would call a natural human, meaning that what you feel is what you feel, you embrace your physical body from the inside out, and you feel comfortable with what your physical body is. How many people in your society feel comfortable with their physical bodies in terms of appearance, to say nothing of trying to control them?

So it has to do with being able to express in the physical body, then, which means to be aware of it, to be healthy, to be free?

Not necessarily to be healthy or to be free, but to simply engage the physical body as you might engage someone with whom you wish to be present, to embrace it not only on the outside (as in wrapping your arms around your shoulders and hugging yourself genuinely, which is good) but also on the inside by taking note of what's moving around, what's gurgling, and so on — not with a cold, dispassionate observation, but by feeling good about it. In short, to embrace the physical self, one also has to observe the feeling self. Maybe there will be a sense of warmth in some part of your physical body, which is love; maybe there will be some tightening of your physical body, which may, you would say, have to do with nervousness. But always when there's some tightening or discomfort in the physical body, the physical body will want to move in some way, and then you allow it to move to the best of your ability.

The main thing is that the physical body is an instrument, which unlike a saxophone (a saxophone cannot play itself; it requires fingers on the keys and air passing through it from your lungs) is working even when you're not paying any attention. When you are paying attention, it has the capacity to deliver *more*. And that is ultimately the intention of what you and I are doing now for the reading public. Good day.

Thank you very much.

Chapter 4

An Unending Parade of Existence

Ssjoooo

July 10, 2000

Greetings. Well, we begin again, eh? I am not quite prepared to give you a name, but there is a sound that is associated with me: "Ssjoooo." I recognize that this does not have much of a literary quality, so we'll see. It is not easy to pick a name that has practically no connotation to anyone, since I do not wish to be seen as anything other than a guide or instructor.

Thirteen is a mystical number on Earth. Does that have anything to do with the thirteen of you?

Thirteen is a mystical number because it recognizes that it may be another step. The actual mystical number is the zero, all right? Which, as Zoosh (I believe) has said, is actually a circle, not a zero. And of course it's a sphere, and of course it's a tube. The further away you get from precreation, the more likely you are to see things (should you look at them with your eyes) as elongated. This does not mean that the finished product, as you might say, is elongated but that the resource available for what you want is elongated. [Draws.] This is from the side 9 (see fig. 4.1), obviously, because this is the resource that's available for that sphere, and it goes way, way back. And that is the precreation aspect of it.

Now that you're able to step back from the worlds within worlds — which overall is spherical, correct? — do you see it as that tube?

Yes. I don't step back; I *am* back. It is my nature to see things, everything, from that distance. I do not see it as a tube, no, but I'm using your eyes because it will be eyes like yours that read this. So there's no point in saying what I see it as because you could not relate to it nor are there many words in the English

Fig. 4.1. Image representing concept of precreation.

49

language that can describe it because it is less of a vision than it is a complete feeling. A complete feeling cannot be described in your terms. Your idea of a complete feeling might be something that you feel inside your body, on the surface of your body, and perhaps the anticipation — meaning in your auric field — of more of the same that's stimulating that feeling. To you, that would be a complete feeling. But from my perspective, an actual complete feeling is so much vaster than that, that there is no point in explaining it.

Yes, okay. I haven't read the first few Explorer Race books for a long time, but when Zoosh talked about the Creator going through this tube, did that have the same connotation to it?

Yes. For creators to create, they must also have the capacity to precreate; therefore they need to have vast reserves available to them. Just think of everything you see here as having a tube that goes beyond it. It is even related to the link, sometimes called the cord, that connects you to your greater being; just expand the concept of that cord into a tube. The tube goes back to your greater being, and your greater being goes back, and so on.

Yet you said that this totality, the worlds within worlds, is complete in itself, and nothing goes back to you or the other twelve. Right now you're in the creation.

No.

How are you communicating? How do you do this?

Everyone and everything has that tube that goes back. Let's say, for the sake of an easy way to talk, that I can stand off at a distance and speak or project, and that individual who is synchronized with me can deliver these words.

So can we say that every human has some sort of a tube to — what? — the outer edge of the worlds within worlds?

Oh, no, it goes beyond that. There is no limit to it. The minute we limit it, we quantify it.

ALL ARE ONE

You told me that the worlds within worlds that you're looking at is all there is. You said that if you look around you, there's nothing else; there's nobody else.

Well, those were opening remarks on the subject. I have to be somewhat cautious; if I did not indicate to you that you could proceed [chuckles], you would have been less interested.

Okay, I'm interested. Tell me more.

Everything is set up with precreation and has a potential for expression before precreation. An idea of precreation might be the moment before you get the inspiration, when it's on its way. That could be precreation.

Now take it to you and the twelve. There's the worlds within worlds, and at that time you said that's all there was. What are you saying now? That it too is connected to something, someone, some where, some — what?

All life — let's call it that — is connected to all other life in an unending parade of existence. The reason that such philosophies have sounded so vague over the years is that the concept of the river of life and other such metaphors all have limits. But let's say you went on a two-dimensional journey, and your journey started here. You were told that your job was to find the end of the road. And you went one way and another way and every other way around the outside of that sphere. You could never find the end of the road because the end of the road is not the beginning; the end of the road is where the road *stops*. You understand? The end of the road is where the road stops. And of course, there *is* no end. The reason I'm using this as an analogy is because this is a pretty good means of understanding the concept of the end of the road, meaning that the end of the road does not exist. If it did exist, if there were an end, all life would have died out a long time ago.

Why?

If the road ended, somebody would have found it. Don't you think they might have? Do you think curiosity ends at my level? Do you think I am not curious?

You told me before you weren't!

But I have my moments, and certainly the others do too. I am not curious at this moment, but there was a time when I was.

What did you do? How did you go about it?

What do you think? That I did not look for the end of the road? Of course I did. I looked and looked, because it is natural to do that. You explore. Once they discover life, what do babies do? They explore. It's natural. I explored; I explored in all directions that were explorable, and of course, all roads went out and then that's as far as they went. And then at some point, just like you, I wanted to go back; I wanted to see what happened before. In short, where did I come from?

I went back farther and farther and farther, and I did not find the end of the road. So I asked the Entirety of Life (yes, I've seen it), "Where did I come from? Where's the end of the road?" And this is the answer I felt, and this is why philosophy exists: The end of the road is also the beginning of the road, and the only way to find the beginning is to *move*. This told me that motion had everything to do with the existence of life. And before this, I had not really considered motion as you understand motion to be, meaning you get up, and you move around. I had not considered it that way. I had considered motion to mean that where I exist, I extend myself from that point, not that where I exist, I actually pick up and move somewhere. So I picked up and moved to look for the end of the road, which I'm sure the inspiration was intended to do. And I went to the end of the road, and there was, illustratively, a dot of light, let's say. That's the best way I can describe it in your terminology. And I went straight into that. I'll give you one guess where I came out.

Where you started.

That's right. This would suggest to any normal being that that's where I was intended to come out. Say you go in a house of mirrors, and when you go out the exit, you find you're in the general area where you went in. To your way of thinking, it also suggests that somebody didn't want me to see what went beyond. I'll tell you why it suggests that. When you are not on Earth, you don't think that way. You think that way when you are on Earth because your limits and boundaries are so obvious and, to you, annoying. In short, it seems that your life is beyond your control, as if somebody else has a finger on the button, and you are unable to do what you want to do to explore life beyond the obvious limitations here, yes? But when you are beyond these limitations, when you are not physical, when you are between lives and can go places and all that, you do not think like that, because you can tell that you do not have to travel in space or, for that matter, in time. You can do quantum travel, which has to do with precreation. Quantum mastery, as Zoosh calls it, has to do with the mastery of dimensions, and another way to say that is it has to do with precreation. Dimensions, after all, are just avenues.

ALL BEINGS ARE CREATORS

Are dimensions everywhere within the totality?

Dimensions are avenues, but they're not everywhere, no. In any event, the realization struck me that if I have created all this — and you could say that too! When beings tell you we are all one, it is very easy to assume that, "You mean I am one with you, Zoosh? You mean I am one with you, Speaks of Many Truths? You mean I am one with you, Ssjoooo?" Yes, yes. But it is difficult to assume, to say, "You mean I created all this?" It's hard to say that as an Earth human at this time. Therefore, when people say prayers or give blessings, they often want to say things at large; they very rarely want to say things, once they become conscious, for themselves only, because they still feel separate from that creation. That's as far as I'm going to go with that statement.

But the point I had to accept was that I created all this, okay? So what is to stop me from creating more? Nothing. Nothing stops me from creating more. How can I find out where I came from? The answer struck me: I have to create where I came from! And this is the only way I can find out where I came from. Yes, this is the way.

You came from the same place everybody came from — you, you! I'm thinking to myself, yes. But you sitting on the couch came from the same place and by the same means as where I came from. We are all one. You created this reality, and so did I. How do we find our way home? We create home. How do you want home to be? Think about it. Think about all the moving pictures you've seen, all the imaginations and visualizations you've had about what is beyond Earth, and all of the stories. "Oh, they go there! They can have everything! Heaven!" You understand? The whole concept of heaven has been given to human beings so that people would be constantly prepared for creating what came before them: "I started out in heaven, and I came to Earth. I go back to heaven when I'm done, and there I can have anything," or "God provides anything for me" (depending on your perspective). And what can you have? Whatever you want. You can create whatever you want. That concept was given intentionally so that you could create your home.

This tells me that the journey I've asked you to take is the *same journey I'm on!* Did someone exist before me? Did someone make me? No. The only way someone could exist before me and the only way someone can exist before *you* — beyond your human being and more — is for you to create that someone, because *nothing really exists before anyone.* This whole idea of space and time is strictly provided to civilizations for whom growth is a desire. But when growth is no longer a desire, then all that you experience is what you create. And the reason it has been so difficult for human beings to accept that is that they're looking for the end of the road, and that's because humans have barriers.

This is very liberating, when you consider it, because this tells you (if you have the concept of heaven here) if that's so, you might reasonably say, "What's to prevent me from creating things differently now so that my world and I and all the people I know on this Earth might have a more benevolent experience?" Nothing! But you cannot do it alone. You can, however, create the potential alone. Remember, people in this world and people in other worlds that the Explorer Race is likely to be interacting with for the next several generations (I don't want to give that in terms of time; obviously, that's a limit) are all going to be involved in growth. That's the whole purpose of the Explorer Race. Therefore, since you are all one, to re-create your reality, there needs to be a consensus. And I'm not going to go through that again, because you've already been down that road and explored it. How can you re-create your personal life? You ask for things, you learn living prayer, and so on, and the extent to which you receive that has everything to do with the cooperation of everybody else.

To the extent that you receive what?

Whatever it is that you've asked for in the living prayer. Say you want a new car. The extent to which you receive that has everything to do with everyone else. It's not that some external source says, "Poof! Here's the new car you want." (I'm just picking a new car because it's something people often ask for.) It's not that. It has to do with cooperation. The advantage of asking for things that you deserve has everything to do with people *believing* and acting on the belief that it's possible. As you know, most people are conditioned to believe that it's not possible to get that car so quickly. But there is a level at which they accept that the impossible is possible, and that's, of course, when they're asleep or if they've been trained in a deep meditative state, when they travel about and can experience their travels not only as a recollection but as an actual conscious experience. That's the deep meditative state to the extent that you can generally do it here.

So you see, one of the main things that all human beings are doing on Earth now is learning how to be cooperative at a level of consciousness. That's why teams are playing baseball; teams are trying to accomplish something, like building the bridge. "We're all going to do this together, and then we'll stand back and admire our handiwork." All this has everything to do with the example of learning how to cooperate at the conscious level.

Wait. You said that when beings become conscious, they have to literally create their reality, but the whole point of the Explorer Race is that the beings are conscious pretty much throughout this whole — what can we call it? — totality and they quit growing, and that's why the Explorer Race is going out to stimulate them.

Yes, but they're ready to grow, so they're still involved in growth. They've quit growing, but they are like a growth medium, and when the Explorer Race hits them — *kapoomph!* — they will start growing. In short, they have included growth in their potential, and growth will be welcome. Maybe the Explorer Race won't always be welcome, but growth will be welcome. Even when you're not growing, growth is a part of your extended choice. Anything that has the potential to expand is involved in growth. But the assumption is — and has been for you on Earth, especially in the past, I think — that if growth is a given, then you cannot be a vast being. One might assume, for example, that the Isis you hear from does not grow. Have you thought about whether Isis grows?

I assume that, with all of the things she's done and the beings she has interacted with, she learned from every one of them, which is growth.

But does she still grow? The idea is whether growth is a potential for you. The assumption for you in the past has been, "Well, who is creating all this growth?" That would be a reasonable question you might have, yes? And that is because you are running up against the wall. But once you are beyond that conceptual wall, you don't say, "Who?" No, no. Your first question is, "How can I do it?" And the attempt here on Earth with the Explorer Race is to move everyone past who and on to how.

When you have the motivation of "How can I do it?" — not just "How can I build the bridge?" or "How can I create the computer program?" but "How can we re-create reality?" — then you can have the motivation. At that point, the consciousness will be accessible on the deep level, but it cannot happen without the motivation. And it can't just be allowance. You might lie on the beach and the waves are coming in one after the other. You wouldn't think of yourself as allowing the waves to come in, but in fact, you are. That's why it's been difficult for beings to crack the conundrum of your question, because your question was based on why and where. Your question was not personally involved with "How can I do that?" But that was your motivation: "How can I do that?" and "How can I get past these limits?" In short, "I'm sick and tired of being stuck in this body. How can I get out of it and do more?" And of course, your natural state *is* to do more; why would you come here to do less? Why would you want to *do* that?

Because we volunteered to come here so that we could cause everything everywhere to expand, ultimately.

All right. Thank you. What's your personal answer? Why did *you* come here?

I have been told that I came here to learn compassion.

All right. But ask yourself now. Don't tell me what you've been told; tell me your personal answer now. Why are you here, now? You don't have to think too deeply, just give me a quick answer. Why are you here now?

Because I'm still alive.

That's a wonderful answer! Most people would have said, "I don't know." I would have done something with that. But "because I'm still alive" is a wonderful answer because it acknowledges that this place has purpose and value. We don't like to think that what is difficult for us to do has value; it just seems as if it's more that we have to endure and get through, and then we can be rewarded. But why would unlimited beings come to a place and purposely limit themselves? Why? You could say, "Well, because of growth!" But why would an unlimited being who doesn't need growth, who has everything and who knows that creation is based on precreation and based on what I create, why would a being like me give up all that I know and come to a place and be a human being on Earth as it is now? Why would I do that?

To get the gift of ignorance. If we don't know what we can't do, we're not limited by the belief that we can't do something, and we just do it.

But the way I would put that would be to learn a new way to create and to create personally, not just impersonally. You know that there is such a thing as personal love — someone we love, someone we adore, and someone who loves us. And then there is universal love, meaning you might love the ocean. "It's so beautiful!" "Oh, the mountains are so beautiful; I love the mountains!" You might love the fresh air, or you might even generally love people in some way (when they're on their best behavior [chuckles]). So that's the universal love. And that universal love exists beyond the school here. But here, you come to learn personal love because all these creations have to do with unconditional, impersonal love. But creations here — and this is one of very few places that I know of for which this is available — can have to do with specific personal conditional love. Although you might judge it and say, "Oh well, that's not as good as the other kind of love," (and I'm not saying that's true, but you might at times choose to say that). At other times you might say, "Oh, it has its advantages!" [Chuckles.] Nevertheless, it gives you a different way to create.

I love that. It's a new way of looking at it.

It's an important way of looking at it because it's very easy to create vast universes with a distant kind of love. But you have talked about the Creator of this universe you are in. Creator, as you know, does not feel pain and has chosen not to feel that and had to be shown what it might be like to understand the result of Its own creation. This tells you that the Creator of this universe has never experienced personal creation and personal love. But you are here doing that right now. So this tells you that your capacity to create will exceed this Creator's abilities, which is exactly what this Creator wanted. This Creator wanted you to be more! And the means for you to be more is to experience personal — granted, conditional [chuckles] — love.

PERSONAL CREATION BRINGS
GENUINE, UNIVERSAL LOVE

You, the Explorer Race, are going to take a greater interest when you create as a creator of a universe. You're going to take a greater interest in how life feels for those you've created as compared to standing off at a distance and saying, "Isn't this *marvelous!*"

But then, by extension, is every creator like that?

No, I wouldn't say that, but your Creator is. What does that suggest? The Creator of this universe is young! There are creators who completely understand personal creation, but they don't all understand impersonal creation. As a matter of fact, once a being has discovered personal creation, then in my experience, it is such a more joyful way of creating because you genuinely care; you have genuine personal love for every being, every atom, every particle, and so on, that you are creating. You have such personal love for each and every individual. You want things to be perfect for all people within the context of their existence. You don't want them to suffer. Or if there is suffering, you want it to be of short duration, which gives them a reward. And it wouldn't be torturous suffering; it would be maybe a struggle or something that's hard to understand, and then they get it. But it is not torturous. In short, you experience personal creation at the level of profound and deep commitment and love for every single being. And once you start creating like that, the idea of universal love that's associated with the impersonal becomes a thing of the distant past. From where you are now, it appears to be marvelous.

The Creator has universal love. It loves us all no matter what we do. Yes, but It doesn't know you all. That's why creators will often say, "Yes, talk to me any time you want." [Chuckles.] They may not necessarily react or know how to respond, because they won't understand your experience on a personal level. When you stub your toe, it hurts. And if you see somebody on the street stub his toe, you know what it feels like. You don't know what it feels like for that person, but you know what it feels like for you. That's personal experience.

Are there creators now who have this ability to personally love their creations?

Yes.

Their growth is stopped too?

No, their growth isn't stopped.

So then it's not that everything has stopped, just most of it.

What the Explorer Race is going to contact as beings — as compared to what the Explorer Race is going to contact as a creator, which is different — are all going to embrace growth. But things that are beyond that are open to growth, should growth be a benevolent experience, those creators understand personal creation, yet if something good can come their way that they're not familiar with, they're open to allowing their creation to be benevolently affected by it. But that's a little different from the people in this creation.

All right, the Explorer Race is going out to contact people in this creation, but when they come together as a creator, are you saying that it will affect other creators?

Yes, in this creation. It is unlikely that you will affect other creators directly. But indirectly? Since they are observing, they might be interested, but once you become a creator and have contact with other creators, your affecting them is not likely — and here I have to use terms of time — in the immediate sense. But it's possible that there might be some effect in the cumulative sense. Now, I have to use those terms because it's really difficult to say, "not now, but maybe then." "Then" could be the past, "then" could be the future, or "then" could be the obverse or the reverse. But sometimes I will use those terms just for the sake of simplicity.

All right. In your experience, this creation started as a thumbnail, and now it's beyond measuring, and it expands all the time, right?

Yes.

Always before, a creator created something that had beings in it. Now we have humans as the Explorer Race coming together to become a creator. That's never been done before?

Yes, and that's possible because of the personal involvement. It's personal as a being who's focused, meaning that you're not creating. You're not trying to create beyond this ... yes, okay, let's just say yes.

EVERY ACTION AFFECTS EVERYONE

I'm assuming that since we have free will, once we become a creator, what we choose to do after we spend a certain amount of time — I guess maintaining this creation — is not exactly fixed. Or do you know? Do you know what the Explorer Race will do after we become a creator?

You have to understand that when you say "free will" on Earth, it means only this: You are free to be self-destructive. When you are beyond Earth, you are simply free, but you do not consider becoming self-destructive because you cannot be self-destructive. Even if you were entirely focused on yourself only, you could not be self-destructive without affecting other beings without their permission. And that's actually true on Earth right now. You cannot be self-destructive on Earth without affecting other beings without their permission — you and everybody else. Everyone is affected.

Say you want something, and you ask for it: "I want a new car." And that car eventually comes to you in some way. It comes not because the gods have given you a new car but because all the beings on Earth have cooperated to bring about that new car for you. But say you decide that you're not good enough (as very often people do in your cultures because of your conditioning), and you say, "Well, this old car is good enough for me. It gets around. It's all right. I can take it." You are saying, "I reject the gift of life." When you say, "Oh, this car's all right for me. I don't need a new car; this is fine," but you look longingly at the new cars and then think to yourself, "Well, this one's good enough," you're rejecting the gift of life. You hurt yourself and others because you are all one here!

During deep sleep, we have all these communicative agreements about everything or we're making agreements. Is that how it works?

You don't make agreements; the agreements are fixed. At that deep level, when your body is deeply asleep, you simply understand the agreements.

What do you mean when you say the agreements are fixed?

The agreements are fixed. You are all one. You help one another to create because you are all one, and you are all one beyond this Earth as well. You are all one, and because you are all one, creation is up to each and every one of you, and everything that you do affects everything that everybody else does, and so on and so forth. And that's a given. That's a given all over other universes, and it's a given here now on Earth as it is. And you understand all of that. You don't make any agreements; those agreements are fixed. It's just that when you're conscious on Earth, when you're awake, you are susceptible to the conditioning that you've had that tells you what you are. This doesn't mean that you are that, but it tells you what you are so that you believe you don't deserve that, or you glorify your suffering and say, "I'm tough; I can take it!" When you do that, you glorify your suffering to make it a wonderful thing. You might even judge other people and say, "Well, they're not tough!" [Laughs.] It is because of the conditioning, you know? It's because you're being forced to do something in your physical life, in your social life.

LOOK TO CHILDREN AS YOUR TEACHERS

In your conditioning as a child and so on, you've been forced to do something that you didn't think you'd have to do. "Oh, I'm a child; I have to do some work, but I can have fun!" "Oh, I'm not a child anymore. I don't deserve to have fun." And then you do it, and they say, "You can do it! Sorry, you can't be a child anymore. We wish you could. But you can do this! How can you do it? Because you're tough! You're one of us. You can do it!" You grow up thinking that being tough is good, but that's how people can kill each other. They say, "I'm tough; I can take it. I can shoot that person and that person falls down dead. So what? I'm tough; I can take it." I'm not saying you're like that, but I'm saying that this is how that happens. When you hurt somebody else like that, you're hurting yourself first. If you are able to shoot people and kill them, you're hurting yourself before the trigger is pulled. The extension of that is you immediately see that you've hurt somebody else, to say nothing of all the people who are going to miss that person. That's a negative example of that cooperation.

But human beings can then look at their lives and pretty much see the judgments that they've made, the conditioning that they have absorbed, and begin to change them, right?

Yes, and that's why the so-called consciousness movement — which you've been exposed to somewhat in the past fifty to sixty years and that has been building steam lately (and the younger generation's taking it into application) — has been very helpful, and it's beginning to join, in more recent years, with philosophy by taking psychology into philosophy. And then of course, the next step is to add science to it, which is happening initially with physics and sciences that are more embracing. But eventually it will become less of a global study and more of an individual, personalized experience.

Children will be raised to not just be imaginative. "Yes, there's a Santa Claus" (that's an adult's creation). The child might say, "Oh, look! I saw a fairy!" And Mom says, "That's wonderful, dear! What does it look like? Can you draw me a picture of it?" Then the child says, "What do fairies do, Mom?" And Mom tells the child what fairies do, as far as she knows. After that, Mom says to the child, "You ask the fairy what it does. Let it tell you! And then we'll know more. This is what I think, but we might know even more if you ask the fairy, and then you tell me what the fairy does!" See? In short, children are encouraged to observe what exists and to report it. Childhood, then, is honored.

Everybody is looking for his or her teacher. Seek no further than childhood. Remember, you are born conscious! [Chuckles.] If you are looking for a teacher in your immediate family, look to a youngster. A lot of parents know this, but it's hard for them to remember when they have to make a living. Eventually that's how it's going to change, because what you consider conscious intelligence will find a way to become personal. Right now, conscious intelligence in your society is largely presented as authority. "This is what it's about: Two and two equals four, and it *never* equals three." But suppose [chuckles] two and two come together; they fly toward each other. These two particularly like each other, and they blend and become one. Then two and two does equal three. That's where philosophy comes in, but more importantly, it's also where imagination comes in. Imagination has been given to you so that you can leap beyond the facts, and you need to do that in order to have personal, conscious, loving creation that will naturally (since there's the tube) go back and forward [chuckles] to create and re-source creation in your own image.

YOU ARE OBLIGATED TO LOVE YOURSELF

Think about it. Religion says God is in your image, or you are in the image of God, depending on which road you're looking at. You want your creation to be in the image of who and what you are. If you are a benevolent being on some other world in some other universe, creation is a reflection of your creator, but it's also a reflection of what you are as existence. There is no violence; there is only beauty. That is creation. But if you are in a world where there is polarization because you are learning consequences and, most importantly, you are learning about personal love, then you discover that creation is the ultimate expression of itself only. You care deeply and personally about your own experience in life because you care for yourself personally and because you are absolutely aware that what you experience personally has everything to do with what the person next to you experiences personally. It is an obligation to others for you to personally love yourself. It's not something you can do, and it's not something you might do; it's something that is an absolute obligation, and you personally choose this not because you're told to but because you know how it feels. When you're doing your meditations and you are loving yourself, you feel so good, and you can compare that to when you're not doing your meditations and you don't feel very good.

When you make the personal choice to re-create your life so that you feel good, even if it is only at the addition of humor (which will help you when you're not feeling very good to feel better and to lighten up, as people say), then you are doing what you can, given your circumstances in life. Say a steel girder falls over your body, you feel numb from the waist down, and you know you're going to die. Rescue workers have stories like this that they tell each other, but they don't say much to the public. It's amazing how often people suffering like this still have humor. You recognize that humor is the link between impersonal love and unconditional love. The link between impersonal, unconditional love and personal, conditional love — the doorway, the road — is humor.

I'm not saying that your suffering is worthy of a joke. You say, "Oh, my back hurts" or "oh, my foot hurts" or "oh, my head hurts," and you make a joke about it. What happens? Other people don't have your pain, and they laugh. Granted, they do so with guilt because they feel compassion for you, perhaps, but they laugh. You say, "Oh, my head hurts," and then you make a joke, and other people laugh. That is because you know at the deepest levels now that your obligation to them is to amuse them even though you are suffering. Of course, you're not supposed to do that all the time, but somehow you know that because you have created it. You have discovered that humor makes you feel better even when you are suffering, even when you are dying, and it allows other people to laugh even though they might be terribly sad that you are suffering. Why, that's come up! You've noticed that before! People make jokes at someone's suffering, and other people laugh; it is a compassionate act on the sufferer's part to make a joke. Sufferers can't always make a joke every time they're suffering, but sometimes they can, and that relieves the others. It breaks the tension in the body of the others so they do not have to embrace your pain and take it on for themselves. Of course, they can't solve it, but they could take it on for themselves. And you know that people will sometimes do that.

That is the reason, I might add, that those kinds of so-called viruses and germs and bacteria exist: so that people will experience things together. You have a cold, and I'm around you, and I get a cold. I don't like it; I wish I hadn't been around you when you had your cold, but okay, I got it. And what happens? We experience something together. That works at certain levels, but in terms of creation and precreation, when you have a cold, it's better that you make a joke about it and turn me away. And then I laugh about it. I feel compassion for you, and I go out and get you some orange juice and set it by your door and knock. [Chuckles.] And I leave you a bottle of orange juice, with a note saying, "Here's some orange juice for you. Drink it down, and you might feel better during your cold." I realize this is simplistic.

YOU'RE HERE TO LEARN SMALLER THINGS

For the past few years, the main thrust of the so-called New Age movement has been "Let's get to unconditional love!" And I say that's wonderful, but that is your nature every place, largely, beyond here. I'm saying let's get to conditional love, which is, in reality, personal love: "I love you as long as you're a certain way." "I love you as long as you're pretty." "I love you as long as you're nice to me." Now, that doesn't make any sense. But this is a school. You're not here to learn universal principles. You know those; you practice those as your normal self, as your self beyond this school. You're here to learn smaller things, but sometimes smaller things are fine points. You sand the surface of the wood, and it's smoother than it was, but you can still feel a few little rough spots, so you polish the surface of the wood. You're here to polish. The polishing is a small thing, but when you're done, the surface of the wood — whew! — feels like a combination of wood and silk! Polished, it feels like glass; it feels like water. It feels magical. So you're here to what? To learn magic! You're polishing your unconditional love by learning something smaller. To have conditional love, you must have what? Discomfort. [Chuckles.]

Why would you see one person as pretty and somebody else as not pretty? A person's pretty or handsome because of the conditions that *you* have or *your* discomforts, all right? Maybe you're skinny and you can't stand skinny people. You don't feel good about being skinny, so you want someone to have a little more meat on the bones. You find that attractive. I'm not saying that one thing is better than the other. What I'm saying is that based on your conditioning, you will perceive somebody as pretty on the surface.

Your culture and little things.

That's right. In short, it is a smaller view. I'm not saying it's better, but it's what you're here to learn. That's another reason why life does not last long here: You're not here to learn it *instead of* unconditional love; you're here to learn it so that you can *add* it to unconditional love so that you then know personal love and can experience other beings personally. Why do you think men and women come together to have sex? It's very personal. Look at life, and you will see how personal everything is. Even people who don't like to go out of their apartments have to interact with other people or they starve to death. You are forced to be personal. You are born through somebody; how much more personal can things be?

So are you saying, then, that people who go away from that level of personal interaction — as you said, the whole New Age movement is attempting to learn unconditional love, loving everyone.

Yes, but you understand that I'm using the New Age movement that way. Ultimately, what people really want to do is to remind themselves that universal love exists so that they can love one another at least in their group. In reality, they need to do this: They need to learn what individual, personal love (IPL) is all about. They need to learn that, and that's why they're here. It's okay to remind yourself what universal love is about, but that's not why you're here. That's perfectly all right.

LOVING YOURSELF RADIATES OUTWARD

So are people who run off to become monks in caves abdicating their lessons and choosing not to?

Most people don't do that anymore. Usually, people who, as you say, run off — and only in the specific example you gave me, all right? — to be monks in caves would do that because their lives are unacceptable, and they need to find something else. They think the best way to do that is to remove as much distraction from their lives as possible. Since very few people do that, it does not mean that they are abdicating their responsibilities, because their whole intention is to calm themselves down, come to peace, and feel better about themselves, and when they do that, they tend to radiate that.

Everything that you are, you radiate all the time. So if you're punishing yourself and being unkind to yourself and humiliating and harming yourself, even without intending to, you radiate that out into the general population and you make it more available for everybody else! That's very important. That's why loving yourself is so important, because then that radiates. You cannot help but radiate; you are a radiating being.

So that's how we hurt others when we suffer. That's very important.

It is very important. It doesn't mean that people should be blamed and vilified for suffering. Obviously, if somebody's going by in the drainage ditch —"Help! Help! Help! Help!" — you rescue that person. You don't say, "You idiot! Drown!" [Laughs.] You don't do that. You don't blame that person; you help him or her. You want that person to be able to breathe and enjoy life, and it's to your advantage to rescue him or her. And it's to that person's advantage to enjoy and appreciate and love life. He or she was rescued. "Oh, I can breathe! Thank you, thank you!" Mostly, those you help will embrace life; they're happy again, and they radiate that. You can't help but radiate.

It's easy to forget. Earlier somebody said that's how everyone all over all the other creations knew how the Explorer Race was doing because we radiated.

That's right, it's easy to forget. But remember that we're talking about personal experience here. You might ask, "So you mean to say that I, as an individual on Earth, am here to learn what it is I'm trying to get away from?" [Laughs.] And I say yes, and that's why you don't stay here very long, because it's school. They don't send you here for a thousand years; it's a short life. You desire to create the life longer, but you're obviously not going to want that. In the coming years, it will be medically possible to extend life to, say, 175 years, and a lot of people will say, "Well, let's just do that for everybody." But it might be better to make it available to those people who would want to extend their lives. Say someone is suffering and crippled up and so on. He or she might think, "Do I want another hundred years of this? No, thank you!" [Chuckles.] But if somebody's life is wonderful, if he or she likes something about life, if life is great and he or she thinks that can continue, that person might think, "Oh, hey, I'll take another twenty-five of this, thank you very much! Drop my coin in the slot, take the shot, and oh, thank you!"

[Laughs.] I had a conversation with the being who set up the planned obsolescence of the bodies we inhabit here, and I asked him how I could stay younger longer. He was outraged that I wanted to skip old age. He said that each segment, each cycle, was planned as an experience, and it was part of the reason we came here, to be a baby and a child and an adolescent and a young adult and, you know, that old age was one of the learning experiences. And why would I ever want to miss that experience?

That's right. It's all part of a master plan.

CREATING WHAT CAME BEFORE

When you went on this journey of exploration that you discussed earlier, were the other twelve beings there with you, or were they coming and going?

We are all one, and I — as you understand yourself to be, as an individual — could not go on this journey without their total, complete cooperation. We all went. Although some of them were less interested, they went. They appreciated my awareness once I realized that it was up to me to create what came before me. [Chuckles.] And they wondered why (as much as you wonder at this level).

They were curious (not enough to ask, but of course, everything they were curious about, I became aware of) why that made a difference to me. And I told them that I didn't have an explanation for that, but in those days (to put it in terms of time), I didn't have an explanation for why curiosity would ever be needed. [Chuckles.] But look at your world! Where would you be in terms of exploring, of being the Explorer Race, if it weren't for curiosity? Obviously, you wouldn't exist. But I didn't think about that then. I just said, "Well, that's how I am!"

This was before you visualized the worlds within worlds, so you had to have that in you. That had to be stimulated so that it would be in you and part of that first creation, correct?

Yes, that's right, everything had to be within all of us in some way. It was just apparently — how can we say? — my job to express that. I will mention that after we went on that journey and my curiosity was satiated, other beings started expressing some feeling as well, because curiosity is a feeling. And I won't go into all of that because basically, you could just list feelings that you know. But I thought it was interesting because I didn't consider that it was any leadership on my part; it's just that this was the starting point of the long journey that never ends. In short, I saw it as a picture around the circle.

CREATION REQUIRES COOPERATION

Would you say that all feelings that are known within all creation were stimulated in the thirteen of you?

No. If I said that, then I would be removing the inclusion of all beings everywhere. You could reasonably ask, "Well, if that happened to you then, before the worlds within worlds, before the totality was created, where were those beings who were yet to come? Where were those universes? Where were they all? Were they from us?" I'm going to tell you something now that may be a little hard to take: None of the beings who exist in the worlds within worlds came from us, nor did they come from without us. If we are all one, you have to ask yourself whether we were any greater or lesser in terms of the sum, the total sum of our being, before you tangibly existed.

I'm not talking about just your physical bodies; I'm talking about your definable immortal personalities. This can be answered only by you creating the answer. The reason you are here is to learn a new way of creation that you will choose to use when you wish to. And that is, ultimately, the answer to all the grander questions, meaning all the vaster questions. And it is sometimes the answer to individual, personal things. Living in the material world that you are living in now, as you see it, you could very easily say that it is possible to get that new car by willing it: "I'm going to get that new car!" But will, as you call it, still has everything to do with the cooperation of others. As a soldier, you might say, "I'm going to bring my unit up to the top of that hill; we're going to fight our way up to the top of that hill!" Everyone who dies to get you to the top of that hill cooperated with you. I grant that is an unpleasant example, but it is not an atypical example in the world in which you live at this time.

Have you looked into the totality and seen feelings or thoughts or behaviors that you were surprised at or that you never felt or saw or thought yourself or among the thirteen?

I have to admit that surprise is something that one of the other twelve brought up. I now understand surprise, you know. Ha! I understand surprise. But have I ever looked and seen or felt something that was a surprise to me? No. And that, you understand, is the motivation that utilizes curiosity. Curiosity wants to know what's on the other side of the door. So I'm curious; I want to know what's on the other side of the door, but I want to be pleasantly surprised. I don't wish to be unpleasantly surprised. But no, I have not. My motivation, however, in the search that I made, was to find the other side of the door. And the motivation of the other being I'm talking about for coming with me was to enjoy the pleasant surprise. But no, I have not.

The other being, or beings?

Well, since we're breaking them into twelve, I'm saying one of the other beings. That being's motivation was to experience pleasant surprise. And of course, it would be pleasant anyway, but I'm saying for the sake of making the experience diminutive so that it makes sense in a linear world. Even the little bump in the wood has to cooperate in the polishing. That little bump goes somewhere. Why does it allow itself to be removed? Because it's cooperating. You might say, "No, no, it allows itself to be removed because we're polishing it; it can't withstand being polished." But suppose it didn't want to go somewhere else. Suppose it had the capacity to resist, and you could polish till you were blue in the face, but you'd always feel that bump. Even if an instrument told you it wasn't there anymore, when you run your hand across that wood — whoop, there it is! You might even polish it below the surface so that there's actually a depression there, but you'd still feel the bump. [Chuckles.]

So everything everywhere cooperates with everything else, right now and always, and that level of cooperation is so profoundly easy to forget when you're living in the school that you're living in right now. It's so easy to forget that because you're surrounded by what appears to be a lack of cooperation. But given your actual feelings based on how you've been conditioned, if you've been conditioned to believe, at the very least, that your world is limited and you could only have what you can have, that's what you're going to believe, unless as an adult you choose to make the effort to change that. And that's the effort that you and all of the readers are making now.

THE THIRTEEN AND THE EXPLORER RACE

The thirteen of you have a creation, an extension, a projection, now of you on Earth, which says to me that the Explorer Race is awesomely important. There is no place else within the totality that you would have extensions of yourself at this time.

If I might make a joke, not that I'm aware of!

When did all of you first put this much attention on Earth, on the Explorer Race?

You know, when you breathe, you're not consciously creating the air that you're breathing. If someone points out to you that you're breathing, you might for a moment become aware of your breath, but you're not mentally creating the air. So I first became aware that I might be going to speak through somebody when I did. But it was something I didn't have to be aware of until, in the case of the example here, someone pointed out to me that I was breathing. I then became aware of my breath. It was the same thing for speaking. I wasn't experiencing it any more than I experience anything else, let's say, for the sake of context, until it began to happen. For example, let's say you want rain. You're waiting for rain, but you can't *will* it to rain; it's going to rain when it's going to rain. After a while, you forget that you're waiting for rain, and then suddenly — whoop! — there's a drop. And then you become aware: "Oh yes, I want it to rain!" [Chuckles.] So it's not that I forget; it's that my attention is somewhere else.

Well then, when was your attention first here? When was the desire to do this or the need? When did you see the need to do it?

No, that's not it. For me to have that motivation, that desire to do it, I would have to be doing something that affects others without their cooperation. No. Say, you're a parent, and your child says, "Gee, it's raining; I wish it were sunny." And you acknowledge that. You nod and say, "Hmm." Of course, you're enjoying the rain. You can't honestly say, "Gee, so do I," or if you want to be slightly dishonest, say, "Oh, I wish it were too," but secretly you're enjoying the rain. That doesn't mean that I wasn't prepared to do it. It means that what I am always prepared to do was suddenly desired by all of those who want to hear it and, in this specific mechanism, those who choose to participate in the actual mechanism, which is the channel and the ground; let's call it that. I don't like to identify you in that electrical terminology, because it would be very easy for you to say, "Well, anybody can be the ground," and then I have to come back and say, no, only *you* can do this because this is something you made available as part of your potential. And when you make it available as part of your potential, it means that all other things have to happen that would allow this to take place. In short, you say you're including that as your potential, but all kinds of other stuff has to happen: Robert and you have to meet, Robert has to be a channel, you have to be bountifully curious and do something with the information, and so on and so forth.

All right. What was the motivation of the other twelve beings to have someone on Earth at this time? What's the word? "Projection?" "Creation?" "Extension?" "Life?"

Any of those. Their motivation was not a motivation so much as an allowance. They are conscious, of course, of everything I'm saying and doing right now. You might see a flower and smell it and experience it and appreciate it, and you might smile a little bit. It's like that. It's not a motivation. They're not going to stamp their feet, as it were, and say no! [Chuckles.]

Are you saying that the need of the Explorer Race pulled this from the thirteen beings? Can you say it like that?

I think that's a good way to say it. You can say that the need created a response. Someone comes up to you and says, "Gee, I'm hungry," and you say, "Oh, here; I have an apple right here, and I really am not hungry myself." Earth was going through so much, and it was like almost crying out for something.

What is the benefit the other twelve who put beings on Earth to Earth? Is it the energy that they bring?.

Oh, they are no different from me when you line us up as individuals (I'm calling them individuals for the sake of understanding).

But they're not channeling through anyone.

But they are! They're channeling through someone just as much as I am. You understand, you are in a world of individuals, and your tendency is to say *you* and *me*. So of course, if I say that there are twelve more of us here, you're going to say, "Okay, there are thirteen of you." But from my perspective, we're all one.

I'm not making my question clear. I'm so sorry. The thirteen of you are channeling through Robert, but the other twelve have beings here on the planet, and I'm assuming that they're not being channeled. But are they bringing some energy? What is the benefit to the Explorer Race or to Earth of the other twelve? I'm not discounting anything; I'm just saying that the other twelve are not acting as channels.

Correct.

But there is obviously a benefit to Earth and to the Explorer Race for these beings being here ...

No greater than or less than any ant or fly or human being anywhere. We are all one. If you eliminate even one of the other twelve, we — everyone — will be, at the very least, different.

What need do they fulfill?

What need to Earth people are they fulfilling? They are part of the one. I understand what you're saying. You're trying to say, "But what are they *doing* other than being part of the one?" I'm not aware that they're doing anything other than existing.

They responded to a need. What was that need? What was the need of the Explorer Race that caused them, suddenly, for the first time ever anywhere, to all be on the same planet at the same time? What was the need they were responding to?

The Explorer Race's needs to create, to understand. You're learning a new version of creation. In short, you needed something. And given your process [see previous Explorer Race books] of going out farther and farther and farther to talk to different beings, we were farther out — we're far out [chuckles] — and speaking about us as a totality, we were available. And were we going to say no, sorry?

All right, I'm still not getting an answer.

Rephrase your question.

What are the extensions of the thirteen radiating that is of value to the Explorer Race and to the totality

I have, in fact, answered the question by simply not saying anything. You want me to define it in a word? I could say, "nothing," but I can't say, "nothing" and be honest, because you would discount their existence. You're saying, "I grant that you're all one, that we're all one, and that all of us together are all one, but what are they *doing* for us?" You're speaking through Robert. "What are the others doing for us?" Is that what you're saying?

Yes.

[Pause.] And that's my answer. Aside from being, they are not doing.

What is their beingness contributing to the Explorer Race?

If you are going to push this to the nth degree, I will say they are allowing the process to go forward, the Explorer Race's process. They are not interfering with it, nor are they trying to create it to be something other than what it's creating itself to be. So they're allowing it. How's that?

But they're here. They're no place else. They're here, all of them.

But everything is here. The outer boundaries of your universe, all right, or if you prefer, the outer boundaries of the farthest universe from you, all of those beings are participating on the cooperative level of creation with you right now. Everything everywhere, without exception, is cooperating in everything that you do right now, here, and in everything that everybody else does. And of course, conversely, everything that they do, you are cooperating with. If you are one, you can't eliminate anything from the one. If you're looking for what's motivating everything else, then you're all motivating it. We're all motivating it; everyone is motivating it. We're all one, but we're different only in the way we define ourselves, and that changes from moment to moment, though the change will be a reflection of what some other portion of the one is. If you think of it as a big ball, that helps.

So the totality is a big sphere.

It is for this example. I'm not saying that if you stood back far enough, you would see it. Of course, you can't stand back far enough, because you're part of it. But theoretically, if you were to, on a quantifying basis, say what it looks like, it doesn't necessarily look like a ball. But for the sake of the example, it's easier to understand a ball because you're born and raised with balls around you. You know what a sphere is, so it's easier to understand it that way.

Okay. So every bit of life force and consciousness within the sphere is cooperating with the experiment of the Explorer Race, is what you're saying.

Yes. And I'm saying that (I wouldn't normally say this) because you are asking what the others are doing. But it's important to broaden your question. To say, "What are the others doing?" is like saying, "Well, is somebody ..." It individuates them in a way that says they're different. The main difference between them and you is that they know, and right now you consciously do not know. But that's it. The body, the physical body, is your temporary vehicle, that's all, which you are personally choosing right now so that you can learn little things. Not little meaning less important, but little meaning that they are details that are very important and will have a profound effect on the bigger picture.

On our ability to create the details in the bigger picture lovingly?

You could say that. Yes, you could say it that way, lovingly in the personal and impersonal way.

YOU'RE ALL HERE TO HELP ONE ANOTHER

You are very patient with all my questions.

Well, one of the most profound realizations that any human being can have on Earth is something that is so patently obvious that it strikes you as humorous when you realize it. Yet people have very often been conditioned — not everyone, but very often — to feel bad about it; they'd rather die than to do it. And that's when you ask for help. When you ask any other person to help you, you are living up to your obligations because you are bringing to consciousness your awareness that you're all here to help one another. Now, the other person may not necessarily give you help. But it's not about what they do; it's about what you do. If you say, "Help me," then you are. The precondition to that question is not only that you are acknowledging that other people can help you but, more importantly, that you are acknowledging the oneness. You might get some pleasure out of helping somebody else. "Oh, I can't find my way. Do you know how to get to such and such?" "Oh yes, just down there, turn right and left, and you'll get there." "Oh, thank you!" It means so much to that person. To you, it's nothing, but it gives you minor pleasure. "I helped someone out." But for you to say, "I can't find my way!" in a nice way [chuckles], not, "I can't find my way!" meaning you're revealing your sense of personal failure. "There's something wrong with me. I hate that about myself," you say, the human being. "I hate that about myself, that I can't find my own way. Will you help me to get there? I'm already mad at you for helping me, even though you haven't helped me yet." You're defeating your obligation; your obligation is to help one another.

You've brought up some extraordinary new points today. It's wonderful.

Let's end on that point for today and continue — what would Zoosh say? — rambling on tomorrow.

Yes.

[Publisher's Note: This series of questions was based on my misunderstanding of something Ssjoooo said that I took to mean that the other twelve personalities of the group were actually physically incarnated on Earth, and I was trying to find out what they were doing and who they were on the Earth. Such a misunderstanding would normally be taken out of the text because it is confusing, but we are leaving it in here because his answers are so interesting and loving.]

Chapter 5

Disentanglement

Ssjoooo

July 12, 2000

Let us proceed. Robert has requested some homework here, and I think that the timing is appropriate. Robert has been doing a process that is called disentanglement. We talked about precreation. To talk about disentanglement, let's talk about postcreation. With postcreation, instead of seeing the tube coming in to the point of creation, let us see the tube exiting the point of creation. Again, try to picture.

It's a cross section of the tube (refer to fig. 4.1), an example, but that does not mean that is how it always is, because it is advantageous to do disentanglement. I will speak of postcreation first. In postcreation, a life lives its life. Seasons change, and a leaf falls from the tree, say, somewhere people don't rake it up [chuckles], and then it gradually disintegrates into the ground. We can say that as it disintegrates and becomes soil, that's postcreation. You can think of a number of other examples, of course. For the human being, however, this form of postcreation does not mean that your body returns to the earth. [Draws.] If this (fig. 5.1), in our cross section of the tube, is creation, then there is a point, which I'll say is just there, where creation of the moment starts to uncreate itself. Though things might or might not actually dissolve, creation starts to move on. Creation can also be something as simple as seeing your friend on

Fig. 5.1. Representation of postcreation.

the street unexpectedly, and you say, "Oh, it's so good to see you!" You give your friend a hug or a pat on the shoulder, or you shake hands and go on. That moment is a creation.

When you go on, it dissipates; it goes away. So let's talk about that as the example for the form of disentanglement we're going to do. You can understand that more easily because it is clearly a moment.

Now, you all have moments throughout your lives when you connect with things, people. Say on the other hand, that there is someone you have been friends with for years, but you had a misunderstanding. You see that person on the street, and you are happy to see him or her, and you give the person a pat on the back and shake hands and so on, yet you are uncomfortable, and so is your friend. You're both rushing somewhere, and you say, "I'll call you!" and off you go. But you have an uncomfortable feeling. This tells you that aside from needing to talk things over with your friend, it would be of value to disentangle from that past situation.

DISENTANGLEMENT EXERCISE

For those of you who meditate or do relaxation exercises, simply do your basic relaxation or meditation. Try not to think of too many words. After you're relaxed, request that gold-light beings come and remove the discomforting cords that are connecting you to all your past discomforts in this life. Period. Say no more than that; that's a good beginning. If you feel that you've had some incident that's upsetting you — someone or maybe a circumstance or a problem at work — you can be specific, but you need to be generally specific, meaning you can ask that the gold-light beings come, and you'll say that opening statement, but instead of requesting disentanglement from all discomforts of the past, you will ask, "Please disentangle me from that argument I had at work today." Period. You don't also say, "That I feel so bad about." You're very specific, but at the same point, you don't give a lot of details, because they'll know. But you need to say it when you're beginning to do this work.

Don't write it; say it out loud. You can take notes if you want to, before and after, about your impressions, but during, you just lie there, and you need to make an effort to not think. For those of you who can do that, just go ahead. For others, I'm going to give you a trick that you can do, and it would be best to be in a darkened room, even if it's daylight. Squeeze your eyes closed tightly and then release them. Do not squeeze so tightly that it's uncomfortable. When you release them, you will be able to see light patterns if you stare at your eyelids. Keep your eyes closed during the process. Look at those light patterns. Or you can imagine standing in front of a white wall and look at that. In short, do things like that, that are inclined to cause you to think less. If you catch yourself thinking, don't worry about it; go back to looking at your eyelids or the white wall as best you can. That's the beginning of disentanglement. It is going to evolve, all right. It is going to evolve, but that's how you begin.

When you're not doing the disentanglement exercise, write down a list of all the people whom you're in any way uncomfortable with. You don't have to write it down in any order, but write down everything that you can think of, including all of the incidents or circumstances you can remember that make you feel uncomfortable when you think about them. When I say uncomfortable, I don't mean sick to your stomach; I mean even annoyed. It can be something that happened and there was a misunderstanding, or you feel someone might have judged you — anything, all right? [Chuckles.] You don't have to write it down in detail; just write down enough so that you know what it's about.

After you've done that — it will take a few weeks because you'll add and remove things — then you can do the second stage of the homework. Before you lie down to do your relaxation, say out loud the disentanglement. Say,

"I request that gold-light beings and light beings who are compatible and comfortable with gold light and/or gold light beings, come now and disentangle me from _____ and their causes." You can say, "All these things I've written down," but you have to glance at the pages. Don't read them; just glance at them. Or you can pick out two or three items (no more than that) and you can say an event. Use a key phrase: "That event that happened in 1987," or something like that. In short, be to the point so that you know what it's about, but don't dwell on it. After a while of doing this homework and saying two or three things a night (you will say, you know, "Disentangle me from _____" say the names or the events), at some point you'll work through your whole list. Then you can just say, "Disentangle me from all my discomforts and their causes." You can go back to the original statement.

Lie down and relax. It will take as long as it takes. You cannot time it and say, "Well, it'll take a half-hour." The best time to do this, actually, is before you go to sleep at night, but you need to lie on your back with your arms down at your sides and with your palms touching the mattress or the couch — whatever you're lying on — or the ground, if you happen to be on that. That's what I recommend.

Some of you will fall asleep during this, so it will be accomplished to some degree or not. I feel that the first stage is the most important because the gold-light beings will find what you need to be disentangled from. They will also tend to take things out of your body that are discomforts, so you could say it's a healing practice. But the reason I want you to consider using it for specific things is that there's a follow-up observation that you could make (it's not something that you need to keep notes on, but you can if you like). You're going to notice that you feel either physically different or attitudinally different, meaning you're not thinking about things the same way you did. It can change your whole life. Most people here on Earth, because it's a school, are an effect of everything that they have created or equally, that they have participated in with others, having to do with the creation of others, which then become, because they participated in it, somewhat their own creation as well — at least a part of it. As a result, because of that school effect, they have situations in which they find that their personalities are driven by the events that have happened in their lives, including the good things, of course. You're not going to ask to be disentangled from benevolent things and good memories; you don't do that. You will most likely notice attitudinal changes. You will also notice many things that might change. I don't want to say too much. You can keep notes on that if you like.

Now, how long might you expect it to take, and what might you expect to feel? Some of you might feel a sense of electricity in your body. It might be difficult to remain perfectly still, which is helpful for the beings who are working on you. This is at all stages that I gave you, not just the second stage we're talking about, so if you feel that and if your body suddenly jerks like that [shakes as if experiencing an electrical tremor], do not worry about it. You might feel, because some of the beings will be working in the electrical realm (those who are working in the magnetic realm will have a different effect on you), as if you have to move, but don't be afraid. Your muscles are being stimulated with electricity, and basic science tells you that when you do that to a muscle, it contracts. So you might feel tense. Don't worry about that; that'll go away.

Ask to be given a sign that you're done for that session. You can do it any time of the day. I recommend before you go to sleep at night as the best time to do it, but that's not best for everybody because of other things you might be doing, to say nothing of the fact that you might be exhausted and fall asleep.

You might turn over on your side or your stomach. They can do a little bit when you're asleep, but they can't really do a lot. So you can lie down in the afternoon or in the early evening, before you would go to sleep (most people sleep at night but not everybody). Or if you sleep during the day, then try to darken the room and proceed. Try to make sure that phones are not going to disturb you, because that will break the flow. I'm not going to go over everything like this because most of you are doing some of these things as it is. If there are questions later, I will respond to them. Now, when you ask for a sign, ask for something benevolent; don't say, "I want the phone to ring" [chuckles]. It will happen. It's better to say, "I would like to have a feeling when it's over." It is most likely going to take anytime from twenty minutes to an hour and a half. As I say, if you manage to stay conscious for the first half-hour to forty-five minutes or so and then you fall asleep, that's all right.

Now there is another matter. Even though electricity stimulates muscles to contract, some of you are more electrical than other people in your basic makeup. Therefore, there are many gold-light beings that are magnetic in nature as well. You will feel the opposite: You will start to feel more relaxed; that is all right as well. Any questions about the process so far, now? You were going to say something?

Exactly what are you saying that we can clear? You use the word "discomforts."

You can clear almost everything. Obviously if you've been in an accident and you're missing a finger or something, you're not going to grow a new one. Or if someone, a loved one, was killed in an accident, that person's not going to reappear in your life. The whole point is to disentangle from the pain that is in your past that is driving you to display certain traits in your personality that are not your actual personality. When your personality is not being driven by past pains and miseries, most of you become much different. You will tend to be very calm, your sense of humor will be much more up, as it were, and you might even notice that you're more polite [chuckles]. It is not politeness that is driven by conditioning or culture, but a greater consciousness of the needs of human beings in general, meaning that you just become gentler with people.

More respectful, more aware?

Yes, but it is not your job to know what everyone is feeling. Rather, it is your job to allow them to feel that way and to offer help when asked, if you choose to and have something to offer that will benefit that person.

Now, when the disentanglement process has gone a long way, when you've gone through your list (over the weeks and months you will think of other things and you'll write those down), many times the gold-light beings will disentangle you from things that you can't remember, things that happened when you were a baby, things that were so traumatic you can't remember anything about it. Everybody has those. They will do that, but they would like to disentangle you first from things that you perceive as priorities. So you don't have to keep a book about how much better you feel after the first night or the first session of doing this. This is a long process.

Even though you might go through your whole list, the disentanglement process has to continue because many times there are things happening in your life that you need to disentangle yourself from that you haven't noticed. Maybe you hurt somebody's feelings without knowing it, or maybe somebody hurt your feelings, but you didn't notice it. This happens profoundly often in your society because people in the United States — of course, in other places too — are used to a certain level of pain. Adults and even young children get used to a level of pain, and it tends to make them somewhat cynical, to say nothing of wearing them out or making them sick.

Very often your body will get sick to tell you, "Hey, something's wrong. Let's remove this pain; let's do some disentanglement." Your body knows how to do disentanglement; you don't have to instruct it on how to do it, but you need the help of beings who can do the disentangling who will not be affected by it. That's why we request gold-light beings: They function very well on Earth, and the gold light contains the other colors of the spectrum.

For the first few weeks, just do stage one of the homework. Then after you go through your list, start keeping notes if you want and if you see that there's a difference in you. Notice that this might make you more sensitive, but that is a good thing.

I want to give you something you can do so that other people's discomforts or the general discomforts around you — an animal's discomforts or Mother Earth's discomfort and so on — do not always affect you. At times, they will. You can radiate, meaning you can do the heat-in-the-chest exercise.[1] Also, if that's hard to assimilate, picture gold light inside you, and make a tone, any tone, and let that gold light radiate out. Always try to start it inside you, and let it radiate out; that way. It will tend to push out discomforts that are in there. If you create a shell around you, it will just trap the discomforts within you [chuckles] in that shell and will sustain that level of pain. The whole point is you want to let go of pain. You want to let go of the things that prompt people to be the way they are:

---

1. The heat-in-the-chest exercise, also referred to as the heart heat exercise, is a practice for feeling love as heat in the chest. Learn more about it and how to do it at http://benevolentmagic.com/disentangle-ment-heart-heat.php.

The Heart-Heat Exercise

Practice feeling love as heat in the chest. Use your hands over your chest to help focus energy but not touching your body.

When you can hold this warmth, add the feeling (not visualization) of gold light.

Keep practicing back and forth until you can feel both at the same time; then hold it for at least 10 or 15 minutes.

After you learn to do this, while you are feeling this heat or love or both, say out loud:

"I give all beings permission to be of love and to be fed, clothed, healed, and comforted."

You can add other appropriate things, but keep it simple. The heart heat will naturally radiate even when the gold light is absent.

Because one of the most important levels of creator training is to be able to feel what others feel, you might have nightmares and wake up with horrible feelings or have other experiences that result in such feelings. As soon as you can, ask:

"Let benevolent love bless and transform all I am feeling."

Then feel gold light. This is alchemical training to transform the pain of others through being aware of their feelings.

When you come together as a group to feel heart heat and gold light,

talk about what's bothering you so that you have some feelings to transform. Focus on the physical warmth in your chest or solar plexus, which is the physical evidence of love.

Strike a chime, or make some signal. Then imagine gold light there while you feel the heat with total focus so that the alchemical transformation can take place.

These feelings are amplified in a group. This exercise can transform any discomfort that arises, and you will feel ecstatic; it is the closest feeling to the Creator energy that you are. The larger the group, the wider the area it will transform to cheerful, loving feelings. Eventually it will become first nature to you, and you will feel it all the time. It will lead to unifying all beings everywhere.

to be submissive, to be bossy, to be angry — just fill in whatever adjective you want to there — to be fearful, enraged, in pain, aggressive, violent, and so on, and to have these, as predominant emotions, drive them.

It's profoundly true that without disentanglement, in most of your societies on Earth — not all, but most — the adults are not really adults but are living out the pain of their childhoods. They might learn to do things as big children [chuckles], but they are still living out the pain that has not been resolved. That's why I do not expect you to remember everything on your list. But once you do the first stage and then make the list and do the second stage and go through that, the gold-light beings will then understand what you are trying to do. And they will continue to do things, meaning that when you get to the second stage, you don't eliminate the first stage's statement. You'll say you want to be disentangled from all your discomforts. We're using discomforts. You can say, "from all my pain," or you can say other things, but you have to be careful not to say "from all my anger." Anger, actually, is useful sometimes. I'm not saying that self-destructive anger is useful, but I am saying that sometimes the energy on a low-key level of anger causes you to be more assertive at a time when you need to be and so on. But it is better to say, "Disentangle me from all my discomforts." A discomfort is something that you know passes. You have something uncomfortable, but you know you've had uncomfortable things pass before that, and you go on.

It's an accessible word. It's a free word, and it means that there's motion in and out, whereas if you say, "Disentangle me from my pain," you can say it only if you have something specific going on. When you say that, your mind might say the word "pain," or it might think, "Gee, I've had that pain for years and years." In short, it might not seem like something that you can go in and out from, you see? So we want to use a word that describes it sufficiently to the gold-light beings but doesn't sound crushing to you. So the choice of word is sometimes useful.

Now, at some point, you're going to feel that you've gone through your list and you can't think of anything else to say. By that time and after all that process, you will have come up with other words. You will have either come up with other words that work for you or been inspired to come up with other words. Always ask for what you want; don't ask for what you don't want. So at some point, then, you will simply say these words that work for you to preset the condition that you want the gold-light beings to do for you. You don't have to be exclusive; if you sense that there are white-light beings or pink-light beings or something like that around, you can welcome them. But you'll need to say something like, "I welcome gold-light beings and other light beings ..." (or you can say white-light beings, whatever) "who can work through the gold light, or through gold-light beings." Say it just like that, because some of you know white-light beings that you'll want to participate; don't call the being by name if you can help it. If you call the beings by name, they will come with lots of other connotations, all right?

There are lots and lots of gold-light beings — and white-light beings, for that matter — who you've never heard of and that you probably never will hear of here, but when you say a name that you might normally feel good about, you might not feel that way at deeper levels. In short, that's what I'd recommend, but you can say what you want and see how it works. My feeling is that it is my job to instruct the way that I feel is best. People might want to say, "Jesus," or they might want to say something that is a deity to them, but when they say that, they will think of that being the way they know that being to be at that time of his or her life, whereas by simply saying "gold-light beings" or "white-light beings," that being, if it can help you, will be there. That's sufficient because those beings will describe that being. But it will be able to come in its entirety, or in its pure state, without being limited by your preconception of what that being is.

Now, at some point you're just going to be saying those words and having yourself disentangled. This process can easily take months. And it is really an ongoing process that is generally something you do on a daily basis. Once it gets going, it's very helpful for you, and you can feel it. Your personality will change, but you will not become someone that you don't know. You will recognize your personality because you will have demonstrated various characteristics of your own that you're conscious of in your personality, not those that other people or you perceived. You will be happy to notice that you are acting and being and feeling so much more like yourself. Some people will react well to this; some of them might be people you don't really know, and they might become new friends. Other people might not react so well, and you will have to decide whether you want to keep them as friends as more of your pure personality comes forth. And when I say "pure," I do not mean something that is more spiritual than other people; I simply mean your actual personality that is not restricted by the pain of the past. You will then have to decide whether you want to continue to see people who might criticize you for not being this pain-filled person that they used to know. You can tell them as much or as little as you think they can hear about your process and why it's working for you and what you're getting out of it. It's up to you. I'm not trying to drag you away from people or break up relationships or friendships; it's just something that you need to know could happen. People who are with you might perceive you in ways that draw relationships closer together, and this is much more likely to happen. But the unexpected is also possible, so you need to know about that.

Now, after several months of doing this, you will most likely notice changes. (I grant that I'm not telling you everything about it, and I or Speaks of Many Truths or Zoosh or Isis will say more about it perhaps at some point in the future. Someone else might comment on it, and that's fine too.) Your whole list will probably be pages and pages and pages long, but don't let that alarm you; it takes a while, but it's worth taking the time. And sometimes you might say two or three names, and the next night you say the same two or three names because you don't feel finished. That could go on for a week. That's all right, and it's not unusual, especially with people in your past or even present. Don't eliminate the present, in which you have a great deal of enmeshment (I think that is the popular word of today) that is uncomfortable. So it could take a long time, but that's all right because it's intended to be homework that you do for the rest of your life. [Chuckles.] It's not temporary. It's homework that you were intended to be able to do when you were born here. In ancient days and societies, people knew about this; they called it something else, but they knew about it. And some societies still know about it today.

CONNECTION EXERCISE

I also want to say a little bit today about the other aspect. It's a little too soon to talk about connection at the moment, so I don't want you to work on connection first. But I want to give you the outline of how connection works. Now the basic connections homework is this: After you have asked for gold-light beings and said your disentanglement words, you say, "I will also request that connections be made for me with beings or other energy sources that will improve the quality of my life." And these connections will be made, and the energies will connect to you. It won't be for specific incidents; it will be an ongoing thing. You add "this," and you add "that." You don't say that just once. Every night or whenever it is that you do your disentanglement work, you say your disentanglement words first, then your connection phrase, and then you lie down, and the work is done. That's it. That's as much as I want to say now, because I've really given you about six months' worth of homework.

The reason we don't do the connections work first or with the disentanglement right away is that it's too complicated for the gold-light beings. Picture yourself inside a ball of yarn or something like that. There's such a massive amount of cords going every which way that they first want to clear you of as much as they can. Afterward, doing the connections is easier for them and better for you. So that's why I've given it in that order. I gave you a little more than I intended to give right now, but it's the basic work, and I feel that it will be very helpful to a great many of you. Through the disentanglement, you let go of all that stuff; it improves your life because you become yourself, and then we improve your life with what you want. You don't say, "I want connections to get a new car." You don't say any of that. The connections will be the energy that will support whatever it is that you want in your life. And later on, maybe other beings or even I, will give you other things you can say for connections. But this is sufficient for now.

DISENTANGLING AND IDENTIFYING CONNECTIONS WERE ONCE ROUTINE

This is absolutely awesome. When you say that some ancient tribes know this, when did you decide to give this to everyone? This is incredible!

When human beings, as you know them today, started running around on the surface of planet Earth, they were much more open to Spirit. They didn't know that they had to be certain ways. [Chuckles.] In short, they were people living by the sacred. And the sacred, in the early days, had to do with paying attention to how things are here and trying to get along with all life. In short, it was harmony. This is often identified in your time by beings who are shamans or mystical people who will almost always have a relationship with such activities that they do with what is called the natural world, meaning earth, plants, animals, elements, rain, lightning, and so forth.

Now these people were given this homework, and you can relate to some of these people. I can't say that all Native American tribes still have this wisdom, but some do. And some have been given the wisdom more than once when the tribes were decimated. The same goes for native peoples who trace their roots to Australia, New Zealand, and other places — obviously, Canada and Africa and all of these places, even peoples in Scotland in the early days, going way back — but in the early days people didn't really populate areas that were cold because they couldn't be there. Granted, the climate was different at the polar icecaps as you know them today. In the early days of human beings, the planet was more temperate. Ice ages, as you know them, came later. So people could live in northern Canada, and it would be balmy year-round. There is scientific evidence for this that I will not discuss, because it's been thoroughly researched and discussed in other books. So I mention this to suggest that the native peoples of those lands were born in those lands not only because their souls chose to be but also because in the early days they were setting the pattern on Earth so that Earth would know how to respond to their needs and set their internal pattern for their culture. Then those born to those cultures all over Earth would be inclined to cooperate with those cultures and would want to embrace the cultures' interactions with Earth and all beings on it. So the disentanglement and connection work was given to them, but in those early days when harmony was much more of a factor of life, disentanglement and connections did not seem any more important than anything else; as a matter of fact, it seemed in some ways less important because of the harmonious condition of life.

So it would be something they were less inclined to pass on. If they did remember to pass things on, that would be something they wouldn't remember, so it fell away after a while. Some peoples managed to maintain it longer, or it was given again in inspirations.

Now, the early peoples had it, and some people have managed to maintain it over the years or had it renewed if they've maintained the contact on a spiritual, inspirational level with the ancients that preceded them. That's how some peoples who still exist here have managed to maintain this wisdom. But a great many people in this modern society, especially those involved in the pursuit of the intellect for its own sake, don't know about it. And in your time and in these conditions, it is vital, and it really can change your life. It requires a great deal of patience because in your societies, you are culturally conditioned to rush-rush, hurry-hurry. "What can I do fast? How long will it take?" But if you know that it's intended to take the rest of your life and if it works for you to pass it on to your children or to those who ask as you become more familiar with how it works, then it doesn't become rush-rush, hurry-hurry. It just becomes something you do on a daily basis because it improves the quality of your life.

DISENTANGLE FROM LESSONS YOU ARE BORN WITH

I find this absolutely astounding because one of the beings through Robert said that a soul comes into this life and wants to do certain things, but it sets up certain lessons first. And then what happens is those lessons create such trauma in the cellular memory of the physical body that the soul can't really do what it wants to do.

But you remember that your friend Zoosh told you some time ago that karma was over. What he didn't say is what I'm saying now.

That the stuff is still there.

That's right. What he didn't say is that karma's over, meaning that you do not have to come in with lessons anymore. Think about what that means. Think when Zoosh said, "Karma is over." It was a while back. That meant that the children who were being born then were being born without lessons. That does not mean that they do not experience things in their lives or that they didn't come in to learn new things, but that they didn't come in with soul lessons in the same sense. That's why people have noticed, "Oh! The New Children! Oh, look how they are!" and so on. I will not divulge too much, but what I will say is that, yes, as you mentioned, you need to disentangle from that stuff, but if lessons are no longer so vitally important, then it is possible to change your life., Those of you who were born earlier could let go of your karma. The whole point of the disentanglement is to disentangle you from your pain, but it also disentangles you from those lessons that you came in with. That's why it takes time. When you are born with those lessons, you continue to do your disentanglement until you die, but when you are born without those lessons, then the disentanglement will be easier for you. So this is a process that youngsters can do, those youngsters that people like to call the New Children, who are not really new, but they're not driven the same way you are. They can sometimes accept things that have been difficult for people to accept in the past. They sometimes see things more clearly. As I like to say, they see things the way they are. This does not make them a separate group, but it allows them to do what they do. I'm going to be vague about that for now. Sometimes when I'm vague about things, it just means I will talk about it later.

BE COMMITTED TO CLEARING
YOUR CELLULAR MEMORY

So the disentanglement process will go differently and at different paces for different people. Youngsters might not even feel the need for it, but if you're a young person and you're experiencing some pain, you can try it. It can't hurt you. It's very benevolent. You don't have to give up your religion to do this. [Chuckles.] I can assure you that one of the first things all religious deities do when they start communicating with those who make notes or try to leave messages or pass on the wisdom that these beings have to offer is to tell them how to live on Earth in a way that is better. [Chuckles.] So this is one of the first things they'll talk about. Disentanglement will clear what we have called cellular memory, where the traumas are very physically in the cells, and we don't know about that, but they still run our attitudes, our emotions, our feelings, and our choices. It will clear it if you maintain it. If you do it a couple or three times and then stop, it won't. If you do it for six months and then stop, it won't.

It's the continuous application ...

That's right. It will clear the drive of that to resolve things, but that doesn't mean things won't happen in your life. It does mean that you will react to them in ways that are more clearly your personality rather than reacting to them in ways other people told you how to. This will allow you to give the gift of your personality to many more people than have seen it. You know, sometimes people say, "Oh, that guy, he's such a jerk." But when you talk to people who know that person better, they say, "Well, he can be annoying sometimes, but if you know him, you'll see at times he does these wonderful things." You'll often find that in relationships people say, "Well, he can be annoying, but I've seen him when he's really on, and he does these great things." When he's doing those things, he might be (not always, but he might be) revealing or exhibiting his true personality. So that's the sort of thing that's going to become more common. You understand that because you are in creation school here, I cannot simply wave a wand and say, "Okay, everything's all better now."

We have to do the work.

You have to do the work because it's school, but to do it, you need to be instructed on how. And the first "hows" always have to do with your own body because your first responsibility is to your body and what you do in it. Obviously you are immortal, meaning your personality goes on, but your body is the vehicle made up of Earth and what she has to offer that allows you to learn these most profound lessons that cannot be learned anywhere else because just exactly the right balance of challenge and discomfort exists here that will allow you to quickly learn lessons. You can learn lessons other places but not quickly. And of course, as more people do disentanglement and are less driven by pain, the percentage of discomfort present will gradually begin to drop (I'm talking about over years, now), and your relationship with animals and Mother Nature and plants and so on will gradually begin to improve. Many of the things that animals and plants and Mother Nature and rain and lightning and so on have been trying to show all of you — not just to mystical, shamanic, and similarly sensitive people — is that you will become clearer not only mentally but also in your feeling self, in your physical self, and even in your spiritual self. Your spiritual self will not have to keep trying to balance you on that one leg of the chair — to do a little of "this," to do a little of "that" — so you don't fall over. In short, it purifies the process over time so that life is simpler and better.

You don't have to give up comforts; you don't have to give things up. You might, in time, do things differently. As time goes on, people begin to notice that some things are less necessary. Obviously, you can't keep building fossil-fuel-consuming cars and using oil indefinitely. In time, people will gradually choose to do other things. But that doesn't happen immediately. You need to do your homework, and it's one step at a time.

NEGATIVITY FLUCTUATES WITH CIRCUMSTANCES

Yes. What is the percentage of the negativity on the planet at this time?

Oh, understanding that it's in constant fluctuation, as taken as a gross potential on the planet, totally, and it does not exceed 47 percent. But this, you understand, means that some places might have a huge amount, and other places won't. The huge amount might be in a war zone, for instance. In a war zone, as you know, death is not uncommon. If you get negativity up around 62 to 68 percent, that creates the conditions where death is sometimes welcome. You don't think of it consciously, but of course, if you're suffering from a terrible wound, death may not look so bad.

But disentanglement (you could call it discreation too, couldn't you?), then, is one of the techniques to get down to the 2 percent negativity?

I'm putting it within the context of what we were doing yesterday when we talked about precreation. I'd rather call it postcreation than discreation because discreation can happen before the fact.

Ah, and disentanglement is only after.

Yes.

Okay. This is one of the gifts that will bring this negativity down to something tolerable before we go out to the stars, right?

That's right. In time it will bring it down, and it gives you something practical and not very complicated that you can do no matter where you are. To use Zoosh's favorite example, you can be in prison and do this, and it can change things for you. It might not let you out of prison, but it's not impossible. It could change circumstances in your life, and if it works for you and others want to know about it, you can tell them. Don't tell them unless they want to know. It's not about a religion. It's not a new religion; it's a way to live.

Can we call it benevolent magic?

You know, I think we don't want to call it benevolent magic because magic has connotations to people. I'd rather talk about it as such a foundational element of life that it can't be something that you add to life to improve it. It has to be something on which you build your life, meaning that this capacity to disentangle and to create connections has to be in place before anybody ever comes here to these kind of societies. So, no, we can't really call it benevolent magic. Benevolent magic is used to improve specific conditions or specific circumstances.

Could we say that once we disentangle to at least a good degree, we are more able to use benevolent magic?

Yes, and it may not even be necessary because the more disentangled you become, the clearer you become, and it is less likely that certain things will continue to happen in your life, especially those things that prompt you say, "Oh, no, not this again." This would be a pattern that you reproduce in your life (granted, very often unconsciously) because of some old pain in this life. By the way, you can do this more than once a day if you want to, but generally no more than twice a day. If something major is going on for you — a temporary major thing — you can do it three times a day. But I would prefer that you do it no more than twice a day, and then, after a while, just do it once a day because I don't want it to take over your life. If you have nothing else to do, all right, but most of you have other things to do. And don't feel that just because you're eighty-five years old and your life is, as you might see it, coming down the home stretch, this won't benefit you; it can benefit you at any age. It's a process that naturally goes on for babies until they're at least six months old, or basically before they start to speak or have any real understanding of what worded language means. They understand what being held and loved means, of course; they have the basics. But this is usually naturally in place for the first five to six months. That is also how you learn to do it; it's not complicated because you were born doing it.

If you disentangle and then you come to the end of your natural cycle, will this eliminate some of the pain of the life review?

It might. It won't eliminate things that you have done in life that need to be felt and understood, but because your personality will change as a result of the disentanglement, it's less likely that you'll be causing pain to others eventually. It's less likely. It very much raises your consciousness and your sensitivity, of course, and it is also less likely that your feelings will be hurt by others because you'll be much clearer when others are not doing this. You will be clearer that something that they're saying or doing is not actually directed toward you. It might be self-destructive impulses on their part. It does not create enlightenment in its own right, but it gives you much more of the natural tools that you were born with without the encumbrances of all of the complications of your past pains and complications of multiple pains. In short, it's a clarifying activity. It probably won't directly change your life review, but it can indirectly change it.

It can, regardless of your religion (it doesn't have any effect on your religion, meaning you don't have to change your religion at all; it's up to you), improve the dying process. That doesn't necessarily mean that you'll have a whole lot less pain, but there might be some pain relief. In the dying process, you can still do disentanglement and your connections. You'll want to be connected to the most benevolent, and in that case, you'll see the connections will be to energies that support you through the death process in perhaps a slightly more benevolent way. So don't assume that if you're toward the end of your life, this can't help you.

Can we add here that because humans are becoming more filled with light that when beings die (Zoosh wanted us to say something) they should ask to go to their own spirits and not into the white light?

It's always best, if you are sitting with someone who is dying or are near someone who is dying and you want something to say to him or her (the dying don't normally have to be instructed), say, "Look for your guide. It will take you on your journey." That's all, something simple. Or you can say, "Look for the loving light from your guide," because the person will see someone. He or she will actually see someone that looks like a person who's radiating gold and white light. And because confusion arises, it's especially useful post-trauma (meaning a car crash or war or something sudden) when you know that the person is dying. If you're an emergency worker, you're probably busy trying to save the patient or to help him or her feel better. In the process, you might not be able to say that. But you might. And if the person is frightened, then you can say, "Look for your guide," or you can say, "Look for your angel," if you like (these are beings that come … of course, they don't really have wings; that was an artistic interpretation that has become popular). You can say either a guide or an angel will take the person on his or her journey. Just say, "On your journey," and the person will get it.

For people who help to release lost souls, rather than telling those souls to go into the light, they can say something similar?

Release lost souls, meaning what specifically here?

Well, people seem to get lost on Earth. Or if they're addicted to the Earth plane, or ...

If you feel that there is a spirit present who is suffering or calling out for your help, you can't really say, "Look for the light; look for your angel." It doesn't work. This is something different. If you're helping these spirits to move on, you probably have a method, all right, that you're working with individual beings. You can't just hurl them out of somebody's body if they're stuck to it, to the body. They'll just go out and get stuck to somebody else — not because they're evil, but because they can't help it. This is a different instruction, and it's probably best for Speaks of Many Truths or others do to it. It is a very lengthy instruction, which we can do tomorrow if you'd like. Either I'll do it or Speaks of Many Truths (or someone who can explain it to those who might be doing this already) can do it. But it is not something that average people can readily do. It's better for them to do their disentanglements. Such beings that might be stuck to you can be removed through disentanglement by the gold-light beings doing disentanglement with you. But if you're helping other beings, these spirits, you probably already know what to do. Nevertheless, I feel that's a valid question, and it is a subject we probably ought to pursue tomorrow.

Okay. It used to be that when even a cat or a dog would die, we would say, "I ask that it go into the white light." I mean, it's just been what we've been told to do, and it looks like we need new instructions.

You need new instructions; that's right. It might very well be you don't really have to instruct cats or dogs, because they're not born with lessons. But if you happen to run across a cat or dog spirit and you can sense this thing, it always means that it's been here with somebody who needed it here. It's been here with a human being. If the human being has moved on and you notice the cat or dog, it is then possible to do something for it. Occasionally cats and dogs also get stuck, but by stuck, I mean there is an actual matrix of stuff that catches them. It's a substance.

EVERYONE DOESN'T HAVE TO EXPERIENCE EVERYTHING

Let's get back to when Zoosh said, "The karma is over." What he said was that everything that could be experienced by a human being had been experienced by at least one human being. So that assumes that in this loop of time, we were attempting to experience everything that we had experienced leading up to our decision that we wanted to look at again with the decision of focusing only on the mental.

You can look at it that way, but you could also say it has to do with the fact that you are all one. So I'm not saying it's either-or. Because you are in fact all one, all of you don't have to experience everything. Yes, it does suggest that it is an attempt to understand everything that you might possibly need to understand on a personal level, meaning someone experiences it personally so that when you come together someday as a creator, you will have the experience you need to be able to personally identify or personally feel and have that personal love for every being you create. So that's why someone somewhere in this loop of time has to have every experience on a personal level. It can't be something you think about or imagine. It has to be personally felt so that you will know — not just think, not just consider because you are a creator, not have the knowledge because of your shared wisdom with other creators — because of your personal circumstances. Because you are all one, what another feels even a hundred years ago (to say nothing of what you felt last week) is personal. You will know what it's like, and you will say, "Oh, my, let's not create that."

But it implied that we had experienced it all before and we need to reexperience it again in this loop of time.

No, that's not it. It might imply that, but that's not true. It will come up during your time as creator. By "coming up" I mean that it may come up as an issue because when you're a creator, you always consider potentials. You don't consider them from a position of "what if," because you know all what ifs. But you do consider potentials: "If this being is here and that being is there, they are basically incompatible. The chances are," you might say, speaking as an Earth human now, "they'll never meet. But what if they do meet?" And you'll know what if. You don't just make a practical, mental decision. You know from your personal experience, so you make sure that something better takes place. You see, that was why you were willing and (going back to the seeds, which refers to a previous book) why you were prepared to come. You would be able to experience something unique that you had not experienced before. And you all were not prepared to come to — how can we say? — just be a creator.

You were prepared to make the travel and were enthusiastic to come because it was made clear to you that you needed to be more than a creator. And of course, that was marvelous, to be more than a creator. So you came.

Who made it clear to the seeds?

The need. The Creator here that was creating this universe, or intending to create this universe, had a need to move on and also had a need, a desire, to have offspring, to generate someone — a child, let's say — that could do more than It could do. So always the condition that sets up creation is a need. Let's just say people on Earth don't always think that creators have needs, but they do. After all, creators create for the joy of creation, yet sometimes their creations have to do with their personal needs to express something. Creation is often joyful. On Earth it is not always joyful. The birth process is not always fun, but the effect after one gets over the trauma is often joyful for mother and child. This basic example is given so that you will notice it. Almost everything you need to know here is symbolized in your life in a way that you cannot ignore. You need to breathe, to eat, and so on. Things like that. Those symbols are profoundly basic so that you will not get away from lessons that you came here to learn.

THE UNEXPRESSED NEED

What was the need that you fulfilled when you and the other twelve created the totality — the felt need for the totality and the need in you? Have you addressed those issues?

Yes, I have. And the need was not within us. This is a bit simplistic, but you can understand. I'm just going to make a point here, just living in our way and not dreaming that we're going to be involved in this massive creation in any way. Then putting it in the simplest terms possible, we start to feel something. Sometimes you get a feeling of precognition, and when I say a feeling, I don't mean that you think something or a word comes into your head. You get a feeling. It's your instinct: You know something's going to happen without having any evidence to show it. Sometimes you get a good feeling: Something good is going to happen. Sometimes you get another feeling: Something's going to happen, but you're not sure what.

What was your feeling?

Our feeling was that something needed to happen. Now think about this. Here we are, if I can put it humorously, innocently living without any idea or consideration to the fact that we're there for something beyond our apparent existence. We start getting a feeling. When you get a feeling, it is the same function, exactly the same. It isn't for all your feelings. Some feelings are driven by other things, which we've already discussed. But sometimes you get a feeling, and your guide is stimulating it. It's intended to help you out, and it's probably something you've discussed with them that you're familiar with, and were familiar with, before all this creation occurs anyway. When we get this feeling, our first reaction is that someone is trying to inspire us in some way. We've already gone on the journey, and we couldn't find anyone, so we know better than to go on the journey. We know better than to look for that. It's not there, not accessible to us. That makes you feel better, I know, to hear me say that.

Then we discover something about the mystery of life: Unexpressed needs are just as powerful and sometimes more powerful than expressed ones. This is a most important realization on our part that we've never had to consider before in this moment, but we consider it because there is no other explanation. There is absolutely no other explanation than there is an unexpressed need going on for which we cannot localize in any way. We consider it for a "long time." And while we're considering it over "time," the feeling is gradually getting stronger.

How would you describe the feeling?

The feeling is a sensation. Have you ever been around a person or a group of people and when you walk in the room, you feel just fine, and then you suddenly feel like you need to be doing something? You will first examine, "What did I forget to do?" You can't think of anything. You look at your organizer. "No, no, I did everything." And then it dawns on you that there's something else. "No," you say, "there's someone in the room who needs me to do something; I wonder what it is." You're very sensitive. After a while, you start doing things. You get Grandma another cup of tea, and you change the baby's diaper. And at some point, you probably fulfill the person's need. But this thing you were feeling might not even have been something that the person knew he or she needed. After all, unless the baby was in dire straits, it didn't know it's diaper needed to be changed [chuckles], and Grandma might not have even been thinking that she would like another cup of tea at all, but it was nice to be offered the cup of tea. Maybe she didn't even want a cup of tea, but it was so nice to be offered.

But their subconsciouses might ...

No, no subconscious. It's an unexpressed need. When I say "unexpressed," I do not mean not verbalized. People do not know about it, nor is it felt anywhere in their unconscious, subconscious, anything. But it is something that, when provided to them, they appreciate and they feel better. That's an unexpressed need. We have to differentiate here, because the unexpressed need presents us with something that is wholly new to us, and a normal interaction has to do with needs that portion of ourselves might say, such as, "I had a need, and we all went and did it, and then that was something we understood, clearly." But an unexpressed need that is expressing has no awareness that it's expressing. What can this mean? It can only mean that the unexpressed need that we were feeling had to do with something that would take place, at some point, that this thing that was broadcasting, this unexpressed need, did not know about nor was it driven in any way to do it. So then we realized that, since there was an unexpressed need by someone or something, we didn't have to go *somewhere* to respond to it, but what we could do is stay in touch with that unexpressed need and flood energy toward that need and see what happens.

So that's what we did. We flooded energy and we waited. And we waited and we waited. [Chuckles.] And then we asked each other (you realize that we don't communicate like this, but to make it more narrative), "Well, is that helping?" And one of us said, "It seems to help a little bit. When we stop," added this portion of ourselves, "I feel the need a bit stronger, don't you?" And we also agreed that we felt the need was stronger when we stopped sending the energy. But when we were sending the energy, we expected at some point to sense something or to have some feeling that the something that was broadcasting this unexpressed need that we felt would respond in some way. And we said, "We flooded this unexpressed need with energy. We can continue flooding it with energy, but what's the point? Let's wait."

We waited quite a while. Then another one of us said, "Do you think we need to actually do something?" And another one of us said, "Let's try. We can create something within that energy where that need is, and it can be the most receptive. Then let's see whether the combination of the unexpressed need and the energy do something. In short, maybe there needs to be some kind of a medium that will allow this unexpressed need to at least become an expressed need so that we know what we're dealing with." So we said okay, and we created something that would appear, for all intents and purposes (it doesn't look like this, but for the sake of the description), to be a ball with windows and doorways to various dimensions, and in short, something like the center of most galaxies. It's a creation device. It's profoundly receptive and also very reactive, all right?

We took this on the basis of what we felt. We discussed it, and everybody contributed, and we said, "We have to create something that's reactive." And we could be reactive to the portions of ourselves.

But you never created anything before.

No, this was new; we hadn't done it.

How did you even know about creating? How did you even know that you could create?

As is often the case with you, very often if you don't know how to do something, you discover you can do it when you've never been in a position to do it before. So we discovered we could do this, and we put that in there, and then we waited. We waited and we waited.

It was in a specific space?

It was in the area where we'd been putting all this energy. We waited and we waited. Nothing. So we waited longer, and then we said, "What is it we're not doing?" All the while, the unexpressed need is getting more so, so we said, "This isn't it," but we didn't take that thing out of there. We said, "There's something else." And then we said to each other (for the sake of the narrative story), "What is it that we need to do" [chuckles] "that we're not doing?" [Snaps fingers.] It's there. And I know you want to hear this: What we were not doing was that we, ourselves, had no personal need to see or experience anything. We were responding to something else entirely, but we, as you might say, had no stake in the matter. It's not that we didn't care. We cared enough to respond, but we were not attached, as you might say, to something showing up. We were just curious and didn't understand why nothing is. So then we had to have a long discussion about what we wanted. And then we finally decided, "We're happy the way we are; we don't need anything! Everything's fine!"

The unexpressed need got stronger! And we said, "That's not it." Then we considered more, and we said, "What if, just for fun, we take a personal interest in something developing here? What might happen if we *want* something to develop?" We had never considered wants before, because we had everything we needed. What would we want that we didn't need, if we had it all? So we had to be honest, and we had to discuss, "What is it we want that we don't have?" We had to agree that there wasn't anything. Then we had to consider whether there was something that somebody else wanted us to want or participate in that we were not aware of. But we immediately had to say, "Wait, wait, wait. We've already been on that trip!"

Then someone says, "What about the point of light? We didn't create the point of light." No, we hadn't. So we had to think about that. "What is it?" we had to ask ourselves. We finally asked ourselves the most important question: "What is it that Creator does?" This, of course, was involved with the question having to do with my search. We asked, "What is the most overwhelming feeling that we're experiencing?" And we suddenly realized that what created us was the unexpressed need! That's what created us! That's why we're here! We're here to serve this unexpressed need in some way. What we're looking for, beyond, is actually this thing that is yet to be!

Our Creator is something that hasn't appeared yet, and it's our job to create It if we're ever going to meet our Creator, which of course I was passionate to do. The others didn't really care, "We're going to have to be personally involved in this creation!" And just like the first blacksmith, we basically had to learn our trade. First, obviously, our first effort at creation was a complete flop. That thing we put in there with all the energy — nothing! So we kept working at it. Eventually we got it going enough on its own.

What we initially did — I can't give you the whole story; it would take forever — was to create something that was really a huge difference and really helped us a lot. Here we are again, the dot. "What can we create that will do it for us? Because we obviously don't know what we're doing." [Chuckles.] We say, "We don't have a personal need to do this; but we know we need to have one. Let's create a being like ourselves, and give that being the potential to create other beings just like itself and that has a personal need to do this creation for us. In short, we created creators.

THE CREATORS OF CREATORS

We created creators, period — from our perspective, in any event. We created creators, and we gave them, of course, impersonal unconditional love. We gave them personal unconditional love. We gave them impersonal, specific, one-to-one love, all right? We created personal love. In short we gave them all the forms of love we could create. What we gave them is motivation.

A being has all this love and all this creative potential, a form of love that we do not express: personal love. With the first creator, that creator immediately had to create another creator so that it could express personal love to something because this creator could express personal love to us, but we couldn't express it back! So that creator needed to immediately create another creator with which it could share personal love, and that happened for quite a while. And then we instructed them at some point. We gave them plenty of time to interact with each other. And we said …

So there were two of them?

There was one, and then that one made two, and then those two made four, and so on. And then we said, "There's this unexpressed need. Can you do anything about that?" That's it. And they started creating. And that is how it started.

But what about worlds within worlds where the atoms would grow larger…

Oh, they took one look at that, and they said, "Pppfff …" They sent that back to us. [Laughs.] They said, "No, thank you! That's not it!" They sent it back to us, and we absorbed it. We said, "Well, that's how much we know!" That told us something vitally important, and that's that a creator, at least at that level in the beginning, cannot function without embracing personal love. You understand, these creators at this stage had personal love for other creators! And many of them took that on to having personal love for the beings they created within their creations and so on, but not all of them did that. Some of them, while they had personal love for other creators, didn't necessarily have personal love for everything that they created. They had unconditional love, of course; they couldn't create without that. They couldn't create without having personal love.

Most of them, in their creations, had personal love for their beings, but because it's young and learning, your Creator in this universe did not apply that in this universe. That doesn't mean there isn't personal love; it exists all over the place because, after all, the creation is a portion of that Creator. But not here where things are so extreme in this highly advanced school of creation. Creator couldn't do that with you here, because then It would have to experience what you were going to experience, in short, your path to becoming more than this Creator.

Okay. I had this nice little visual about this thing that was going to expand. Did the creators they create then create their own creations?

First they were working together, as you might with your companions, and then of course, someone got an idea that others said, "No, I don't think we want to do that in our creation." So this thing went over here, and they started creating that. They didn't go away mad. They said, "Well, I'll just go over here."

Is this all in this totality you talked about?

Oh, yes, it's all in the totality that we can perceive from where we are. Where we are is not within that totality in the sense that we are involved in some ongoing creation, but of course it's involved in it because we're involved.

My feeling was that there wasn't anything in it that you felt was new to you.

I'll tell you something, and this might surprise you: We haven't paid that much attention. Remember, I said we're pretty much complete unto ourselves. I suppose if we had a personal need to examine it, we would, but we don't. [Chuckles.]

So how are you complete unto yourselves?

I think it would be very difficult to say anything other than that because our state of existence is so marvelously complete for us. We want for nothing that could improve us. This doesn't mean we're egocentric in that sense; it just means that of everything that's been created in this mass of creation, we haven't felt anything that we want that we've taken from it or that we've re-created for ourselves. We responded to the unexpressed need, but we're waiting. Perhaps when the Explorer Race does its thing, we will then be able to meet our Creator. Perhaps it will happen beyond that.

Maybe you will experience more potential too!

We don't see how, but we're not motivated to. The main thing is, my portion of us would like to meet that which came before us, as I said, in the journey. But it wasn't possible because what came before us [chuckles] hasn't existed yet. So that's why I've said before, and I know other beings have said before (and this is not always a good explanation) that creation is a circle. That actually works in some ways for understanding some levels of mathematics, because the saying that you create something and you meet yourself coming is a joke, but it's true.

Yes, and see, it makes a lot of sense of some of the earlier books, because at that time I was asking about things at the center of creation, but we didn't have any idea what the words meant, or we were told things, like the place that creates creators is at the center of creation. But you know, there was no frame of reference at that time for what the totality was.

That's right; it was defining itself through the use of the term, which doesn't work.

But we didn't know what it was the center of.

Well, that's right.

So that's why ...

You had to go on your path. It's at the center within the context of who you are and what you're doing, recognizing that it's constantly changing shapes and forms, and Earth might not always be at the center. But it's at the center in terms of what you're doing. A wheel has to be round with spokes and so on, yes? But a wheel could also look like this and have spokes; it just doesn't roll. [Chuckles.] A wheel could be a lot of different shapes, and at any given time the axle could be here or it could be there. It could be here; it could be there.

Chapter 6

Disentangling Cords of Discomfort

The Spirit of Transformation

I am the Spirit of Transformation. It is my intention to help you understand the meaning of disentanglement as compared to its impact on you. It is not my job to analyze it but rather to help you appreciate how it works.

Disentanglement is intended to extricate you from the uncomfortable ties that bind you to portions of your demonstrated personality, which for the most part have very little to do with who you actually are and who you will show yourself to be once disentanglement is well under way. You might say that it performs a clarifying function, but clarity in your time is often associated with the mind. Disentanglement, however, is more associated with the physical body, the feeling self, the spirit self, the inspirational self, and the instinctual self.

You haven't heard about the inspirational self before because this has largely been referred to as the soul self or the spiritual self. The inspirational self is that which can act quickly on the best feelings and instincts passed to you from all sources who respect and appreciate you as you are without having to be something to please others. In short, it is what is focused to you as a unique personality, as an individual designed to reflect that portion of Creator.

The inspirational self works like this [holds index and middle finger together straight up] with the soul self, or the spirit body. But it also works just as compatibly with the feeling body and the physical body. It tends to think of the mental body as a child and does not indulge it but rather will simply ignore it if the mind wishes to exert its will. The inspirational self will disregard that will, which it can do, and provide the pathways for inspiration. I am talking about the mechanism by which your instinctual self can pass wisdom or awareness to you that you might need to apply in your physical life. Equally, it functions to create a welcoming atmosphere for benevolent beings, guides, angels, and others who might wish to pass on a message, either felt or heard as a word or two in the mental process. This is to inspire the best quality of life for you and perhaps even for others around you. That is how it functions. The circuit from the spirit-self comes from one direction and the instinctual self from another.

I am coming through to speak now in order to provide the necessary understanding of the *value* of disentanglement, because the value allows you to gently, without trauma, release the portions of you that are the masks you have taken on to survive in your culture, family, or society. Disentanglement allows you to gradually, gently remove these masks while gradually, gently counterbalancing that removal as the weights and measures tilt toward balance. You understand that disentanglement allows this process to take place slowly so that as the mask is gradually removed the feeling that is generated is one of the emerging natural personality you were born with.

This is directly connected to the essence of your true self, meaning that which bears the marks of your immortal personality. These are the marks by which you might be recognized by someone you never met in a given life because there is a familiarity, a sense of feeling exchanged between you and someone else. You come up to someone in a crowd, you begin to chat, and pretty soon you're like old friends. Without doubt, that kind of connection allows you to disentangle from the old timeline of the third dimension and directly connect to the new timeline in the most easy, gentle, and accessible way. The attempt to grab on to the new timeline does not become a hit-or-miss thing, something there is no apparent way to accomplish other than what may sound insufficiently substantial. When you do that, it then becomes easy to make the shift, even though your body might still be in that old timeline with others in that society.

Here is the old timeline [draws line on the left, see fig. 6.1] and here is the new [draws line on the right]; you have these dotted lines here. The disentanglement essentially allows you to do this [draws an X with broken lines].

It does not disenfranchise you from your world, but it allows you to move flexibly between the old and the new, similar to the way alternating current pulses. Alternating current is essentially like a switch: It's on; it's of. It's on; it's off. The process of disentanglement is not a matter of being on or off, but the switch can happen so quickly that those in the old time with whom you may very well be interacting on a daily basis are not aware that you are, in some senses, between worlds. And those in the new time line with whom you interact

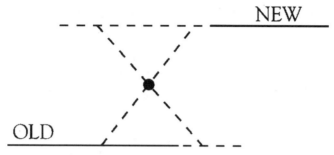

Fig. 6.1. Disentanglement helps you access the new timeline.

in your day-to-day life are not aware that you are also available to access the old world (using "old world" interchangeably with "old time line").

So it allows you a greater degree of flexibility and, perhaps most importantly, safety; that is a key factor. When one feels safe, one is much more inclined to reveal the personality qualities that one treasures or feels shy about in a group of unknown people. Therefore, the safer you feel, the more likely you are to demonstrate that "new" disentangled personality, which is your actual personality. ("New" is in quotes here because it's not really new. It's the personality you came in with when you were born out of your mother.) Disentanglement essentially sheds that which does not serve you. But — and this is important — it does *not* shed the valuable experience that provides for you the necessary discernment to live your life. In short, it does not shed your wisdom.

Wisdom is the key here. You are here as the Explorer Race largely to assimilate wisdom that can be applied on many different levels, and that works in concert with responsibility for consequences. You have, then, an ideal situation in which something you would do to improve the quality of your life anyway is actually easing your way to a newer, better world, a world in which complications, discomforts, and other things that seem random (but really are not) are much less a portion of your day-to-day life.

Disentanglement does another important thing: It helps you to feel less attached to the behavior of others as a reflection of your own. So many people feel the need to apologize for the acts of family members or of someone else, even if that person is not even related to you in given circumstances. I grant that there are times when such apologies are appropriate, but when this is done all the time, it simply allows that rebellious family member to be constantly offensive, because he or she has an explainer, a person saying, "Oh, please forgive him" or "Don't pay any attention to him."

Disentanglement allows you to feel more complete as an individual and gives you much greater flexibility and motion. Perhaps it also allows you to feel what is an opportunity and what will simply lead you down a path to unhappiness. In short, it clarifies your body's physical messages to you through feelings you can understand, not something vague. A warmth is love or good for you in that moment, whereas a tightness or discomfort might mean it's not good for you in that moment.

Such clear and simple *feeling* messages take the place of an analytical process, which can always and only be based on the manners, mores, and values of the culture you are in — not just the ideal manners, mores, and values, but the actual ones you live in. That's the key. Even though a given society might say wonderful things and might have ideals that are definitely worth looking into and striving for, what occurs on the day-to-day level are the real values.

One can always be clear about what those values are when one observes twelve- to thirteen-year-olds, because it is at this age that they are moving away from their parents as their models for behavior, albeit temporarily. They are adapting not only to their peers but also to the values presented to them en masse — not just religious, spiritual, or personal values from parents and other concerned family members. When you observe the behavior of the average twelve- to thirteen-year-old in your society, whatever that society is, you will be able to quickly understand that the actual values of your society may not directly connect to the ideals you were raised with. Of course, when these youngsters get older and begin consciously or unconsciously to emulate their parents or the adults who raised them, they may shed some of this apparent rebelliousness. But I call it "apparent" because rebelliousness is usually a direct reflection of actual values, not promoted ones.

I am telling you this to help you appreciate and apply the means of disentanglement and to allow you to rationalize these means so that your minds can feel they are being given an understanding of either the value of disentanglement, which your mind is not clear about, or its purpose and function, which the mind will accept over value anytime. This is why the physical body and the feeling body provide a much better way of knowing heat, warmth, and other good feelings within you. This is a much better way of knowing whether something serves you — and hence others — than what your mind tells you, which is always based on something abstract, such as words or motivations compelled by having to adapt to a given society's rules or, more often the case, behaviors and reactions to what you've been exposed to as a youngster. What we have here, then, is a mental explanation of disentanglement, which is my intention to give you tonight.

EXERCISE TO CONNECT TO YOUR PERSONAL AND PROFESSIONAL GOALS

Say,

> "I am asking ("I am asking" is in the present) that cords of support, nurturance, love, and strength be brought to me and connected to me in the most loving and gentle way to bring energy from resources who have a great abundance themselves, who wish to lovingly support me and provide strength and insight, and who support my wisdom process in the most gentle way for me, so that I may achieve my personal and professional goals."

Now, here's a little homework to do before this request. Briefly write down your personal and professional goals. Make sure they are practical and things you can live with. Your goals can't be pie in the sky. They have to be something down-to-earth that you would like to experience on a regular basis, not something you think you *should* experience.

Say more about "pie in the sky." Do you mean unrealistic?

Yes, not grounded, as people sometimes say. Make sure that your goals are grounded in reality. Say what you want, but make sure that it is a real thing, not something that is associated with, for example, "I want to fly around in spaceships with all my space friends."

The gold-light beings can do a great deal. They do their best work if you are lying on your back with no folded arms or legs. If you fall asleep, you might tend to roll over on your side, in which case they can do some things, but every time you fall asleep during the process, you might have to add a few more nights.

Are they basically untangling the solar plexus? Is that where most of the stored trauma is?

Oh, no. It's all over your body and your auric field, everywhere. It is a worthy process and it's not difficult. You give yourself permission, then basically other beings do it for you, but you must be receptive. Not everyone can be receptive right away, so it takes time. Over time, you develop a degree of trust and faith in the process. It is not something you do for a year and then go on to do something else. It is essentially a lifetime thing, because it performs its initial task and then functions as maintenance for you — the gold-light beings can remove discomforts that have become attached to you during the day on a daily basis, not just cords and connections rooted in the past.

Let me go back to the drawing (fig. 6.1). Now, the bottom triangle extends up and the upper one connects to the new timeline.

Not a solid triangle, you understand; it's a broken line.

But are we at any moment physically or mentally or in any other way conscious of being on that other timeline, or does the movement happen so fast that it doesn't have a chance to filter down to the mental body?

It's not intended that it feel like anything other than a benevolent change in your personality that you feel better with and that very often others react to in a better way. The world around you does not apparently change, though your attitude about the world around you will. So it is a subtle difference but also profound in that it greatly improves the quality of your life and often the lives of those immediately around you — family, friends, and so on.

I'm hoping facilitators will pick it up, use it, teach it, and share it.

That process has already begun. I do not intend to speak only to the mind, but since the mind is that portion of the total being that can withhold permission because of the way you've been conditioned, it is my intention to soothe its fears. In this way, the mind can potentially, at least, offer permission without feeling it is being coerced. The mind often feels coerced and then becomes truculent in terms of allowing benevolent change for any individual who might desire that change.

When you are going through this process, sometimes you will feel angry and resentful because those feelings were happening when you were donning a mask and suppressing your actual personality. So as you disentangle, some of those feelings are released. It will, for the most part, have nothing to do with what is going on in your life, though it might seem like that sometimes, and this might be a minor influence. But largely it has to do with the release of those feelings you are actually feeling. Because you are actually feeling them, they can be processed. But when you suppress them and stubbornly wear the mask, the feelings cannot be processed, resolved, nurtured, or healed, and they build up into a coagulated and often destructive mask.

Is it okay for the reader to ask the Spirit of Transformation to help with this? Or is that not something you want to get involved with?

No. It is my job to inform, to educate, and to enumerate, but it is not my job to activate.

SOME EFFECTS OF DISENTANGLEMENT

You've given some side effects, but are there other results of disentanglement that people should be aware of so that they don't think something strange is happening to them as they go deeper into this process?

It is possible to experience a change in attitude toward those around you. For instance, in a relationship, perhaps your loved one does something maddening, something that might have driven you to the edge many times. It is very possible that this maddening thing will either no longer bother you or will trigger a decision that prompts you to seek other companions or, more likely, friendships, so that you no longer require your companion to fulfill all things for you.

Very often in relationships in your time, there is the mistaken impression that the husband or the wife must also be the best friend. I do not feel that this is required. It is required that he or she be a friend, and a good friend, but not the best friend. The best friend is usually someone a bit more objective in terms of the relationship, someone you can speak things to that you would never say to your companion because it might hurt his or her feelings. Therefore, know that such things might come up. It is equally possible that the behavior, whatever it is, however small or great it might be, will simply become something you have less of a feeling about. You don't really take it as seriously anymore. It doesn't bother you. Furthermore, you have no desire to change it, so you will stop trying over and over again in direct and indirect ways to change this behavior. You might even come to find it amusing, which is a very good way to break the tension, as you know.

It is also possible that you will change your attitude toward animals and plants — in short, toward nature all around you. You will probably begin to feel better about it even if you are living in the middle of a city that is all concrete and steel. You might, when you see the weed growing up through the sidewalk, find beauty in it instead of seeing it as something that needs to be removed. You may have a different attitude about your lawn. In short, you will stop seeking artificial perfection in what you are creating — in your lawn, your children, your companion, your students. Instead, you will begin to allow and encourage the nature of the true personality of those beings to emerge.

You might also find that your wardrobe can change. Certain colors once favored by you might go out of favor for a time. Sometimes you wear certain colors as a way to support or nurture some condition that is beyond your means to take action on, or this becomes a compensating factor. As you begin to experience this disentanglement process over a period of months, you might notice that although you were once attracted to wearing, for example, purple or red or black, you suddenly are enchanted with orange, yellow, or pink. You begin to integrate these colors into your daily wardrobe regardless of whether they are in fashion or not. It doesn't necessarily sharpen your fashion sense, but it will very likely affect the colors and possibly even the fabrics you choose to wear.

How do the colors you wear reflect your level of development or your feelings?

Let's not call it your level of development. Rather, let's say that the colors you wear might support what you are feeling in a given moment. For instance, if you are feeling stressed or put upon to do much more than you want to do or are even capable of doing, you might be attracted to a given color. It is not the same for everyone. The assumption is "this" means "this" and "that" means "that," but "this" is not so, just as a dream symbol for one person might be different for another. Granted, many dream symbols are similar for all people, but all dream symbols are not the same for all people. Therefore, it is not good to say that this color means this and that color means that.

So just enjoy it; don't analyze it.

It's important not to analyze because in analyzing you support the mind's desire to be approved of at all costs. You are not born with that desire, but it is conditioned into you by your physical environment, not only in the formative years, but as you come into your teenage years and so on. You want to please and be approved of by those peers you admire or at least want to be liked by. So I would say that the demonstration of personality is a fragile issue and must be treated gently.

You must understand that personality requires nurturance in order to feel confident about demonstrating itself, especially in a world of polarity. One cannot stand in front of the mirror and demand, "Be yourself." You can say other things, but the mind, remember, has been conditioned to make demands. Those in authority when you were a youngster — your parents or grandparents, your teachers at school, those you had to look up to or that you did look up to — often made demands that might have seemed completely reasonable to those adults. The adult does not always know how to explain the reason to the child or does not feel the child can understand it, so the adult will simply make a demand. Thus the child learns, in a very powerful way, that making demands is appropriate behavior and ought to be emulated for the sake of approval and love. That is why little children will often sound authoritarian to their younger siblings or to dogs and cats around them, and it is cute up to a point. But as they get older, that authoritarianism can constrict the demonstration of their true personalities, to say nothing of how it might constrict those around them.

Can you give us words to use for disentangling from the authority issue?

Why don't you say, "I am asking that unnatural-for-me authorities who make demands on me that are not natural and not in my best interest easily fall away from me by a mechanism supported within me by loving, generous, and nurturing gold-light beings and other light beings." Understand that I am stating this in a clear way because I am speaking to your mental bodies. This might not be the most heart-centered thing to say, but the whole point at this time is to get the mental body or the mind to release restrictive control and to allow the process to go forward in the most nurturing and gentle way rather than demand that the process, even the disentanglement process, be done in the fastest, strongest, and most authoritarian way.

It will be fun for people to see who's under their masks.

Most of you are much more gentle, spontaneous, artistic, and affectionate than you now know. Many of the qualities that you and others like about you will remain in some form, but many of the qualities that make you feel guilty will fall away. That is because those qualities are conditioned into you but are not part of you. That is how the gold-light beings can remove, in that sense, a cord you have sent out to something because you are trying to understand your world.

Cords can be with you for a lifetime. A child sends out cords all the time to parents and peers that are intended to help that child to understand, because very rarely can parents communicate in the way the child needs to hear and understand. A child does not learn only from the pronunciation of words; a child learns from feeling and touch. These cords provide a more profound connection to the child's learning mechanism. This is understood nowadays in special education classes where children who have been unable to learn in conventional ways are nurtured and perhaps touched by those who are attempting to teach them life skills. This nurturing helps them survive easier, get along on their own, or perhaps learn things not unlike what other children are learning, but in such a way that the child feels safe to learn and does not feel a demand to perform like a trained being.

CORDING AT BIRTH

Say more about these cords.

You completely understand the function and value of cords when you are born, even while inside your mother, because there is the tube from your mother's body to your body. As an infant within your mother's body, you understand that cords are good, that your life depends on cords, that you are corded to something greater, some spiritual thing beyond you. Often you understand it much better in your early years, as well as in utero, than you might as an adult. The infant inside the mother is presented with obvious physical lessons. And at that stage, you are not interested in complexities and complications; you are interested only in what is pure, clear, and true. Therefore, since there is a cord that you can clearly understand is supporting your life, you will immediately assume that life is supported by cords.

The child growing in the mother is not only receiving from the mother but also giving back, so the cord is going both ways. The child, the boy or the girl, reaches out along the cord for what it needs, but also tends to give back a sense of personal enjoyment about life. The mother is much more aware of this when the child is kicking inside, flexing its muscles, but sometimes she is simply happily aware of the happy being inside her. Sometimes the glow (as it's called) of a pregnant woman is equally prompted not only by the mother's feelings about being pregnant but also by the child within. So the glow is real.

Once the baby is born, does the child put cords out?

Think about it. The child is raised in a water environment, inside the mother in a saline environment, so it is essentially at that stage of its life a water being, not an air breather. Picture an extraterrestrial who normally lives under the water coming to Earth. It's as if you are demanding, in the baby's physical process, that the extraterrestrial suddenly become a terrestrial — with very little warning. The child suddenly goes from a water being to something else, an air breather. This is startling and often done in ways that are not so nurturing, though it can be done in more nurturing ways, such as water birth. When it is done in this nurturing way, the quality of life greatly improves because the child learns as it emerges from the mother that life on Earth is an extension of the mother, not something other than the mother.

When the child believes that life on Earth is something other than its mother, the first thing it does is send out cords to understand what it is. The infant will plant those cords in whatever adults are around it in those first few hours of life, as you understand it. Therefore, it might quickly cord the doctor, the nurse, and the midwife — and the child may not ever pull those cords out. So whatever the doctor, the nurse, or the midwife go through, the child might be feeling that on a stimulating level.

To the same degree, the child might cord the parents. This is why some children demonstrate qualities beyond their years, whereas others seem to have great difficulty in learning simple things about acceptable and unacceptable behaviors from parents and siblings. What often happens here is that the child gets mixed messages along the lines of the cords. Remember, if you are suddenly thrust into the unknown world of Earth, you don't go, as in water birth, from being a water being inside your mother to being a water being on Earth who can choose to be an air breather as well. Water birth is best done in a large tank so that the child can swim out of its mother. It will swim naturally; it doesn't have to be taught. If you are presented with a loving water birth, then you are much more likely to send cords out to beings who demonstrate an ongoing love for you. For instance, you will send a cord out to your mother and perhaps your father or brother or sister, but you will tend to send it out that way to beings who have an immediate sense of connection to you.

But if you don't know where you are and you are thrown into a world that is completely unfamiliar, you will do what people do (whether they are adults or children) when they are thrown into an unknown situation: You will either withdraw or you will seek anywhere and everywhere for stimulation to understand what it is and where it is you exist in that moment. In short, you will use no discrimination whatsoever. But if the child, for instance, swims out of the mother or is gently welcomed by loving family members and sung to and cooed to and so on — it doesn't always have to be a water birth, though that's the easiest way; it can be a nurturing birth in other ways too — then the child is more likely to feel that this air world is safe compared to the water world.

HOW WE CORD IN CHILDHOOD

Okay, but let's consider the typical case in the hospital. The infant cords to people in the hospital. It goes home and cords to people at home. Then it goes to school and it cords, and it just keeps going through life cording, then?

Yes. Just think about it. In your modern culture, in a society where a child's education is often more academic than based on values and principles, the child becomes confused. The child thinks that learning about the life of Abraham Lincoln or George Washington may be exactly the same value, no greater or less, as learning how to be a good citizen — meaning how to share your toys with your brothers and sisters. At that level, citizenship training immediately takes place. So in terms of cording, when understood in a spiritual, mystical, or medicinal society, it is understood that one is asking to have these things gently resolved in some way. A disentanglement is more direct in the mental society of your time. You are, in that sense, demanding that children be mental and insisting that they be mental above all else. It is small wonder that so few relationships are lasting, in terms of husbands and wives, girlfriends and boyfriends, and even among friends. Because if you approach a relationship on an intellectual level, aside from a sexual one in the case of an intimate relationship, you are missing the vast reservoir that can be given and shared and appreciated. In short, what do people want in intimate relationships? They want to be loved for who they are. But by the time most people come to the age where intimate relationships are acceptable, they are already confused about who they are. However, they know when someone is being kind and loving to them as compared to when that person is being cruel.

I'm bringing water birth up because it will become increasingly common in the future. One of the reasons for this is so people can begin to regard water as something that not only keeps them alive, that entertains and amuses them, and that fosters growth in the plants and animals they need but also is a sacred fluid that welcomes them into the world and therefore must be allowed to be itself. The whole water-birth impact is going to encourage people to allow water to be safe and to find technological means to transform pollution. And this, of course, will be very good for economies. Those technological means all exist right now; people just need to want to do them. These technologies will certainly give many people a lot of work and create good businesses for many, and of course over time they will improve the water and the earth and human relationships with both. Now, in order to embrace physical life on Earth, you need to feel safe and nurtured by life around you. Water birth will provide that means to allow the connection between the academic, the technological, and the heart-centered worlds. I realize this is not a new thing; people have been giving birth in the water for hundreds of years, which has been documented in your time. Only recently has it come into greater popularity once again. So it is not something unnatural; it is just something that requires a different shift, an allowance.

I want to understand these cords. So as the child, the adolescent, and the young adult, we send these cords out all during life to things or to people or what?

You might even think of your childhood, how sometimes you had a favorite chair or a bicycle. You may have very well sent a cord to that object because it is something you drew a string from or felt nurtured in. In short, you have no limit to the amount of cords you can send out.

So you might have cords to your motorcycle, automobile, and all the houses you've lived in?

That's right.

CORDING IN ADULTHOOD

So here's the adult now, and there are cords to everything the person ever contacted?

Possibly. Only possibly.

How do those cords affect the person now? Are they pulling on her energy? Are they confusing her? How does it work?

It tends to keep people in the past, and if your past was loving, nurturing, and supportive, then that is fine. But this is not the case for most people in your society in your time.

So everything traumatic that's ever happened, you have a cord to that trauma?

Not necessarily a cord to an event, no.

To the person who caused the trauma?

Or even to someone who witnessed the trauma. Maybe you were spanked for something as a child, and you did not understand, as children often don't, the mental concept of what you did and why you were being punished. You might not, in that circumstance, send a cord to your father or mother who's spanking you, but you might very well send one out to your brother or sister or your dog or cat because they are there and you're hurting. You're fighting tears and trying to understand. Perhaps later, the parent found a way to explain it to you that you could understand, but the cord is still there.

Are there many cords to the same person — for instance, to parents or siblings or if you are married a long time, to people in relationships?

Let me just give you an idea. Let's take an average forty-five-year-old adult in the United States in the average social and workplace conditions. In your time, this average person could have several thousand cords.

The purpose of disentanglement is to disentangle you from the pain, discomfort, and restrictiveness — in short, from the discomforting aspect of whatever that cord was connected to. Therefore, you might easily be able to change attitudes without someone saying, "You should forgive your brother or your sister or your uncle or your aunt. That happened thirty years ago. Why are you still angry at him or her?" You will try to mentally rationalize why you are still angry because you feel the anger, and it's real, but you may not be able to say it in a rational way to another person. Maybe you can, but most often you cannot. Therefore, regardless of the best intentions of those who are trying to convince you to let go of this old grudge, you don't know how because you are corded to the pain and the anger of the time. You are not corded to the pain and the anger per se, but you are corded to something physical of the time. *Cords go to physical things*, whether they are physical in this dimension or other dimensions. They are, in fact, things of substance. That's why I say one does not cord an idea.

DISENTANGLING YOUR CORDS

Since cords represent your vast means of understanding the world around you, then what happens during disentanglement when these cords are removed? Not all cords are removed, you understand. Obviously the connection cord between you and Creator is never removed; however it might be clarified or purified so that discomforting things attached to it are removed. But *all* cords are not removed. Some cords are simply clarified and nurtured, meaning that some cords might be going to things that are nurturing you right now. In that sense, one never says to gold-light beings, "Please remove all cords." One does not do that because some cords are feeding you in the moment, especially if you have asked for something to be fed to you to support and nurture you in some specific way or for some specific circumstance. If you ask for all cords to be removed, you can unintentionally have those removed as well, because the beings will tend to follow what you say — not because they are stupid, but because it is their job, just like all other beings in your society, to serve your learning process as well as your needs.

So they don't just remove the discomfort. They actually remove the cord?

If a cord was sent out prompted by discomfort, then the cord itself will be removed, purified, and allowed to come back to your body in a purified state. It is not cut off and discarded. They never do that.

So you get the energy back that you used to send out the cord?

That's right, and that's why often over time with disentanglement, you begin to feel physically stronger or mentally clearer, or you find it easier to adapt and accomplish spiritual goals. In short, you have more energy to do more things.

So at this moment the cords are physical, but we can't see them or feel them?

Sometimes you can. Occasionally you will get a stinging vibrational feeling, and unless it is associated with a disease, it might be associated with your bellybutton. Sometimes in your bellybutton — being the initial physical cord through which you understood the cording process inside your mother (aside from your spiritual connection to Creator) — you might get a resonating pang, as it were, like an echo, when you are being corded by someone else. You will sometimes get a discomforting feeling.

It works both ways?

That's right. So if this resonant feeling suddenly occurs and you get this discomforting feeling at the root of your bellybutton, which goes inside your body, it is your physical body's way of telling you that something has just entered your body that needs to be released.

The gold-light beings remove the discomforting cords you send out, but what about all the ones that are sent to you?

There are just as many. When I said that the average forty-five-year-old might have thousands of cords, I was including cords from others. Now, animals do not cord, so you're not going to be corded by your dog or cat. You might cord them, but they won't cord you. They don't do that, because they aren't here to learn anything. Human beings are the ones who are here to learn.

If you're asking to remove the discomfort from a cord from someone else, will the gold-light beings remove that from you and send it back to that person? Is that how it works?

That's right. They will extract it from you and resolve the physical discomfort around it to the best of their ability, unless it has festered into something over the years, in which case a trip to the physician might be necessary before or after, but you will usually know that. You may have an ongoing discomfort, but I won't go into that; you can resolve that on your own. In short, the cord will be removed, purified, and clarified and sent back to that other person.

Even though they didn't ask for it to be sent back?

They might not want it, and they might very well try to cord you again, which is why disentanglement needs to be an ongoing thing indefinitely. In some societies, when children are nurtured and welcomed as one often hears about with extraterrestrials and so on, the cording process does not take place, because one is nurtured and loved and raised that way. And nothing ever happens to the child, even as it grows up, becoming a young person and then an adult. Nothing ever happens to it that is not easily and nurturingly and lovingly felt as well as mentally understood, if there is a mental body. Therefore, the cording process is not only unnecessary, but does not take place, even if the physical birthing mechanism is similar (meaning that in utero, one has a cord in the mother). But that cord is understood. It is often suggested in the religions and philosophies of those cultures that that cord is the connection to your mother in that stage, and that your mother's cord is connected to the Creator. It is thought that your mother splits her cord, and that when you come out of your mother she essentially shares or gives life to your cord to the Creator.

You need to understand the sacredness of mother herself. Mother becomes part of Creator during conception and the entire birth cycle. This allows Creator to come as close as a creator would like to come to joining the human race through the mother as a representative. Of course during this time, mother must be herself, so this is why she often has mood swings, sometimes even major ones. It is also why on occasion mothers take a long time recovering their own personalities, even well after the birth.

All souls who become women on this planet are instructed by their teachers before life that they will have a special obligation to Creator to carry a portion of Creator's consciousness during conception and birth. Of course before life, this sounds and feels wonderful to the souls. During their lives, it does not always feel so good, however. If the mother was treated and honored as bearing a portion of Creator as well as the soul of the child, most women would have a better pregnancy experience. It is unfortunate that during your time and in your culture a mother does not receive this respect and, perhaps even more importantly, does not receive the guidance that she needs to comfortably accommodate Creator's personality within her own.

Now, I'm not saying that this is necessarily always and only true. But I'm saying that in cultures not associated with Earth at this time, if birth takes place in a similar fashion, it is usually considered to be that way. This allows the child to feel that its mother is not only a wonderful being that the child loves but also a sacred instrument.

CORD REMOVAL AFTER PHYSICAL DEATH

Let's get back to Earth. What happens when someone dies and all these cords are running back and forth?

Often what happens is a long period of resolution after death. That means the soul, the essence of one's personality, leaves the body, but the soul still has somewhat of a responsibility. Remember, these cords are physical; you don't see them, but some sensitive people might sometimes see them. I really do not recommend preserving the body — let it return to Earth without boxes and concrete bunkers around it. As the body returns to Earth, it gradually dissolves all those cords, not only the ones it sent out when the personality was in it, when the soul was in the body, but the connections that others sent. In other words, it dissolves cords coming in from the outside, but only if the body is allowed to decompose in a natural way. If the body is preserved, then those cords you may have sent to that person can create a problem. The soul will tend to stick close to Earth when that problem exists if the body is unnaturally preserved. It might hang around, maybe thirty days in Earth time, hoping to resolve it, working with teachers, guides, angels, and so on to continue removing those cords, which can be done very quickly since the personality is no longer in the body. But it requires the soul to hang around to do that, whereas if the body naturally dissolves on its own, then the soul can leave. It might hang around for a short time but not very often. If you, for instance, sent out a cord, you did not necessarily send out that cord hatefully. The vast majority of cords are sent out simply because you need or want something. If you've sent out a cord to this person when he was alive and then he dies and his body is preserved, it becomes harder for you, the individual who consciously or unconsciously sent the cord, to let go of that person. In short, grief might take longer, and the natural process of transformation is greatly slowed down because of the desire to unnaturally preserve the apparent innocence of life.

Aside from commercial and industrial motives, the whole idea and appeal of preserving the physical body — so one can gaze on it not only at a funeral, which is understandable, but when the body is in the earth and no one's ever going to see it again — is that the body is formed by after-death artists at the mortician's, and they are artists. The face especially is formed into something that looks idealistic, not unlike the way one considers babies to be. The babies are idealistic. They are pure. Likewise, this is an attempt to re-create that pure innocence of childhood so that the friends and relatives can have the memory, the last memory (if one goes to the funeral and looks in the coffin) of seeing the pure innocence of this person. This is the appeal on the deepest level. I am not saying that this is a bad desire, but I feel that you are greatly complicating your lives by it, from my perspective. It is the unnatural desire to preserve the quality of life for the passed-over loved one rather than putting enough attention toward the quality of life for the living. That is why one often overdoes a funeral. But you know, it is not my job to criticize your society; it is my job to help you to understand it better.

What about cremation?

Cremation is acceptable, but only marginally so, because it is not natural. The natural way is for the body to decompose on or under the surface of the earth. Under is acceptable, but the purely natural way is for the body to be *on* the surface of the earth and decompose. Now I realize that in your time this is not acceptable; too many people are on the surface of the earth, and thus you would be tripping over bodies. The smell would not be pleasant. But think about the societies you have read about where a bier of some form is built and the body is laid upon it and allowed to gradually decompose in nature. Even though the animals might come and do things, this is allowed because it is considered a returning to the earth. I am not, in this sense, trying to tell you how to live your lives. That is entirely up to you. But in time, I feel that death will be celebrated in a different way, that the recollection of the loved one and all these things going on in the funeral ceremony — be they religious, philosophical or heart-centered — will evolve on their own. But it would be best if the physical body was placed in such a way, perhaps wrapped in a sheet or something, on or within the earth so that it can simply dissolve on its own.

You said cremation was barely acceptable. How does that affect the cording process?

In the sense of the soul hanging around Earth, with cremation it might hang around for twenty-eight instead of thirty days. So it is better than preservative and wooden boxes and concrete bunkers and all that but only marginally. Now I will give you another choice: Burial at sea is considered completely natural, but only if the body is wrapped and dropped into the ocean as one often finds in seagoing societies or navies. This is also considered natural and completely acceptable.

CORD CONNECTIONS AND DISENTANGLEMENT

Let's say a man or woman has many sexual relationships over the course of his or her life. Is he or she corded to every one of those?

Oh, certainly.

What effect does that have on his or her life, then?

Well, of course, every succeeding relationship is still tied to the one in the past, to say nothing of being tied to your parents and so on. This tends to color the ongoing relationship cycle, which is why people often have similar experiences from one relationship to the next. It's the cording, not the karma. Karma, to my understanding, is a philosophical way of explaining the circumstances of your life, but it is not, nor was it ever, intended to become an iron rule.

What about those we read about who are contactees, or as they're now called, abductees? Are they corded to the ETs on ships?

If they are little children, it is less likely they will cord unless they are in that moment missing mom or dad, or dog or cat or something. It is less likely that they will cord, because if they are, say, three, four, five, six, or seven years old, and especially if they've been nurtured by their parents to accept and appreciate different appearances of other human beings, they will simply accept the appearance of the extraterrestrial at face value. When they are older and have to deal with the complexities of society, or if they were raised to feel afraid of other people in general, they will always and immediately not only cord all the extraterrestrials they see but also run cords around the vehicle and cord beings they don't see as well as attempt to cord the ship itself. In most cases, if the extraterrestrial society is advanced enough, the ship will have a living element to it and will reject the cord. The extraterrestrials will probably have the cord in them and accept it during the time the individual is actually on the ship, or they will integrate it into their society in some way — sometimes contactees are taken to the place of culture of these beings — so the cord will be allowed. But once the person is returned to Earth, the extraterrestrials will release that cord so that they can go on with their lives, using a process not unlike the one you are being taught now.

How do people ask for disentanglement when they don't know the names or descriptions of the beings who corded them?

Just let the gold-light beings do their work. If the cord does not support you, if it is associated with discomfort in any way, it will be removed and resolved. You do not have to specify ETs unless you want to, but sometimes cords connected to ETs might be nurturing. Still, ETs do not cord you. Nevertheless, if you ask for certain energies and supports, one might liberally interpret that to mean energy coming from ETs. Therefore, if you ask for all cords connected to all ETs to be removed …

You are shooting yourself in the foot.

So it might be good to be specific, asking for only the discomforting cords — either from you to extraterrestrials or from them to you — to be disentangled from you (which is unlikely, but you can say it like that). Adapt it. It doesn't have to be what I said per se.

This will also help the person who may have an attitude, such as an individual who believes ETs are dangerous. Granted, this might be fostered by fictionalisms in your society, but if you have that attitude, you need to honor it within you. If the gold-light beings do not see any ET cords running to you, they will simply ignore it.

If you go into a public place and see thousands of people who each have thousands of cords and they are walking down halls and in and out of rooms, or they go to the opera or to the baseball stadium, how does all this work as far as keeping cords straight?

You understand that the cords, while they are physical, are not of the same kind of physicality you experience as a solid substance. If they were, you obviously wouldn't be able to move. But they are physical in the sense that they prompt physical experience and, of course, they are associated with feeling.

So they're very flexible? You can travel around the world and cords still connect you with others?

That's right. Of course, once you begin disentanglement, that number reduces quite a bit. Eventually, if you do disentanglement long enough, cords will essentially be down to a single digit on any given day. But you must remember, it's not that you are exclusively cording others or that others are exclusively cording you. It happens all over. You do them; they do you. It might be unconscious because you've been trained in your society to do it and you weren't sufficiently nurtured to *not* do it. Don't feel bad; just allow the gold-light beings to resolve it for you as you ask them to do it in the way you prefer. That's why it needs to be an ongoing process. Initially, of course, for the first year, year and a half or so, a lot is going on. But after a while, when there are very few cords connected to you, less goes on, and the disentanglement becomes a maintenance procedure.

At that point, when the cords are down to very few, is that when you can start asking to be corded to abundance and energy connections? You don't say how to do it yet, but what are the possibilities ahead relating to connections?

I think it's best for the first six months to not become overly involved in asking for connections. But if you feel tired and feel the need for connections, you can ask for them within three months. Now, some people will ask for connections immediately, but what will happen is that they won't be made.

So there's discernment on the part of the gold-light beings as to which of our requests to honor?

That's right, the gold-light beings know how to do their work. They are not subservient to your requests.

When people try to use this for some purpose that is not benevolent to themselves and others, will the gold-light beings ignore that?

They will ignore it.

So there's a fail-safe?

Yes, there is. And if one even asked light beings to do the work without the use of gold-light beings — light beings might be benevolent, wonderful beings, but given the specific light they are — they may not be able to protect you during the process. That's why you can ask for gold-light beings or for light beings who can work through gold-light beings or radiate or emanate toward them for your greater good. You can use your name. But gold-light beings *need* to be present. Simply by their presence and by working on you, gold light tends to protect you like a shield during the procedure. When cords are being removed or brought back to you, this creates a vulnerability. If it is only, say, white-light beings, they can give you all the love that exists, but they cannot protect you. They may very well have the wisdom or the experience, but the mechanism of protection is not a portion of white light. White light loves everything all the time, no matter what. So you can ask light beings to support the process, but gold-light beings must do the process so that you are safe.

I think we have contributed vastly to the understanding of this process. You are wonderful.

We may talk again about the process as time goes on and as you develop other curiosities, but for now I will say good night.

Good night. Thank you.

Chapter 7

All Creation Responds to Need

Ssjoooo

July 12, 2000

Those first few creators that you created, have we ever heard anything about them as deities or in mythology or anything?

That's a very good question, but no, you haven't. Really many thousands of creators existed before anybody started identifying deities. Now, you understand, I'm taking into account when you say, "we," you mean on Earth. No.

What about the rest? Well, it's irrelevant, the rest of the totality. We're not concerned with that right now.

Yes, because after all, their history is discussed for them.

Yes. And the thirteen, you haven't interacted enough to have shown up anywhere in our history or mythology or anything?

Not yours, no. Perhaps other planets but not in terms of interacting in the way you're talking about. We might be known on other planets but not on the basis of our interaction with them. Perhaps they were told.

THE BIRTH OF CREATING CREATIONS

Okay. So those first creators created creators, and it went on. They just created beings like themselves? They didn't actually create creations? I mean, who invented creating creations?

It came about largely because it is in the nature of creators to create, and after a while, one creates another creator, you understand. After a while, the beings began to realize that was not their function, so because they were all this creative energy, they began to notice things they could do, like when a child notices its abilities. The child can smell and taste. You've seen babies in cribs. They experiment; they make sounds. It's not at all unusual. And creators did this too, in their own way, perhaps a little vaster compared to a child, but the comparison is very appropriate. So they began doing similar things.

119

When a creator makes a sound, usually something happens, all right? So they noticed what was happening, and it basically started out as self-discovery like a child's self-discovery. So when things started happening, of course, they all got enthusiastically interested, and they all started doing it, and before you know it, you had creations — at least in the beginning. Once they started, they noticed that each of their creations was slightly different, so they got an introduction to the concept of individuality. Therefore, they would get fairly enthusiastic about their own creations and talk, as creators talk to each other, about the uniqueness of it. It wasn't competitive, of course.

More like, "Hey, look what happened! Look! When I do this, that happens!"

That's right; they were enthusiastic, joyful. And so that was really how that got started.

ALL CREATION RESPONDS TO NEED
So how did it all get encompassed within a totality? The creators started out there in space and made their creations?

Well, you understand that a lot of what I tell you is put into space and time connotations because that's the language. The basic language that exists here is space and time, and it's a limiting thing. So for me to say, "Well, there's creation, and we're beyond it," is just the simplest way to put it. It's a little difficult to conceptually describe something that is a feeling, so I can't really answer that question without misleading you.

Okay. But for our purposes, just to get a visual of it, we can imagine it as a sphere.

Yes, you can imagine it as something that exists, and then we're ...

Back a little bit.

Yes, but that's just a way to imagine it. It doesn't actually look like that.

At the center of creation, there is this place where creators seem to be formed. Remember the void? It was so noisy where they went in these tubes that the creator created the void where everything was quiet to get away from that.

Yes.

How did creators creating each other get to the point where there seemed to be an automatic function or a process there to create creators?

It is not the only place like that. Any time you talk to beings, as you know, they will speak on the basis of what they know, but they also might speak on the basis of what they feel is relevant to you. They might not necessarily tell you everything if they feel it has no meaning to you or would not do anything other than complicate your understanding of things — or worse, lead you astray as you try to understand something from a point of view meant for others. In short, they are also taking into account the reader.

You know that, generally speaking, all creation is responding to a need.

That's basic. And if you understand that, if this is the spot where creation is taking place, or creators are being created, then there is no reason why creators can't be created over there, if there is a need for that spatially. But remember that creation, or the place where creators are being produced, is described to you as one place, even though it might be another simultaneously and even though it might be everywhere at once. Now, recognize this as an example: We know that love exists everywhere, but it is not localized. It does not mean that the beings in those places are producing love or have love for each other and therefore love exists everywhere. It is within the massive creation itself; love exists there and everywhere else. Therefore, you can conceptualize that love is a feeling and that it exists everywhere.

It is no different for creators being generated. It happens on the feeling level, and it can happen simultaneously everywhere because love is everywhere. Also, creators can be generated everywhere. If you understand that, you will have a much better grasp of the whole definition of what happens in different places. The point of creation might easily be here, and we're calling that the center, but the center is not really the center; it's the focus. If we change the word "center" to the word "focus," then it works a lot better.

Ah! That changes things! Yes, good. We're close to the focus of creation because of the importance of the Explorer Race.

Not quite. When you think of focus, you might think of your eye. You see [through] the pupil of your eye, and your vision focuses. The pupil might be in the center, but sometimes the eye might drift to one side and focus over there. That's not the center. So the focus of what you are doing, yes, that's fine, but you have to understand that not everyone in all creations everywhere has any idea of what you're doing, nor (to put it bluntly), do they necessarily care. They might be affected by it, but they might not know anything about it, or it's not important for them to know. For the vast majority of beings, it's not important for them to know. Think about it: It might be important for creators to know, but for the beings in their creations, why would it even be important for them to know? So the vast majority of beings have no knowledge, and it is not necessary for them to know. If they knew, it would just complicate their lives.

If you take what we've been told so far through just love's creations (I think there are thirty-five to thirty-seven of them) and then the level of Jesus and Quah, who say they created just that part of it, could you give a percentage of the total, or is it so minuscule that it wouldn't even get to a thousandth of a percent or something?

It is what one cell might be to your physical body. This does not mean it is not vast. For the sake of the example only and not in an attempt to say "this is how big all that exists is," consider that the actual size of that cell — including all times, all dimensions, all space, and beyond, since that is really a very limited focus of existence. If you were able to simply fly in space across that cell, it might very easily take you 1,000 or 1,500 average lifetimes to do so traveling at a velocity that is three times the speed of light. Now, if you understand the distance ...

That's just up to Quah and Jesus; that's just ...

When they talk about what they have done and what they're doing, they've done that in that vast area, but there is much more.

That's why the Adventurer has to move so fast, trying to see it all! [Laughter.]

Yes. Of course, as you know from your experience living life here on Earth, it is moving fast that keeps you from seeing it all. The walker is much more likely to notice a beautiful flower or a charming child than someone speeding down the highway.

Then why is the Adventurer going so fast?

Because the Adventurer does not know that, and the Adventurer is impatient. The Adventurer is motivated by getting there to find out. But you know that the trip is what it's all about. The Adventurer does not know this yet. But you will add this to the Adventurer's knowledge, and then the Adventurer can have the pleasure. It won't be like, "Oh, no!" It will be the pleasure of beginning again. It's like, "Oh!" Fortunately the Adventurer will remember where it's been and will go back and begin again and, as you say, smell the flowers.

[Laughter.] All right. That satisfies my curiosity. But you really want to focus this on humans, so ...

Well, it's all right to ask these questions. I don't want you to feel shy to ask questions that are personally related, because very often they will bring up material for the book.

THE DIRECTIONS OF LOVE

All right. I thought that possibly the thirteen beings had extensions on Earth and perhaps they wanted to learn personal love?

No. I'll tell you why not. We have noticed this: The function of personal love ... because you are loving. Say, that's someone you love, and the circle is you. So that occurs, say, during a life in which you love someone, whoever that might be, including animals or your favorite plant and obviously husband or wife or child, and so on. After the limits are removed and you go beyond the veil, this happens. It's a bit more complicated, but I need to indicate direction. This happens as a result of your experience of personal love. You understand, this is actually spherical.

Okay. First it all goes in, afterward the love goes around, and then it radiates out.

That's right; it goes around in several different projections. That's the diagram of personal love. Also, impersonal love might simply be moving in all directions at the same time. Of course, there's unconditional love, which might not be moving but is everywhere at the same time. And it is possible, as you know on Earth, to have unconditional love on a personal level, meaning you love someone or something unconditionally.

It's rare.

But it happens, and that's possible. It is more often the case that unconditional love is impersonal, where you might have unconditional love for all beings, and it might be a conceptual thought. As you work on it through life, you manage to create moments when you can do that, sometimes in deep meditations, sometimes with great joy, and other times you actually achieve it functionally in your life. It's not common in the past or recent years, but it's getting there. So these functions you understand more clearly.

PERSONAL LOVE AND THE THIRTEEN

For us, we find that because we are waiting for contact with what we believe has created us, if we become involved in personal love, we will be drawn into the creation itself. But we feel that we have fulfilled our duty, what we are here for, by getting things going. There is no advantage for us to go into the creation to find something that hasn't come up. Remember, the whole thing started for us with that feeling of need radiating to us. Once the creation got going, when all these creations got going, we did not feel that need any more. But we expect some other feeling to radiate to us.

So if you're in the middle of it, you might not feel it.

That's right. We might not feel it the same way. So we're waiting, to put it simply, in the same place we were. Since we initially felt that feeling of need where we were, we have no reason to believe we will not feel what it is we expect to feel when that is generated. So that is why we are avoiding personal love. I don't think we can get involved in personal love without wanting to express it.

Yet you created beings with personal love, so you have to have it in you.

Well, it's like this: You might say, reasonably, that men and women create children, yet this is not something you can do by taking the chemicals, the organic compounds, and say, "Okay, let's assemble a child here on the table." As much as human beings are trying to create that concept, even in cloning, you still won't do that. Even in test-tube babies, you're still not doing it. You're not taking the ingredients — so many minerals, so much water — and assembling a child. Yet you can say that man and woman come together and in nine months or so out comes a child. Human beings create children. Of course, because you have concepts that are religious or spiritual, you will say, "We do that, but we can't explain it. We can't create a child any other way; we can only do it by man and woman coming together." So you say that God is something beyond you. In short, you adamantly refuse to believe that you are a portion of the One Being, the portion of everything, which means that you are God. Now, religious leaders over the years have noted from their point of view the pitfall of allowing people to believe that they are God because then they might feel omnipotent and do whatever they care to do and say, "I am God; I can do what I want." I support that they are trying to teach some kind of moral values and principles; this is a worthy effort. Yet it is true that you are a portion of the God-being, which does not mean that you are separate from the God-being. It is very difficult for a person to grasp that if he or she is a portion of something, he or she is it.

CREATOR-LIKE QUALITIES

Imagine that you had a bowl of chocolate pudding in front of you [chuckles]. You took a toothpick and stuck it into the chocolate pudding and then pulled out the toothpick. Isn't the pudding that stuck to the toothpick a portion of the chocolate pudding? Is it any less of a portion? When you put the toothpick back into the pudding, is that pudding that you pulled out any less of a portion? Is it something other than chocolate pudding? It may have traveled on the toothpick, but it went back in. In short, you can be a portion of the Creator and be the Creator. The Creator did not intend for you to ever think of yourselves as anything other than a portion of Itself. But because this Creator, as you know, is not as personally involved with Its creation — oh, It's personally involved with all of the benevolent aspects of Its creation, but It's not personally involved with this school you're in, the suffering — you have a situation in which you feel you're cut off more from the Creator. You're not. You don't feel that the Creator is personally involved in your life. It's very impersonal, and this is the problem. This is why you do not easily identify not just with being the Creator but, most importantly, having creator-like qualities.

That's the key. A lot of what Zoosh and Speaks of Many Truths have been doing in recent books — some of which is not published, some of which is especially from Speaks of Many Truths — is to remind you of your Creator-like qualities that you can access, all right? Yet the going has been slow because the attempt is being made that creators do not do whatever they want whenever they want. As anybody who is in business management knows, if you did whatever you want whenever you want, the business would fall down around you. If you were the entrepreneur, this would not only be a disaster for you personally but also for everyone who works for you. Furthermore, everyone the business serves would be affected. On a larger scale, that's similar to what creators do. They might be the creators of the creation, but they are responsible to the creation just as a mother and father are responsible to the child that they have, and most mothers and fathers are pretty responsible. As a result, the creator-like qualities (of course, with most creators, the first one is love in what you know as personal love and unconditional love and so on, all these things we've been talking about) must begin with that and expand into other things. But the foundation is that.

Because your Creator cannot be as personally involved with Earth and the Earth School (because of the nature of its being), it is not surprising that you might attribute human qualities on the basis of human desires to your gods. In short, your gods can do things that humans want to do and that you, of course, can do (for the most part) when you are not on Earth and are in your spirit form. The idea of turning to light and rising up into the sky is not something that one normally sees with a human being, so that's, of course, seen as a godlike quality. Yet even though this is something that is ascribed to the Christian religion, what the Christian God does is very similar to the recent interest in the ascension idea: It is turning to light and rising up. Even though the broader ideal of ascension is to raise others up in the process, still this is a desired quality by human beings because they are cut off from a personal interaction with the Creator of this universe.

If you weren't cut off from that personal interaction, you would understand that creator qualities are foundationally love in feeling, meaning that how you feel about yourself, how you react and act with yourself and others and so on — all of the things that have been talked about over and over, so I'm not going to exhaust that topic. But it is a feeling, and then it is an action. Love is always a feeling first, and then an action might follow, especially in the case of animated beings. If we understand that, then we recognize that the qualities of creators are really not understood on Earth, and that creators are not ...

Gods.

That's right.

BE MORE THAN YOUR CREATOR

When you think about that, it looks profoundly simple. But if creators are not gods, then what is a creator? That is the big misunderstanding. Then we get back to your original statement. After I showed you this, you said, "Who are the gods?" There are no gods. I realize we're playing with words here a bit, but let's say you all are a portion of the Creator, but since personal love is separate from that Creator, what does that suggest to you? Why, oh why, is everybody on this planet beyond infatuation desperately seeking personal love? "Where is my mate? Where is my lover? Oh, you're it! Oh, wonderful, wonderful, wonderful! Oh! Oh, you're not it! Where's my lover? Where's my mate?" Everyone says that. Children are raised to seek that. What does that suggest? You are desperately seeking personal love. Why?

Because we're not getting it from the Creator.

You're not getting it from the Creator, and you also know that on a deeper level, you are the Explorer Race and you are intended to become a creator at some point. What must you have that this Creator does not have for you? Not just personal love, because this Creator has personal love for the rest of Its creation because that's benign!

But we're separate.

You're separate, and your Creator cannot express personal love to you the way It expresses to the rest of Its creation — right? — because of the energies, the suffering, the pain on Earth. It's a school. It's Creation School, but it's a Creation School that this Creator never went to! That's something that's easy to forget. So what we're dealing with here, then, is that you are seeking the personal love that you're not getting from Creator, but you know at the deeper level that you are seeking a personal love that this Creator knows nothing about. It is your job to be more than this Creator, meaning that the kind of personal love that this Creator expresses unconditionally for all other beings in Its creation (and to some extent, in this creation It expresses personal love to the planets and so on) is not sufficient for you. That's why almost everybody (human beings) runs all over the planet seeking out personal love and trying to find something that is idealistic, meaning that goes beyond the kind of personal love that might suit other beings at other times in other places. In short, you're trying to re-create the wheel, as you say.

You're trying to create a personal love that does not exist in this Creator's universe. That's a big thing! That's why you're overwhelmed by it. That's why men and women have hormones that sometimes drive you, and that's why you assume that sex is associated with personal love: lovers have sex. It doesn't have anything to do with it. While you might celebrate your personal love by having sex, and that's perfectly acceptable, it doesn't necessarily have anything to do with real personal love.

First there's unconditional love; personal love comes after that, all right? So we know that personal love is built on a foundation of unconditional love.

Real personal love means (and we covered this a little bit already) that you have experienced in some way what the beings in your creation have already experienced, meaning you have on Earth (taking that from the creator level, as we've talked about already) the understanding of the human condition: Every human being knows that every other human being has a lot in common with him or her. Even though you don't always remember it and you get angry with each other sometimes — sometimes violently angry — in your clearer moments, you look at other human beings and know that basically they're a lot like you. So you're conscious of the human condition, and if life has been not too awful for you, you very often have a sense of humor about it. Without a sense of humor, you are definitely handicapped. A sense of humor is, to some extent, cultured into you, conditioned into you. Some people are born with a sense of humor; even if they're discouraged, they still have a sense of humor. Others come to find out about it.

Now, for you to experience personal love that comes from one of you to somebody else (from the concept in your minds), first we can do the mental. "This person has a lot in common with me, and if I find him (or her) attractive, maybe he (or she) will find me attractive too." At least, you hope that person will. However, first there is an attraction on the energetic level. That's kind of universal. You know, part of the confusion of being born in your time is that very often the first people a baby sees are doctors and nurses or maybe a midwife. If it's a midwife, she knows that one of the first things she needs to do, aside from all of the other things she's doing, is to be happy and loving and cheerful to see the baby come out. Doctors don't often know this, and because of hospital procedures, they might wear masks, so when the baby comes out, it doesn't know what it's coming into. "What is this? It's not what I expected." So there's that.

When births originally took place here, two people received the baby, not just one: the midwife, perhaps, and the father. The father was there. The midwife didn't just take the baby out, wrap it up in something, and hand it to the father. No, no. The midwife guided the baby out, and the midwife and father brought the baby out of the mother so that the baby would immediately see at least one of the beings who had love and wonderment for it. A father cannot have anything but wonderment when he sees his child delivered from its human mother. It's an amazing, wonderful thing, and it is certainly creator-like.

So, I'm trying to tie all of these things into the idea that personal love has to do with the fact that you as the baby are being delivered under more ideal circumstances (maybe with a doctor standing by in case there's a problem):

The baby sees people that love him or her right away. The baby has been in the mother, so very protected in ideal circumstances and even, in the vast majority of circumstances, essentially protected. When the baby comes out, it needs to see somebody that loves it. In short, the baby is attached to feeling personal love immediately and gets personal love. The sooner the baby can get personal love, the better adjusted that baby's going to be in life.

Otherwise, he spends all his life looking for it.

Yes. That's why when a baby is born in hospital conditions only, it might be confused for a little while. I'm saying this, really, for the benefit of physicians, because I honor the desire of medical personnel to maintain sterility; I honor the need to do that. However, it is absolutely essential to have someone there — at least one person — who knows that the baby needs love. You've got to start honoring those midwives and letting them right into that place where the baby is born because most midwives will know how to welcome the baby. It is very unusual for experienced midwives to not know that. This is why very often (sometimes to the dismay of the mother) a midwife seems to be laughing and cheerful even though the mother's not necessarily feeling cheerful as she gives birth. But the midwife is welcoming the baby.

So you know that babies, then, are born seeking personal love. Once you get past the point when parents' love is all you need, you get to the hormonal stage when you need to become your own person and separate from parents, but your need for personal love does not cease. You can no longer accept personal love only from parents or from siblings. You need to find personal love other places. From that point on, you are largely driven to find personal love not because it has just been removed from you as I've described it but more importantly because you are born seeking it. Remember, where you came from before you're born is a place of unconditional love; so it's unconditional all the way, largely — with the exception of some cases of not feeling that inside mother, but largely you do. And mothers will often notice a feeling, a sensation of well-being when baby is in there. That's the unconditional love that the baby experiences.

But it's radiating; the mother feels it.

That's right, but it's radiating to baby from the baby's prebirth sources and radiating out from baby to mother. That's why in a mother's quieter moments, it's hard to feel anything but just wonderful about this — unless there's some reason she doesn't feel wonderful about giving birth, which happens sometimes.

So people seek personal love not only because it's an obvious need of life but also because on the deeper levels you know that it is your job to demonstrate personal love when you become a creator — to say nothing of on your journey to become that — to beings who might otherwise not attract your love. Because as a creator, this Creator is limited. It cannot provide personal love, period, to you on Earth. Creator loves you. This is not to say that Creator does not love you; Creator has unconditional love, but it is impersonal.

Was this part of the plan, or did this sort of develop and then the ones working with this experiment realize, "Uh-oh"?

No, it wasn't an uh-oh. Remember that the idea — as it was described before, yes? — was that the stream of what could become the Explorer Race was around for a long time. It's not as if the creator of this universe happened along when it was first emerging. That was floating around for a long time, and only this Creator of this universe found it appealing. So it wasn't an accident or that it was put out there with the idea. Let's say (for the sake of the mental construct of the narrative), that this Creator would, at some point, find it, and It might not even notice it or care about it right away. But It might at some point notice it, care about it, and take action.

The Creator was going to become more by creating this universe because the Creator was going to notice Its shortcoming. It was going to notice that It couldn't personally react to beings on a place that would require that Creator to personally feel pain. That Creator could not personally feel pain, so the vast amount of the creation is this pain-free, benevolent place. On the occasions when Creator has experimented with polarity and some pain and all that, the Creator immediately had to withdraw from it, which showed the shortcomings of this universe. And the universe would be in imbalance if this Creator stayed with it, always experiencing.

This Creator knows that It needs to experience some kind of polarity in a way that It can assimilate it, but It has come to realize that It cannot assimilate it here in this creation, so sees you as offspring, all right, and it is your job to do that. And that is why you are so focused in personal love, in a climate on this planet (I'm not talking about weather conditions, but circumstances) in which love is kind of an up-the-down staircase. It's not always easy; the people that you love personally do not always live up to your expectations and needs, and sometimes you make demands of them, or they make demands of you. "Why aren't you this way? Why aren't you that way?" In short, you experiment in every way you can find to love something that isn't always very lovable.

So you see, what you have here, then, is explanations not only for why you are the way you are but most importantly, for it's ultimate reward. When you, the Explorer Race as a creator take over this creation, you will be able to personally accept and love the beings on Earth that are going through some sort of Creator School, if Earth chooses to do that or if it's another planet. Maybe Earth will recover, and another planet will become Creator School, will volunteer to do that. But you as creator will be able to personally love those beings, so even though those beings will be in Creator School and even though there will be some discomfort, they will be conscious of Creator as a personal experience in their lives. They won't have to create gods with qualities that humans aspire to and that you actually have when you're spiritual beings, and they will understand that the creators that they can have as gods (as it were, instead of gods), that Creator will be their ideal because they will feel Creator as a personal presence in their lives, even though they are in a polarized place. And of course, when you "offspring" a creator, it will be able to carry on.

So you're saying we're going to create another Creator School to create the creator to replace us?

Very likely, because you will want to go on and go other places. You are going to want to create your own creation. Here you are, as it were, in middle management. And you're going to move up to management, and then you're going to want to say, "Well, this is great, and we love it, but we'd like ..."

"But we can do so much better!"

That's right. "We want to create our own thing." Then you will reproduce the process in a better way than this Creator did not because this creator is not as good as you but because this Creator did not have a quality that it needed for you to have. And that's why, of course, parents always want their children to be more than they are.

But will this Creator, once He understands this (and I think He's beginning to understand it now), at some point find a way to express that or create a creation where He can express that? Or how would you say that?

Maybe or maybe not. You have to recognize that the vast amount of creations everywhere have nothing to do with discomfort. That is something that you haven't considered.

That's it. He might go off and create one that has only comfort, only love?

There's more to it than that, and I'm glad you asked that question. You know that it is your job as the Explorer Race to go out and contact the civilizations you will contact and to bring them a low-key level of polarity that they can interact with in order to have growth, the growth that they want. But it has to be a very small amount of polarity so that it does not overly disrupt their society. But we need to extrapolate that. When this Creator of this universe goes on, It will simply rejoin the other creators and create only benevolent creations, as you indicated, but what about you? You as a creator are going to be different.

The critical factor is not when this Creator leaves this creation. When this Creator leaves this creation, It will go out and re-create things that are only benevolent and will enjoy that. But what happens when you, as the Explorer Race, are a creator — not when you take over this creation and do something — and go out as a creator after you've created somebody else to take your place? What happens when you, as a creator who has had experience with polarity and who has had capacities to interact on a personal, loving basis with beings who are not always so lovable [chuckles], go out and join the other creators? You affect them, of course! All creators are naturally affected, and then, all creators will expand. It will be a diluted impact, and all creators will suddenly have the capacity to love, on a personal level, beings that are not always so lovable, and that is what is going to cure almost everybody.

Remember you asked a question years ago to the negative being that came with Creator, "How is that being going to be able, when it …" That negative being, you know, is not going to hang around here. When this Creator goes off, it's just going to go on its merry way! It's not going to hang around for you; you don't need to have it hang around because you will have already experienced polarity for yourself. You know what it's all about. It won't be needed as a consultant. It will go off into the creation somewhere. But when creators everywhere suddenly can experience polarity and love things that are not so lovable, that being will be redeemed! And there will never again be in creation intense discomfort because that being will be loved for being exactly who and what it is, even though it's not very lovable. The intensity of its discomfort will immediately fall away and be transformed, and it will only have that same level of discomfort that you might deposit on other planets, 1 percent, something like that. It will be no more or no less than the level of discomfort that exists in all creators everywhere, which means it will then be able to be a creator itself!

Oh, how wonderful, how beautiful!

So it's exciting, is it not?

It's much bigger than we thought!

I get excited about it myself! But I must demonstrate that with the energy, because the energy comes through, you know.

That's great. The Explorer Race thread itself was still from within the creation; it didn't come from you guys. You didn't inspire it or anything?

That thread had been generated in the creation itself, the mass creation itself, because …

Of the need.

That's right! Because there was the need. You could easily say from your perception of creation here that without needs, nothing gets done. On the other hand, from our point of view, we were doing just fine before that need, but we can always experience more.

Well, you've experienced more since then, haven't you? [Chuckles.]

Indeed! Is it not thrilling?

It's awesome. And we have a context for all of this now, but you couldn't have talked to us without all the others before. It wouldn't have meant anything.

That's right. It wouldn't have been thrilling without taking all those steps because when you take the journey, you appreciate the value of the journey. The journey itself becomes the main thing. Then when you discover the answer, it's euphoric!

Yes!

Yet you look back on the journey, and the journey doesn't seem like work anymore; it seems like a labor of love.

Yes, yes. My attitude has changed. [Laughs.]

Chapter 8

Every Action Has a Reaction: It's Mother Nature's Plan

Ssjoooo

July 13, 2000

You said there were tubes leading from the creators, from the thirteen on the outside into every single part of every single being in the creation. We've talked before about how the Council of Creators doesn't have to move; it just knows everything that's going on, or when someone gets its attention, the creators know. Is there some kind of a tube system, grid system? How would you describe this method of everybody knowing everything?

The tube was just a narrative means to explain to you so that you understand, but there aren't tubes. None of that exists. That's just a means of explaining it. This explanation is profoundly simple, but it requires that you move past a mental concept to a feeling to understand it or at least be able to imagine the feeling. So if everything is one and if you are completely conscious of the one, as some of the beings on the Council of Creators might be, who have said this, if you are aware that on the feeling level everything that happens everywhere is happening within you because you have that awareness, you would know every time someone sneezes.

If you wanted to pay that much attention to it.

No, no. It's not if you wanted to pay that much attention to it; you would know. Period. On the feeling level, you are one. There is no barrier. Individuality is homework, but it's not real. There is no individuality. Individuality does not involve barriers. It only appears to involve barriers here for the sake of your personalities doing your homework, but there are no real barriers.

THERE IS NO BARRIER IN ONENESS

The whole issue of people on Earth wanting to keep their private lives private and details about themselves private will only be active until there's more of a feeling of oneness, then?

Yes, you might say that, and any desire for anything being private is only based on a person's discomfort with being judged. Usually that comes about as the result of learning judgment, meaning judgment has been put on you, and you might perpetuate that and judge others, consciously or otherwise, and as a result the idea of being judged is not a pleasant idea. Therefore, you might find that privacy would be to your advantage in your feelings and in your thoughts. Also while some people know that there really are no secrets, nevertheless, one likes to pretend that there are, given the nature of the culturization and conditioning on this planet. Therefore, when you are in other places where judgment does not exist (though discernment may exist), then not only are you unconcerned about others knowing what there is to know about you but you also embrace it. You know about them too, and you still like each other. [Chuckles.]

Your culture can't embrace being one without changing. You can't go on being as you are. You can't be nationalistic. You can't say, "My people, right or wrong." You can't say, "My group, right or wrong." You can't do any of this without embracing all beings, including animals and plants and Earth and everything. You can't do that and move forward on the plane that you are required to move forward on in your education here, to say nothing of rejoining spiritual life everywhere either at the end of your natural cycle or as a group moving onward in spiritual evolution, as you say, which is actually not so much moving onward as gradually returning to your true nature. So it is a passing thing, but it is a real thing, because people's concern about having their private lives kept private is based on not wishing to be ridiculed or judged by others or not wishing to have things that they would prefer to be known by few to be known by many. You can think of many examples.

Oh, absolutely, but we're not looking at that many years. This is a cycle that we're going through to expose our worst fears before we expand a little bit, right?

Yes, but you understand, it's not a cycle measured in years at all; it's a cycle measured in feeling. It's all feeling, and to embrace your natural feeling, you have to change your societies. To change your societies, you have to change yourselves, meaning that you change yourself. It starts individually and then moves into society, not the other way around. That's why these books, all these books, are geared to the individual and in some cases geared to groups, but they are not geared to whole societies with the idea of setting up an authoritarian system to exert change.

They're saying, "If you understand this, then you will just naturally allow yourself to change."

Or with given instructions and manners and mores and principles and homework, you can remind yourself of your true nature.

THE COSTS AND BENEFITS OF RELIGION

Christianity, as it was practiced twenty or thirty years ago (since it has been undergoing its revolution for the past twenty or thirty years, really), could be referred to as the world's most successful business because it is set up like a business in some of its aspects. It could also be referred to as one of the world's most successful public services, but as for the more economic aspects, not all the churches but some of them certainly would be analogous to a successful business.

Another thing that's important is there are elements of control in these religions that make people afraid to die and afraid to take their power, and that needs to be brought out.

Well, that's certainly true. Fortunately many people are becoming more conscious of that in your time, which is part of the reason that church attendance has been in decline not just in the U.S. but other places (not everywhere, of course). It's a religion whose gift to the people is not as appreciated as it once was. This does not mean that religions do not offer something benevolent to the people, but the trappings of religion make for problems, and of course, ultimately the biggest problem of your religions today is competition.

They don't all see themselves as competing, but enough of them do. At the core of competition is "We're right, and you're wrong," and as a result, if you see something that you perceive as wrong, you're going to want to make it right if you've been raised in a competitive, conditioned system. A lot of systems around the world are that way but not all. It's a bit of a shame because for most religions, their basic core principles are still valid and offer worthwhile things, but the practices are not always the same as the doctrine. The doctrine is often based on an accumulated manual of what works as compared to the intention. The intention is often lost. But then people within the organizations frequently know this.

In the days when such religions as Christianity were started, it was well understood that you couldn't just offer people a method of living if you were not going to improve their living conditions unless you were offering them something authoritarian as well. If something were going to be authoritarian, why would people who are otherwise desperately struggling just to survive stop what they're doing and pay homage to you and your religion and you and your god unless they either saw that there was some value in it for them or were afraid of it?

It was a political understanding that set up the foundation for many of today's religions in your time. Equally, it will be the change in political understanding that will not only liberate the religions to seek their own level but also encourage people to be more — how can we say? — receptive to other philosophies. People are looking to other philosophies and explanations these days, and of course science is one of those. Science, as it's currently practiced, has the trappings of religion in a lot of ways, and people are looking to these things because they have the option. Not everybody now faces as much hunger and as many struggles for survival as people once did (although more people are doing so than is, let's say, necessary in your time), and as a result, the politics do not function the way they once did, so people can look for answers that are more fulfilling and nurturing than answers that come with a stick: "Do it or else." This tells you something important about your times: The changes going on for people en masse, which have to do with their internal changes and spiritual changes and feeling changes, are going to affect the way they live. And religions that cannot change and adapt with that, religions that are rigid, will fall by the wayside, regardless of how much they struggle to maintain control. Struggling to maintain control will be a guarantee of falling by the wayside, but if the religion can become flexible, it may carry on for a time.

Beyond Earth, are there religions? Are there deities? Are there religious feelings? How does it work when one is conscious? You don't look to a middle authority or a hierarchy, certainly.

No, because you feel there the presence. There is no reason to not feel. On your planet, there is every justifiable reason to not feel. I'm not saying you shouldn't; I'm just saying that you can make a very convincing argument for not feeling, because of all of the discomforts around you, to say nothing of your own. On other planets, that doesn't exist for the most part, you understand. Therefore, the presence, the omnipresence of the awareness of all other beings, is a religion in its own right. Without judgment, the awareness of those beings and the acceptance and universal love of those beings create sufficient consciousness, as well as good feeling, that you do not require someone to tell you or explain to you the meaning of life, as a religion might wish to do according to its perception of that query. As a result, religion is not the same. But if we can define religion a little more broadly and say that it might encompass social practices and ceremonies and celebrations to welcome enlightenment, instruction or even interaction with other beings from other planets or other universes, then you might say that religion is more of a social experience. There is, of course, an acceptance of teachers, spirit teachers, so one might say it's a social experience inclusive of spirituality and without doctrine.

In the context of control and politics?

That's right, in the context of control and politics, as you say, which is not really a function of necessity. It is perceived as a function of necessity here for reasons that can be rationally argued, but there it cannot be rationally argued, and you would not argue, period.

Right. So is it fair to say that religion of the kind we have, controlling political religion, was invented on this planet?

No. It is not fair to say that. You understand that you're a traveling group. The Explorer Race has been traveling for a long time. When you do not find what you are looking for and even when what you are looking for is a fallacy, it is in your nature as reincarnating souls to travel somewhere else to find it. In such travels when something is being sought after, whatever it may be — whether it is something minor or something broad — there is a tendency to see the local environment in the light of your desired answers. As a result, the tendency is to turn the local environment into something that you can identify with, which might very well corrupt it, meaning turn it from being what it is naturally or turn it away from its natural beauty. Of course, you can look at Earth and see the Garden of Eden is in fact actually the way Earth was in its natural state, regardless of geological references to ancient planetary awakenings and so on. But I'm talking about long after, when most volcanoes were less active and life on Earth was quite tropical for the most part and much more benign in a lot of ways.

That circumstance is something that in reality creates an entirely different situation. So as a result, as times evolved and as humankind became more controlling on other planets (humankind in this case referring to the Explorer Race, for the sake of simplicity) you would attempt to re-create your doctrinaire desires: "I want to know ..." essentially. So over the years, with such a focus and in your passage from one planet to another, you have gradually seen the value in your own mind of setting up certain strata, meaning you thought, "To do 'this,' we have to do 'that,'" taking not a direct route but an indirect route. "To understand what we came here to understand, to find what we came here to find, we have to first control things so that we can live here." [Chuckles.] The minute that happens, hierarchies and political establishments are likely to follow swiftly.

PREDATORS ARE NO ACCIDENT

Now I want to talk about something before it's too late within this concept, something Zoosh wanted to talk about, but I'll get to it first. You can always ask him later if you want to. Human beings are seriously concerned about how many human predators there are now and how unsafe it is as a result and how much more extreme things seem to be not only in your own society but also globally. I will say this: It is not an accident that this planet has animal predators; one lives with such beings. Dogs and cats are truly predators. Cats might demonstrate it more apparently, but dogs are also predators in their own right. And the numbers of dogs and cats globally are as high as they are because a certain predation here is a necessary function of Earth and her makeup to keep physical life in constant circulation.

You may not know this, but one of Mother Earth's basic rules is that she will loan you the material from her body to reproduce a body of your own, whether you be a plant or an animal or a human being, but that is of short duration. She doesn't just want it back quickly from a human being, she wants it back generally — sometimes more quickly — from human beings because the gamut of feelings that human beings have and what they are trying to learn and so on overwhelm her materials. It is why some scientists say that there is a change in the cellular structure of the body every so many years, and so on.[1] The fact of the matter is that Mother Earth has a fixed rule. Even if a tree is 10,000 years old, it is expected to return the material of Earth to Earth. So predators were not something that you brought with you as a belief that it might winnow out the weak, meaning the strong survive. It's not that at all. There have been some philosophies that would support that. Darwinism describes evolution as the strong survive, the weak fall away, and as a result, the species becomes stronger.[2] Social Darwinism justifies that: "If we're stronger than you and we survive because of destroying you, then we deserve that."[3]

I'm not saying that's a good thing; I'm just saying that that's something that is often around. Now, Earth requires so many predators to be among you, and because you are no longer living as you did, say, in North America or various other places, you don't have lions and sharks in as great a number as you used to have, or other creatures that not only defend themselves when attacked but also have predatory natures toward human beings as well. It's very important to differentiate that because many animals might be perceived as human predators, but I'm talking about predators that might attack human beings on the basis of hunting them for food or because they do not abide human beings. They do not care for human beings, or their culture says, "Let's get rid of those human beings," which is not common among animals, but it has existed in the past. This is something Mother Earth has set up and invited, all right? So if you know that, it will help you to understand why there are so many human predators among you now, to say nothing of (and

1. The cells of the body regenerate at varying rates. See http://science.howstuffworks.com/life/cellular-microscopic/does-body-really-replace-seven-years2.htm to learn more about cells in the human body and how often they regenerate.
2. Darwinism is the theory that evolution occurs through natural selection. See https://en.wikipedia.org/wiki/Darwinism for more information.
3. Herbert Spencer, a nineteenth-century philosopher, promoted Social Darwinism by applying the premise of Darwinism to social, political, and economic issues. See http://www.allaboutscience.org/what-is-social-darwinism-faq.htm.

this is the crux of the matter that Zoosh wanted to talk about) bacterial and viral predators.

GENETIC ADVANCES HAVE CONSEQUENCES

You might reasonably ask, "How can human beings continue to extend their life cycles from twenty-five (if we go back far enough) to forty to sixty to eighty to one hundred and beyond when we keep discovering new diseases?" These diseases — as has been mentioned before, I think, in previous books — truly are a portion of Mother Earth. They are not raining down on the planet from the stars, though one might make a case for certain rays coming through the atmosphere of Mother Earth. For the most part, bacteria and diseases and viruses are part of her system for keeping the physical bodies of all beings on the Earth in a cyclic rate to return to her body. She knows that only she can purify portions of her body in the way that works for her. This is why it is in your nature, being made up of Mother Earth's body, to think in terms of recycling, whether you do it as a technological society, and to perceive the recycling nature in society. You see the leaves gradually turn into the soil, and it makes sense to you. You consider that the bodies of all beings will gradually turn into the soil. "From the soil they come, and to the soil they return," is a reasonable and acceptable concept (and I'm speaking from a spiritual, religious, and scientific perspective).

The number of predators is fixed by Mother Earth, so as you kill off the bears and the tigers and the sharks, then new predators are made apparent to you that you can eliminate diseases on the basis of genetic reproduction, which is bound to happen globally, initially in the form of in vitro fertilization. You could say, for instance, "Well, heart disease and the propensity for heart disease run in my family," or encephalitis and the propensity toward that or epilepsy or even an appearance or the tendency to become obese — anything that might be cosmetic as well as hazardous to your health — asthma, whatever, things that are well known. The doctor could say to you, "You know, we can eliminate that in your offspring by using in vitro fertilization when you decide to have children; we will simply eliminate that potential genetically." Those who can afford it initially will do it. But in the long run, it will become part of your society (not in the long, long run, but in the long run, say, for a few hundred years, at least, it will become part of your society) because society will then consider it to be benevolent. Why should anybody ever get asthma or hay fever? Why should anybody ever become obese regardless of how much he or she eats or his or her level of activity?

It will become something much broader than the elimination of disease not because it's mandated but because it can be done. There will be many explanations to justify its worthiness; fortunately, there will also be those who are preserving every bit of the former genetics. They will say, "Oh, for study," and at some point, it will become part of the genetic library. You can look at other planets and find that they have a thorough genetic library for their species that goes back to the point when they started getting involved in genetics, or whatever method they use on that planet. In some cases, bodies and genetics don't count, but in terms of what makes sense to you here, what's relevant, you will find that kind of genetic library, and your scientists have already begun that. That's to the advantage, because at some point people will say, "Well, wait a minute. We've eliminated asthma and hay fever. We've eliminated the propensity for heart disease, and we've eliminated any potential for a person ever to get tuberculosis even without the inoculations. We've eliminated any potential for any disease that we can locate at all, so even if we're exposed to the microorganisms, we wouldn't get them."

Even so, you would eventually notice that other traits have been unintentionally eliminated as well because sometimes a person might come in with a propensity for a disease, but attached to that disease, genetically, would be a propensity for profound genius or insight or talents or abilities that are unintentionally eliminated as well. And this will not be recognized immediately, because it will require time to show.

How can insights and genius be attached to a disease?

It's not attached to the disease as, for instance, a requirement of being expressed in that sense, but say you've got a chain of molecules, or let's call it a chain of genes. So then you don't have to do the cost-benefit analysis. Some people will say, "Well, if we eliminate a gene, who knows what else we're eliminating. We don't exactly know what they do." That will be talked about, and as a result, many samples of the gene will be kept in their original condition for further testing and understanding in the gene bank. And imagine we see these genes as separate, floating things. First there were no connections, but the actual reality is different and there are connections.

Oh. The insight or brilliance is in one of the connections that gets cut off.

Well, you see, you can have things like that. The connection is severed, perhaps, in this case. But in the process, since it is a circuit, as you might say, and any time you take something out of a circuit, it might affect other things. It is wired in such a way as other things will undoubtedly be affected. The whole creature that develops out of this basic gene will feel as if it's been wounded. This has been noticed over the years, particularly in certain breeding techniques of animals or plants. Sometimes you can do the breeding in specific ways and produce, say, a certain kind of dog, maybe a smaller dog, or a smaller horse for people who want to have a horse in the house, something like that. Often these beings are not quite right. They don't live very long, their personalities are not the same as the full-sized versions, and they are nervous and upset. They don't feel right. When you extend into their bodies, you find that they are nervous because they can tell they're not quite right. Something is missing.

So that's what happens. It's not that the disease is a requirement of Mother Earth's loaning that body to you; rather, the way it works out is that she loans it to you with the guarantee to herself that she can depend on that body being something you will have temporarily. So she fixes it.

So when scientists fix it, there's something wrong with it!

That's right. This is all intended to show you that things are really perfect in their own right, which doesn't mean that people should get heart disease or should change how they eat, but that the cure, while it initially seems to be genetic, is not. This doesn't mean that you won't experiment with genetics, as many, many cultures do.

THE ZETA RETICULANS: A CASE STUDY IN GENETIC EXPERIMENTATION

A culture that is known for its genetic experimentation and has been involved for years and years and years in terms of your experience — or as Zoosh likes to say, "experiential years," which are obviously much longer than actual years but in some cases are shorter — is that of the Zeta Reticulans. The Zeta Reticuli beings have so refined their genetic code over the years that they have unintentionally eliminated a great many of their potential qualities, some of which they don't even remember. They had the full range of feelings readily available to them, and they could still bring those feelings up now if they wanted to, but it would take a certain amount of teaching. When they had some things that they would recognize as diseases (although you wouldn't recognize it as such, but in their society in days gone by, before they refined their genetic code to the current state, they would have seen anger that results in self-destructive violence or violence on another being as being a disease), they were determined to eliminate them. They also had other qualities that were connected to those things. Again, from the cost-benefit analysis position, they might still today say, "Well, it was worth it," but it has also prevented them from expressing to others things that are at the core of their personalities. They are fairly well-known for being particularly fond of beings who are innocent, such as children, or the elderly who are less attached to the expression of conditioned manners and mores. They are known for being fun loving or being their innocent selves with children, but they are not known (at least in your society) for having the capacity to interact in a complex way or in various complex social systems that are known to adults. They have trouble with that. This is not because they are unsophisticated, but it is primarily because they cannot build or maintain the capacity for such complex interactions in a way that flows smoothly for both groups because of their genetic refinement. They unintentionally refined their capacity for such flexibility.

I give you that example because many people in your society have heard that Zeta Reticulans who interact with people do not always understand that the people experience discomfort when it seems so profoundly or at least patently obvious. How could they not know that? Well, there it is: They don't know it because they have unintentionally refined that quality.

LITTLE CHANGES CAN
HAVE BIG CONSEQUENCES

You are going to travel, as a society, through this technological voyage going on in medicine right now. You're going to travel on that same path, but you're not necessarily going to be fixed to it in terms of time sequence. However, you're probably going to travel on that same path because the benefit is going to far outweigh the cost in the minds of those pursuing it not just because of the money (although that will be a factor to those who go through the monetary costs and expenses to develop these technologies) but also for the thrill of saying, "Well, here it is! We've genetically cured any potential, down to a very small fraction indeed, of anyone ever getting cancer again!" You know, that's going to be profound, and as a matter of fact, aside from projects that various drug companies began a long time ago and are ongoing, the bulk of the long-range outlook to eliminate disease is now genetic and has been for a while. Even though there's still a lot of work going on with chemicals, the drug companies and public health services recognize that genetic research is the quickest way for the greatest value.

Aren't we supposed to be learning to not just use our heads but to make these decisions from our hearts? Isn't that why we're redoing this in the loop of time?

That's right, but I'm talking about the long run, also known as the short run. You might go through this for a few hundred years. This does not mean you'll go through it for thousands of years or millions of years. It doesn't mean that you'll do that, but what it does mean is that you will necessarily see the wonderment of it all. Look at what's going on genetically and otherwise with agriculture. For years people have been researching plants that don't require as much water or that are disease resistant or insect resistant and so on. The same thing is going to happen with people. It will become very clear that there is only so much water and food to go around given the population.

This is not to say that there won't be people working on spiritual manifestations and benevolent magic and all of this. But I'm talking about the short long run, meaning the next few hundred years. People will say, "Well, how can we create a human being who is genetically less dependent on these things, who doesn't need as much food." I'm not saying it will be possible or that people will actually do it, but it might very well be possible. The potential is there. For example, let's say you don't need meat to survive. Then a great deal of land that is now used in raising cattle could be used for other purposes. I'm not trying to cast any value judgments here; I'm simply saying that much acreage could be devoted to something else. I think, for the next many years, you'll still consume fish because you will be able to farm them and raise them underground and so on, but they won't have as much nutritive value as a wild fish. You've been farming fish for a time, and they fill you up. They don't necessarily give you the energy you need, but that will come as more conscious farming evolves.

I'm mentioning these things not to cover a wide gamut of potentials for the future so much as to show you that even small changes create bigger changes than you've realized. For example, people get married. At least in the early days, the husband sees the wife in largely benevolent terms, and the wife sees the husband in largely benevolent terms, but they both look at each other and say to themselves, "Now, if I can only change these two or three things he (or she) does, he (or she) would be perfect!" Of course, when you can change those things, it has a vast effect on the way the person is. You think you've changed somebody by training them or encouraging them to discipline themselves not to do something (or conversely, to do something), but in fact, it just puts a control on a behavior, and that's going to come out some other way. People have known through the years that it doesn't really change things only in one area. I mention that because it's something you can all relate to. You can encourage your dog to go outside to go to the bathroom or your cat to use a litter box. But when the cat does that (and I'm not saying this is bad or that you should change what you do if you live with cats), it will become a little less wild. In some ways, of course, that would be perceived as a benefit. You wouldn't necessarily want wild cats living indoors. At the same time, it changes their personality; I'm not going to say for the better or for the worse. In short, you are put here at this time to experience consequences so that you can learn and grow. I'm not saying that consequences are bad; I am saying that consequences exist as a result of everything, including genetics.

What you're saying is they exist in ways that we don't even expect and that we don't understand, and there might be hidden consequences that we still have to deal with.

That's right. You'll also have totally surprising consequences, meaning as certain things happen for the human genome, as the changes happen there to ostensibly make people less prone to disease and perhaps even more cheerful, it's possible that other things might happen as well, not just things that are unpleasant, but surprises might happen, meaning people might become more intelligent. Conversely, people might become less intelligent. People might become more loving or more austere. People might become more spiritual or something else. You do not understand the full impact of everything that a gene or a portion of the gene does. You do not understand what the portions do, nor do you understand what the whole does. And you do not understand what all of the wholes of all of the genes in all of your bodies do as a combined total, the micro and the macro.

THE SOUL MUST ACCEPT
THE CIRCUMSTANCES OF LIFE

We don't just create human beings. I mean, the soul comes in to inhabit them. Are there agreements on the part of the soul that comes in that agree with the altered genes? How does that work?

It is always the case that, given the circumstance of the society and the planet, the soul must agree to accept the circumstance of life. If the soul does not agree, then the soul goes elsewhere. It's a requirement. This way, no one can be sent somewhere on the basis of some arbitrary circumstance.

The soul, or the immortal personality, as Zoosh says, will probably not see the life the same way, at least on Earth, as the actual embodied personality with the soul sees it. The soul sees it as an objective, something attempting to be accomplished, and can easily live in the circumstances offered and even proffered, meaning offered by Earth and proffered by society. In that way, the soul can say, "Oh, sure. Fine." But the embodied personality might feel entirely different, as you live in something. The soul might look at something, a situation that the embodied personality might say, "This is awful. Why did I come here?" and still perceive it as something in which the goal of the soul can still be achieved regardless of the circumstances, and in most cases, because of them. So the soul's management approach may not always feel so wonderful to the worker.

You're saying right now that the viruses and the predators are to recycle the material bodies back to Earth.

Yes.

But you're saying there was a time when Earth was more benign.

Even so, there would have been a degree of predation if the people who were living on Earth were born here of her material. Now, she would not have the same requirement of people who visit, as they were born somewhere else. So for extraterrestrials that might come and live on Earth, from her perception there is no need. That material is going to return to where they came from, at least from her perspective.

When the beings born on Earth were living in harmony, due to their spiritual instructions through their inspirations and culturalization to that effect, conditions were such that Mother Earth still required the recycling of bodies. Now, some of your holy documents refer to people who lived a thousand years, but when the population is small, Mother Earth does not perceive that as a problem. After all, she can accept a 10,000-year-old tree's life cycle.

It's not the length of time, it's the length of time combined with the number, the quantity. You might have many 10,000-year-old trees for a time before too many human beings are present, but after a while, you don't have too many of them. If you have millions and millions and then billions of human beings, she's going to require a shorter life span because this requires much more material from her body to be loaned to you.

So how is this going to balance out? As science and genetics extend the life cycle, there will be more and more human predators or bacteria?

They will genetically code that out as well. You'll be surprised. It's not going to be too long before they find genes that are involved in aggressive acts. It's one of the big motivators, to find that, not because the research is being capitalized by those who are trying to create a nation of controllable beings but rather that it will be perceived as a general benefit, and good and rational arguments can be made for that.

Chapter 9

Love and Care for Others to Embrace the Totality

Isis

July 14, 2000

I always believe there's a beyond, but now that we have somebody who says he created all this, when did you become aware of what the thirteen say they created, or that they instigated, which then became this totality?

I'm not conscious of ever not being aware of it.

Were you part of one of the early creators or something?

No, it's very much the way they explained it. When you are connected on the feeling level to all beings — not just all people but also the space between them, meaning it's a continuity — it's not when it is no longer a factor. When we become aware of it, it's as if we always knew it. That's why I might answer in ways that seem vague to you, and other spirits might answer that way too. "When did you know that?" you ask. We always knew that. "How did you know that?" Well, we felt it.

Okay, what was here?

Felt experiences cannot be measured by time. I'm going to give you an example in the instinctual body as Speaks of Many Truths talks about it. When you remember something, you remember like that [snaps fingers]. In the instinctual body, once you become aware or you have the instinct that you need something or that you need to do something differently — that you need to do it this way — you'll have to sit down and think hard to remember that you ever did it differently. Perhaps you suddenly feel the need to smell a leaf; you can't just look at it anymore. The instinctual self is not based on thought; it's based on feeling directed through the physical body. I do not have a physical body as you know it, but I have feeling, so there is no way for me to say *when* something happened. I've always known it. You might think, "I've always smelled the leaf," and then someone tells you, "Well, once upon a time, you just looked at the leaf." After a while, you don't remember that; you can't conceive of it.

That's based on feeling, and that's why Zoosh and other beings have been telling you that what you're all coming into now is a time of feeling, which is why the past memory is hard to remember. Zoosh has described this as vertical time just to give you a bridge from the concept and experience of time into feeling. If Zoosh went on at too great a length on what he might have felt about feeling, people would immediately hear this as emotions, and it becomes something hard to grasp. You have to make the steps slowly. "Vertical time" sounds somewhat more mentally acceptable.

THE RULES OF TOTALITY APPLY TO EVERYONE

When you became aware of yourself, aware of anything, of all the stuff that we understand this totality to be, how much of it was there? How much had been created, then?

Not that much. [Chuckles.]

So you're one of the early ones.

That's right. There wasn't that much that had been created in tangible ways that you can understand. There was a vast amount of what you might call precreation or not exactly potential. "Potential" is a word that you use that has a certain amount of authoritarianism in it. Precreation is very open — anything is possible — but there is no attachment, no motivation, nothing like that.

So there were some creators floating around?

Yes.

So what have you been doing? You've been watching them create stuff?

Well, of course I interact; I help when people ask. Occasionally I have my own projects, like my students here on Earth. Just being is enough, and you will understand this completely when you rejoin your whole being and when you're beyond this body. The whole idea of *doing* simply disappears. Here, doing feels like *being*. You measure your being in what you're doing, even by measuring how many breaths you take per minute. But beyond here, you enjoy being with no requirement to do anything, ever. And it is a pleasure, and everybody loves you just for being. [Chuckles.] No one says, "What have you done lately?" [Laughs.]

I see. So are you considered an elder, then? Do people come to you for advice?

No, I receive no more respect, and appropriately so, than the youngest. Everyone, as part of the one, meaning as part of the total, receives the same amount of respect as everyone else, and this is appropriate. If you have no respect for a portion of your body, after a while it will get upset and demonstrate something to you that will affect your whole being. It has to be equal not because someone said it has to be but because if you do not love all parts of yourself, not only are you being unkind but you are also hurting yourself. When people on Earth are starving, it is not only unkind to allow them to starve, but you are hurting yourself because it actually has a physical impact on you. This is not obvious to you, as you (meaning the general public) are not as connected to the consciousness of that because of the apparent individuality here and being cut off from your sense of totality. This doesn't alter the facts. The basic rules that apply all over the universe apply here as well. That's important to note. Even if there are different rules for you in this area, you have those rules while you have the same set of rules that everybody else has. It's an addition, not something else.

Like Earth School.

Yes, that's right, and that's very important to remember. So the basic reality is for you as well. That's why we say when someone is starving across the street or on the other side of the world, it affects you whether you know it or not.

Is it also your understanding that these thirteen beings began the creation by creating the creators? As far as you know, there's nothing beyond them?

Yes, that is my understanding. And as they said, to have created it from the new thing that they felt is the only way they could do it. Obviously if they created it from themselves, they would not have had the capacity to produce anything other than what they were. That's why when the Creator of this universe created you as offspring to be more than Itself, It needed something from somewhere else; otherwise, It would have been creating something like Itself. It might have been able to create something less than Itself, but that's not what It really needed to do. It needed to create something that would be more than Itself, so it needed help from somewhere else.

PRECREATION

If I connected to one of those beings, and you said I wanted to know where creation came from, so you took me to precreation, how does that work?

Precreation bathes you in this welcome nurturing. It bathes you in such a feeling that prompts you to feel profoundly safe. Generally speaking, the safer people or beings feel, the more likely they can access every single memory that they might have and remember everything, because when you are surrounded and bathed in this nurturance and love, you feel safe to remember everything. It's a very good place to take beings who cannot access something that they need to remember, not just as a thought, but that they need to remember as an experience so that they can understand their present situation.

Precreation is a wonderful place for this because in precreation nothing permanent happens. There are these feelings, meaning the feeling is present and it prompts you to have them, but since it's in precreation, whatever you remember or whatever goes on there isn't fixed. So you can remember everything, and you have everything in context and in whatever continuity that you need in order to appreciate what it might mean without having to live with the consequences. When you remember things here, you very often have consequences, meaning things happen and then you have to do other things. But in precreation, things do not happen; you simply have the recollection.

Chapter 10

Feel Heat to Learn Oneness

Ssjoooo

July 17, 2000

Greetings. We continue.

Welcome. You said you would explain the meaning of existence.

We have been doing that because when you explain how existence, as you know it, has come about, it defines a great deal of your purpose and intention, whereas if you want to know why we exist, it is really a misnomer. That question is off. The desire to know why always comes about because you don't know what your existence is about. But we, and others, have explained that quite a bit. It would be like asking, "Why does love exist?" You don't really have to ask that because you know and appreciate its value. So if love exists, then that is existence at its foundation. You wouldn't ask why love exists.

All right, I thought it was something you wanted to discuss because you had made a point of saying, "I'll tell you the meaning of existence."

But we have done this; it is the meaning of existence. When you hear "meaning of existence," you hear ...

Mental.

That's right. You are not asking for a meaning of existence; you are asking for me to mentally justify the value of existence. That's what the mind asks because the mind weighs things in mathematic values, not values in terms of good or bad. The mind does not understand good or bad. It might be taught it, but it resists because the mind's tendency, and what it is set up to do, is to quantify things. That's why a mathematical understanding of the mind makes much more sense: "This has so many x's and o's, and that has so many x's and o's; therefore, this might be appropriate for this circumstance, and that is for something else."

151

Minds and the mental bodies in general resist the idea of good and bad because it constricts the mind from its job as it sees it, which is to measure, quantify, and apply that knowledge to practical, day-to-day life. I'm not saying that values in terms of good and bad are not worthy; what I'm saying is that they can never truly be explored in a way that might influence your values in terms of what you would do, or better yet, for you to understand what you might be capable of doing given certain circumstances. That's why very often either warriors or those who have performed criminal acts might say, "Well, you're not in my shoes; you don't know how I am" or "Put yourself in my circumstances; you might have done the same thing." It is, granted, a justification, and I know it sounds like an excuse, but it is clearly mind asserting its right of how it perceives its existence. This is why a society that puts too much value or weight on the mind as a means of solution walks into a minefield.

Regardless of whether your values are indeed benign, somebody else's values very easily might not be so benign, and the mind can justify it either way. Whereas feelings are always very clear as to what they are feeling, the clarity can be measured in the way your body demonstrates those feelings to you. You may not always know when you're angry, but you know when you are experiencing nurturing love, and you also might know when you are experiencing enraged anger. Clearly, the way to understand existence at its most basic is to explore feelings and to follow the thread of feelings to understanding. The mind can never understand; it can only relax, immerse itself in feeling, feel loved, and feel as if it is not required to do anything other than perhaps make observations for later recollection.

CREATION SEEKS BALANCE

What about the rest of creation? We've never asked about that. Do all creations have dimensions?

They only have dimensions if they desire to. Dimensions, remember, are not really a physical thing; dimensions are a way of saying it is normal to have more than one thing in the same place at the same time. This is another reason your physical bodies are set up in such a way. Regardless of who is analyzing them — a psychologist, a social scientist, a microbiologist, a physicist — that person will, according to his or her profession, define your physical body along the lines of that specialty. After you read one after another of these definitions and explanations, you will say, "Well, there is clearly more than one thing happening inside me at the same time." It is intended to show you that many things can happen in the same space at the same time.

"Dimensions" is a convenient word to explain that reality. To put it simply, dimensions are a natural state. If one wished to have a limited number of dimensions, then one might, as a creator, define a function for those connections, or there might be some other means. Maybe certain beings experience certain dimensions. And yes, your question has value because it seeks not only to find common ground but also the manners and methods of creation.

The interesting thing about creation is that it is easy to create vast variables of life in a creation. What is more difficult in a given creation is to limit creation. For example (always these things given are examples that are not necessarily examples of what is, but are examples for the sake of illustration), as a creator, you might have a creation shaped like that [draws], and you wish it to perform only certain functions. Is it that you start somewhere in this creation and build the functions? No. It is in the nature of creations to be creative. Even if you just begin a space where there is a creation, creation essentially takes off on its own. In short, it will create. The only way you can, as a creator, create certain defined things is to put limits on creation. Imagine you have a bowl of water and you say that the water is creation. If you stick your hand or a book or something into the water, it displaces the water, it displaces the creation, and you have to do something to make it *less*.

This is something largely not understood, because where you live now, to create something in your own conscious mind's understanding of quantification, you start at the beginning or you take the component parts and you do something. It's one step after another. But actual creation is entirely different; you create the creation, and it tends to be self-perpetuating because the nature of life is to continue. So it's not so much that you define your creation by what you put into it; it is that you focus your creation based almost entirely on what you remove from it or what you keep it from doing for a time. When you keep a creation from doing something for a time, you necessarily put it out of balance. No creation can exist out of balance for very long before it needs to have something put it back into balance.

With your creation and your Creator, it was understood that your Creator would not be able to create a creation — using that ribbon of an idea, as we're calling it — to create anything other than a creation that would be out of balance. This tells you that it was a setup, as you might say, from the beginning, to encourage the Creator to add more, to be more Itself, and to allow that to move on to others. But it also ultimately raises the question whether it is a creation's nature to be more and this Creator set up Its creation to be less, then who prompted the creation to be less and essentially prompted and stimulated the idea of the Explorer Race in order to not cause all existence (as you understand it) to become more, but to become more in a balanced way, meaning that once this creation became balanced by what you do, that would radiate out. If everything else were balanced in that opening, meaning that what you are doing here is more, it would not be affected. If on the other hand, it is not balanced, it will be affected in some way, as has already been discussed at length.

So it is an important question because it comes back to who, and I wanted to lead the discussion toward who today because not only is this your underlying question about existence but more importantly it leads you to the most important question. When you ask the question, "What is the nature of existence?" you're really asking "Why do I exist?" It is ultimately a very profoundly personal question. You can say, "Well, I have lessons and things I am learning," but you can go back before that and say, "Is this even a reality?"

A JOURNEY FOR THE JOURNEY'S SAKE

If all life is truly a circle — or in the more real aspect of it, a sphere, and then a constantly revolving sphere, turning inside out and outside in, and open to other shapes and so on (if all life is this) — then what is the meaning of becoming more when it is your natural state of condition? Might this be a journey for the sake of the journey? For example, imagine you started somewhere, and right then you were more — you were all that could be, meaning you were total love and, to your mind's way of knowledge, total knowledge as well — and you wanted to find out whether there would be value in discovering yourself, even though you already existed. The only way you could do that would be to forget who you were and go through a series of experiences that would cause you to forget more and more and more until you not only didn't know who you were but were on the journey for its own sake. Now this has been brought up before, but I remind you of it because it is so pervasive in your existence that it is difficult to keep this in mind. It literally affects all that you are.

So the explanation for life becomes mostly a reminder of what life isn't. Life is not a mystery. To create a mystery out of life, you must become less. In your natural state of being, since you all exist as one here, mystery does not exist in terms of an experience, so this tells you that regardless of all the steps that were taken to get to wherever you got — and this is just an example — all those steps were designed not to help you to remember, which is what you pursue now, but to help you forget.

What is the meaning of life? In order to steer "What is the meaning of life?" onto a path that you can recognize, we have to make it personal. The purpose of the Explorer Race is simply to bring things to balance, to remind, you might say in the mental context, everyone of who he or she is. Of course, if people already know who they are, they will simply say, "Oh yes, we know that." [Chuckle.] On the other hand, if they don't know who they are, or there are any portions of them that do not know who they are, then they must be reminded if not of who they are, then at least of the tools by which they can remember in their own way. You do not wish to interfere in anyone's journey, because the journey was the intention of the original passage out of all natural existence.

This universe is unbalanced, though. Is the rest of creation balanced? Isn't that boring and stultified and stagnant?

It may be balanced, but I wouldn't use those words. If you were living in heaven, where everything is wonderful, you wouldn't think of it as boring, stultifying, and stagnant. You would not think at all; you would be in your feelings, and it would be marvelous, and the idea of becoming less, of having less of that would seem completely unnatural. So none of those words that you used apply except to — what? — the mind, which has been given the job of creating understanding. But understanding is not fully available to the mind; it is only available to the feelings. Feelings, especially when one feels nurtured and supported or when one feels the truth of something, are pure experience. They do not require the mind to say, "I feel love." The mind might *react* and say, "I feel love," but it is only an observation on the part of the mind.

So the key to understanding the meaning of existence is not only to experience the foundational physical feeling of love, which you can generate yourself, but also to recognize the pleasure of a story that children hear (not a scary story, a fun story; it can be an adventure but not frightening). The pleasure of a story is in the telling, not so much the ending. The Peter Pan story, for example, was not considered sufficiently stimulating without the evil captain, but the original concept of the story did not include anything evil. It was just the adventurous travels with Peter and the children.

The true nature of the meaning of existence is the pleasure of the story that is felt. Mentally, the meaning of existence is that the mind can relax, be nurtured, be loved, and make observations that might or might not be called on, and the mind is loved either way. The meaning of existence is not a word, "love," but a feeling. It is important to remember this because it is so easy to become distracted not by the mind's need to know but by the mind's need to define and quantify, and because of the extra effect of being in a polarized world such as yours, the mind's desire to define, quantify, and control.

Explanations to oneself might be of value to the mind, but explanations to others, without their asking, will probably interfere with their stories. This does not mean we do not expose people to these talks that we have, but we do not grab them off the street, twist their arms behind their backs, and say, "You must read this," although that has been done by many. It is called control in its many faces. Control is always based in fear, yet fear is always showing the one who fears the way past fear. Fear is a guide, as your friend Zoosh has said, and it represents its guidance in your physical self. If you do not allow your physical self to respond (maybe for a good reason or maybe simply because you are afraid to show fear or perhaps for another good reason or many other explanations), then the mind will take over and will attempt to control your fear, which it cannot do. It can only fool others when they wish to be fooled, or it can suppress the feelings sufficiently, not so that the feelings are not felt, but when the mind wishes to control something, it ceases quantifying it. So it makes it an "unexperience"; the mind ceases to recognize it and places no more value on it (value being, remember, so many x's and so many o's, meaning quantification). Once the mind starts quantifying something in a mental society, the meaning of existence, which is always rooted in your evidentiary body, your physical body, is excluded in order to explain the question the mind has of the meaning of life. Therefore, the meaning of life can never be found in mental terms, because it has already been excluded. That is why the attempt to search mentally in this circumstance will be fruitless unless one uses the actual engine of the meaning of life, which is made up of the physical body, the feelings, the inspiration, the instincts — and all those things — and loves the mind regardless.

This does not mean you necessarily take actions based on what the mind says; the mind needs to be loved sufficiently so that it comes to recognize that it is no longer being given the responsibility — not just the authority, but the responsibility — to define something when the definition is unavailable to it. This is why minds go crazy even in sane people. This is why thinkers and so on become terribly frustrated: "Well, what is the meaning of life?" Yet you have the meaning of life locked in a box for which there is no key or combination available to your mind.

I'm not saying it is a conundrum. What I am saying is that the solution is powerfully simple, but it won't have mental satisfaction. Mental satisfaction does not come from the mind. What did I say about creation? Creation is natural; it moves on its own, and it can only be limited or defined based on creating less. This tells you that since all creation is like that and your mind is a portion of creation, mental satisfaction cannot come from the mind as a separate thing. The mind is, in fact, an actual part of creation. This tells you something profoundly important. It is normal for the mind to be satisfied, it is typical, and it is the way things are. But when you try to set up an artificial system where the mind is not part of everything and you lock that love and the answer to everything in the box, then the mind desperately searches. The mind is here, and it is there. It is running all over the place in creation, trying to find that which it has been restricted from finding.

FEELING IS THE KEY TO DISCOVERY

So all of this is only true here with the Explorer Race? The rest of creation is not like this?

Not even all of the Explorer Race is.

Just the ones on Earth at this time?

The ones on Earth who do not have this wisdom. That's why it's important to put these ideas out. It has been said by other beings that feeling is the key to discovery, regardless of what is being discovered. However, it's important to indicate what an important key it is. It's not just the key to discovery but also that which is needed to be discovered in the first place. So one does not only unlock the box but everything inside it as well. It's important to know these things, yet it is easy to forget on a day-to-day basis. Philosophically, feelings tend to create within your mind the consideration of the point of asking questions. You've been asking questions based on your personal interests (not all the time), and you've been moving on a steady path toward having more understanding.

What happens, though, when I give you an answer like that, and you consider, at least at some point, "Well, then, why do I need to ask questions at all when, in fact, all the answers are in this feeling I can create for myself?" When you ask questions, it changes to something else. The questions (and this is really self-defining, but I'm saying it for you because it's something you need to consider) cease to be personal. They become unconditional; they also are asked not for your interest but rather for service. It has been in your nature to ask many questions for service, meaning you ask about things that you're not particularly interested in because you feel other people might be interested in the answers, and this is fine. So you will find that when these truths are revealed to you and when you actually begin to practice them in terms of feelings, when you are feeling that warmth and that love inside of you, there is a tendency to become immersed in them the more you bathe in them. That's why a warm bath often feels more comfortable than a cold one.

I do not feel that you have to stop the process. The process then becomes less personal and more unconditional, and you feel, during it, that the pathway is to help others. You've done this a great deal, but the inner drive fades away.

This can only be done, however, through significant time — much experiential time, but time, okay — for you to understand, to experience that heat, which over time, extends throughout your physical body. So here's some homework.

Feel this heat, and notice when you are thinking. Make no effort to stop thinking, but focus your complete attention on the heat. Get the heat so that it is felt so strongly within you that you tell it out loud, "Now I would like the heat." All the while you are talking, you won't be able to say it in these words, but you might simply be able to say, "Spread." This is going to mean that you are mentally giving permission for the heat to spread throughout your body. You might not be able to do it all in one lesson, but I'll tell you the result of the homework when you are able to accomplish it. Remember, the thought does not only happen in the mind but is something you understand, so as you are able to spread the heat, all the while you'll be having thoughts. Whatever they are, that's fine; don't try to control them. Let them be there. As the heat spreads and you get to the point where you feel the heat throughout your whole body, it will be as if the thoughts gradually submerge. It won't be as if they're not there, but they become less of a conscious awareness. They, as you might say, submerge to the subconscious. In fact, the subconscious is just that part of the mental self that desires to be embraced by love, which can only be stimulated by the physical self telling you that the mind is seeking the physical, that the mind will not consider life on Earth under any circumstances unless it is in a physical body that can love it. So the purpose of the homework is not to stop the mind from thinking but to notice as the heat spreads throughout the self that the mind's thoughts tend to submerge.

The true purpose of the subconscious, then, is not to keep something from the conscious mind but to allow the mind to attempt to soak into love. If love is not there, then the subconscious becomes polarized and upset and agitated, but the reason thoughts sink from the consciousness into something less conscious is that the mind is seeking to be embraced by love. Not only will this ultimately quiet the mind in terms of your consciousness, but there will also be, from time to time, thoughts or fragments of thoughts that you become aware of. You don't judge them, whatever they are; you just focus entirely in the heat, which is, of course, love on the physically felt level. So what occurs, then, is that the so-called subconscious is given what it has been set up to seek; it relaxes, and the more one practices this exercise, thought in general becomes less of a driving force. In short, this question mark becomes infinity. True infinity is the assumption of perfect thought, but perfect thought cannot be defined in this mental concept because it is a feeling. Perfect thought is the feeling of love embracing the mental being so that it knows it's loved and can still be itself.

Exploring questions like these allows us to explore the meaning of existence. The meaning of existence is a feeling.

ALL EXISTENCE WILL FEEL PERSONAL

All right, this relates to the Explorer Race: Now we have bodies, but what happens in higher dimensions as we move back up the ladder and we don't have physical bodies anymore?

You will feel the substance of your being. Even if you do not have a man's or a woman's body, you will feel the substance of your being, and you will simply not personalize your body as your being. You will personalize it — maybe you will be a light being, so maybe you will simply be a personality, not unlike the one I am donning for this communication — but all existence everywhere will feel personal. The bodies of others will feel no more or no less like the body of yourself. Existence itself has fewer barriers, and this is safe because you feel benevolent. If there is something that you do not feel you can easily accept or experience in this loving being that you are, this feeling of love that you are, then you will stick a finger in the dike's hole to hold the water back. In short, you will simply not take that in, but generally you will feel all beings as yourself, and it will be personal. When I say that we are all one, it is an unconditional love, but it is no less personal, I feel your body right now as part of my own in this communion. I do not feel that it is anything less than my own, but I do not feel it the same way you feel it because I do not have personal things that I'm attempting to accomplish. It is just part of the one. So that's how you feel things in, what you say, upper dimensions.

So we'll feel that by the time we become the creator?

Oh, well before that.

How does it work in terms we can understand?

When you are in a society that is total love, you feel that way because there is no reason not to. You maintain a border around you that you might go beyond sometimes when there is something that is not compatible with the feeling that you are experiencing of total love and for which you are unable to embrace, meaning feel a part of, and still maintain the feeling of love. So that thing might be floating about in your midst, but you don't feel it. It is not part of you. This does not mean that it is not actually part of you; it means that you are not feeling it, and you are not engaging it.

All right, again in a way that we can understand, is that like the fifth dimension, the sixth, the seventh? Can we quantify it?

The mind can easily quantify it, but of course, it's not true. It might be easier to say that you have a bath, and when you run your hands and your body through the bath, the water feels personal; it feels connected to you. When you drop a rubber duck in there, it might not feel the same, meaning the rubber duck might not feel as personally connected to you as the water. Not that you wouldn't enjoy the rubber duck. [Chuckles.]

[Laughing.] All right. The Explorer Race, now, is unbalanced, at least the ones on Earth.

Yes, it is intended to be so that you can push to find your way home. And of course being physical, your understanding of finding your way home is to physically go from one place to another.

We've been told that everything that we can see with our eyes and our telescopes and our Hubble telescope is the third dimension in this Creator's universe; I mean, there's much more of it, but at least what we can see is the third dimension.

Or it is the dimension in which you are occupying. It is not a matter of quantification. It is where you are; you can see where you are. If you could see the other side of the universe, you would only see it in the terms of where you are. You would see planets and so on and so forth. It's like rose-colored or blue-colored glasses: You would see it through the tint of where you are.

Oh, that's brilliant! All right. If we could travel, we would see the dimension, if we can use that word, that we're in!

You would see things within the definition of what you are experiencing, yes. You would see it only in what you are personally experiencing.

So when we become the fourth dimension, we won't see the third anywhere?

That's right, you won't unless there is some reason for you to be shown it, which is very unlikely. You will see it, then, through those eyes.

Are there third dimensions everywhere, then?

No, that's a mental construct. You're asking whether there are dimensions like the one you're experiencing or places like the one you're experiencing wherever you go. No. It is important for you to have this place of potential consequences, even though if you transported people from Earth right now in a vehicle to the other side of the universe, you would bring those consequences with you, meaning you would see things, your world, in that construct regardless of whether you were in the nineteenth dimension (which does not exist). Mainly, what I am trying to help you do is not to define but to feel the function. So, no, this is available to you here for you to accomplish what you are attempting to accomplish, which is, in the long run, to find your way back home and, in the short run, to accomplish the goals of the Explorer Race so as to make them available to other races.

Okay, but then, in the rest of the totality, creators had never felt the need to create these dimensions as limits?

Remember, it's not happening yet.

CREATIONS CAN JOIN TOGETHER

Creation is naturally what it is when it is created, and it can only be limited by defining it. It can only be made less, and this tells you that the nature of creation does not come from the inside out. If something comes from the inside out, you could say, "Well, out is just a matter of which way is out." Now, if it is natural for this to be everything it is, why do you need dimensions? Dimensions are a means of limiting it.

You asked whether it's natural for all beings to step through the dimension process. The answer is no, because that's not happening here, either. Remember, it is vitally important for you not to get hung up in the concept that the mind has created. Even though we've discussed it and you felt the truth of what we discussed, you're going right back to saying, "But ..."

The question is this: Have any other creators ever limited anything? And they might have used other things besides dimensions.

Yes. They have, from time to time, when they desired for a creation to do something that was not in its nature. This was done once that I know of, when two creators desired to have their creations join each other. It's not unusual for a creation to embrace another creation. The creators decided that they would like their creations to connect on the basis of one creation joining the other while the other was not aware of the one. So one comes to the other, and the other one's not aware of it until the joining takes place.

It is not my intention to create confusion for you when you have a well-laid-out system for understanding, but your system for understanding is mental, and from time to time I need to grab you and shake you and say, "This is a concept! It does not have anything to do with reality."

NOTHING AFFECTS YOU
UNLESS YOU WANT IT TO

All right. So when the Explorer Race goes and does its expansion, it's only going to create more potential?

It will create more potential within those who desire that potential. If a society desires growth, then it will provide the means by which that society can achieve that growth, but if they are very happy being who they are and they have achieved what it is they attempt to achieve, it will just pass through them without affecting them in any way.

But I thought the whole point of many of them was that they didn't realize they had ceased growing, because they had reached a level of perfection. So it's not going to affect them unless they want to?

Nothing affects you unless you want it to. If it affected them against their desires, what would that be?

Control.

Yes. But if they ever desired growth, because it had passed through them, it would be the means by which they achieved it. If they did not desire growth, it doesn't mean that it didn't pass through them. When it passes through them, it then becomes available for them if they ever desire it. If they ever desire it, it will be right there as a means. They may never desire it; therefore, it will never be activated. This way there is no control; it is only a gift.

Right. So it's only for expansion, then. The only place that's going to get balanced is the deliberately unbalanced Explorer Race on Earth?

No, that's not really true. There will be, as you know, other beings who desire growth who will be expanded. They will return by some journey — maybe not yours but maybe their journey — to the state of natural balance. You understand, you can be in balance, go through some journey by which you might seem to be out of balance, and then become balanced again. This does not mean you have necessarily become more; you've achieved balance. You might understand this more easily by simply imagining that you are sitting in a chair and it's leaning one way or the other. When you finally get it to sit just right, you're balancing. As another example, perhaps you're holding something, such as a spinning basketball, and then you balance it just right. You have it balanced just right, and that lasts for a while, but then it falls off. Then you get it going again, just right, and it spins on your fingertip.

But that has nothing to do with growth necessarily.

It might not have anything to do with growth, but it has to do with feeling good, and that's good. It's important to remind you of that so that we do not take a long, circuitous journey on that one. I am not talking to you in any way to try to make you feel foolish or feel less-than. Rather, it is my intention to expand your questions from the loving place.

COME FROM A PLACE OF LOVE

Now we get to something important for all beings, as well as for you personally, as you have considered it many times before. "How do I ask the question?" you think to yourself. "If only I would ask the question the right way." You've had many occasions when you've asked a question in a certain way, and floods of information came out. This will happen.

But how can we profoundly change the means by which you ask the question? Ultimately, when you get to the true unconditional place of asking the question where you're in service, you don't ask the question in the same way because you're focused in the heat. You are experiencing the heat. While you are talking, the heat is present. You will not be able to ask the question in the same way; you will not have all the words. The mind will be soothed and loved; it will not have anything that it needs to know. The question, therefore, comes through love. In short, the question will be what others need. It will reveal what they need. It will also give them the tools that they can immediately grasp because it is what they need. It will be the means by which you can provide to others what they are crying out for, which comes through you as a question.

You might consider it channeling, but it's not something that is actually channeling. It is easier than that. You are experiencing the heat; the words come through the heat. You will know they're not coming through the heat when you ask words and the heat goes away. Then it's not coming through the heat. It gives you physical evidence right away, so it is simple to understand immediately: "Oh, the heat's gone; this isn't coming from there." So then you say, No, wait," and you get the heat back. Then I (or someone else, whoever is coming through Robert) wait, and then you ask the question. This is the question you ask for others; it is the means by which you ask it. I am not trying to say you must do that now, but I am suggesting that the homework I gave you earlier is a means to begin. It is a way for you to understand how it is you will be asking those questions when you yourself have no personal desire or interest. How is it possible to do that? Then you will be channeling the questions on the basis of the needs of others, which is what you're doing. I am channeling answers to questions on the basis of that need. And in its very nature, it will feel profoundly rewarding. It will give answers that are profoundly enlightening. But you, not unlike Robert if he wants to know what's going on, will only really be able to understand it mentally when you listen to the tape later. You won't be attached to understanding it mentally during the session because you won't need to; you won't need to follow it consciously in your mind so that you have to listen to perform the functions that you perform and be able to run that ahead so that you can ask the next question. There will be no need to do any of that.

Now, how does this relate to others? When people talk to each other — for instance a couple, or two coworkers who feel they might be talking at cross-purposes, have the same goal — they are attempting to understand each other and to make sense out of something. In short, they are attempting to merge with something so that they totally understand each other. Such arguments often happen with couples, but in business they happen almost as often, to say nothing of conversations you have with others — friends, people you barely know, and so on. If you can focus on that heat, that love (which every individual can do), then you speak a question that is focused on the same type of love because this love/heat is felt in the same way by all beings. The question ceases to be threatening because it is felt as heat and is focused through heat into your heat by another. Even if the other is not generating the heat, it will still feel safe. It will make more sense to them. They will be able to answer the question, and you, as the person generating the heat in that moment, will be able to understand completely what they say back. If there is still some problem, then you can share with them the method of generating the heat, and then you both ask questions through the heat to each other. The answers will make complete sense because they are felt. Misunderstanding becomes a thing of the past, and we can talk more about that in the future, should you feel that you wish to ask about it.

It certainly will help as we start dealing globally, and then off-planet in that communication.

Yes. At some point books as you know them will no longer be printed on paper and so on; they will simply be on the computer. There will be a means by which publishers can be compensated, but this way anybody who wants to read your book at any time can do so, anytime they wish. This will take a while to develop; it's in its infancy now, but it's coming out. It's coming.

Electronic downloading — e-books,

That's right, and it will work. It will take a while for people to find the means to make it work. If all creation is turning inside out and outside in at the same time, how can anything remain apparently fixed? If your body were turning inside out and outside in right now, how could you live? Because the means of actually having no boundaries — your skin appears to be your boundary — would not allow you to have physical existence. But what if I told you that the means by which all beings — myself included — feel a part of all other beings, everywhere, is that everything is turning inside out and outside in at a fantastic rate of speed? You know that when you put pictures on something and flip through them, what happens?

Yes, they appear to move.

That's right, they appear to move. So this tells you something very important. This tells you that the only way other beings can feel you all, here, as something that is a part of themselves, is because you are turning outside in and inside out also, but so quickly that you do not notice it, and it doesn't interfere with the means by which you are conducting school here.

But that's here, to go from the third to the fourth dimension.

No, no, it happens everywhere.

Zoosh said it was to get us from the third to the fourth dimension without breaking the veil.

I do not feel the necessity of agreeing with everything that you were told from square one to the present. You are told things from time to time that make sense to you in that moment based on who you are in that moment. And the more mentally attached you are to certain ideas in that moment, the more something will make complete sense to you then. But what I'm telling you now is not intended to say that is wrong; what I am telling you now is that by doing this it is expanding.

It is important from time to time to grab your mind and shake it so that you do not become overly enamored with one, two, three, four, five, six, seven, eight, or nine steps. And it is very easy not only for you to do that but for others, because everything in your world supports that as you've now set it up. Everything in your world supports what I am saying too; it's just that it's not being given its natural place in your awareness. You must embrace your physical body as the profound mystical teacher it is set up to be. How would you ever know how to feel the heat if you did not have a physical body in which to do it? You come here to learn material mastery, and you cannot learn material mastery here without having a body available for your personality to occupy. Therefore the body is a gift to you. Of course, it was you before it was given to you, and it will be you after it moves on and becomes part of something else.

Everything is you all the time without exception. Because you are living in a circumstance in which your mind seeks to fulfill the responsibility that has been given to it (which is not its own), it is sometimes difficult to grasp that you are everything else. Yet the simplest, most rewarding way to notice how you are everything else is to experience that heat in your body and then look at someone or something else while you're experiencing it. If it is another form of life that lives now (not something people have created, even though that is alive too), such as a plant or an animal, the heat will increase, and it will be easier to sustain. Then if you look at many plants and animals (who naturally do this very easily because they are not here to learn and are not part of the Explorer Race), then the heat becomes even more defined. It doesn't get hotter and hotter so that you burn up; it just becomes more defined so that you more easily feel it in every portion of your body.

So how does this help you in your homework? Practice your homework when you're lying down and you're relaxed. When you are out somewhere walking or driving, stop and look at a tree. If it's not busy, the heat will come up more strongly. In short, the way to find your way to understand that you are part of all beings is not the mental. The mind cannot grasp this because it is not set up to do that, but your love can join easily when other people or beings or plants or animals are experiencing that love, and there is no problem with that at all. And it becomes more easily definable and fills your body more easily. That's a hint for how to do your homework more easily.

Union on the felt, feeling, love path is [snaps fingers] easily accomplished. You can easily feel being a part of all things. But thinking is where the conundrum comes in. The mind is not set up to do that, not because you are foolish and you cannot get it, but because you're trying to get it with something that was not set up to get it: the mind. The mind was set up to be loved and to make its observations, which may or may not ever be called on. The feelings were set up to unite you with yourself and with all that is around you, which is also yourself. That is why union is possible, and easily so, through these feelings.

VERTICAL WISDOM

Animals and plants don't really need to use their minds at all because they — what does Zoosh say? — know what they need to know when they need to know it. And if they don't need to know it anymore, then they don't.

That's what he called vertical wisdom.

He calls it that, but that was to give you a mental construct to put into your mind. But in fact, if we think of it that way, that the animals (the ants, the fish, the cows, and so on) are not here to learn anything, then they must be here only to help, and it's true. When you are focused in the heat, and you look at a grasshopper, it might be able to focus very quickly on the heat as well, and you feel it more strongly. You feel it no more strongly than if it was a giant redwood tree or a tiny grasshopper. Love is always equal in its quantity and application. Remember that. Write it down, and keep it handy. Carry it somewhere where you can look at it from time to time — not because you don't remember it mentally, but to remind you that it is a feeling, not only the feeling of love, but the statement is a feeling. Love is this spot; the statement is intended to do that. We'll do this for the sake of the mental construct, but don't be attached to its being always and only this direction.

All right, but what about the mind? We've been told that the mind is from Andromeda, but what about all the other beings in this creation and other creations? They don't have minds? They use their minds differently?

It is different and more like what Zoosh was trying to define when he said they know what they need to know when they need to know it, but not needing to have a linear memory to retain it when they don't need to know it. Think of all the things that you know, things you've experienced, maybe things you've watched in entertainment. Sometimes you get images that you wouldn't like to have anymore, memories that are all part of the linear memory. When you think of these things, they actually make you feel bad. In short, you don't need to bring up those bad feelings. Feelings in their own right are not bad, you understand, but you don't need to bring up those discomforts. You do need, from time to time, to know something.

From time to time because when your world is set up in such a way that everything is natural, it flows like a dance. For the sake of your understanding, within the context of your life here, imagine you walk down the hall and you flow through the door, meaning the door is there and you walk through it (probably you wouldn't have a door, but I'm putting it that way, doorway) because that's what you naturally do. You do not need to think, "Me walk, door open."

That's why I say that you don't necessarily need to think in a linear context, but you might know something. An animal might meet another animal, and it is in the nature of the animal (or your aura, for that matter) that the other being's existence, who it is readily available. They know that, then, about each other. Sometimes an animal will meet a human being and will slow this process down. The animal broadcasts who it is, and if you are open, you pick up certain pictures: maybe what the animal did that day, maybe a quick flash of its parents, if it's a baby, and so on. Maybe you don't get any of that; maybe you just look at the animal and react to it from the outside: "Oh, bear! Frightening!" But if you are open to things, then you feel, "Oh, a bear walking through the woods today found something to eat." You don't *think* of it that way; you see these pictures. So it presents itself to you that way. You actually do that to each other.

Now, you present that in your auric field to others, and they either get it or they don't. That would be, in that moment, an example of knowledge that you would need to know that you wouldn't necessarily need to know again later, okay? You might never meet that bear again, but you meet it here, and it might be useful to know what the bear did. On other planets (since that's what we're talking about but I'm trying to bring it down to Earth), you actually always broadcast: Every human being, every animal, every plant, every stone, every seed, every speck of dust, every planet, and so on, broadcasts the nature of its existence not because its sending something out but because it's emanating it. It is your personality. It is who you are, and it all makes you up. The other beings get as much or as little as they need to get to relate to you in the way they need to relate to you in that moment, or maybe they don't need to relate to you at all, but you acknowledge the others' existence, and off you go.

That's how it works everywhere. It does not mean that there is not more, but that exists for me as well. I'm not saying there isn't more, but that is part of what there is too. And it makes sense when you think of it, doesn't it?

Well, the reason I tried to bring it down to Earth, as you say, is because it's happening here now and very few people are taking advantage of it. That tells you something very important: It can happen. That so-called vertical wisdom is readily available here right now, and it's necessary for that to be the case so that you do not have to find something that you need to improve the quality of your life on a day-to-day level. It has to be available. And it will be available to the other planets that might wish to grow someday, just like it is here. If you wish to assimilate in a different way, the means is available right now. That makes it much easier to do.

DO NOT LIMIT THE HEAT

When you say the heat in the chest, that is the soul connection, what we call the soul?

The heat in the chest is no more or less. You cannot say it's a soul anything; that limits it. The heat you feel in the chest is just the same, as it's possible for you to go up to a rock and feel heat, and that particular rock can feel heat from you. Then you feel more heat.

So is it Earth's soul that Mother Earth lends us or the immortal personality or the combination that broadcasts the heat?

It's everything. Everything has the heat all the time. The way you don't feel the heat is to limit it. All beings, all cells have the heat, which is, in short, love that we're defining as heat because we need to give you a trackable means of physical evidence so that you can notice that something is present. The heat is omnipresent. Love and heat are the same thing in this context.

We're saying heat manifesting as love and love manifesting as heat.

That's what you're really saying: Love manifests as heat when focused that way. I cannot say, "Go inside your body and find love," but I can say, "Go inside your body and find or generate heat, a physical heat that you can feel." Then you go into the heat, and you feel it more, and it feels wonderful. What if I say, "Go into your body and find cold," and you generate cold? You might be able to do that, but it might not feel wonderful, and not just because it's cold. Maybe you're in a hot place, and you'd like to feel colder. Under some circumstances, it might feel all right.

The yogis can do that, so we know it's a potential.

Anyone can do it. Yogis do it because they have been taught and they practice. It's not good enough to be taught; you have to practice. The reason they do that, the reason they can do it, is not to say, "Look how wonderful we are." They don't do that. It's to say, "Look, I am doing this; you can, too." They are reminders to the general population that anyone can do this too. They might not necessarily say that, but you are expected to get it. If they say it, they are trying to exert their opinion on you, but if they demonstrate it, they are saying "Look, this is what I am." Just like when a bird flies, it doesn't say, "And you can do it too." It just says, "This is what I am."

You understand, I will not talk to you this way every day. But I talk to you like this sometimes because it is necessary to remind you that the way you think is not the way you normally function, "normally" meaning not on Earth but also meaning normal function on Earth. It can be embraced on Earth. I'm trying to say, "Look, you are "that," even though it may seem to be that you are in fact "this." Even though these appear to be two separate things, in fact what's really here is that and of course there are no real boundaries.

SEEK ANSWERS THROUGH THE HEAT
All right, let me ask this. I have always wanted to bring what I call my higher self, my God-self or something, into Earth expression. Is that possible now, while still maintaining the lessons of humanity?

Yes, and the easiest way to do it is to feel the heat.

Really? I've been looking for some much more complicated thing.

Well, it's much simpler than that. When you look for things in a complicated way, you will always find, what?

A complicated way.

If you taste everything to understand what it is, as a child does, you will understand things only on the basis of how it tastes. The means will give you a reflection within the context of the means. But if you do the love thing, you will focus through that; you will feel the warmth, and then (and this is best done with another) you have the communion, the heat-to-heat, and the question changes. It might even be your questions, in the beginning, certainly; and the answer feels vastly different. What? What did I say? The answer feels vastly different; there is no dissatisfaction, though there might be question after question. You absorb the answer on a much broader scale because you are here to discover — what? — material mastery, which is about feeling. I'm not saying that you're asking the question wrong; what I am saying is that this gives you personal satisfaction. At some point, you no longer have questions that you ask in a personal way, and it gives you a great deal more personal freedom. You may not always do things like that, but it is your normal way. [Chuckles.] I like to redefine the word "normal" because in a social scientific way, you might say that if everybody's yelling for a cab, it is normal to yell for a cab. But let us take the word "normal" and make it something that is not only healthy but also benevolent.

Chapter 11

Expand Your Understanding

Ssjoooo

July 18, 2000

S-S-J-O-O-O-O. [Ssjoooo write his name.]

So how do we say it?

It's "sssss-ssssshhhhhhhooooooooo" or it could be "ssssss-jjjjooooo." I want the "o" sound to taper off at the end. "Sssss-shhhhjjjjjjooooooo." Now, the reason I'm picking this as a name is that it's very noncommittal. It's not that far from my sound, but the "j" makes it a bit more acceptable on Earth, and it was also my intention to make it sound a bit more international in its flavor. And it doesn't prompt the reader to have any divinity questions. If it seems appropriate, I could give a different name later, but don't you think that would be sufficiently worthwhile?

That's fine. It's just a tag, something to identify who's talking.

It is a tag. It's not exactly a catchy word. I'm afraid no nicknames will be immediately forthcoming.

DISENTANGLEMENT DETAILS

Okay, in the disentanglement exercise, is it better to do it at night before you go to sleep? Some people are just going to fall asleep. Is it better to treat it as a meditation, like you do not do it after you've eaten? Are there any contraindications that we could put out, like a few more tips about it or anything?

Yes. It would be good to do it at least three hours after a meal, but it's not critical. It can be done within a half-hour after eating, and mechanically speaking, it can be done anytime. But I think it's better to be in a completely relaxed state, if at all possible. Lie on your back with your arms at your sides, palms down, and don't cross your legs. It would be best to have your hands not touch the sides of your body, but they don't have to be stretched out, just slightly away from the sides of your legs or your hips, wherever your hands normally touch.

Is it possible to combine that with the heart-in-the-chest exercise, or is there no reason to do that?

It is not necessary to do that, but if you want to, you can try. I feel that it is not necessary. If you don't have much time or you think you might fall asleep, I would say the disentanglement might be best, but then during the day sometime, practice the heart exercise.

Because the heat can be done anytime, anywhere?

Well, it is a physical thing. It's hard to do, so you focus on it. Ideally, you do the heart thing first, and then you might speak through the warmth of the heart to ask for the disentanglement, but that would be very hard to do for the average person. It would be better to do the heart thing first for a few minutes, then relax, and then request the disentanglement. The reason to do this is that it prepares your body for something good to happen. It's a way to nurture your body as you see yourself in component parts, and the average reader will see him- or herself that way. It's also a way to allow your body to nurture you, the love that loves the mind. While you might think during disentanglement (and it's best to try not to, but it might come up), the mind needs to feel as if it is accepted as it is. It is important to try to not worry or have thoughts like that; if you catch yourself worrying, just go back to looking at your eyelids (closed, of course) or something in which you might see light patterns. It's just a way of remaining focused. I don't want you to look at your eyelids to the point of giving yourself a headache by concentrating; it's a way to remain in your body and to be awake and receptive.

But if some people are just lying there and they don't see anything and it's dark, should they focus on being quiet?

It's hard to focus on being quiet, in my experience of your experience. [Chuckles.] My understanding is that it's easier for you to do something than to do nothing. So that's the reason for looking at the eyelids while they are closed. If your eyes are open, something you see will stimulate you to think excessively, but if your eyelids are closed and you are looking at the inside of them, your brain knows that you're not looking at something with a need to think about it.

Or respond to it.

That's right. Your brain knows that this is not something that it is required to interpret; therefore, if you see light patterns — and this is not a spiritual thing; it is a physical phenomenon — just enjoy them. While it may have spiritual connotations, I do not want to burden the reader with that right now. By "burden" I mean I do not want the reader to feel he or she should do this or that. If you see light patterns, enjoy them. If you don't, that's fine. It gives your mind permission to relax because it gives you something to do.

Would it be helpful to say that? "I give my mind permission to relax"?

It isn't necessary. If you feel it would be helpful, you can say it before you do your disentanglement, but the mind does not function on the basis of its own permission. The mind functions on how it's been trained since childhood; therefore, it is inclined to do something. If your eyelids are closed and you are staring at them from the inside out, your mind knows that you are doing something but that the requirement is minimal, which is why you might find yourself thinking.

All right. How long do you do it generically before you start introducing lists of things? Is it a feeling?

Do it for three to five days while you're getting used to the idea of it. You're training yourself in the mechanics. And like I say, you might feel some sense of touch. You might feel electrical, you might feel a sense of relaxation, or you might feel nothing. Do it for three to five days, and then start introducing statements that work for you, as I think we discussed. Ask for the gold-light beings and so on. This would be helpful to disentangle you from all of your discomforts that harm you in your life at this time. Something like that.

Then when you say that, it will be easy. You want to say this *before* you lie down. So you have the light on, you say these things, and then you lie down and begin your procedure. You *can* say them after you lie down. In the beginning when you're going through all these elaborate things, you might have a long list to read, and I'd rather you not have to try to remember anything. I'd rather that you have your list written up with the names or the events or the circumstances you want them to work on. You might feel that they will need to work on those more than one day, and it's certainly possible. So if you add things to that list, you can also say, "I'd like you to continue working on whatever else you see that I need to be disentangled from." You can add that as an addendum or to lead off with. Then say, "I would especially like you to disentangle me from _____." Then you glance at your items for that day that you've thought about. It doesn't have to be a word or a name. It can be, for example, "I would especially like you to disentangle me from that time that I_____."

YOU GRANT PERMISSION

You can be as explanatory as you wish. Don't be cryptic; you're not trying to tell them as little as possible so that they can dazzle you with their abilities. That works entirely against you because what you are doing when you're asking them to do these things is basically giving them permission, but you are also preparing your physical body, your feeling body, and the portions of you that retain the memory of these things chemically, physically, and mentally, and you're giving yourself permission to have these things disentangled from you in ways that don't harm you. You might still have the recollection. It might fade in time, but when the recollection comes up at some point in the future after you've been disentangled from it, it won't cause you as much pain, or it might not cause you any pain at all. You'll think of it, and you'll let it go. It's nothing; it doesn't bother you anymore. That's the key to understanding how it works. It's not intended to wipe your mind clear of recollection, but it might have that effect because your mind is not bringing something up to you that needs to be resolved anymore.

So to experience it fully, the idea is to give yourself permission as well as to give the beings permission. In short, be as clear as you want. When you disentangle from a person, it doesn't mean that the person goes out of your life. That person with whom you have a history (some of which you don't like) might very well still be in your life.

One has to be cautious with this. I don't recommend you disentangle from husbands and wives immediately; I prefer that you disentangle from, say, beings who used to be in your life more dominantly, such as parents, uncles, children you knew at school, people you've known at work, and so on. But you know, if you're younger, then it can be kids you know at school and teachers, and so on. In short, there might be people that you still see, but you are disentangling from painful experiences. The idea is that you disentangle from the pain of the past with these beings and that whatever relationship you establish in the present with these beings will not be affected, at least on your part, by the pain of the past. So you will not be driven by the pain of the past in this avenue, and you don't continue to perpetuate the same problems with this person on the basis of what you are doing for yourself.

This does not mean that the person won't do something, but of course, if you are both doing the disentanglement, your relationship such as it is will be on more comfortable grounds or at least will not be weighted by anger and pain from the past and can establish itself on a daily basis. This is an example only and is not the way everything works. I need to give you examples that are practical in your life because you might very well have somebody, especially a relative, that you see from time to time or even regularly with whom the pain from the past is affecting the relationship, such as it is.

HOW TO MAKE YOUR LIST

If we look again at the analogy of the ball of string, do we assume, then, that we should start with more recent things in our asking and work backward?

No, just bring up whatever comes up first. When you're writing your list, write it down in the order in which it comes up. Don't try to organize it. If you notice once you've been writing your list for a while that you want to ask about things further down on the list, go ahead. Just circle those things or check them off after you've asked about them. Even after you've gone on and asked about other things, once you've asked about something with these beings, they will continue to monitor that thing. That's why as you talk to the beings who may be present, you might say, "And if you see anything else that I need to be disentangled from." You don't have to give them any more specific instructions than that. Then you might say, "Please do so." That allows them to continue to work on things that you've brought up in the past that you might, by that time, already be sufficiently disentangled from and don't consider a problem anymore.

But there might be residue.

That's right, the people on your list might still be doing things. The experience that was painful with them might have been based on something that wasn't necessarily painful for you, or it might have grown out of an experience that was similar with somebody else. In short, experiences tend to be connected to other experiences. It gives them more latitude on the basis of what to pursue. They are attempting to disentangle you from the pains of the past. You can, if you like, ask to disentangle not just your physical "body"; you can ask to disentangle your "bodies." You might say "my bodies in this life" if you wish, or just leave it as "my bodies," in which case, if they feel that it's from another life, they will go ahead and do that if they feel that that life is in any way affecting your current life.

If we have a feeling that something that happened in our childhood is really working on us now, even though it's under layers and layers of other stuff, we can ask for it to be worked on at the beginning, then?

That's right. You can say in your overall statement that you're asking to be disentangled from any pains and discomforts that you have experienced in your life. Say it like that, "In my life, whether I am aware of the cause or not."

While practicing disentanglement, you may in time develop your own words that work for you. If your guides speak to you, they will probably give you words that they feel might work for you, but you will know whether the words work because when you say them, they will feel all right, meaning that you won't have any discomforts.

Now, of course, if there is a great deal of pain and discomfort around something that you're asking to be disentangled from, that pain or discomfort may make itself known. But you know when you say something, even to each other, and you realize that you've misspoken or you've said something that isn't quite right, you get a funny feeling. If you get the funny feeling when you say something, then you could stop for a moment and ask yourself, "Is there a better way to say this?" Any time you are concerned about a better way to say this, always finish up the statement with, "And if you see anything that I need to be disentangled from, that I am not aware of at this time, please go ahead and do that." Of course, you can say, "anything painful or discomforting."

THE NEED FOR DISENTANGLEMENT ON EARTH
This is a major boon to humanity! Is this somebody's project? How did this come into being?

It is actually a typical application on other planets where there is communication from one species to another, usually from another planet, sometimes on your planet, where you may have offended someone but do not know it, or you may have been offended, but the other beings did not know they offended you and certainly meant you no offense. Therefore, it is established in many other places, but applying it to Earth is something that I feel is important to do at this time because right now the average person, and this includes young and old alike and all walks of life and in all situations, has his or her feelings hurt forty to fifty times on an average day. Because the average person is out of touch with his or her feelings, he or she is not necessarily aware of it, but that does not mean that it isn't happening.

That's why disentanglement is an ongoing thing. You essentially do it for the rest of your life not because you're so messed up that it takes the rest of your life to get you to feel better but because discomforts are somewhat consistent; even though they might be slight, they are cumulative. Something that is uncomfortable might be slight, but if enough of those slights build up, they have an overall effect, and that overall effect usually causes you to restrict your behavior. One of the primary ways you restrict your behavior — and this is vital in understanding the value of disentanglement — is that you restrict the way you receive. This is why so many people in your society desire so much but experience so little within the context of their desires: They've already restricted the way they receive to a tiny thing that feels safe. Because of hurt feelings that they knew about when they were youngsters and then over time developed a sense of cutting themselves off from that so that they weren't overwhelmed by those feelings and had no means to resolve them in a way that works for them, they become — how can we say? — handicapped on the basis of being able to change in a natural, healthy way. A disadvantage of the way they experience individuality in recent years (though this is going to change these days) is that the more they see themselves as individuals, the less inclined they are to embrace help that comes from beyond their own individuality.

Many of you have been trained to be rugged individualists, but I'm talking about that which goes beyond even physical help from another physical being. It is natural for spirit beings to help beings who are in other forms just as it is natural for you, when you are in deep sleep, to help other beings — sometimes human beings, sometimes beings on other planets or worlds or galaxies — in ways that you can offer. You travel; you are not restricted. You are tethered because your body is still alive, and you are expected to have that personality in your body when your body wakes up in its entirety that's normally in there, but you travel and help other beings as well, just as they travel and help you. You are all part of the one; you help each other all the time, no matter what you are doing.

So in the past ("past" meaning any time before this) when you cut yourself off from receiving, you might have been cutting yourself off from the beings who can do you the most good. Therefore, the way you receive some help is when you are in deep sleep because then your personality tends to go where it is nurtured and comforted, where you are reminded of who you are, and where your body does not feel the same level of restriction that you might feel when you are awake and conscious and moving about. So some spirit beings who present themselves to your body while the bulk of your personality is elsewhere can interact in some helpful way with your physical body as long as they present themselves in a way that is entirely safe to your physical body. If there is any fear or alarm whatsoever, even if the beings are totally benevolent, you will wake up; you will pull your personality back from whatever it's doing and wake up. "Oh, what's that?" You have all experienced this, whether the being was benevolent or not. In most cases, it's benevolent; sometimes it's otherwise, especially if you are in a physically dangerous environment. This happens for people.

ALLOW THE GOLD-LIGHT BEINGS TO DO THEIR WORK

Why are we receiving this now? But it's time to wake up, and this is one of the tools that we're being given?

Exactly. You're being given something that you normally use elsewhere and that some beings may use in some way now here, but I'm trying to disseminate it more broadly because it has the capacity and capability to do so much good. Because of the nature of creativity of other beings and other spiritual practices, spirits and humans as well, you will build on it. People will come up with things that work for their ways, and that's intended. The whole point is to not complicate it too much. You remember that the point is to give yourself, meaning your personality, permission to allow these beings to help you to disentangle from that.

It's much easier to be disentangled than for you to mentally let go. You can mentally let go of something, but you have to physically let go as well. You have to let go on the feeling body, and you have to let go sufficiently so that your spiritual body isn't reminding you that you need to let go. [Laughs.] So it's better to get help from these gold-light beings who can do the most good for you, and of course, other light beings who can work through the gold light, or work through other gold-light beings. We do not want to reject other light beings, but we cannot have anything but gold-light beings working on you directly, for instance, white-light beings might work through the gold-light beings, and that would be fine with the gold-light beings. That happens with the gold-light beings because of the extremes that you are exposed to in this Earth School. White-light beings may be able to easily work on you without gold-light beings there, but that level of light may attract beings that do not have the sophistication. They may want to work on you, but they may not have the sophistication to work on you in ways that are benevolent for you and might actually in some ways be harmful for you, but they do not know that. The white-light beings will not keep them away, because they are unconditionally loving. But if gold-light beings are there, these unsophisticated beings are kept away because gold light and the energy of the gold-light beings — but gold light in its own right — will just radiate in such a way as to keep all those unsophisticated beings away. It will not harm these unsophisticated beings; they can keep at a distance, watch what's going on, and learn. So it is good for everyone.

The more people do this, the more good spreads around the world. And of course, in this day and age of people speaking to other people on the other side of the world on a moment-to-moment basis, it can be a wonderful thing, if you like to do it.

YOUR PERSONALITY MOVES FROM VEHICLE TO VEHICLE TO EXPRESS ITSELF

There are souls that ensoul our bodies, there's spirit, and there are high selves, and even though we're part of the one, there's some unique somebody somewhere that we're connected to. From your perspective, talk about this. Supposedly there's a physical and then the soul creates the physical, the spirit creates the soul, and it goes back somewhere. How do you see all this?

That is just a way of explaining things to people that isn't overwhelming. If I tell you the room is filled with loving energy, you do not point to a place in the room and say, "Is there loving energy right there?" Nor do you point to some other place and say that. If the room is filled with loving energy and you can feel it, you will accept the fact that the room is filled with loving energy. You won't ask what the beings look like in the room; it is loving energy.

"Energy" is a word that has come to be applied to a broad spectrum of things, including the human being, who broadcasts energy as well. People have been trained on hierarchical methods of understanding, and in your time and in your country most people have been exposed to that, if not through religion then through the scholastic enterprise or the business enterprise. So your basic concept of understanding comes in a hierarchical method: this, this, this, this, this, this, this, and then we get this. That's the means by which beings in the past have chosen to speak to you, and they chose to speak to you that way because that's the way you understand things.

Who you are, of course, would be your personality, and regardless of who you are, you can differentiate your personality from the personality of somebody else even if you are attempting to emulate them or if they want you to emulate them in some way. You can still differentiate your personality from theirs, regardless of the value judgment that you or they place on it.

The reality is that your personality, as you know yourself to be (even in this life, not just in the wider sense), moves from vehicle to vehicle as a means of expressing it. On one planet, you might look like a humanoid but not like an Earth human; that would be your vehicle. On another planet, you might look entirely different. On this planet, this is your vehicle; this is how you look.

It looks like a bullseye.

You are in the physical center of whatever vehicle you are in. Is it like this? Not exactly, but that's closer. This is you, but it is you in that proverbial room of love, meaning off the paper, but for the paper used for the sake of putting a dot, you, and everything, meaning your personality focused in your vehicle with nothing above you, but everything around you and everywhere around you. The next galaxy is around you because it's part of the whole being. The whole everything is that this is the closest one to what it is. On a piece of paper, it looks like an individual all by itself, but in fact, the dot is just to give you a representation of your personality's presence in its vehicle. It is you within everything everywhere else, so there are not only other dots, but there is everything. It's more like that. There is no hierarchy.

When you go into those deep levels of sleep where you go to talk to individual teachers, those teachers are remembered sometimes, or in your visions or meditations you can remember them personified as teacher. In fact, when you are there, there is no personification. The absorption is happening without that physical personification, but when you come back into your body and make some effort, should you do that on the meditative level of some sort to remember that, you will screen everything through the manner and means by which life is conducted wherever you are. In short, everything here is personified, even if it is a leaf. It is a leaf regardless of how you feel about the leaf, whether it is a sacred thing or something to rake up when there are too many of them. It is still personified, meaning individualized. In short, from my perception, there is no hierarchy. That is why I say your body is a part of my body; I don't see any difference. I don't consider myself any grander than you or you grander than me. We are literally one, to my understanding.

THE MIND CONSTANTLY SEARCHES FOR MORE
When what we call a human body dies, there is a thin, shimmery film that clairvoyants can see that leaves the body. That, you're saying, is the immortal personality.

That which you or sensitives see is in fact that which is the essential you. You see it, perhaps, in a form, yet the form that it will take shortly after the point at which you might not see it anymore or might not personify it anymore (even if you are a sensitive or a clairvoyant, you're still a human being, in the human vehicle, and you're still going to personify) will eventually be a smaller, more concentrated circle of light.

Okay, but this film is shimmery and iridescent, translucent. They called it "mass." It has some mass to it.

Yes, it has mass. It appears to be going through something and to be going somewhere. Why does it appear to be going somewhere? Because your world is focused in space and time. And it is moving. If it is moving, it must be going somewhere. What if I told you that when it is no longer visible that doesn't mean that it went somewhere beyond the sensitive's ability to follow it but that it had re-embraced its natural way of being? In short, it became. It rejoined, in its total consciousness sense, being a portion of all beings.

Now, you could say, "Well, what about these people who have after-death experiences?" The reason you know about those is that they didn't go away completely; they came back. What about people who have visions? This is all true, but these visions are intended to remind people who are still living or focused in the vehicle of the human being that there is more; this isn't all there is. The mind is constantly searching for more, for the way that it can understand the more. But the mind, because it has been trained to understand and look for hierarchies or minutiae, will continue to see things comparatively: "What's bigger? What's smaller?" It will continue to see things in that form because that's how it's been trained. This does not mean the mind cannot be trained to do other things; it does not have to be trained to see things only that way. If your minds were not trained that way from childhood, you wouldn't think that way. It's not that the mind thinks that way; it has been conditioned. If you know that, it's very important, because it tells you that your brain, as it exists, and your mind (which has connections to the brain but is not only the brain) do not have to evolve physiologically for you to make strides in spirit, meaning to embrace your whole being, to have the capabilities of your whole being, and to have the potentials that you can apply to your whole being. No physiological change is necessary.

All right. This essence has to go somewhere because it has to go beyond the veil; there's a veil around this planet.

That is, again, a story. Remember, you see your teachers personified, but are they physical? You say, "This thing has to go somewhere." You understand that I'm shaking you.

But there's a veil around the planet, and everybody says you go beyond the veil. In fact, you can't even get out by yourself; you have to have guides take you out, and then we become "more."

I'm not saying this is false; I'm just trying to stretch you past that because what you're telling me is, you're saying, "No! I want my hierarchy!" [Chuckles.]

I don't want a hierarchy, I just ...

Yes, you do.

We're limited, so therefore we're limited by coming through the veil. Zoosh has been talking about this for fifteen years, the gift of ignorance.

It's all true, but I'm trying to expand your point of view. How, given the nature of creation, is it possible to isolate anything?

You said that the only way to learn is to put limits on something.

How is it possible to do that?

Well, what I understood is that the veil around Earth limits us.

No, no, no, not the way it was done; that's the mechanics. How is it possible?

Only if we agree to do it?

How is it possible? That's the mechanics. To put it in different terms, imagine you have two bowls of food: One is salty, and the other is sweet. Your teacher says, "Now change the salty one to sweet and the sweet one to salty,"

You cannot mix one with the other. You must only work with what's in the bowls, and you cannot use magic. How do you do it? You do not have to answer that question.

I don't know! [Laughs.]

Thank you. I want you to put "I don't know" into your repertoire more because "I don't know" does not mean it can't be done. "I don't know" means you do not consciously know at this moment. Now, this is not my way of reprimanding you; what I am saying is that sometimes the question can stimulate you more than the answer.

What I am saying is this: If all those things that Zoosh and those other beings have said are absolutely true, how can what I'm saying also be true? If the teacher tells you to change sugary to salty and salty to sugary, is the teacher trying to present you with a conundrum? What you are presented with is less important than what the teacher is motivated by. What does the teacher want you to learn? Does he or she actually want you to do this? No, the teacher wants you to think about what is being asked, not to accomplish what has been requested. If you understand that, you realize it's not intended to complicate the process but rather to move the student past the limits in front of him or her. You notice that when you are going through the whole thing — this creation to that creation to love's creation and so on — you are essentially going through what one might call levels or hierarchies. The explanation is being presented to you within your mental conditioning. But you also notice that you have never yet come to the answer that you could say, "This is it; seek no further," have you?

Well, I thought I did when you said you created the first creator, but I think there's more out there somewhere, so I don't think I made it to the end yet.

That's right. This tells you something important: Is it that there's more to be told, or is it that the means by which you're attempting to understand, the machine, is flawed? If it is flawed, does that mean there's something wrong with it or that you need to understand what the flaw is? You look at the crystal, and it might be very clear, not a flaw in it. You look through it, and it's beautiful, and if you shine light through it, maybe you can see the colors of the rainbow. Then you look at another crystal, and it's flawed. Your mind is triggered to wonder how the crystal got that way. Yet if you turn it, you can see the colors inside the crystal because the flaw creates the potential for a beauty within what you're looking at, and you don't have to go through the trouble of shining the light, and all of this business, through the crystal to try to get it just right. In short, pick up the crystal, hold it up to the light, and see the colors. The beauty is more readily accessible. Is the flaw the problem? Or is the flaw the solution? [Chuckles.]

The key to understanding the way I speak to you is to understand that what appears to be the problem is the gift. The blank spot, the difficulty, the place where you can get no further because let's say you're worn out or you've gone as far as you can go using that method. That method itself is limited, and what appears to be the flaw, the limit, is actually the gift. When you realize the method is limited, what do you do? You immediately look for another method.

RETRAIN YOUR MIND

The mind has absolute capacity to grasp what is going on within the feelings, but it must be retrained. This is why you have a feeling. You accept your mind exactly the way it is; maybe it's thinking, and maybe it isn't. You start with love because that's going to nurture the mind; it absorbs whatever's going on in the mind and loves it regardless. The mind goes, "Ahhhhh, I am loved for being myself! I can think whatever I want, even in mathematical concepts, x's and o's [chuckles], and I am loved." It relaxes. In short, you learn not only a new way to think but, more importantly, to liberate the mind from the responsibility that is not its own. The means of understanding moves from an exclusively mental process to include the feelings, which necessarily includes the physical body because the physical body gives you the feeling in a physical way that you can understand. And out of this you might have instincts. Before this, you might have inspirations, as a spirit, and since it's delivered by spiritual means, it's spirit also. You must go beyond the means by which you understand and move into something that is felt to have an understanding. What is obvious to one is not always so obvious to another.

Those of you who completely understand that the benevolent feelings you have are the answers can, from time to time tell others, "If you're looking for the answers, go into your feelings of love or joy or happiness; they will not give you the words, but they will give you the feeling that you seek to have when you get the answer." Remember, if you follow something on a path from here to there, from A to B, and you eventually get to your destination, there is an exultant feeling that follows. Or you could — remember, space and time are changing — just have the feeling. The journey is not about the thought that inspires the feeling; it is about the feeling. Why go anywhere? [Chuckles.] But I'm not trying to talk you out of our conversations; I am trying to expand your means of understanding. What you perceive as a limit is the little bell saying, "But this isn't the way to find it!"

All right. If I could feel it, I would feel that everything was here, now; is that what you're saying?

All of the things that you are trying to achieve through the ecstasy that is capable through the mind (meaning we can achieve these feelings if only we have these answers) are available right now without the answers. Nevertheless, because you are here to learn, I do not want to take the answers away from you. So let's get back to your original question: Where does the personality go? It blends in with everything. Let's say that the veil is not real; let's just say that the veil is a means to understand how you become completely aware of everything, one more time, meaning once you've left the vehicle of the body behind and have that awareness available to you, you then can choose either the vehicle of a body or not.

So that which is perceived of, that which was stated in all the books, is all true, as far as it goes. Yet in reality, it is personified in that way. All the planets, the love — everything — all those creators, and so on, are essentially personified to give you permission to know that life goes on, that you are a portion of something larger and more wonderful, that your nature is a portion of that, and perhaps, in the way that's most important, that it is easy to acquire it. Ultimately, the whole point of telling you that is not to give you a bedtime story but to give you permission to have access to those levels while you are in the vehicle of the body. That's why you are told about these levels of things, not only because you're conditioned to seek levels, to seek things because of space ("If I am here, I go there") or to see things in terms of time ("If it is now, I'll get it then") but also to help you to expand, to have access to all of those things in a way that is personified. "This" has to do with "this," and "this" has to do with "that," but it all has to do with the means to help you to feel safe and comfortable as you acquire those things while you are here in the vehicle of the body and to do it in a safe way and all together. That's why I'm giving out these methods, so that you can do various things together. It's not just to become aware, as Zoosh and other beings have said, of how much more you have in common than in differences but to eventually give you something that you might all find yourselves doing in the same moment at the same time, even though that time might not be in the same second or even in the same hour. If you're all doing it within, say, a cycle or as you call a day (twenty-four hours), that might be sufficiently close to doing something in the same moment, at the same time, so that you can move beyond what you've been. [Chuckles.]

You know, you do that right now. Very often, all of you do things at the same moment, at the same time; it's just that the things you're doing aren't improving your life. [Laughs.] You might be uncomfortable at the same moment at the same time within a daily period. Forty to fifty times a day, you become uncomfortable even though you might not be aware of it. You might get your feelings hurt, and you might not be aware of it, and that tends to perpetuate that for all beings. But if you do something that makes you feel better, that also tends to perpetuate that for all beings. You can have that too. So I'm trying to add something here; I'm not trying to take it away. It looks as if I'm trying to take away what has been given before, but I'm not. I'm attempting to add an understanding of how the flaw helps and does not hinder. The flaw is a doorway to something that does not go beyond what you have already learned but adds something to the way you have learned so that the thing that looks like this edge of my hand and that you have only seen from this edge is a revelation when you then see the rest of the hand. That does not mean that you forget about the edge of the hand, all right? You still have that, and you still appreciate its value, but when you see the hand full on, palm forward, toward you, you then have more. So what looks like a limit is sometimes the doorway to more.

THE CHANNEL AND THE BEING

All right. Allow me my limits for a minute, here.

Yes, of course.

If I could see, would I see that same filmy translucent mass that we see leaving the body at death when you come into Robert's body?

No, probably not. What actually happens with Robert's body is that Robert tends to assimilate more. He takes me in, although he steps out. You might see his lightbody step out, but he assimilates more. In short, you might see something that looks like a switch. Robert steps out, and I step in. But in the larger picture, Robert may step out, but he is part of the whole. During the times he is out of the body, he is more conscious of being part of a whole thing. He is more conscious of being the whole being, which is why when one channels this way, the way Robert channels, over time, as the channel begins to feel more and more part of all things, he or she does not become overshadowed. It's important for the channel to maintain his or her personality. The channel does not have to become overshadowed by the beings who speak, but he or she begins to have more personal identification with them not because the beings are better than the channel but because the channel experiences more time when he or she is aware of the beings as a portion of him- or herself.

The disentanglement is actually a variance on that. These beings help you, but they come to help you easily without you having to say, "If you come, I'll give you sweets!" [Laughs.] It's not about that; it's about having manners and means to improve the quality of your life, which necessarily joins you to other beings. But I bring that up about people who do this level of channeling — I'm not trying to say greater than but rather what is commonly referred to as deep trance channeling — because the longer the channel can do that and the more he or she can assimilate this, the more the channel can assimilate all that exists.

All that exists, of course, in this case, refers to all that has ever existed, all that will ever exist, and so on. In short, there are no limits on that, but speaking in precise terms tends to define limits where there are none, even if you do not wish to. If I say, "Aaaaaaaa," it certainly appears that I'm not saying, "Oooooo." But if A and O are in the same existence, am I necessarily excluding one or the other? I seem to be trying to drag you away from something, but I'm really just trying to add something.

YOUR PERCEPTION IS LIMITED

Did you come around here to train the Zen masters?

The whole idea of the Zen masters was to help people to see that life can be simpler and divine, the physical can be divine, and all life can be divine when one sees it in a different way. It's all about perceptions, values, and context. That's what I'm doing with you, and that's, of course, what the Zen masters are attempting to do with others. That's an advantage. We want to expand people's perceptions not because we want to complicate their lives with more but because we want to simplify their lives with less, in the sense of fewer complications.

This way of being that I thought existed, where there was a piece of me on the third dimension and a piece on the fourth and a piece on the fifth and pieces all over the place and then some ultimate home for me somewhere, are you saying that's not true, either?

No, I'm not saying that any of this is not true. By saying "either," you suggest that I've said it's not true. I'm not saying any of that. I'm saying there's more to it than that. Remember the reason I gave you the example of seeing the edge of the hand. When I turned the hand and put the palm toward you, if you say, "Ah! That's what it looks like, really," are you then saying that the edge of the hand isn't real or that it's wrong? I'm not saying that it's wrong; I'm saying I want to show you more so that you can see more, not that I want to play with your mind and say the edge of the hand isn't there or that it never was!

So is it true that every human has, as part of their immortal personality, parts of them that experience various places at the same time?

Yes. You cannot be here in the vehicle of the human being without having some portion of you at all times in your natural state. You think of this very often when you're dreaming and you're tethered, and I will support that when I say it sometimes. But you cannot be here in your entirety because it is unnatural for you to be cut off. It is unnatural for anyone to be cut off from their natural being. So you extend a portion of yourself to this place that is a school so that you can learn, and you cut yourself off — you cut off your conscious mind, though you're not really cut off — at least temporarily from your normal state of being so that your vehicle here that you occupy might be able to do things in a way that allows you to understand the gifts that other people do. Are you really here to learn something entirely new, or are you here to learn things that are done by others? Imagine this, again, is everything (which is arbitrary) and you, in that everything, are your immortal personality and have certain skills and benefits. Others in that whole thing are aware of you, and you feel like a part of them; therefore they know that that exists and they can do it, but they don't have to, because you do it. Are you really here to learn something new? Or are you really here to learn, in some way, more intimately what others do so that you can experience on a more personal level the unconditional awareness and love that you have for other beings and to learn what you don't do because they can do it better, even though you feel that as a portion of yourself? You learn more personally what they can do not because you have to replace them but because it creates greater intimacy between all beings everywhere. In short, you move the all into a greater sense of personal love as well as unconditional love.

So that might be an easier way to understand what I am attempting to communicate. It is a different way of experiencing. It doesn't mean that you do not have all of these different versions of yourself and all of these different levels. It means that from my perception, you are learning something on a personal level, which is loving, that you know on an unconditional level, which is loving but not in the same way that somebody else knows it and does it. You know it also, and you might do it in your own way. When everybody knows not just unconditionally but personally what others do (and you don't have to know what everybody does, but it might happen), when something like that takes off, everybody might want to know it, and then everything necessarily has to expand because you increase not only your capabilities and potentials but also your desires. So you are no longer necessarily satisfied with having your own talents and abilities while other people have their own talents and abilities (I say "people" for the sake of understanding your personification and the all), but you learn more about what others do in a different way. When you have that, you don't love them any more, but you want to know more. So when you and everybody else start to do things in a different way, then you want to know more and you become more. In short, more is possible. Even though the level of satisfaction, the level of love, does not increase, the pleasure of life might very well increase. So ultimately that's what's going on here: The pleasure of life is increasing.

DISENTANGLEMENT RE-CREATES THE PAST
It's a strange recipe, to limit and suffer.

Suffering is not really intended; it has happened. It was a calculated risk by the Creator of the universe you are in, and you might easily say the Creator was set up. You might easily say that, yet you will be disentangled from it all.

Since all creators were created to feel personal love, how did the Creator go through that tube with Zoosh so that He'd be disentangled from personal love? How did we get a Creator who didn't experience personal love? Somebody had to tweak something. You told me that that's why creators were created.

Yes. It was necessary to create more. If you have perfection that you love, why would you want to change it? The only reason you might possibly want to change perfection that you love is because you might consider whether there is more.

Wait a minute, I'd forgotten about this! Zoosh said way back in the beginning that the Creator didn't want to ask us to do anything He didn't do, and He separated from a portion of His being. Is that how He became disconnected from personal love?

To accomplish what the Creator needed to accomplish, He had to separate. He had to limit Himself, which tells you everything in this creation is limited. But it's limited on purpose so that it will have motivation to find the rest of itself. He gave Himself the same motivation.

Of course, in the larger picture, the Creator was apparently set up to fail because to create something that is mostly beauty but has some discomfort in it intensified to a great degree there. All that needs to be disentangled will be disentangled in a way. Say you and another person come together and caused each other pain. How will disentanglement happen? Not only are you disentangled from the pain, but also when the light beings are no longer focused on disentangling you from the pain, the disentanglement procedure continues because they disentangle the circumstances that brought you two together and generated that pain in the first place. So if you two come together in that past time, pain would not have been generated. In short, they are re-creating the past. Disentanglement functions to re-create all of the past. You have asked in the past, if I might use that term, how all the pain and discomfort is going to be re-created on Earth.

They used the word "discreate," but I like your "disentanglement."

"Disentanglement" gives you a better understanding that you can embrace and be involved in personally. The so-called discreation was a word that served you in the past to understand this, but now you can be personally involved in the process. And that's what we want; that's part of Creator School. The Creator School that you are in is to be personally involved in your creation.

ASK WHATEVER YOU WANT

Can I ask to somehow change the disentanglement that caused me not to be able to see properly? Is that possible?

Ask whatever you want.

If I hadn't fallen down the stairs and the Zetas hadn't been emotionally constricted, I would be able to see physically.

Perhaps. Although one of the things it forced you to do was to see in a different way. When things like this happen (even though the vision problems really became more constrictive later on) what you experience in your overall life that drives you, your feeling that drives you, is, "If I cannot see clearly this way, I will see clearly another way." So it has also helped to create your personality to constantly look for answers that are not obvious.

Well, I don't want to lose that, but I would like to be able to see a little better. You can ask.

Remember, write down anything on your list that are discomforting. You may or may not be able to improve your vision, but there is no reason not to ask. But ask it in the way that you want to be disentangled from; you could always say, "from the injury that has reduced my capability to see with my eyes as I would like to." Something like that. You have to be specific. In the beginning, very often one is general with disentanglement, but as time goes on, you become more specific. And then as time goes on even further, you become more general.

Many, many people for a long time were into something called pattern removal. For people who are familiar with that, this is similar in a way, disentangling from limiting patterns.

Yes, but instead of being something that you do only on your own, this is being done by others for you, so you don't have to rethink it.

But a lot of people can ask for things on their list of disentanglement that are similar to some of these patterns that we used to work on.

Yes, but I think you need to go beyond that. You might say, for instance, "I behave in a certain way, and I know that I need to behave in some other way. I request to be disentangled from that which prompts me to do this." In short, you want the gold-light beings to work on the causes as well as the symptoms. The behavior is the symptom; you want them to work on the cause.

Right. And much of the cause is the stuff we took in, which caused each of us to create how life is, the rules for life, which has limited us so much.

Yes, but it's very important to not make it only spiritually focused or only psychologically focused. It's important to allow it to be of the feelings. "So-and-so hurt my feelings." It's okay to be like that. You can say, "I want to be disentangled from all the pain I've had with this person." It might sound as if you are blaming, but it's okay to say that. Or you can ask to be disentangled from an individual. It doesn't mean that you'll never see that individual again if he or she is alive and you're likely to see him or her, but you'll be disentangled from the pain of it. Remember, you're always asking to be disentangled from the pain and discomfort. You don't even have to say "pain"; you can say "discomfort." It's up to you. It's optional.

All right, I'm still seeking to understand. You're saying that the soul that went out of the body goes into everything.

It rejoins everything; everything becomes a part of it. Remember that you are focused in the physical vehicle here, but that does not mean you need to stay focused. You might be in what appears to be a hierarchical system, but it's a hierarchical system in order to work as a teaching technique to understand consequences of actions and thoughts. It's part of the school. But just because a bell rings in school to let you know when to go to your next class does not mean that bells will ring everywhere you go beyond this school. [Chuckles.]

So you're saying that the part that takes with it the feelings and the lessons it learned joins the all, and then everybody knows everything that it learned. At some point, mustn't it reconnect with itself?

But it might not, in fact, have learned something. It, meaning the person, might not have learned something that was not known by others, but it will personally understand it. Remember now, this is a creator — we're attempting to create — that has personal identification with the beings. The more personal love it can engage, even with things that are discomforting, the more personal love it can engage with every portion of that creator and with every portion, of course, of all that exists. The more it can engage that on a personal level, the better for that personality. In short, the creator becomes — *you* become — more versatile. Just for the sake of understanding (not that this is the way it works), imagine that the creator has different parts of itself that do different things. Why should the creator have everything, every part of itself, that can do everything and understand what every other part of itself does in the most personal, intimate way? Why? Because then the creator can become more. That's why.

We're talking about the Creator who created this creation, not the humans becoming the new creator?

No, I am talking about the creator that you are going to become. You are learning something that appears to be small that will enhance something that appears to be big. None of you is learning anything here that is not known by someone else where as a part of the all, but you are learning in a way that feels intensely personal. It's not something that you know as a distant thing but do not have any personal feeling about. You are learning it in a way that is personal so that you will have a personal feeling for all beings you create or are already created and you inherit.

As a creator in training, you are learning how to personally identify yourself as a creator with all parts of your creation without exception. And while you, as an individual member of the Explorer Race, might not be learning something that isn't known somewhere else, you are learning it in such a way — the way you are learning it, the way you will embrace it, and the way it will become a portion of you — that is new. For example, you have a bowl of ice cream. You've never tasted ice cream. You look at it; you observe it completely. It sits there, and it changes form; it melts. If it sits there long enough, it rots and eventually turns to dust. You can define it very well as something you observe, just as you might look at a rock and observe it over time. But here, you're learning how to taste the ice cream. It's a revelation when you suddenly discover that it is not strictly something that is observed, acknowledged as having value, and present within you and your greater being; it has an entire other function that is gloriously satisfying.

Good analogy! [Laughs.] So, it's going to be highly interesting to see what the Explorer Race as a creator creates after the maintenance of this creation.

Well, that's the whole point. And to some extent, you might say that it's an experiment: Will it actually be more? Will it be a different flavor? Will it be something that is similar? It falls under the heading of "we'll see."

Now, if I consciously could get out of my body and go look at orbs and realms and love's creation and the Council of Creators and the levels, would I see it?

You would see it. Yes. It's there. But if you're going on the trip with the question, you might not get the answer to the question by taking the trip, but you would certainly see it as beautiful and marvelous and wonderful. And then, of course, you could pull back and see it from a different perspective. If you put your hand over your eyes, you cannot see it any more, but it's still there; you know it is. You can feel it; it's all there. It's just from a different perspective. In short, why are you having trouble in this life with your eyes?

Because I'm trying to see with my eyes, and I was trying to force myself to feel.

Exactly!

Chapter 12

You Planned Your Journey

Ssjoooo, Seven of Thirteen, and Zoosh

July 19, 2000

Greetings. Now I want to acquaint you with something today. There is more than one reason I chose the name I gave you. It's not really unpronounceable, and it is a name that works for me. Saying it has an effect, so anyone who says it in the way it's intended to be said will be able to experience this benevolence. So to start with today, I want to train you on how to say the name [chuckles]: Ssssjjjjjjoooo[w], putting in that *w*, because it sounds like there's a finishing-off sound to those oo's. That rounds it off rather than just having open-ended oo's: Ssssjjjjjjoooo[w] is the quick way to say it but Sjjjjjjoooooooooo[w].

There's S-S-J-O-O-O-O. It fades off — Ssjoooo. Now, I want you to experiment with it. Eventually you might get a good feeling. Find out the way you can say it that produces a benevolent feeling in your body. It actually is intended to activate something, so it performs a function. Now, many people will look at the spelling and give up, but quite a few people will try to pronounce it. Of course, because it's hard to pronounce, at least by just looking at it, they'll experiment with it, and they might just activate that portion of themselves. You might ask, "What is that?" For some people it will be the feeling part of their bodies, where the feeling is centered (what the native peoples might call the feeling heart). It will activate the feelings to benevolently support the physical in tangible ways. In short, it performs a function. You might feel the benevolent feeling the first time or the second time or the third time. After that, you might not feel the feeling any more or you'll feel it as long as you feel it until it's activated. Once it's activated, you might not feel it anymore, but it's still a good sound to say.

You might have a pleasant physical feeling, such as warmth in some part of your body; if you do, just feel it. You can go into it and feel it if you want to, but you don't have to. So practice saying it, and if I feel you need to say it in a different way from time to time, I'll correct you. But it is actually something to say that is better than the tag you've been using, which was perfectly adequate for a tag. But this is actually something that will benefit.

BE RECEPTIVE TO THE WORK

Very quickly, before we get on to other things, let's go back to the disentanglement. You say to lie on our backs, but some people are more comfortable on their sides or their stomachs. Is there some specific reason they need to lie on their backs?

Lying on the back is best so that the beings who work on you can work on the part of you that feels the most vulnerable to you. Remember, it feels the most vulnerable because it tends to be the most receptive. When people are suddenly frightened of something, they close up even though this direction might be an area that you could be injured from. The vulnerability is always associated with receptiveness, so it is much better to go with the front even though you might fall asleep and turn over on your side. The beings might still be able to do something when you're on your side, but it's better to give them full access.

You might say, "Well, why can't they come around and work through the bed?" They can, but it doesn't train you to discover the value of being receptive, vulnerable. A long time ago, Zoosh and others talked about feminine wisdom, and one feminine wisdom alluded to with very little explanation was vulnerability. You do not often consider vulnerability to be a wisdom or a trait to acquire for its benefit. You usually use the term "vulnerability" to describe something that is at the very least tender for you. In fact, vulnerability is keyed directly to receptiveness, and to change your life to become more beneficial and benevolent and to work for you, you need to become more receptive to the energies that can assist you in bringing that about.

Of course, your interaction with them after a while becomes a circle. It's not just receiving, then; it's things that you do. When you do something physical toward creating what you want, that action goes out, and you're still receptive toward something benevolent. You do something that will help you to get that, and it becomes something that is of the feminine and of the masculine and is wedded in perfect harmony.

These steps build on each other, and they support each other as is intended here. Most importantly, they provide you with physical evidence for the value of the process. You have been conditioned to do otherwise, to not be vulnerable, but there will be times when you will feel, "It doesn't work for me this way."

That's why you've been trained by other beings to do the heat and so on in your body and even to put your hands up like this [puts his hands about a foot in front of the heart] to support the heat and to feel safer. That will help you to feel loved and safer.

When you do that, it doesn't just hold the energy in but deflects the energy that naturally flows out of you so that it heightens the feeling in your physical body. It's easier for some people to find the heat in their bodies that way. You move your hands around in front of you slowly until you find the heat, which you can usually find much quicker that way, and then you don't try to move that heat. You just go into it and feel it more. It's a good system. Sometimes you feel so loaded with the strife of the day that you need some help.

Mm-hmm. That's good, all right. Now, can you communicate to the being I'm connected to? Will the being, one of the thirteen that I'm supposedly connected to, communicate with you?

Of course. It won't sound any different than my voice talking.

Did she come to me when I was four or five years old and I thought it was a knight in shining armor? Did she come to try to give me comfort or something?

No. She wouldn't interfere directly with your life. Oh, you want to hear from her directly, I forgot. Pardon me.

✳   ✳   ✳

I wouldn't interfere directly with your life, but I know who came to you.

Who was it?

It was a combination of your most benevolent past life personified in the way a child would enjoy and your most benevolent future life also personified in a way a child would enjoy to inform you that, no matter what came in your life, you would be protected, you would be safe, you would survive — sometimes even the most unlikely situations — and you would succeed, all said in a way that a child could hear and feel. And even at that young age, success was vitally important to you because of the conditioning you'd already received. So it was to encourage you.

The toughing-it-out part was the way you were conditioned. You can say, "Well, I couldn't have done "this" and "this" and "this" without toughing it out." Nevertheless, toughing it out has been the thing you were exposed to in this life so that you could understand the conflicts human beings work through on a daily basis. It wasn't intended for you to embrace as your own philosophy, quite the opposite, but because of the conditioning.

YOU PLAN YOUR LIFE

Do you plan the life? Who plans this life?

Oh, potentials are presented to you before the life, and then you choose. This means slightly before your actual personification inside the body of mother but in a mode that is already prepared for Earth life when the soul, as you call it, or the personality is still connected and understands what it is attempting to accomplish. Equally, there is the understanding of the challenges of Earth life, but not complete understanding. There is no physical experience yet, given that life. At that stage, you don't draw on the experiences of other lives, so you're not all that you normally are, and you're not what you're going to be on Earth. You're in between. This is done so that you can decide based on Earth potential, since you're already focused somewhat in Earth. You make the decision that way rather than making it in some way that you would believe you have access to your normal capabilities. So you decide, interacting with your teachers and some guides, that this would be what you would do because you would be able to have a greater, more compassionate understanding of the human being's process, provided you could survive long enough to assimilate it, and that it would be your nature to be fairly strong and athletic, if you choose.

But was it your desire to experience this?

No. I am not attached to that. For the sake of your understanding who we are, there is no individuality whatsoever, you understand? You are saying One of Thirteen; let's say Seven of Thirteen. It is better for you to just throw that one out. Those ideas are given to you when you hang on to your hierarchical mindset. One tends to learn things like that in childhood. You don't find that as often in families where there are fewer children, but for those who grew up in families with a lot of children who range in rank and authority — in short, a pecking order — that concept can be hard to let go.

What is the connection between the part of you that's the part of that totality and me? Is there a line of connection? What I'm learning is not helping you to learn?

No.

Then why am I learning this?

Because as you like to say, or as someone you talk to likes to say, this motivation occurred for you further down the line, meaning that in the process of being involved in this kind of activity, you have accumulated over time certain motivations on your personality level that did not originate here. So you might be connected here. This is something we might have some knowledge about but don't really. We don't tend to tap into individual's life histories.

Isis said there was a question whether I was projected from you, or whether I was from the inside and reaching up to connect to you.

No, it might have looked that way, the way she drew it.

All right. I'm just looking for where I'm from and who I am.

You're trying to find out not only who you are but also who you're *not*. Very often you look at things, you observe things, you don't feel good about things (which is typical for a human being at this point, where you are), and you deflect it. But you cannot get away from the fact that everything is connected, everything is united. You cannot be from one place without being from another. You are from all places at once all the time. Everybody is. But you do not identify with that in life here because it would almost immediately take away your motivation to live, to be individuals, and to do anything. Why would you want to? You'd be born, you'd lie there and say, "This is wonderful!" and you'd die, just like that. You wouldn't go anywhere, and you wouldn't be interested in learning how to walk — not anything. You'd say, "Well, this is what it is!" and that's it. In short, it would be very unsuccessful if you remembered the school here and if you remembered who you were.

Well, your counterpart said that I'm down here because it's too boring up there. But you're up there, and you're happy.

It would be too boring for you given who you are right now. You're condensing what was said. In fact, what was said is if you were here now, you would be bored. That means the you who you are, the you who you know yourself to be. It's true: If you were here right now, you would enjoy it for five minutes, and then you would say, "Now what?" And essentially you would feel, "No, now what? This is it?" You would be bored because you are motivated. You are in school. Even when you go beyond this school, you will still be motivated. You'll want to do something, because you are engaged. You are engaged in the activity here, and by "here" I mean where all creations are, different things happening; you are engaged in the adventure of living. Even in larger personifications, you are still experiencing yourself. After all, when you become fully conscious — meaning feeling, not thinking; you can't do it through thinking — you can feel all the portions of yourself. You can feel your heartbeat, you can feel the blood going through your veins, and you can go in and feel every molecule, every atom. I'm not saying you ought to do that; what I am saying is that it is no different doing that than being a creator and feeling all the beings one has "created."

One does not actually create things in a creation as a creator; one actually personifies them. One takes what is necessarily there — everywhere, all the time — and says (they don't talk like this, but for the sake of the illustration), "Okay now, everything here that wants to be a planet the way I see this planet, come together and be that planet." They don't take a scoop of this and a dab of that and a pinch of this. This way, it's voluntary, and then the planet stays together. It doesn't say, "But I was busy; I need to go somewhere." [Chuckling.]

They talked about lightships, and I assumed that it extrapolated out into creation that way.

THE DENSITY OF YOUR DIMENSION

All right, I had a vision yesterday or today. That need that you saw that started everything, could it be a black hole?

No. Black holes, as they are called here, are really just doorways. They are doorways that are acquiring material for a creation elsewhere. "Black hole" is not a good term. It's black because it's not easily defined, so it's given a description, and it appears to have greater density. But I'll tell you something interesting about the density. Scientists detect density, and they say, "Oh, it's very hot, it's very powerful." What they miss, and what's very interesting, is that they're actually detecting the difference between the density of the third dimension that they're in and the density of the dimension that is usually higher, that goes beyond. They're not detecting, say, second-dimensional density beyond that; they're detecting the difference in your dimension. In short, your dimension's material is concentrating there, and because it's concentrated, you can feel more profoundly, meaning the instruments used can more profoundly detect the concentrated density of your own dimension because there is intended leakage around the so-called black hole as compared to the density beyond. The hole acquires energy from your dimension, but the energy might not go through the center; it might just as easily go around the hole. And it's not actually a hole, but that's how I'm describing it. At the same time, what is beyond the hole is something of a different dimension.

So it is a tip-off to scientists who use those instruments that something is going on here. It will ultimately become an attraction point for scientists working on propulsion systems. It will tip them off as to how they can use systems for attraction instead of propulsion, which will gradually move them into something less polarized to the masculine. When you look at your culture and your society and almost everything that your society creates, almost all that you create on your own (you do not create the method of birth) tends to be masculine, meaning done without the permission of that material that is used to create it, which is why it doesn't last; that material has a bias to becoming what it was before or at least continuing on a natural existence when it becomes one thing and then changes form and becomes another, as a seed changes form and becomes a tree over time, falls down, returns to the earth, becomes soil, and goes on to become something else. It's the cycle of life.

But here, oil is taken at a certain cycle and made into plastic, and then it's just put there indefinitely.

Well, it's not indefinitely, even though it appears to be indefinite. At some point, Mother Earth will say, "Well, that's enough of that," and she will reclaim it. She will not say, "Okay, this piece of oil that turned into this piece of plastic has to come back to the exact place it was taken." She won't do that. She'll just gradually convert other elements in her body to oil, as you call it, and over time convert that plastic back to something or into something that is more natural or akin to her through her natural elements: fire, water, wind, cold, hot, and so on.

GAIN COMPASSION FROM UNDERSTANDING THE EXPERIENCES OF OTHERS

Remember, you cannot appreciate the compassion that you might feel for somebody else unless you can identify in some small way (it doesn't have to be every way) with his or her experience. So part of the reason you've suffered in the past in this life is so that you could completely understand that person on a personal level. It's to completely identify, on the personal level (just like Creator), with what it's all about. What it's about in terms of how it is for people. So much of what you're doing here has to do with feeling better after you've suffered, even when it's the temporary way you feel better. "It's been a tough, day! Ugh! Have a bowl of ice cream!" It might not be society's approved manner to feel better, but often it is.

Do you see places of business where people pay to go in and swing a sledgehammer and break up concrete and do hard work? Of course not. But you see ice-cream parlors! You see restaurants that serve ice cream because it not only is enjoyable to eat but also always feels like a treat or a reward. So, there's nothing wrong with ice cream. You could say that it clogs the arteries and so on, and it might very well, but you go on with life.

Always expand your vision. When you're looking for someone to not only blame but also interact with, it is a long journey that goes from place to place and being to being, and you never have the feeling of satisfaction. Even if you have satisfaction for a short time, it passes, and then you feel like there's more. There is more, because no matter how far out you go or how far in you go to the minuscule, you still have to come to communion with yourself. You are all there is of you right now.

I do not see you sitting here in this body, on this piece of furniture; I do not see you as the boundaries of your physical body. I see you right now as all. I feel you as all that you are everywhere. Even though your conscious mind is focused on you right now, that does not mean that you are not all of these things. It does mean that to find you, you need to expand your definition of you, and the mind cannot really do that. The mind cannot fully grasp the idea of so many apples that you can't count them. The mind can only tangentially grasp that. But on the feeling level, enough apples for everyone *feels* like loving abundance. So we come back to *where you are.* You are your feelings. They are not only the means — here, you discover feelings as a means — but you *are* your feelings. What leaves the body at the point of death? The condensed feelings.

After the personality moves out, the body on its own can only generate feelings based on the component parts that are left; the tissues and so on might have their feelings as they gradually return to Earth. What exits the body (if you could examine it and say, "What's this stuff made of?") are feelings. Initially it's all your feelings: those that are resolved and benevolent as well as those that are not resolved and are uncomfortable. That's why that mass of feeling passes through, as has been described (and I'm using that description, even though it is a description and not an ironclad series of walls and barriers, but it's a good description to understand things when you're in space and time).

Those feelings move through a winnowing system, which helps you to resolve the unresolved feelings in some way, even if that means turning around and having another physical life right away, which usually doesn't, but it occasionally does. It helps you to work through those feelings in some way that is still understandable to life in Earth terms.

You might see beings that you've known on Earth and resolve those feelings you had regarding them. You might see beings that you identify as deities and love them and hug them, and they love you and hug you and so on. There are many other possibilities. As you work through this series of winnowing-through — not unlike the way water moves through stones — eventually you come out the other end with those uncomfortable feelings resolved, and then it is strictly the benevolent feelings. Those feelings are the stuff of your personality. This is why you're never very far from yourself in totality: You can access yourself through your benevolent feelings, such as that love, that heat. That love, that heat, feels so good. Why does heat feel good? On a hot day that makes you sweat, the heat doesn't feel so good. Why does *this* heat feel good? This heat feels good because this love represents the you you're looking for.

Remember, almost everyone — not everyone, but almost everyone — who comes to Earth to live a life will ask the question (and it is almost always misunderstood by parents), "Where did I come from?" They get a physical answer. "Well, the mother and the father _____" That's not what they're asking.

They want to know *where* they came from. And when people know how to describe that, they will say (instead of giving a physical description), "Would you like to find out right now?" And the child will say, "Yes!"

"Would you like to feel where you came from, right now?"

"Yes! Yes!"

Then they do the love exercise. And it feels good to them, and they say, "Ooooooo …" It will give them a lot of confidence as children. It builds their confidence on the foundation of who they are rather than having them cast about and say, "Oh, what can I be like so people will love me?" which everybody does now. We need to bring that onto your nature. That's how things are done elsewhere. It will be done here someday too, because that's how life is lived elsewhere.

That quickly achieves a sense of personal support, a sense of personal confidence, and most importantly for children, a sense of home, wherever they are. How many people sit around and long, "Oh, I want to go home"? It's a real need, but when you work on that heat within yourself (maybe plug the ears or go to some quiet place where there is no other stimulation) and gets totally into that heat to completely feel just the heat, it *is* home. It's home in your physical body. When more people do it, it's home in your neighborhood. When more people do it on Earth, it's home on Earth. So home moves. It isn't that you have to go home; we bring home here! It's a feeling, so there is no sense of, "But where is home *really*?" because it's physical evidence of home and who you are.

The feeling is so similar to what is produced by other human beings, to say nothing of the plants and the animals and Earth herself, that you feel absolutely your commonness in how you are together — not how you are plain [chuckles], but how you are part of the same one being and how that one is mutually supportive. And that is something that you rarely feel. But when we get people to feel it (how you mutually support yourselves), a bunch of people in a room doing this, it feels so much better when other people are doing it too. Maybe a cat or a dog in the room would feel it too. Everybody doing this together would be wonderful. It feels great. And you can see the physical evidence of how it works. It's personal *and* unconditional.

LEARN FELT-CONFIDENCE

We need to change that term "self-confident" because when you say "self-confident," the assumption is that it has to do with the mental process, and that's what separated the mind from the body and why people say "the body" instead of "my body." That's common. "Where am I?" you say. You are here, in the feelings. So "self-confidence" moves to "felt-confidence." That's a confidence that is often felt by people who are professionals. You are confident in your capability as a publisher and as a printer. Other people are confident in their capability to run the mile quickly, and they exude confidence on that, but in some other point (it is a human situation), maybe how they relate to people, crash! The confidence falls away because it isn't based on who you are in feeling. So we need to change mental confidence to felt-confidence. And it's very simple; it's not complicated. The complicated part is doing it the other way. Doing it on the felt level [snaps fingers] …

No matter what we put on with our minds, we still radiate confidence when we know we can do something, but we're only fooling ourselves?

That's right, but you are trained to do that. In short, you are trained to be limited when, in fact, what you want is to be unlimited. So you are often unconsciously driven to be unlimited, and many things you do are to encourage yourself to be unlimited, which is why some children are adventurous. All children are adventurous in one way or another, even if they're not swinging on ropes across the creek. They might be adventurous in terms of using the computer in a new way or learning something musically that they didn't know before and used to feel like they could never do.

So you're always being brought back to the physical; that's what you're here to learn about, which is why you find your "who" inside a physical body. That's not [chuckles] anything other than part of your schooling. So when your mind is thinking, thinking, thinking, always know that you can come back to your center, which is everywhere but most easily accessible with physical evidence inside your physical body with this wonderful warmth that you can actually feel. It's not a tingling. Some people say, "I feel a tingling." That's because they've been trained that failure isn't acceptable and they're afraid to say, "I don't feel it." The honest thing to say is, "I don't feel it." But people are afraid to say it, because they're afraid they're doing something wrong or they're less than other people. Other people are saying, "Oh, I feel it! I feel it!" and "I feel a tingling!" [Chuckles.] That's understandable, that people want to say that; they're afraid of being judged or afraid of judging themselves, which is more often the case. So there it is: It's okay to say, "I don't know."

You can show me how to do that; it's like "help me."

I can, or I can give you techniques. Hold your hands here. Try it for a while; if you don't feel the heat, hold your hand here.

He's going first in front of the heart chakra, then more by the solar plexus.

Yes, and it's not really chakras; you can hold your hand over your side, if you want to, over your kidneys, whatever. In short, you can move your hands around. That, as I say, tends to stimulate what you're feeling.

FEELINGS EVENTUALLY RESOLVE

All right. I still would like to finish the day with some type of an understanding or visualization. The feelings of someone leaving Earth after death, you said, were winnowed through until they got beyond what we're told is the veil, and then ...

No, this happens after the veil. Not that the veil is there, you understand; always these things are analogies, stories. These are stories to help beings who are in space and time to understand how it works. So don't be attached to the idea that there's a veil.

But there's something there to keep other people from feeling the suffering on Earth, isn't there?

Don't be attached to that. Think of it as a story that explains something that's very difficult to understand but very easy to understand. In short, it functions on a felt level. Imagine you are in a place that is secured, as they say. You have to have a key, or you have to have your eyeball, your retina, looked at, or you have to say, "My name is thus-and-such, and I can be here," or you have to show your ID. This is no different. Certain feelings can go through. Other feelings are not bad, but when they are uncomfortable, they are recognized as *needing resolution*. So the resolution happens as you are going through, and then those feelings are transformed. They are not eliminated; they are transformed. Once they are transformed, they join with the other feelings, the feelings that make you up, and eventually when all of that resolution takes place (of course, if all the resolution to all the problems in your life took place right now, you wouldn't feel very attached to going on living), you are easily able to let go of your Earth life, and you move on, to say nothing of being stimulated by what you experience around you.

YOU KEEP YOUR UNIQUENESS

Okay, but let's look at those feelings, now. That's the immortal personality, somebody's immortal personality.

Yes.

All right. Now, in that being's totality, there are other little groups of these feelings somewhere. Do they all come together, or do they continue, each little group, being separate?

They're not separate; they're together even when they're trillions of miles apart or more. They're together immediately; they don't have to be in one place. If you are part of the whole being, does this mean that you individually (again, this is the story boundary) are part of the whole being?

All right. I can understand intellectually but not feeling. And I think it's a fear of losing my individuality.

There you are. You found it. It's a fear not just of losing your individuality but also of becoming like others who you do not wish to be like for whatever reasons — not just because they look some way that you don't feel good about, but because you don't want to be them. You want to be *you*; "Where am I?" you say. "I don't want to be *them*. I want to be *me!*"

So I thought we kept our uniqueness in the oneness.

You do keep it. You have it; you're aware of who you are. Everyone is aware of everyone else's personality, but it is — how can we say? — homogenized. You have your unique personality, you have your personality that blends with other beings, you have combinations of personalities should you wish to, but you never lose yourself within the context of a personal identity, even though, what's the line from the famous movie the Wizard of Oz? "Well, that's you all over!"[1]

Is there ever a coagulation or a coming together of all those parts of that being?

Yes.

Oh, they become parts of ... they become totally altogether uniquely themselves, plus become one with everything.

Again, these are space-time questions. You do not need to have everything in one place to be everything of yourself. I'll give you an example of that. You have memories of events in this life on Earth, some pleasant. Those memories are rooted in a different time and place. Those places and times are part of you, but they are not physically, provably in your culture now, not part of your present. Yet you can remember them, so they exist and are parts of you. But they are not present; they are not with you. You recall them. They are parts of you even though they are years behind you and maybe on the other side of Earth or hundreds or thousands of miles away. They are still parts of you on Earth that are thousands of miles away in a different time. You remember them in your present, so they are connected with you; they are you.

So by analogy, you're saying that the being beyond the veil, the being ... whatever ... who left Earth remembers all those other parts of itself wherever they are, then?

The being is aware of all those other parts. It doesn't have to remember, but if it makes it better for you, it remembers. We're simplifying it, but right now you're stuck on the idea that this has to be when a being goes beyond Earth. Of course, I can remind you. When you're at your deep levels of sleep, you're aware then too. Because you want to be more now, here, you're attempting to become aware of that on a feeling level while conscious.

People wonder, "When will I be forcibly expanded again? I'd better be *ready!*" [Chuckles.] And how does one get ready? By accepting the value of flexibility. That's the mental thing you do. You say, "Flexibility can be valuable. There are times when I need to be rigid: If I'm holding something up and it's

---

1. In the *Wizard of Oz*, the scarecrow is lamenting that the flying monkeys have torn him apart and scattered his sections in various locales. The tin man responds with the quip mentioned here. See http://www.imdb.com/title/tt0032138/quotes.

not easy to hold, I've got to be stiff and rigid to hold it up." But there are other times that being flexible is very helpful. So this says that flexibility has value. That's the mental thing, and then of course, there are physical parts of being flexible as well as feeling parts of being flexible.

✳ ✳ ✳

[Zoosh]: All right! What did I know and when did I know it, eh?
Yes. You've always known you can wander in and out of what we're calling the totality, because it's a group of separate things, right?
That's right. It's not much different from, "What did you think about a moment ago, and what are you thinking now? In short, where is your attention?
Ah! So were you one of the early creators? You've been here a long time.
You know, I don't really like to think of myself as a creator, because it's not my focus.
Well, okay. What was here when you became aware of yourself?
[Chuckles.] You mean what was here substantively? Well, there was love …
No. I mean, we've established that there are thirteen who were one who were out there and who created the first creators, and then by the time you became aware, were there tons of creations, or was the place half created compared to what it is now?
I know what you're asking. When I became aware, I didn't immediately pay attention to my surroundings, so I cannot tell you the length of time in measure that you can identify with or how long things went on around me without my paying any attention to them. But once I started to notice things, I was aware of the being you are communicating with and not much else.
Had they created some creators?
If they did, I wasn't aware of them, which doesn't mean to say they hadn't, because once I initially started paying some attention, as you might say, to that which was around me rather than being focused totally within myself — it's possible that my awareness didn't range out that far — but I didn't see anything other than what I identify as them today.
Do you see them as separate beings?
Only if I need to …
If they move?
Well, they don't move, and they're everywhere, but I see them in their personality. If I were to see out of eyes, I would see them in the same spot, but they are also everywhere, so it's really a question that I cannot answer and be accurate.
So that's why you couldn't say, when we first started talking, how far back you went, because you would have talked about them, and they wanted to talk about themselves, right?

That's right. Most of the time I *can't* say more than I *can* say not because I'm keeping secrets but because whoever is asking the question is not prepared to hear what I might offer honestly. I don't actually have to think about it, but what comes through Robert is inclined to what person asking the question is prepared to hear — not just what they want to hear, but what they are prepared to hear. Very often what I say is intended to prompt other questions, which the questioner might or might not pursue at that time, which is why people say after they listen to their tapes, "Oh, I should have asked this, I should have asked that." Well, you ask that next time.

So it doesn't really matter; it's just my natural curiosity. Do you feel they created you?

I don't get that feeling, but that doesn't mean it isn't so. But I do not get that feeling.

So you're part of the more that we're looking for, then?

That's not necessarily so; I said that I don't get that feeling. I'd be interested to hear what they say to you.

When I ask, okay. Well, I don't want Robert to go through another being, so when I come back, that's the first thing I'll ask. [Laughter.] So there's something throbbing somewhere. There's something where everybody is from, you know. There's somebody back around the corner.

You have to remember too that it isn't always of value to know from whom you come, especially when a being is attempting to identify itself for any reason. If you're attempting to identify who you are as a human being, for example, you don't necessarily feel assisted by knowing that you came from your physical mother. "Oh, who am I?" And then someone says, "Well, you came from your physical mother," oh, well …

Yes, but the way he says it, though, they don't really create the way humans do.

I'm not saying they do; I'm trying to put it in terms that are clearly grounded because I don't want you to rethink what you're saying but to *feel* it. We really have to stop.

Let's stop. Okay, all right. Thank you so much.

Chapter 13

The Reservoir of Being

Ssjoooo and Zoosh

August 7, 2000

Greetings.

The first question I have today is for Zoosh, with his permission: When did you first become aware of him?

After he no longer existed. [Chuckles.] Well, very often I become aware of things when they are no longer a factor because I notice their absence. When one is used to all things being present, one gets used to things being a certain way. You notice that things feel a certain way, and then you notice something is missing. It's not unlike having a big pie that is complete, but one day you notice that an infinitesimal piece of the pie is missing. The piece is so small that you couldn't see that it was missing, but you notice something's not there anymore.

That's when I became aware of Zoosh — when he was no longer present in the way that he was before. And I looked for him then. I didn't know I was looking for him; I was looking for something that was no longer there. He had left, what would you say, is a signature. Have you ever seen these things that people scrawl on the wall that say, "So-and-so was here"? It was like that, but energetically, and I thought any being that would do that has the kind of personality I'd like to get to know better and to make a more personal connection with. So I made the search because I thought it was humorous. That's when I made the search to locate Zoosh as an individual. Before that time, I had not put much energy into individuality per se; rather, I looked for complete things from time to time, when it was necessary to look at one thing, but not often. So I looked at him and where he'd been and what he'd done, and of course I was doing this with the bias of wondering where he was now and why he wasn't here. It was my whole awareness. I do not isolate things. You might say that you have a chair in your house, and that's where the chair is. And you have a desk in your office, and that's where the desk is. But for me, the chair and the desk are in the same space. So I do not individuate things.

SEEKING ZOOSH

You had created creators and creators. There were all kinds of creations out there: there's a totality. At what stage in the evolution of just being the thirteen and then there being everything that's there now, did you started looking for Zoosh?

The point was when everything that you now know exists and more but also much, much more in terms of taking in the concept of moment-to-moment experience, meaning things become more, and then they change their form. You know, like the physicist says that energy cannot be destroyed, but it takes a different form. It's not about destruction; it takes a different form. And that's true.

So there was a moment when there was more form than there is now in the totality? Is that what you're saying?

For the sake of simplicity, I will say there were times before now, in this moment, when there was less form and more form, and there are times after this that there is significantly more form. In short, it was the latter.

It was after this point when you were looking at it. All right.

Yes. I was looking for him because he wasn't there anymore, and that's when I became aware of him. Was that your question, when I became aware of him?

Yes. Where did you find him?

I found him in the present as you know the present to be, meaning (to put it simply) he's not always going to be here. Where you now understand "here" to be, he's not always going to be. At some point he's going ...

Is he from the future?

No. Don't be locked into time. That's why I was saying experience, not past or future. At some point — I have to use your terms as such, as always — he's no longer here, but I became acquainted with him by focusing on times when he was here. Is that clear?

THE RESERVOIR OF BEING

He feels that he was not necessarily created by the thirteen.

Oh, I have to agree with that.

You have to agree with that?

Oh, yes. I don't really think of him as having been created. When I became aware of him no longer being here, in my "here," I, like you, traced him back — let's say "back," use time — until I could trace him no further. When you trace something back and can trace it back no further, you in the world of time and space say, "Well then, I've found the beginning." But when you're dealing with beings who are not only functioning in time and space but in other things as well — they can function here — they don't necessarily trace it back to the beginning. They trace it back until they can go no further back and find any more; they just reach this reservoir of total existence, meaning that looking for any more is pointless. So I was not able to trace him back in your time context, here, to a point of origin.

So how did he get here? He doesn't know.

That's a question you can ask him or — he doesn't know? Well, there must be ...

He said he asked you once, and I understood him to say he thought that he'd like a little more clarification on the answer.

All existence is very similar to Zoosh's experience in that we always draw a circle because that's so easily understood and is probably the first shape that anyone becomes aware of in this world.

In this world, or in all creation?

Oh, in this world. The totality of being, or the reservoir of being.

Okay, what I'm calling the "totality" of everything that's there — except you, the thirteen, who are beyond it — you're calling the "reservoir"?

No, let's not exclude me; I am a portion of the totality of being. If things do not have a beginning or an ending and they are a constant, then how can you find the point of origin when origin is a constant? The answer is very clear. The answer is you have to change the question. The question in its own right is limited, because if you say, "What's the origin?" you're speaking a question within the context of space-time. It is very difficult for you to speak within any other context. You could try to rephrase that, saying, "When did you become aware of yourself?" but you understand that you're trying to get away with something, there. You're laughing up your sleeve; you're saying, "Well, I'm really asking, 'When did you start,'" But that's not true to all beings, including you, who have been told that when they became aware of themselves was their beginning. That's not true at all. "When you became aware of yourself" simply means that you in some form, as you recognize yourself in your personality that you can access now, even in some minuscule form, became aware of yourself then. But you existed well before then.

THERE IS NO BOUNDARY

But take that back, for instance, to the Council of Creators or to the various beings. When I asked, "When did you become aware of yourself?" could they have been re-created before then, or ... ?

That was their answer within the context of your question.

Ah, but they could have had other incarnations.

No, no, no. "Another incarnation" is oriented to space and time because it sustains sequence. "Another incarnation" is a sequence phrase. Sequence, just saying it. What you will have to accept is that existence is a constant. No thing, whether it is the smallest or the biggest, has ever not existed. There was never a beginning, and there is no ending; only the perception changes. Perception is what you perceive, how others perceive, what form something takes, and what form it's seen as. As you know, the way you see yourself might be entirely different from how someone else sees you. This tells you something that you must know to achieve peace as a personal experience: Not only have you always existed, but you will also never end. You change the form and your awareness of how you exist, meaning you have a little bit of awareness and you have lots of awareness. You change the form, how you look, how you present yourself to yourself and others, for the pleasure of variety.

Can you do that without knowing there were previous expressions of yourself?

You can if you choose to do so, and you are choosing to do that now.

Oh, but that's the situation now with humans. I was talking about Zoosh.

Anyone can! You choose to do that when there is something you are attempting to create that's new. So the fact that Zoosh tells you to ask me something for which Zoosh says he has no awareness of in that moment, honestly, that tells you that he has engaged the Explorer Race phenomenon as part of his own personality and has chosen to forget his own constant so that he might have the joy and share in the joy of the Explorer Race experience.

Well, it wasn't quite like that. He said that when he became aware, he could see the thirteen out there, but he didn't feel he had been created by them. I don't think there was anybody else there.

If I traced him back to his reservoir of being (I didn't say I traced him through us) and if we had had anything to do with the creation, I would have said so. All beings can be traced back to their reservoir of being. I understood after a time that the point of light that I looked for before to find out where I'd come from, I went through that point of light very quickly [snaps fingers], as you'd go through an open door, but I didn't stop to examine it. Since then, I've been back to examine it; it's my reservoir of being. Everyone has a shared reservoir of being. If you looked at it under a microscope, you could see it like this, where everybody has a reservoir of being that seems to overlap each other.

KNOWLEDGE EXPANDS SPHERICALLY

We have on Earth the idea that there are forms, and then we have the idea that there are souls or spirits that ensoul them or enliven them.

That's acceptable.

So could you say that when you created the first creators, and they created, what enlivened them? It came through that same source of being?

Oh, absolutely, but it's not a linear progression that is in existence now. In space-time, one sees that as a thread that runs from here to there, but that's not true. You're in that right now. Picture yourself for a moment in a theater. There is only one seat, and it swivels any way you want to look. Or maybe you have spherical eyes, and you don't have to turn; you can see the entire screen all the time. And there are multiple pictures going on, and you have the control to watch multiple things at the same time all the time by just twiddling the control. You are showing only pictures of variations of yourself that are in existence somewhere, but because you can change them, they change where they are, and where they are, they change. You are doing it. You did this for yourself so that you could enjoy the variety of what you can be. But it's happening in the same space. With the analogy of you being in a theater, you can see it that way, but there are no theaters, and there are no boundaries. This is a story to illustrate a point. All of that is happening in the same space at once, but equally, for those who wish to find and to experience a pathway from one place to another — in short, people living in space-time — all those pathways are available so that you might find your way.

In *my* reality, none of those things are fixed; they are only available, much the same way a fictional story is available to illustrate a point that you might not get otherwise without the story. For that matter, it's much the same as an experience or a repetition of experience that might make a statement to you all the more understandable and part of your actual philosophy, as the statement makes sense because of your experience — not because of its truth, which you could have admitted before you had the experience, but because after you've had the experiences, you can feel the truth of them. It's so much more profound than simply saying, "Yes, that sounds like it's true."

I'm not trying to talk you out of anything you've been told up to this point because the progression of the books has just as much to do with your personal path of understanding. You as the questioner have been representative of all the readers. Your context of space and time was essential to present this material by these various beings to the readers, who are all space-time people. Therefore, there is no advantage in anyone having said to you before what I say to you now, but this will broaden what you've been told and will bring it closer to what reality is.

The whole point is, even though it seems as if we're just going around and around in a circle and coming back to the same point, it's not really true. That's the two-dimensional representation. What's also going on is a spiral, only you don't see that from the top down. We're going around, all right, and it seems we're coming to the same point, but in fact, we're going around and expanding in the spiral in both directions, not just going in one way. We're going around and around in many directions. It's not just a fixed spiral. In short, your knowledge expands spherically.

YOU ARE PURPOSELY RESTRICTED

All right. But you know more now than you did before. The last time I talked to you, you were looking for your creator in that throbbing need out there in front of you, which is now at the middle of the totality.

The more we work together, the more I am able to reveal to you because your needs put my attention in different places. That's why I said in the beginning that the link here is important: your needs or your curiosities that you feel the readers might be interested in will cause me to put my attention in certain places in the same way Zoosh caused me to seek him out when I noticed that his energy was no longer present in the totality that I had felt in that moment. And this works very much the same for all of you as well, but it makes more sense if I say it works that way for me.

So you put your attention back on that point of light, again, which you now know is the source of the reservoir of your total being.

In fact, that reservoir is of everyone; I can trace myself back to a certain place in that reservoir, you understand? You might trace yourself back, and even though we'd be conscious that we were in the same reservoir, if we — how can we say? — waved to each other, I might not see you waving, but I would be very aware that you were there, meaning the reservoir is vast.

Does it have another side to it? Does it come out the other side?

Only if you're attached to space-time. No. That is a space-time question, because you're asking, "Where's the beginning?" I am trying to explain the constant to you, but you are searching for the beginning, and when you search for the beginning like that, you are enslaved to this process. You are enslaved, then. Yes, you are enslaved to the process here that becomes only two-dimensional. It's two-dimensional in this case, around and around and around and around, looking for the beginning, it's two-dimensional because you are not supposed to have that greater awareness here on Earth. I'm not saying that Earth is two-dimensional; I'm saying that you're supposed to put your energy here not only for yourself but also for the other beings who are not present here that you are representing, the readers, per se.

All right. So you found your source in that reservoir of being, and all beings, then, are in that. To answer Zoosh's question, then, he has his source in that reservoir of being with everybody else?

He did. And I expect it would still be there, but I do not know, because I became aware of Zoosh when I noticed he was absent. I looked for my self. No, I only traced it now; he is not there.

He is not in the reservoir of being?

No.

How is he speaking to us, then?

I can say more about this in the future, but I will not say it now, because you will again become attached to the idea that there is something that preceded the reservoir of being.

Oh, there's more; there's always more.

Well, there is always more when you are living in a bag. I know that it feels like that to you sometimes. "I want to get out of the bag. Let me see the more; let me experience the more." But you are purposely restricted in the conceptual being here, but not, of course, at the deep-sleep state when you move beyond all boundaries. Every time you go into the deep-sleep state — you are not just dreaming but are very deep and connected with all beings, understanding the joy of that connection in that moment — every time you achieve it (not just once, not just the first time, every time) it gives you that exultant feeling of being out of the bag, and it is a feeling you retain when you wake up. It is the thing that you are always looking for, the feeling; however you cannot get it in words. Words might trigger it, but it is a feeling. Everybody has that feeling. You personally and others who are annoyed with the apparent limits of space-time know that it is only part of the school system here. It is not a fact.

Can that point of light speak through Robert?

Well, it is possible, but I don't think you could hear it. For a moment, I will focus myself there, and let's see. Now many voices, not all of them, are speaking through Robert, but I don't think you will be able to hear them all, though the energy has shifted.

Oh, what is happening?

I'm going to stop, because we don't want to do that indefinitely. But if you had heard that completely, it would have been like an experience of hearing a great many things at once and then later being able to sort out a few voices, this and that and so on.

You almost faded into light. Robert's hardly there. I'm just seeing this glimmer of light, and it's wonderful.

It is who you are and all beings. It's good to be reminded of that sometimes because it is very difficult in the world of space and time to remember that you are that; that is not part of the scholastic system here. [Chuckles.] You don't have to learn anything when you're focused in that, but here, you apparently do, meaning it is apparent to you that you need to, not to me.

All right, now just before we cut off, can Zoosh come in just for a few minutes? I'll talk to you tomorrow.

All right.

Thank you for everything.

※   ※   ※

Well, you paid your nickel, and you took your ride, eh?

[Laughs.] What do you think about that?

I think it makes complete sense. And I must admit, there is a point at which I know I am no longer here, and I think that there could be two explanations: One, the obvious one, is I go somewhere else; two, I become something else. I think it would be worth pursuing that with your friend. And on that note, I'll say good day.

[Laughs.] All right.

Chapter 14

Take Your Journey

Ssjoooo

August 8, 2000

Let us continue. This is Ssjoooo.

You went into the point of light, and there were billions of voices. Can whatever contains or holds or created that speak?

It's not so much what created it. Think of it more as a vessel. When you think of a vessel in your world, it is natural to think of something that holds something else. But you will have to expand your concept of a vessel. What if a vessel didn't hold something? Picture this: You go into a room, and there are people of many shapes and sizes. Some are youngsters, some are oldsters, and everything in between. Some are thin, and some are stout. You have to hug the little ones like this [puts arms to chest]. You have to hug the big ones like this [spreads arms out wide]; you can't even get all the way around them!

It is an arrangement in which you essentially find yourself embracing, but the embracing is not to hold people in. When you hug them, you are not trying to say, "Grow out this far and no farther" [chuckles]; you are just embracing them. So picture a vessel that does not hold or contain but hugs, meaning it expands infinitely and does not have a boundary that holds or protects. It is more of a feeling of embrace. And this is vital to understand: a feeling that embraces. You've heard many times that when you pass beyond the veils, the first feeling you notice is unconditional love. If you have a feeling of unconditional love, the first and immediate response of all beings — regardless of how they've lived on Earth or anywhere else — is to go toward that feeling.

You have, then, this vessel that embraces all these beings and also encourages them to live and express themselves in life because they are in not only the vessel experiencing and sharing unconditional love but also what you might call the outer reaches of the vessel. It is more like something that reaches out, experiencing and broadcasting unconditional love so that the beings who are lovingly nurtured within the vessel, the total reservoir of being, want to go. They want to go out and experience life. So it is a vessel that loves and encourages. This is why you feel that unconditional love when you travel through the veils. The assumption, of course, is that this has to do with whatever deity you feel good about in any given life. It might present itself that way for your comfort, but in reality it has to do with this love. It is love and nurturance. And what about as you go beyond that point? You will go into this more and more and experience it more and more. I want to put it to you like this so that you don't think it's something that's far away. It's something that's readily accessible in about the same time as it takes to snap your fingers.

It's something that is readily accessible, and it not only has everything to do with the nurturance that you need at the end of a life in this difficult school but also nurtures you and encourages you to go on to have another life. Many Earth dwellers might ask, "Well, after such a difficult life, why would I want to even consider immediately having another?" That is a perfectly reasonable question. Why, indeed? You might wish to bask in that unconditional love for some passage of experience or, let's say for the sake of convenience, for some time. And that's acceptable too. But why, after that, would you want to go on and have another life on Earth? It is because of the function of that loving embrace; it is an embrace that loves and, most importantly, nurtures, encourages, replenishes, and revitalizes. When you feel that way, you are happy to go and live life because you know not only that you will return to this wonderful place but also that wherever you go, you will have some good experience. Of course, most of the time you do not return directly to Earth, but if you do, you know for certain it will be of short duration, and you'll be back to this wonderful place.

EVERYONE EXPERIENCES THE POINT OF LIGHT
Are you saying that between lives we actually go to that point of light that you went through when you were looking for the Creator?

Almost everyone goes to that point between lives. The only beings that do not are those who desire to complete something in an immediate sense. Sometimes people are told, "Well, if you do not do this in a given life, you'll turn around, come right back to Earth, and have another life to complete this." This is not common, but it happens sometimes. Those would be the exception. Almost all beings, to my understanding, go to this place between lives. And it is not so much a place in the sense of a physical location; it is a place that embraces all physical locations and could be referred to as the spaces within things, all around and about things, and everything. But I'm trying to keep the description of this from being too cryptic, and that's a bit cryptic even though it's an attempt to be inclusive. It still sounds cryptic in a space-time world, so I prefer for you to think of it as a place with a general shape. But it really is everywhere.

But the first time you went through it as a point of light, you just went through it as a point of light. You didn't see anybody?

It didn't occur to me that it was anything other than a doorway. But on further consideration, it occurred to me since I came back to my point of origin, that there might be more to it; in short, it was worth a second look.

Because I was nagging you?

You were not nagging me; you had a question that I felt, again, as the absence of Zoosh brought my attention to my awareness of Zoosh. So the absence of my curiosity was heightened by your question, which reinvigorated my curiosity and caused me to have another look, at which time I recognized — it's not "realized," exactly; it's more of where you put your attention — that there was more to this space than I had first noticed.

So you feel that your thread runs back to there and that you came from there also?

I didn't come from there; nobody comes from there. You see, this is something that you're attached to because of space-time, and you are looking for points of origin. Here is the best way for you to understand point of origin, even though it may seem completely ridiculous on the surface. [Draws.] This is but one line, you understand (see fig. 8.1). Well, let's do it like this so there isn't any doubt about what the purpose is, here. The purpose of this is to perpetuate — if the artist is curious, just have him or her draw a daisy pattern, where the lines appear to continue to go in and out without any apparent ending, not unlike a mandala. If you think of your point of origin as a place, then of course you will be looking for something that begins at point A and travels some journey to point B. In fact, your point of origin encompasses all points. If your point of origin were in one place and then went to other places, it would establish linear space-time as the ultimate truth. But we know that this is not so; therefore, we know that you do not have a singular point of origin but plural points of origin. If we know that, that means that you are — and how many times have you heard beings say this? — from every place and every time all at once. This goes for every single being that you know now or have ever heard of or can imagine and beyond. I have never seen an exception.

It is important to recognize this because often beings will say to you that there is no difference between us other than — what did they say? —we remember who we are, and you don't. But this does not make me superior; it only allows me to jog your memory.

So that vessel, that nurturance, that feeling, cannot speak as an entity, as a personality?

It can only broadcast, as I demonstrated. It can demonstrate a feeling, but I do not think it can broadcast in a singular voice. Nevertheless, the feeling is something worth broadcasting, and I would certainly be open to broadcasting that feeling again sometime to you or others in short spurts.

Yes, to a group, if possible. This may be the same thing. When I wrote this down, they were two different things. The space that you and the totality and that point of light are in, I was looking to have that space speak, but it sounds like what you're saying is that that point of light is indeed everywhere, that that feeling that comes from that point of light is the space that you created your first creator in, and that all the totality is in it.

You cannot separate it. It is that and more. You might go to the ocean and fly over it for a moment, and you could address a single molecule of water, but you couldn't address it as if it were an individual separate from the rest of the ocean; you could only address it as if it were an individual inclusive, meaning the molecule might feel a sense of individuality, as all molecules might, but it

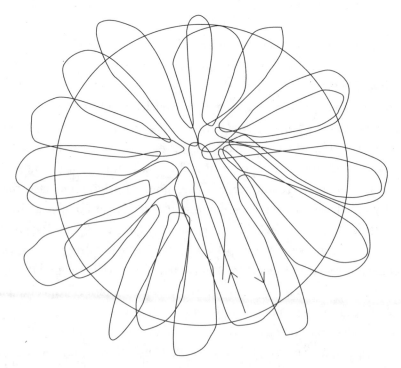

Fig. 8.1. Instead of one point of origin, we are from every place and every time all at once.

would identify with the rest of the ocean as being its place of beginning and ending, even though as a molecule of water it would certainly evaporate and come down in the form of rain and cycle all over the surface and under the surface of the world. Yet it would always identify with being water as long as it was in that form. You would not be able to say, "Get out of that water and stand over here where I can talk to you! Shape up, and let me talk to you! Stop being that ocean right now." [Chuckles.] You can't separate it really.

We've learned a lot now! We learned that that's an emanation of that point of light; we didn't know that before.

That's right.

Can the unexpressed need speak? Does it have a voice?

The unexpressed need?

That you responded to, yes.

I think, again, we're dealing with a feeling. It's important to identify these things as feelings, because feelings do not speak. If actual feelings that are felt spoke, they could only limit themselves by speaking. It is not that much different for anyone speaking. Have you not had the experience yourself, when someone asks your opinion of something personal (meaning you have a personal opinion as well as, perhaps, a mental understanding), that no matter how much you talk, you could not express everything that you feel about that? I am not saying it cannot be done; what I am saying is that I question whether it would be of value to do so.

All right. Can Zoosh talk from where he went? You said he either went somewhere else or he became something else. Can he speak from where he went, if that's what he did?

You'd have to ask him about that.

He asked me to pursue it with my "friend."

He may be able to communicate in a way that is verbal, but you'd have to ask him while Robert is attempting to connect with him, or you'd have to ask him through Robert. While Robert is channeling Zoosh, ask Zoosh to put himself in that place and see whether words can come through or if a feeling comes through or if nothing comes through. In short, you would have to experience that through the Zoosh connection.

I'd like to do that before we quit, if that's possible. If not, okay.

You understand, Zoosh and I are not playing a game with you, here; it is important to recognize that each of us has the knowledge and wisdom at all times, but it is of value to present this knowledge and wisdom to you in a sequential manner because sequence is something you are all here to learn. In lessons of a creator, you cannot learn about responsibility and consequences that will affect physical worlds without experiencing down to your very bones the constant of sequence. If you do not experience it as a constant, you will find a way to escape it. Because it's constant, it can be aggravating. Personally, you can feel it as a limit. Yes, it is a limit, but it is also a profound teaching tool that you would escape if you could. The intention is that you do not escape it. Obviously, you're only here for a short time, and if you could escape it, you most certainly would. When you embrace living here, you are forced to accept the lessons of this place, regardless of what lessons you've brought in to learn or that you might embrace separately from them. You must accept the basic parameters. There are some people, by the way, who simply cannot.

Accept physical sequence, you mean?

Yes, as a constant — not just to accept it as an idea, as something that one experiences, but as an absolute constant, all the time. For people who cannot, there are certain exits; death is obviously one, but another is sometimes what is known as madness. Have you ever observed or become aware of an individual who appears to be in a completely altered state but is not in a state that can present itself (meaning the person cannot present him- or herself) in any sequence? What that person talks about jumps around from one thing to the next, and even his or her therapist cannot follow the conversation. The therapist will just pick up bits and snatches.

But that's what the person is doing: jumping all over the place!

The individual is not accepting sequence. When he or she cannot accept it, the so-called madness will almost always take this form: The words spoken, if there are words, are without any apparent context.

HOW TO HELP SOMEONE WHO CANNOT ACCEPT PHYSICAL SEQUENCE

Is there anything that anyone can do?

Yes. There is something that you can do therapeutically that will often help the individual to experience sequence. One might assume it would be music, but it is not quite music; it is tone. However, the tone must be something that actually moves the air. One cannot move the air with, say, a speaker or through headphones. One could take a child's chimes, or xylophone, or one might even take the kind of chimes one hangs from an eve to catch the wind and gently strike it near the person. Or you could even have something mechanical strike it from time to time, not constantly. Perhaps the chime is struck, and it vibrates first loudly then tapers off much more quietly. Let it be perhaps three to five minutes before each strike. This allows the person to experience a constant in a benevolent way.

You could experiment. Do not use the highest tones but high tones and low tones. The lowest tones might be acceptable, but not the highest tones. Lower tones tend to create more of an embrace of the physical life not because physical life is low but because tones broadcast by the mountains — part of Mother Earth's body — tend to be in the lower tonal range. Since, as Speaks of Many Truths says, your bodies are made up of Mother Earth's body, the lower tonal ranges can be calming, relaxing, and soothing and can be a wonderful way to introduce a person who cannot accept sequence to the joys it offers.

It is a useful therapy, but do not rush the effects. Give the person plenty of time, and see what develops. Don't try to do other therapies once this begins to work, and you will notice it's working when the way the person talks or the actions he or she performs (sometimes people make motions) will change. As the therapist, you will notice that whatever stream that is discussed will go on longer than it used to or that the motions the person makes might have a certain rhythm, and that rhythm might last longer. In short, there will be direct physical evidence of some acceptance of the value of sequence as a constant. When you see this, it's too soon to begin other therapies, but you might try adding to it. Don't take away the first tone, because that will be the foundation on which the person learns to embrace sequence, albeit to a limited context. Add another tone that is, perhaps, close to the initial tone. Don't experiment by adding a high tone; that could destroy the whole experience, and then the person could retreat into his or her former shell of existence. Rather, add another tone that is, as they say, perhaps a full musical note lower or higher.

Make the initial tone and wait three to five minutes. Do that for perhaps four or five cycles. Then add the new tone, but you only strike it once and let it go for that three to five minutes. Next, return to the previous tone for three to five cycles of that tonal moment, all right? The three to five minutes are what I'm calling a cycle. Then you again do one chime of the new tone. You do that so that when you introduce the new tone, it is struck no more than three to five times.

You notice I am saying three to five a lot. That is because it is within this range that the human being in such a condition can accept sequence. Therefore, that's what I'd recommend. If you notice an improvement (it might not necessarily be a marked improvement, but you might see that in some cases), then every ten to twelve days, say, you can add another tone. The reason we only go one note at a time is so that it won't be a shock to the system. If you notice that a note does not seem to be well received by the person, you can do one of two things: You can skip to the next note or go back to the original note and go one note in the other direction, either higher or lower. You are essentially establishing a language of feeling because tonal notes struck in this way induce within these people a physical feeling. When this therapy is at its most successful, you are establishing a means by which this person can find a way to accept the value of sequence and in time can be around other people, which the family of this individual might find marvelous; the family might be able to come in as long as the tones are going on. The person might sit calmly or make repetitious motions, but the family will not cause an interruption or distraction or an unhealthy excitement within the therapeutic parameters of the treatment for the patient. It might even be possible, as the therapy becomes a constant in the person's life, for family members to hug the person, and other things could develop.

THE ORIGINS OF THOSE WHO HAVE NEVER EXPERIENCED SEQUENCE

Wonderful. What kind of lives would a person have lived on other planets or in other existences that would cause that strong reaction to sequence?

If a person has never experienced sequence and wishes to experience it just in the slightest way, one way would be to occupy, say, the egg within the mother. The mother might be pregnant for two or three days and is most likely not aware that she is pregnant. The pregnancy is not a strong one, and it does not take root in the wall of the uterus. Even at this stage of the union of the egg and the sperm, there is the potential for the personality to enter and to conjoin with that, but if the birth were to somehow go to its full term, it would not be what this individual would have wanted. What occurs, then, is that they have two or three days to experience sequence in a very nonthreatening way. This happens very often; it is not at all unusual for beings who have never experienced sequence to have this experience at least once. I might add that, to give you an idea of how common it is, for people in your time, human beings on Earth now who've never experienced sequence before might be perhaps 1 to 2 percent of the population. Every one of this 1 to 2 percent will have done this thing, on the two- to three-day basis, within a woman before they chose to come to Earth to live some type of life.

How is it possible that such a person, such a personality that has such a lack of understanding or cannot embrace sequence, could actually be born? Occasionally, that sperm and egg combination goes to full term and that person is born. In at least one-third of such cases, these people will be inclined toward such madness. Now, this does not mean they will experience it, but they would have, say, a fifty-fifty chance of going into that. The parents might notice that the child has become like this in situations of extreme stress in a given life, or a person might go into this behavior as an adult. Of course, most therapists will attempt to treat the person by addressing the shock or trauma that put them into this behavior, not realizing that the individual had the potential to become this way from the moment of birth. The best treatment that I would recommend is the one I mentioned already. The reason these therapies based on the shock or the trauma are not always successful (sometimes they are) is because that tendency was present from birth.

Now, to expand on that further, how is it possible for a personality who comes into a mother for a completely safe two- or three-day exposure to sequence to experience such an occurrence? This isn't a question of how it is biologically possible; that's obvious that in some unexpected way, perhaps as a result of exercise or some unexpected impact on the womb, that fertilized egg becomes attached to the wall of the uterus. That's the biological way. But spiritually speaking, how is it possible? It's possible because the personality may decide as a result of its two-or three-day experience that it is interested in experiencing more sequence, even knowing that this is not the best way to do it. It is considered by guides and teachers that this two- or three-day experience is the best way to prepare for a life of sequence, as you experience here, and then a simple exit; the mother, in most cases, has no idea she was ever pregnant for such a short time.

Of the initial 1 to 2 percent, maybe 8 to 9, and occasionally 10, percent might say, "Oh, sequence is wonderful; I don't want to give it up! I want it to go on." They embrace it. They do not wish to follow the advice of their teachers and guides, who tell them to only go in for a taste, as it were. It's as if you go to a gourmet tasting, or someone says, "This soup is not ready, but taste it. How does it taste?" The soup is far from being ready — maybe the meat is still bubbling or the vegetables haven't even been put in yet — but you taste it and say, "Oh, it's heaven! Can't we keep it like it is?" The person who's making the soup says, "Oh, we can't serve it like this!" When the soup is ready, you politely say, "Well, it's fine," but you thought it was heaven before. It's very much like that. These personalities love sequence so much that they can't give it up.

They make it happen.

They make it happen, or they embrace its happening, and sometimes it will happen, and then they can be born. But they will always have that tendency for this to happen. Many are the time these people will go through life and not have this madness, but they could have it. When they do, it will usually take the form discussed.

WHAT WE LEARN FROM SPACE-TIME SEQUENCING

Okay, but my question was what kind of life had they led before? I assumed that most beings have had some kind of sequence in their lives.

Oh, no. You're completely mistaken.

Okay, please talk about that because this is a whole new understanding. This is not something we know about.

Beings who might come here perhaps will go somewhere there is an understanding of sequence, of variation of time and space. Beings like that require some initial experience of sequence because they might choose at some point, even if they hadn't planned on it, to experience sequence. In my experience, the vast majority of beings do not experience sequence that is in any way related to space-time as you understand it from your personal experience now. This kind of space-time sequencing is a part of Creator School to experience lessons of responsibility and consequences and all of this other stuff. It's not necessary for most beings to learn that because they are not going to become, on their own, creators. They might be part of the body of some other creator, lending their general energy to the allowance of creation, as you all are now, but they are not in and of their own personality choosing to become a portion of a specific creator, as the Explorer Race is, or choosing on their own, in their unique personalities, to expand into being creators on their own. This can be done, but they are not choosing to do that.

Now, since the vast majority of beings are not in creator training nor do they choose to experience any form of sequence for spiritual or personal growth, they will simply not experience sequence. Their lives are constant, and beings like this will often use terms of the moment you are in. For instance, Zoosh understands sequence, having, as he said, been a planet, but he does not personally embrace it as part of his life and will struggle sometimes when he tries to describe things in his terms and apply them to your terms. (I'm not trying to say Zoosh is a limited being, but he must be.) Sometimes Zoosh must be Zoosh, so he might say, "This moment," and then as your time goes by, he will say, "And this is now, the now moment." Do you understand what I am saying? He will attempt to describe his time in a moment experience: The present is the moment, and it is only the present, and so on, because you cannot directly interpret nonsequential time into nonsequential experience (I'm trying to use the right words here for you) into sequential time in any other way than to talk about the present moment. Nonsequential experience is always in the present moment, whereas sequential experience experiences moments in the present, but they tick along on a scale, measured perhaps from second to second (for the sake of the illustration), though they occur between seconds as well. That is why they struggle to speak to you of these matters: They are in another form of experience, and the present moment is the only common ground between those two realities. So the majority of beings live, have a life, and exist outside of the boundaries.

Outside of the body, outside of time, but in space somewhere, I'm assuming?

Yes, you could say that. It may not be the space you see between the stars, but they live in this other form of existence, which you all, of course, are much more familiar with than living in space-time. That is why very often you personally, as well as many others — not everyone, but many others — are frustrated at the slowness of things. "Why does it take forever?" You are here to learn this, and you get frustrated because you are used to the other way. In the other way, you do not become frustrated because things need to take time. That is a one-way experience because this is not your natural way to live; this is school.

YOU CAN FOCUS ON EVERYTHING AT ONCE

All right. So just describe your life a little. Whatever you're doing is what you're doing, and when you're not doing that, you're doing something else. Is it whatever you're interested in?

There's never any sense of the past. To try to put it in your terms, the past is the present, and the future is the present. You never leave anything behind you; you never go to something that is in front of you. It is all there in the present, in the same moment. This does not mean you cannot enjoy different things, but everything else is there at the same time.

So it's what you focus on, what interests you, what calls you, what attracts you. Is it something like that?

Yes and no. Let's say it this way, even though it is an analogy. Everything else is there and is just as loud as the thing that you might be doing, and you do not resent it. It is not distracting. What makes you up are all these things, and you would no more put one of these things aside because you want to put your attention over here ("here" meaning I am pointing to another direction). You would not put something aside from your total being, your makeup, what you are, because you experience your so-called past, your so-called future, and your so-called present (for the sake of adapting this to time). If you focused on, as you say, one thing, you would have to set all this other stuff aside. It would be as if you said, "I want to examine my right hand, and I want no distractions," and you took the rest of your body and set it aside and just laid your eyes on your hand. You can't even imagine doing such a thing. It would be against life.

So you have the ability to focus on everything at one time?

You have the ability, and it is natural. The idea of not having the ability would seem terribly unnatural, and that is why when you are here in sequence of space and time, you very often feel frustrated. It is not just a matter of being frustrated when things take so long, but it doesn't feel right; it feels unnatural. There's something unnatural about it, yet your logical mind tells you, "That's ridiculous!" Your logical mind is rooted in the sequence of space and time to encourage you to stay here. If your mind weren't rooted in this, you would be out and about all over the place. You would return to your natural state of being. But your mind, as you like to say, grounds you because it is anchored; it is the mental self that is anchored to space and time because it is this form of your mental body (which takes a different form in your natural state) that in fact is loving space and time and is enamored of it and is fulfilled by it, and it can't imagine why anyone would want to experience anything else. It is the part of the baby that when it is born loves space and time. It is that mental self. Granted, the physical self is loving it too, because the baby is more united with its total being, but the mental self is the constant in the human life that continues to find some joy and pleasure in experiencing space and time. For example, you are at work, it's hard, and you think, "Oh my, I can't wait to get home, (in the future) so that I can do _____" whatever, visit with family, have a bowl of ice cream, watch TV, read a book, anything that you look forward to. In short, it is the mind that embraces the expectation — always in the future, you understand — and then equally, the mind might remember something in the past that was wonderful, that was marvelous. It is the mind that embraces this memory. It is the mind that keeps you here.

PSYCHOLOGY WILL EXPAND YOUR ABILITY TO COMMUNICATE

That is absolutely brilliant! So this person is escaping when we call it "going mad." He's just becoming his natural self, even though he's imprisoned in a body.

That's correct. He or she is demonstrating the natural self to the best of his or her ability, even though the vehicle for demonstrating it is not adequate to the task. So he or she appears to be absolutely crazy but is, in fact, simply demonstrating a normal state of being as best as he or she can. Such people feel perfectly all right, and usually people like this become so disconnected from the world around them that if they didn't have someone taking care of their bodily functions and needs — feeding them and giving them water and so on — they would simply die. In the past, they did so without care, but nowadays with more benevolent treatment, they are cared for and live long lives.

Even though they don't want to!

They don't want to; that's right. When they are in that state, they would much prefer to be allowed to die, and perhaps in the larger sense, it would be kind to let that happen, but I do not feel that your current morals and values and principles would accept that at this time. I think in the future that you will be less inclined to think of death as something to fear but as just part of life.

Often to understand things, you have to look at people who do not fit into society, such as the example I use of the mad person. These people do not fit in society because they are somewhere and something else. You can follow the sequence I laid out for you very easily because you see how it fits. Sometimes these people, while they would rather be elsewhere, are demonstrating to their therapists and psychologists another way of living, and that is why I suggested the therapy with the vibrating tones. Your astronaut programs are developing these programs now and, as is to be expected, will be much more interested in psychological interpretations. For a long time, psychologists have interviewed astronauts and cosmonauts to get the astronauts' actual impressions. Sometimes this has been caught up in a bureaucracy, and the purpose of the discussion has been subverted, meaning the astronaut or cosmonaut might have felt that if he or she didn't give the right answer, he or she wouldn't be able to stay in the program.

So they keep the more interesting parts to themselves.

That's right; they have. But perhaps when they retire or talk among each other, they discuss it, and as more people in these various space programs embrace the purpose of basic psychological research, individual reactions to space travel will provide profound insights to encourage future space travelers. And commercial space travel, meaning one who goes into space is not an astronaut, is just around the corner. Astronauts take the ship up, but a passenger is there to be encouraged to experience the psychological differences, the feeling of freedom, and the elation. In short, travelers will have an entertaining voyage. Even though the initial trips will not be very long, they will be long enough to create tremendous excitement and desire by many, many, many people who will want to experience this entertainment.

Pure psychology is to discover, to explain, and to help; that is it's purpose, but it gets subverted sometimes for various completely understandable reasons. Psychology will return to its core purpose, which is to help, yes, but it is ultimately designed to unite. Very often the psychologist can even be the mediator. If the psychologist understands what's going on with the patient, the psychologist can mediate between the family and the patient, meaning that the psychologist explains the patient's behavior to the family and, if the psychologist has a relationship with the patient, the family's behavior to the patient. This goes on now. In the future, general society will embrace the role of psychologists, which will start in various fields (one being the space travel field. Unlike how they are perceived today, the psychologist will not try to control you and turn you into a rubber-stamped "approved" individual but rather will attempt, as psychology returns to its core purpose, to liberate you so that you can share your uniqueness (and feel safe in doing so) with all beings around you. That is the ultimate spiritual and physical and mental goal of psychology.

So do I hear you saying that an astronaut has feelings of euphoria and freedom that, if he explained it to the psychologist, is afraid the psychologist might say he's mad?

In the beginning, yes, especially in the first five to ten years of the programs. In recent years, that's been moderated somewhat because psychologists are working for other people. Yes, the psychologist would love to be included in the loop of sharing information of what the astronaut actually felt, and sometimes astronauts are completely frank with the psychologist or therapist. I don't want to make it sound like astronauts are universally holding out on psychologists, but very often they do not feel comfortable sharing these intimate feelings with someone who is ultimately a portion of the certification process to make sure that they can stay in the program, which is understandable.

Psychology will become more heart-centered, which was its original intention, rather than mind-centered (of course, it must use the tool of the mind and it is grounded in the mind). Most importantly, it will be perceived by the general public as being heart-centered. One can only perceive this from one's own heart; when you talk to a psychologist, and your heart feels warm, you have physical evidence. The psychologist will not be able to fool you with words; you must have the feeling. The psychologist might even talk on TV or use some other manner of communication, and you will get a warm, loving feeling that's physical, and you will say, "This person is perfectly genuine."

Psychology will come more into other fields, meaning that what are now considered politicians will gradually become psychologists. Future presidents and congressmen and senators will become — how can we say? — more like psychologists and therapists and teachers and, in short, nurturers of society. This is a step you will take. You will discover why, so very often, when human beings have had contact with extraterrestrials or spiritual beings who were benevolent, they felt as if they were talking to someone that seemed a lot like therapists or psychologists. It is because this form of communication, heart-centered psychology that utilizes the mind, is the best way to nurture and to know how to nurture people individually. You cannot apply the same psychological principles in structure or form to every individual. That is why psychology must be considered an art. Even though people at this time want to consider it a science, that is its false face. It is an art. Many aspects of medicine are art. You learn by doing. You discover what works with one and not with another. You have certain basic guidelines, but these are guidelines only, not rigid formats or protocols that you follow absolutely. No, in the future, government as you now know it will become more and more nurturing to people. That is why one often finds profound nurturing in extraterrestrial places.

I wanted to give you a glimpse into your future so that you would not become fixed in the idea that psychologists are the enemy. It might be that they are caught up in the moment, in a loop that is not natural to the pursuits of psychology in the most nurturing state, but that will pass. Many psychologists even now are very heart-centered, and this is known by their patients and often their colleagues.

I like to talk about professions like this from time to time, because it's important for you to be able to gauge (in space and time, you *must* gauge) your progress. Very often people look at society around them in a moment and, feeling rather sad, say, "How have things really changed? Have human beings really changed so much? Look at all these bad things." Then they go on to easily enumerate those things. But you have changed. There have been changes, and you are moving toward a more enlightened society. And the reason I have discussed psychologists here is to give you a means by which to gauge your progress and to know that this form, this profession that intrigues and interests people so much is intended to excite and stimulate them. It is not an accident that college students are fascinated by introductory psychology. How many people have had the experience with the so-called Psych 101 student who wants to analyze them? It is amusing and annoying in the same moment. Yet when you were initially exposed to Psych 101, you were just as fascinated and attached to your new insights as others are. It is not an accident that these insights and revelations to students excite and stimulate them; it is a step on the path toward enlightenment. It is not enlightenment in its own right, but speaking of these matters gives you a means by which you can gauge your progress as a society and gives you something to look forward to.

BEINGS ADAPT TO ONE ANOTHER

You don't live in time and space. How are you able, then, to adapt explanations into time and space?

There is a good explanation for that. As you may know, it is in the function of a channel such as Robert that the more he works with an individual entity, the more trust develops. Between Robert and me, in that sense, I am learning how to utilize his body, his consciousness, and his mentality to speak and communicate more easily. You remember, perhaps, that when we first started talking it was slow, and it was difficult because the energy had to be adapted to. Robert had to adapt to my energy, and I had to adapt to his; in short, the adaptation process builds up so that the accommodation of each other is more complete. That is the answer to your question.

You had said Zoosh was focused in the moment and had trouble with sequence. I was really looking at the difference between you and him.

You have to ask that, then. Ask it of Zoosh, and I will say from my point of view in discussing Zoosh that Zoosh must be who and what he is to you right now so that he can deliver on his job. But the way you've experienced Zoosh throughout all these books, while being profound and helpful to the extreme for people, is not Zoosh's natural state.

The place that Zoosh goes after this point — or this state of being, depending on how you wish to see it — is much closer to Zoosh's actual personality, but he has decided, and accepted, the decision that to communicate with you in the best way for himself, of course, and to fulfill your needs and the needs of the reader, he must present himself in the way he has. And I agree.

You've heard Zoosh say before, and it is maddening and annoying and also amusing, that he will purposely make mistakes. You might ask, "Is this just because Zoosh does not want to be deified?" That is part of it; that's how he's presented himself to you. But the other part is so that he can be closer to you. You make mistakes, and that's how you learn. If Zoosh also makes mistakes and appears to learn, he does not seem to be so far removed from you.

Like a teacher who is with us.

He is, yes, more of a living teacher than someone so far afield that his advice seems remote.

What else would you like to discuss?

I couldn't understand how you could create creators that had personal love when you said you chose not to experience that. But it's because what you created them out of, the renown of being, is suffused with personal love.

That's right — and with the emanations. It had that within it. I can only tell you that because of hindsight, but at that time I would not have been able to say, "It is this concept that is included." But yes, that is my impression.

If you are living in that same place, how can you say that you do not experience personal love?

At the time that I said that, it was true. Again we come back to the point of attention: It depends where I put my attention, and it is part of the "contract of services," you might say, of Robert's channeling that he prefers to channel loving beings; therefore, I need to adapt. Just because I do not consider this part of my personality does not mean I cannot adapt. As you adapt, so I am also able. And it is necessary for me to do so to be able to channel smoothly through Robert because of the contract's being that way and your need. Anyone would prefer to speak to someone who has some degree of affection or friendliness toward him or her, even though some people do not think that they need or want it. But underneath all of that, when they go somewhere and relax and are allowed to be themselves — they can just relax and be — they're going to not only want and desire friendliness and such from other beings but need it. The more relaxed you get with me, the more it follows.

Well, you're doing a good job there. The concept of precreation was discussed in the past, prior to your arrival, and I've never really understood that. Could this point of light be considered precreation?

Yes. It could be considered it because it is not possible to have precreation without it being enmeshed with postcreation. And this is that place that is everywhere. It's not a portal because that would take you from one place to another or from one space to another or from one way to another or more.

You went around and came back out near where you started, so it didn't go anywhere else, but that's maybe just your journey?

Not just that I came back to here, but I came back to where I began exactly. And you know, you can measure things; I don't, but let's give it to you within that context. If you started a journey, and you came back to the exact physical parameters of your point of being, including the motion you started it with, it would strike you. You would notice it. I noticed it. I noticed it, but I did not. Because it is my natural existence to be accepting, I took it. My initial experience was to just accept it, but I did not immediately realize, using your terms, that there was more. So on my second voyage there, I investigated what else was going on there.

You don't think you could go through there into somewhere else, somewhen else?

Oh, certainly!

It leads ...

No, it doesn't lead; that's a sequence in space and time. But as a reservoir, it leads to all places and all times because it's job is to embrace, nurture, and essentially encourage beings to go out from there to rejoin life in some form. You are welcome to be here and stay here as long as you want, and when you're ready to go, go out and enjoy life, and we'll look forward to hearing from you should you return.

EVERY OPTION IS AVAILABLE

But within all of that, they're nurturing what we call, for lack of a better word, the "totality," and where you are, as far as you're concerned, there isn't any more that they connect to except what you saw when you started.

There is always more.

That's my line! You said this was all there was!

But this is all there is, and there is more. It is not possible for it to be any other way. Now, you have discovered this in your journey with these books: You have gone in, and you have gone out. There is always more. Yet the more is encompassed by that which I have mentioned. It is hard for you to understand, and it is difficult to describe to you. It is like this: Imagine a rubber band that can stretch infinitely without ever having to snap back. You have this rubber band that you're holding on to. You pull it out a ways, and nothing happens. You keep pulling, and then you can feel it beginning to stretch. It doesn't bind on you; it doesn't want to snap back, but it can lead you back. So you go out and you're stretching from this rubber band as far as you want to go, to infinity; there will always be more. Yet as much as you can ever discover on that journey will also be located in the exact same spot from which you began. And that is a direct analogy to my statement before, how beings who are one thing — their past is their present and their future is their present; their moment in that moment is their total being — could not or would not want to remove some portion of themselves to examine some other portion. It is a direct analogy to that. You would not wish to set your body aside and place your eyes on the palm of your hand to examine them. Obviously that's against life.

So when you, as a being who needs to be more (and of course, it is your natural state to be more, and that's why you're driven; it is a personal need on your part), go searching for more, you will always find it. That's a given, because it is a personal need. You might ask yourself, "If that's true, suppose I didn't have that need. If I did not need to go out and look for more, would I have less?" No, you would have all the mores that exist, but you could examine them within the palm of your hand instead of having to physically go anywhere. Just as you could examine them within your thoughts the way thoughts can examine, you could examine them in your physical feelings the way physical feelings can examine. You can use your senses, all right, as you know senses to be.

You're talking in the physical body.

Yes. I'm pointing to your nose and your mouth and your eyes and your ears and so on. You can examine these things in every means you have available, but they are never any more or less than their total being. But if you go looking for more, you will find it. And there are some beings for whom their world is too much, and what do they want? They might say they want to simplify their lives, but they want less, yet you all have the same amount, which is often referred to — given to you in this word, which is intended to encourage you — as potential. "Potential" simply is an encouraging word that means you have as much or as little as you desire, and it is all present, immediately available for you to express, to discover, to experience in any way you wish, right now. You understand that someone could say this to you; you could be a teenager who wants a car, and you can say, "Yeah, well, that's no help to me, because I need a car to drive to the other side of town!" And I might say (wanting to encourage you as a youngster), "You are absolutely right, but the potential is there. Someday you can have a car, and you can drive not only to the end of town but also to another town or anywhere else you want to go where you can drive." And you as the teenager might say, "Yeah!"

In short, you must communicate with people within their capacity to communicate not because they are foolish or are not expanded in spiritual reality but because you are focused. You are amazing beings, but you are focused here, in creator school. Our job as beings who are not focused there is to encourage you but not to delude you.

I cannot tell you that you can find something that is unavailable to others if only you know how to ask or to proceed; it is not unavailable to others. It is available to all beings all the time, but you have been indulged in your journey to find more because your personal journey serves others so well. Those who are looking in similar places find answers that nurture and encourage them as they read the books. The books, as you know, are largely a personal odyssey of your own explorations, just like Homer's poem *The Odyssey*. It's called *The Odyssey* because of the unusual things found by the character, yet that character was but a vehicle for the famous author to express how anyone journeys through life and to encourage the reader to expand his or her journey, to look at things in a new way, and to move beyond how he or she sees him- or herself to how he or she *could* see him- or herself. That was the author's intention at the time, which is why the author was, at least in part of the poem, inspired. The book is not channeled, but it is certainly inspired. There is a fine line between the two, but the line exists in this form. This is channeling, but inspiration, you had earlier today; a guide gave you inspiration, and you followed it.

Is The Odyssey *based on a real trip?*

I would not say that is not so, but I would say that it is not based on one person's trip. It is based on the trips of many, including the stories of many, including the inspirations that came to the author, including the author's imagination and what could be and what might be, and so on. And that's why the poem has stood the test of time: It is not only a marvelous and entertaining a story but it also speaks so presently in your own times to the needs of all people — not to journey that journey but to journey your own journey.

Chapter 15

You Must Qualify for Physicality

Zoosh

August 10, 2000

All right, Zoosh speaking. Greetings.

Greetings!

Now as you were discussing with Robert before the session, what's going on with everybody? Why are people having experiences, shocks to their bodies, sicknesses, frightening things, and so on? There's a reason. The reason is simply this: It is a push-pull that's going on now between people. People are being pulled and pushed, not only by the senses of who they are, but by their experiences of who they wish to be. And who they wish to be is less associated with their experiences of themselves, meaning how they see themselves, than it is associated with their future and their more benign selves in future lives. So what is occurring is that their future lives are attempting to support them to become their natural selves in this life. Their past lives that were discomforted and not resolved through the disentanglement process and other processes are pushing them to change.

What's happening is that you are beginning to connect on the spirit — or light level, as you might say — with all the other people on Earth. It is not just the pull into the future or the push from the past but also a desire to conjoin, to reunite with everybody on the surface of the planet one more time, as you have reunited with these beings before you came here as part of the Explorer Race, and to have the freedom to do that without the bounds of the physical body holding you here. It's as if you're all being reminded at the same time in your deep-sleep states that you are these light bodies, and you are in physical bodies to learn, but it is not anything other than that. The physical body is to teach you. So there is that exultancy of recollection that you *are* these light bodies. The physical body is the only means that has been found that is successful in teaching your consciousnesses. So why is there so much discomfiture in the physical body? In the past three to five months inclusive and ongoing for a time yet (at least another eight months), it is as if you discovered a part of you that wants to come together with others. When you discover that conjoining again of the light bodies, you want to do it *now* because light bodies do not know anything about next week or maybe tomorrow. [Chuckles.]

It's an immediate state of being in an immediate now state all the time. So the physical, as it is set up here on Earth, is one thing at a time or many things at a time, but you are doing things in time and in sequence to learn. In short, it is slow enough so that you can understand, at the very least, that consequences are a part of life. They're not all bad; some are good. So your physical bodies are essentially waving a flag and saying, "Hey! I am why you are here." And for this to make sense and function in the way that will work for you, you need to make an effort to not rise up out of your physical body but to rise up into your physical body. If we say that your physical body is the means to spiritual and material mastery, then you are attempting to *achieve* physicality.

Just because you're born in a physical body does not mean that you're guaranteed that you have that. You can pour water into a water pitcher, but the water pitcher does not *have* the water; the water will evaporate, or someone will pour a glass of water. The water is not part of the pitcher. You pour your lightbody and your guides, and so on, into your physical body, but you (meaning the immortal you) do not *have* physicality. You have not qualified for or achieved physicality. You must qualify, and you're not doing it yet. When your physical bodies remind you with discomforts, those discomforts sometimes represent things you haven't processed that you need to take care of or things you need to take a look at in your life. But suddenly, all over, you hear from people, from friends, "Oh, this person is 'this,' that person is 'that.'" There are great and unexpected things going on with physical bodies, regardless of their apparent scientific causes. The reason for it — you have mentioned that it's going on — is that your physical bodies are demanding that you qualify to be in them.

How to do this? You cannot see the physical world only as a school; you must see it as something that can deliver profound rewards. When I tell you that when you're in your lightbody, you can create something in a snap [snaps fingers], you say, "Wow, gosh, I can't do that in my physical body; I'd rather be in my lightbody!" And of course there is a great desire by many people to be in their light bodies, and to say, "Okay, enough of this physical school now! I want to be in my lightbody and have some fun and be natural." But you know, you had lots of fun in your light bodies, and you were natural. The reason you're here in these physical bodies is not to do all the things we've talked about in Creator School; you were essentially bored. "What's the next thing?" (I'm interpreting this in colloquial language.) "Where do we go from here? This is fun, but what else is there?"

You were told that you could go and experience physicality on Earth, and you would be placed in a physical vessel, but you would have to find your own reason to want to be in that vessel. And you will have to do that without remembering who you are, without having that recollection of the desire to be physical and to have the opportunity to discover what's so divine about the physical. You will also only remember this desire to be physical at certain times. There will be times when you will love being physical because you'll be having so much fun. But what will cause you to want to be physical and to desperately want to not give it up? You will be given one thing that is available there. You will not be given memory; if you remember who you are, you will no longer have the desire to be physical. You'll say, "That's enough! I'm ready to go back to my lightbody now; I've found out what physicality is about! No, thank you! No, thank you! Let me be in my lightbody again!" No, no, no, no, no. If you come here, you have to accept that it's a school that you've desired to come to and that you have to go through when you're here. You will be given the fear of dying, and you will not only experience this in moments of obvious mortality, such as when you are injured or have frightening experiences, but you will also experience this feeling of your impending mortality — coming to an end, a mortal fear, and so on — when you are embarrassed. You will have it at times when the risk is small, but your personal feeling is that it is great.

In short, you have the gift of mortal fear, and this gift causes you to feel attached to your physical body as exactly what that pitcher is to the water — but only while the water is in the pitcher. When the water is in the pitcher, it's comfortably surrounded by something that contains it, even though it knows it can achieve freedom by evaporation or by moving from one place to another, and flow is natural for water. So your lightbody is conscious of the stream of its being. But when you are awake and running around in your physical body (even in the slightly subconscious state, such as when you are going into or coming out of sleep), you will not have that liquid reference that the lightbody has, as water has. Water is a direct analogy to the lightbody that way.

So your physical body is there for your lightbody, but you have to find out what's so wonderful or, as I've said before, what's so divine (it's intended to be a part of the divine, okay?) about the physical for yourselves, each and every one of you. When you know that this is what you're here for, you'll stop struggling to get out. As I've said before, it's a gift to be here; you wanted to know what's next. "I'm bored, now, Zoosh! What's next? Is there something else I can do? This is fun. I'm loving it! It's great, but I'm getting kind of bored now, Zoosh!" [Chuckles.] Of course you said that to other beings too.

We told you there's something next. "There's something next, but [chuckles] it won't be as easy as it is to be a lightbody!"

You said, "That's okay; we want to do the new thing!" [Chuckles.]

We said, "Okay, you can do the new thing, but you can't stay there very long."

You replied, "Oh, let us stay there! We want to be there forever, we want to do the new thing!"

We said, "No, no, no. In order to do the new thing, you'll have to just be there for a little while to see whether you can embrace it so much that the new thing can work with you the same way that you can work with your lightbody and be your lightbody."

It needs to be something like that, so you have to start off slow and have brief encounters with physicality on Earth in this way. You as an individual and you as a society on Earth can all find that the physical body can be a great, wonderful thing, just as the lightbody is, but the physical body will be able to do more.

"That's all we want!" you said. "More!"

We said, "You will be able to do more, do your lightbody things in your physical body, and do the more that the physical body can do because the physical body can do what your lightbody can do and more than you can do now. After you discover that personally, you will have to discover it as a society so that you can achieve physicality."

You said, "Well, how are we going to learn that if we can't remember who we are?"

Other beings — your teachers, myself, and so on — said you will have to find that out on your own. Over the years, of course, many people have discovered this embrace of the physical body, and some have even discovered how to interact with the physical body in a divine way. Robert has explained and others spirits have explained to Robert about the heat exercise. Let's bring that exercise into context now.

THE REASON TO DO
THE HEART-HEAT EXERCISE

When you learn how to do the heat in your chest or in your solar plexus or generally in your body, that is a physical heat that you can feel, and it's wonderful; it has many benefits. When you share that, meaning when you do it along with others, you feel the heat more intensely. You do not feel it in an uncomfortable way; it just feels more wonderful. Increased numbers of beings who do this, whether those others are human beings or trees or animals — whatever — make not only the feeling within your body feel more wonderful but you can also do more with it. You can connect easily to benevolent magic, and you can change your lives in benevolent ways, not just ways your mind says people ought to be or should be, but ways that are benevolent for all beings.

You will know this because when you try to use the magic (which is really just a statement or a living prayer) in ways that are controlling, manipulative, or harmful for other beings while you are experiencing this heat, it will simply cause that warmth to decrease enough for you to notice it. In the beginning it might just go away, but in time you will notice a significant reduction, and you will have to change what you have said. You cannot just say, no; you have to change it. Of course the animals and the plants and Mother Earth's body are doing it now. Only you as human beings in physical vessels do not do it, even though the organisms in your physical body have the complete capacity to do it, the heat. That's why, when you attempt to do the heat, it can be done physically; your body does not have to learn how to do it because it's made up of Mother Earth, who can do it now and who does it now. But you, as you think of yourself as being separate from your physical body (almost all of you do), have to do it. You have to trigger it, and your physical body will wait to be triggered.

Now we come to what you need to understand. If your physical body is waiting to be triggered and you're trying to get out of your physical body — "Zoosh! I've had enough of this! Time to go back to my lightbody where everything is fun, life is fun, and everything's fun and easy!" — then I and others say to you, sorry. You have to go back when the cycle is actually over. Then what comes up is that to achieve this blessing of the heat that allows you to unite with all beings and gives you creator skills, you have to begin to speak as your physical body and as your conscious mind. The mind can trigger the physical body to do the heat, but the physical body is not instructed by the mind. The mind learns to accept that the physical body can do this, but the physical body is in a state like that of an on switch, meaning the physical body has thrown the switch to do these things already.

For the thousands of years and more that people have been here, the switch has been thrown, but you must throw your switch to complete the circuit. You must say, "All right, now I'm ready to do this," and go into your body to feel the heat or to find the heat or, as is sometimes said, to generate the heat. You're not really generating it; you're just joining your physical body in a process it has begun, meaning it begins before you even come into your physical body, before your physical body is even formed, because it is made up of Mother Earth. She does it, and all the animals and plants do it; in short, all the other forms of life on Earth do it. You must join all these other forms of life to discover the divine here because the divine here is representative of what it is to be a creator, not just as an analogy or a story or illustration. This is Creator School, level one, but it isn't just Creator School, level one. As any apprentice will tell you, you do not apprentice by reading books. You apprentice by doing. Oh, you might read the books before you apprentice, but apprenticing puts you right into the place where the thing you want to do is being done. So you not only learn but must also do, even if you don't do it very well. So this is not only Creator School but also being a creator. Of course, to work, to actually achieve its purpose, it is a Creator School.

So in short, to accomplish what you came here to do, it's not really about leaving to join your light bodies; the Explorer Race is waiting for you elsewhere! That was a step. Everything I say and everything other beings tell you are steps along the path for you to understand your greater you. We can't explain the greater you to you, even through feeling, in a way that you can consciously understand how to get there without revealing the steps to you one at a time. It's not only about that. It's about taking the next step, and the next step is to understand that when you embrace the physical, when the physical is part of the divine to your mind, then and only then can you begin to sweep the shop, to become the apprentice of Creator.

Right now you're sitting in the chair. You can see Creator's shop, and you can see the broom against the wall. You don't know what that broom is doing there, but you embrace the world you're in, not for all its ugliness. You don't have to do that, because there is that here (discomfort, disease, misery). That's not what you embrace. What you embrace is the physical itself. You hug yourself, as it were, from the inside out, with this love exercise because the heat is about loving yourself. It's also about loving the physical. It is also the first "word" that is exchanged between all natural beings on Earth. Animal does it to plant, earth, rock, right? Water to desert to animal or plant. In short, first there is the warmth, and then there might be some communication about whom one is or is not, but there is the warmth, the foundation on which all else is built. It is why so many basic lessons are given to you that you cannot ignore.

You are not cold-blooded; you are warm-blooded. It is not an accident. It's not just, "Oh, that's the scientific way you are because you're this, not that." It's because you are intended to have clues to find out who you are. First there is the warmth. You generate that warmth inside you with your mind, and you get back this wonderful feeling of warmth. You find out not only that being in the physical can be wonderful but that you will be able to do all the things you do in your lightbody and more by being physical, and the impact is greater.

There are light bodies of beings around you everywhere, right now. They can do things that have an impact on other light bodies around them, but that impact might or might not have any impact on you, the physical being, or the impact might not be noticed by you in a way that you can directly access. But you, when you've embraced the physical, will be able to affect not only light bodies around you but also other physical creations. You will be able to begin physically, tangibly, creating not only on the physical level but also on the light level as well, thus achieving material mastery. You do not have to go somewhere else to demonstrate material mastery; this is where you find out how to not only be a material master but also become one. That's why it has been given to you by many, many teachers for years: "If you can only get Earth to the fourth dimension, then you can do these things." But you have to remember that all of these statements — 3.47 and so on — are intended to be an analogy, a story, to help you to find where you're going. Dimensions, as I and many other beings have said, are not real; it is a means for you to understand, very simply, the word "more."

So if you now are prepared to hear that, then you must embrace your body. I do not care whether your body is 500 pounds or 50 pounds; it's not about how you look, how big or small you are — even though I grant that that is important in other ways to you personally. Your physical body is your creator body now, and to be that, you have to find out what's so divine about the physical. That's the reason for the heat exercise. It's an exercise, yes, but it's not an exercise on the way to something else. It's a foundation.

All right. To relate this to all the people who we started talking about who are feeling sick and ill at ease, their first step toward healing or getting better is to embrace the physical?

The first step to their feeling better is to not insist that they feel better. If you approach everything on the basis of how you feel or what you're going to get out of it immediately, you might be disappointed in life in general. Rather, do the heat foundational exercise, and see how you feel. Do it as much as you can if you're not feeling well. Do it, and if you feel the heat somewhere in your body, go into it, and feel it more. It's intended to be simple. If you focus on the heat when you're not feeling well — perhaps you're able to lie down for extended periods of time — then go into it and feel it more, and do nothing else. Make sure the phone won't ring; make sure your distractions are minimal. Just go in and feel the heat, and do it for as long as you can. If you notice that it spreads to other parts of your body, go into it and feel it more; you won't have to go into it and feel it more when it spreads to your hip. If you're feeling it more in your chest, you will feel it more in your hip too. It is simply an exercise of foundational embrace of the divine. I can assure you that Creator would not have created physical bodies the way they are in this world if Creator does not find these physical bodies to be divine right now. You don't have to shape up; what you need to do is to shape in.

So do the exercise, recognize that it is not something you do to get stronger, and then go on. It is a foundation. The best buildings have good foundations, and you build on that. By "building on that," I do not mean you do it for a while and then go on to other things; you do it as long as you can. If you are ill, do it; it can only cause you to feel better, even if you have injuries or conditions in which things are missing in your body, taken out for one reason or another or you were born that way. It can only cause you to feel better to feel that warmth. It's not just a tingling; it's not just "maybe I feel it." You'll know when you feel it because it will feel like a physical warmth on the inside of your body, so keep it simple. Lie down, and do it as much as you can. If you can't lie down, if your disease takes that form, then whatever position you're in, do it as much as you can. It will cause you to feel better; it may not cure you, but it might.

NOTHING IS EVER EXTERNAL

Okay. This desire to join with others is going to go on until May [2001]. By that time, are most of us going to accept that our bodies are divine? Or are there major cycles ending now?

That's up to you. Nothing is ever external. Cycles are a means of seeing the rhythm of all beings. When you are flying above a river, you can see it differently from when you're standing next to it. You can see how that bend in the river came to be. In short, you can see the path of the river. It is a way to understand how rivers move. Cycles are no different; they are ways to understand how the rhythm of life — all beings — is functioning. But the attachment that is easy to make and easy to fall into is to believe that you are encompassed by something larger than you, and it is this exact thing that people have clung to in order to remove responsibility from themselves for their actions as well as to remove responsibility from themselves for their own well-being. If we externalize anything, we say that life is not sacred. Life must be sacred not because Uncle Zoosh says so, of that heat. Remember, that heat is the foundational rhythm of all life; it is love.

We call it love so that you will appreciate its value. It is unconditional love, it is nurturance, and it is all these things. That's why, when you feel the heat in your body, it will feel relaxing, calming, and nurturing. So it's necessary for everyone to personalize all things, all beings. You can discuss the means, meaning you can look at a pile of papers and you can discuss different ways on how to file these documents, and you can even put them in different files, but all the discussions about the filing techniques do not address what's written on the paper. Yes? So all of our discussions about "this" creation, "that" creation, "this" cycle, and "that" cycle are all filing techniques. But it does not change the absolute of everything or everyone being united. I say this to you because the attachment to being a part of something bigger is so profound. Seeing yourself as a part of this bigger thing externalized, you think you are a part of this bigger thing. No, no, no. You *are* this bigger thing.

You all attach such importance to being a portion of some larger thing and that you are in that larger thing's stream. If you think like that, you will always be attached to external things affecting you, over which you have no control. And I put it to you that way with that word, "control." It's not a word I generally use, but I put it to you that way because that's something you can all identify with. Even if you try to discipline yourselves out of using that word, you can identify with the feeling and the thought. So in order for you to embrace being part of everything, you must exclude nothing, and that begins with your physical body. Don't exclude it. You all will, even the most beautiful among you, even the most gorgeous physically who other people admire and praise for their beauty. Those people too (and we all have those beliefs about externals, okay?) find fault with their beauty. Rarely do they look at themselves and not only see beauty but feel the beauty as well. So this tells you that appearance is not the means to permanently achieve the feeling of beauty that you try to achieve; feeling is the fast track. But as you see yourself externally — "How do I look to others?" — is that the fast track to beauty? No. It's a very long track, and it will still come back to feeling, no matter how long a journey you take. I'm not trying to give you a hard time, as you like to kid around and say. I'm trying to keep you on track so that you can find your way rather than taking the long way around. The long way around has been helpful, with you as the questioner, because everyone else is taking that long way around too. I want to, from time to time, give you the opportunity to take a shortcut, but to claim the opportunity is up to you.

You could say, "Since disease and discomfort and pain are being demonstrated by so many people that I know and even others that I do not know, how can I best accommodate the fact of this disease and this pain in the most comfortable way for me?" You see, the question sounds paradoxical: "How can I accommodate pain in the most comfortable way for me?" Of course, the most comfortable way is to not feel pain at all but rather to feel wonderful. The question is a material mastery question because the question itself imposes the challenge: "How can I possibly feel wonderful when I'm in a river of pain and discomfort?" And of course, the physical is demonstrating that when you're united with and even linked (see it as an umbrella, if you wish) to all other light beings on this planet, you are linked to not only the beings that are in balance (the animals, the plants, Mother Earth herself, and so on) but also to all other beings who are not in balance. You are linked to those who are suffering, who are miserable, and who are unhappy or in pain. "Since I am in this, how can I accommodate it," meaning it's part of the stream — you're in it; it's not separate from you — "in a way that is most comfortable to me?" which means, "What can I do?" "Most comfortable" means no pain: "What can I do to have no pain? But more than that, what can I do to feel wonderful in this?" You go into that heat; that's what you do.

It's simple. You experience the heat; you share the idea and the value with others not in a messianic way — "Have I got a way of life for you!" — but when others notice it. You might be able to accomplish doing the heat, and they notice it. They'll feel something about you, and they'll want to be close to you because they'll feel the heat. Don't send it to them; share the means. Invent, create, means; make up ideas on how to explain to them so that they can do it. When they get good at it, tell them. Share it with others. It matters not what you call it, by what word, by what spoken language, by how you define it religiously; it is still the same feeling for all beings. Do this, and understand that you will be giving them the means to feel better. How do creators feel good when surrounded by discomfort? If you, the creator, are all things, how can a creator feel discomfort and feel good? Only when you focus in this feeling as your foundation — but not just your foundation — and build on that. When a mind, a mental being, thinks a profound thought, you build on that thought, but you do not think of that one thought all the time. You then think other things. Even though it's spreading from that one thought, you do not continue thinking that thought while you go on to other thoughts. No, it cannot be done in the mental fashion. What you can do to improve your life and the lives of others is to do this heat and to learn how to speak, act, and live while you're feeling this heat. It will take time, but it's worth doing because that's how you can accommodate the pain.

Picture yourself in a blood vessel. You are flowing in the vessel, and there are other things flowing in the vessel (see it scientifically), cells — this one does this; that one does that. They don't all look the same, but you're in the same stream. It doesn't have to be that, that's an analogy, but look at it that way. Some of those things floating in there are pain. How can you accommodate? How can you be in the same vessel? How can you flow in something? How can you encompass something that is pain without feeling the pain? The way to do it is to feel this heat, and then all pain, all discomfort, all misery, all fear, and everything will be there with you, but you will not feel it. You will not be it. It changes your life; it changes the life of all beings who ask for the heart-heat energy. Animals will look at you; maybe a grasshopper flies up to you, a butterfly, a bird. They look at you. Everybody has the same feelings that radiate from your eyes. Many of you have noticed that the expression in a dog's eyes, in a cow's eyes, in a deer's eyes, in all these different animals' eyes, is the same expression; the same feeling is radiated through their eyes as are flowing through the eyes of human beings. You can get the same feelings by looking at the eyes of a grasshopper. You may not be able to understand the feelings the way you do when you look at eyes that are like yours, such as the eyes of your dog, but you will still get the same impression of feelings.

Why? It's to remind you that feelings are the means, they are the union, they are the bond, they are the stream, and they are the encompassing union of all things. You must be a constant, as your other friend says. You must have the constant. When you are doing physical mastery or material mastery, it is not the inspired thought that then goes to other thoughts, and you don't think the inspired thought all the time. It is that you have the feeling of heat, and all the other things you do in your life, including what you think, included in this physical heat. You are the physical heat all the time. If something that you think of or that you are doing suddenly decreases the physical heat, then do something else, think something else, or say something else so that you can have the heat and maintain it at that comfortable level.

It is something you learn on your own, as an individual, and as you join with others, you will still feel it the same way. Except in this case, you will all feel the reduction if you do something that isn't quite right. It's the same way you learn how to sing as a professional singer. You train your voice, and you learn how to sing the notes that you can achieve. As you join a chorus or another group or a band, you learn how to sing your part in the range that you can achieve that sounds good with the others who are singing their parts. It is the universal choir, it is material mastery, and it is the sound you hear in the background. When you move beyond the veils of life that you know, you hear the universal choir; you're not sure what they're singing, but it feels good. You're not sure what they're saying, but it feels good. You can have that here and now; you don't have to move beyond the veils of physical life.

Why wait? It is the means. Think about it. If you are doing the physical heat for yourself and training as an individual, when you get good at feeling the heat in your body, you can begin slowly to practice while doing something else. Don't start practicing by writing; do something simple. Maybe try to wash the dishes or even something simpler. Move your body around while you are feeling the heat. Move your arm back and forth to see whether you can still feel the heat. Move your leg back and forth, and ask yourself, "Can I still feel the heat?" In short, start small. Work up incrementally, one thing after another. "Can I speak and feel the heat? Yes!" But you will not be able to say everything that you say now. "Can I think my thoughts and feel the heat? Yes." But you will not be able to think everything that you think now nor will you want to. When you feel the heat, it is such a wonderful feeling that you'll want to maintain it when you do everything. How can you do that when something doesn't feel good? If it doesn't feel good, the heat reduces greatly or it leaves, and you have to generate it again. Then you know that that is not something you can do and feel the heat.

We must keep it simple. Achieving creator status is not something that is externally given to you; it's not that others say, "Now you are ready to be a creator." It's that you feel it. It is something that you can do in your body. Your life changes because what you've been doing no longer seems very important. It doesn't mean that you stop loving the people around you, and it doesn't mean that you abandon your work, but it might mean that you do your work differently. It might mean that you interact with the people around you differently — in a better way that is love for you and that they will probably like better. If they don't, then you will need to be with other people until they are ready, on their own, to embrace this heat in whatever way it is introduced to them. I am not saying to run away from your families; I am saying, learn this as an individual, and when you find others who are doing it, do the heat with them. It will feel wonderful. If you don't know others who can do this or want to, then try it with a tree. Some trees will do it with you; others will be busy doing other things. But begin.

It is the way to material mastery. You will find that the creation of what you need in your life can appear much more easily in your life when you are feeling the heat. You might say, as you feel the heat, "I need a new car," and the heat will decrease, even though you know for a fact that you need a new car. The heat decreases; does it mean you are afraid of getting a new car? No. It means that's not it. Then how do you say it? Do you say, "I need a new car?" No, the heat goes down. You say, "The way I am getting around now in my car isn't working so well for me. I need a different way to get around that works better for me," or something like that. In other words, you broaden it. Saying "a new car" is limited; you might need to say, "I need a better way to get around than I'm getting around now." You don't ask for a new car; it's not the goose with the golden egg. When you say that, you might not be able to say the words that I said.

Maintain the heat, and say the words that come through you. As long as the heat is present, the means to get around in that new and better way will be there. You say, "I need a better way to get around than I'm getting around now," and that's it. That better way will come because you are in the heat, and you are in the stream.

You do not experience externals in any way. Money doesn't stand between you and a new car. Maybe it's not a car at all. Maybe there's something else entirely that you do not know about, but because it is focused in the heat, meaning the love (but I'm saying "heat" because that's how it will feel to you, to other beings, and it's a landmark to recognize; I'm honoring your need for physical evidence, as you were created to seek physical evidence intentionally), when you say it, it will happen.

You won't have to say it over and over again, but you can say it more than once. Don't say it every day. If you still need your transportation to improve, you can say it in a different way, but always maintain the heat while you're saying it. Then the words that come out, that you can say — you won't be able to think or to say it in a different way — will be the words in the flow of that heat and will be a living prayer and benevolent magic. Benevolent magic is just a way of describing what is in the flow of the union of all creation. This is not for the reader only but for beings who are present. It is for all beings and both beings who are present. If you can do this, do it. Begin. And practice, practice, practice. Life will get better.

Chapter 16

Beyond

Zoosh

August 17, 2000

Zoosh here.

Greetings!

Well, you are interested in beyond. What is beyond all of this is a complete lack — of course it doesn't feel like a lack; it feels like a gain — of any sense of personal identity. When you are here and in the soup of the light, even though you are in the light and there's all this sort of gentle motion in the soup, in that reservoir, you might at moments feel completely united and connected with everyone and everything. But you would still have a sense of personal identity, a sense of self — not enough to cause any feeling of separation, but a sense of personality that is still present.

On the other side, in the beyond where I am speaking to you from, the personality that you feel on the other side, all of that is gone. So where I am now does not utilize light, sound, or color. No sense that you now have ready access to would be useful except for your sense, which you can acknowledge feeling in your body, of absolute peace and calm. Now, this is something I personally find profoundly relaxing. When I go from your space to that space, I completely relax. It is restorative because within that energy not only is there utterly no demands whatsoever — no requirements — but there is also no urgency, no personal motivation. In short, there is no personal agenda whatsoever.

THE UNDERLYING JOY OF BEING

As sometimes happens after a traumatic life or a traumatic death, people go within this creation, somewhere in total creation, and they might go to a

249

place where they have what I'm describing. However, they would still have their sense of personality. It is the personality that requires the restoration, not the beingness. The particle book[1] shows you that no matter what the particle is doing, there is always an underlying joy of being. Now I'm going to do something that Ssjoooo did to see the extent to which you might feel it. I will attempt to radiate the energy to you that I feel; it might or might not work.
Mm, wonderful ...

Do you notice the complete lack of any urgency or desire to do anything? Right now I want you to say out loud, if you can, how it felt.

First everything in my body loosened up. It's as if all the chakras opened and I expanded and then sank back into that, and it was so peaceful and so loving. I could hear the street noises, but it was as if I were in a different world. It felt beyond peace. It was loving. It was wonderful.

Thank you. It is important to say things like that from time to time because, as you transfer a feeling to words to the best of your ability (and that was very, very good), your descriptions of these experiences will help the reader to identify with them. But there's more to it than that.

You know, when a person is passing over at the end of their time, light beings (sometimes referred to as angels) come to them to help them cross to the other side. These light beings are given an energy. They are corded to all the energy sources that the individual coming over, or being escorted over, might require, and there are also a lot of cords that allow the light being to do this constantly. You have to remember that they move from one dimension to another. They are not just beings that you meet when you go through the tunnel or beings that are suddenly there. They are not beings that greet you as you've passed through something but beings that actually come to fetch you. This happens sometimes when people are lost or there's been a sudden death. Crossing in a crosswalk, a person didn't see the bus. *Bang!* Sometimes people don't realize they're dead, and they're dazed. In such cases, they need to have light beings or angels come to them. As you said (which was why I wanted you to give the talk), you could hear the street noise around you, but it didn't affect you, meaning that you could be in both worlds at the same time. In that moment, you were in two worlds. So given what these types of light beings or angels do, they must be able to simultaneously be in two worlds.

THE OUTER BOUNDARY AND BEYOND

The reason I'm bringing this up is to point out their capacity to do that on a constant basis. Granted, in the world that they are from, constant is a factor

---

1. *Particle Personalities*, Explorer Race series, book 5 (Flagstaff, AZ: Light Technology Publishing, 1997).

rather than time. Nevertheless, they must have the capacity to do that constantly: They take you through and then stay with you or go on to somebody else. It's one thing after another; there's no rest, and there's no time off to put up your feet or to have tea and crumpets. It's just ongoing. The energy that supports them is like this: There is, within this mass creation and all the creations here, a reservoir. It's a different kind of reservoir; it's a reservoir that strictly supports angelic-type light beings who do this duty. But it's within this space, the general totality.

Now, as that goes out to each individual, there is a cord back beyond this totality to where I am, moving back, which Ssjoooo has shared with you a bit. Imagine a dotted line, and say that this is the outer boundary, for the sake of simplicity (but there is no line; it's not literal). Let's say it goes back to what's beyond. Here are angels, or light beings, here's the reservoir, and here's how the reservoir is recharged, going out to the outer boundary and beyond. That might be clear enough. The reason it's helpful to know what is going on out there is not only to know the nature of it but to also recognize that even between things that might seem separated because of the differences going on in them, there is never such a radical difference that interconnectedness is not allowed. So you can see that although this reservoir represents one of the few permanent interconnections, there is some degree of motion available through these boundaries, through these areas that keep things where they need to be. So this is the space that I'm calling the outer boundary.

Around the totality or the reservoir, as if there were a circle around all of creation?

That's right, as if there were an actual membrane. What I'm saying is that there is something within that "membrane" that keeps what needs to be elsewhere, elsewhere — keeps things separate. That separation has to do with the fact that there is a significant difference between the two places. This is not to say that there are not beings in your totality that might have the energy you experienced that is completely devoid of any sense of attachment to personality or that is even completely devoid of any personality of their own, ever. That means they might have either come from that place that I am now in or, after going and spending some moments there, found it to be so pleasant that when they returned to this totality in which you are encompassed at the moment, they decided to bring that with them. And that is allowed.

The allowance, then, is essentially one-way. You can experience where I am now and do what I am doing now, actually, which is to bring the beyond into the totality, but you cannot take what is in your totality and bring it into where I am now unless you're doing it with the purpose of shedding it. Generally speaking, when I go into this other space — because I've been in this space — I essentially shed before I get there, and the shedding takes place before I get to the membrane. If you hadn't ever been to that other space, the shedding would take place in the membrane so that you wouldn't bring anything from the totality with you. There's no real membrane, but there is a means, like a gate or whatever you want to call it. So you go through there, and the shedding takes place so that by the time you get into this other space, the beyond, you are no longer feeling in any way anything like what you would feel in the totality other than the feelings you've described.

So how are you able to talk from there?

Because I'm corded.

Back to this side, which connects you to who you are?

That's right. I'm running a cord now so that I can translate this energy from over here into where you are. So I'm just running a special cord that is not normally there. This is so that you can see, feel, and describe it.

Thank you. So now let's get to the adventure part. Ssjoooo went in there.

Ssjoooo did not come over to where I am now; Ssjoooo went into the reservoir. Remember, Ssjoooo went to the point of light that was the reservoir. He didn't notice that at the time. Then on his second trip through, he slowly noticed what it was. The reservoir essentially spun him back out where he had been in the totality, of which he is largely responsible for having altered into what you now know. But from where he was, he didn't go through the reservoir, beyond the membrane, and into where I am. If he had done so, he would never have started the totality as you know it. He's the key being in that sense. The energy of need was felt by Ssjoooo, and he responded in the only way that made reasonable sense to him. If he had not done that, well, there would be nothing. It would be peaceful but empty. To beings who have interest in something beyond peace, it would be somewhere that isn't.

Well, we wouldn't be here, so we're grateful to him. How does this work? You were a member of what was created in this totality, and then you explored beyond the reservoir, or were you there first?

Oh, no, I was there first and beyond there.

What's beyond there, Zoosh?

Beyond there I do not think is translatable to you in any means you have of receiving at the moment. Where I am now, as I said, I could transmit to you in feeling, and you could describe the feeling. But what is beyond — several stages beyond beyond and beyond and beyond — there is no means of communicating that to you *in any way* as you are now, you understand, as humans.

Now I will say this: It is possible for some beings on Earth, though they have no interest, to feel the next stage beyond, to understand what's beyond, to grasp it, but I do not think that humans have anywhere near the tools to do so, because the reason you are humans, in your bodies as they exist now, is that it's very clearly set up for you to learn what you want to learn. And a great many of your other capacities have been overshadowed so that you do not get distracted by who you are. To want to know who you are, that's fine. That's a good motivation for you. But to be distracted by it would simply cancel out all the value of your having come here in the first place. Obviously, if you had any glimmer as to who you *really* are, why would you hang around this place? And that's only natural. That's not just natural for human beings; that's natural for anybody.

BEINGS WHO TRANSFER ENERGY TO EARTH
There are a few creatures that have the capacity to understand the next stage, which isn't really a stage or a level, but there isn't any other word that falls from the tongue at the moment. Let me identify a couple beings: the praying mantis; there's a sea creature, and I believe it's the eel; and the earthworm. I think cats can get it but not consciously. These other three beings can get it consciously, but cats can get it on the dream level, and dogs too, but not dogs as you know them — the ones going back a ways from which present dogs sprang. Wolves can also get it at the dream level. There are a few others, but those are the main beings who can access that feeling readily, which tells you that the nature of their beingness and their capacities run very deep indeed. Some beings also have the capacity to do other things, such as go to the reservoir and to emanate a great many energies that you need here on Earth. Generally speaking, the beings who are the most commonly seen or who you are aware of in great number are usually emanating or more often transferring, as one of their duties that they freely accept, some energy that you human beings need. But to this totality, they transfer it from various points.

It would be an energy that Earth would not normally acquire for anything she needs. It would also be an energy that your souls or your immortal personalities also would not acquire but that you would need to be exposed to in order to help you find your way. Ants, of course, are one of these beings because they have, as you've noticed, great strength (to say nothing of strength of character). It is not an accident that an ant can lift something significantly greater than its own weight. Furthermore, they're very good at maneuvering, and they're excellent at teamwork. If you want to learn about teamwork, just observe ants. These profound capacities compared with the ant's size provide a hint; they tell you that if ants have those physical capacities, what might they have spiritually? Yet if you were to hear from ants directly, they will tell you many things: They have great depth, and they have profound culture, but they have a much greater capacity than they need for their own purposes. The reason they have that greater capacity — which, as I say, you get the hint of by seeing what they can do physically — is so that they can transfer energies for other beings to this planet. But most of the time they're transferring energies for human beings, and that is why they sometimes come up to the surface — just to radiate. Other times, they bring things up to the surface when they do not wish to be here. Obviously, at the opening of their surface aperture, they bring up rocks and sand and other little bits. Sometimes they charge these things purposely with an energy that allows them to put it on the surface for you, and it will gradually emanate this energy until it's depleted without the ants actually having to stand on the surface and take the risk of doing so, which, around most human beings, is still a significant risk. If you as human beings had any idea of the profound good that ants do for human beings, I daresay you would be much more tolerant and perhaps even welcome them.

EVERYONE IS EVERYWHERE ALL THE TIME

Where did all those beings in the reservoir come from? They ensouled everyone in the totality?

All that really came from the initial triggering that Ssjoooo did. Remember, Ssjoooo started something like a chain reaction. Ssjoooo started something that kept on rolling, and every time, creators came along. But I understand; you're asking where the energy came from. What is very often misunderstood in your time is not just the function of need, but the capacity of need. The capacity of need is to create, as a magician might, out of thin air that which has no components present. If you realize that, if you think about what I just said, you will understand the foundational building block of material mastery (in terms of the application of material mastery) to create not just the understanding of how beings work in harmony and how to continue that harmony and so on but how the actual mechanics of creation has everything to do with the capacity of need to create literally out of thin air.

I understand that because the throbbing need that the thirteen felt is what started all this.

That's right. So Ssjoooo essentially created the focus of the need by adding a little bit of its own personal agenda, you might say, to that which was felt. That first little thing that Ssjoooo launched that literally not only gave need permission to create on its own but also gave it definition and granted a broad but still agenda.

But where did the need come from?

Need is always present when life chooses to reinvent itself, yet if you understand that all things, without exception, exist at all time and in all ways, then what's really happening? Is something new being created? In the larger sense, nothing new is being created, but the process of creation itself might be different.

So if we look back at what the Explorer Race intends to do (in the largest sense that you can grasp), it is the process of creation — the individual process, the scenarios, the whole thing — that is different, not that any idea that is now known as the Explorer Race is something that was unknown before then. It can't be unknown. Maybe you are an artist. You have so many colors to work with. You have primary colors, and you have shadings of those colors; but at some point, you reach an end to the tones that you can make based on the colors you have.

So when the artist runs out of tones, then what?

That's it. He's made as many as he can make, given what he had. That's the end; there's no more to that. What I'm actually saying is this: The sequence is what changed, but the actual idea of the Explorer Race per se was always around.

There was a need. First, we have to address the issue of where Ssjoooo came from. Are you using Ssjoooo as a name for all thirteen of the personalities within that being?

Yes, yes.

We have to address first where they came from. You said they were always there, but ...

It's a sequencing question; I'm going to end up using the words that Ssjoooo uses with you. Ssjoooo was always there in the nature of the personality by which you know him/her/it. He was always there. And before that, you were where you are and beyond. But you could say the same thing of Ssjoooo. Ssjoooo was always there and beyond. You could say the same thing of you right now.

You've seen the fisherman with his hand on the fishing pole. And then there are the components: the reel, the cord, the bobber, the sinker, the hook, and the bait. Ultimately, there's the fish. When you cast that bait on the hook — especially if it's a worm that would rather be elsewhere — it has absolutely no sense of personal identification with the hook other than as the thing that's torturing it. (It is a sad state of affairs, and someday you will fish differently, in the old way, as was done here on these islands, I might add.) The worm does not identify the hook as being part of itself, really, because it's suffering. If it is sitting somewhere in its own world and sees a hook on the ground, it might appreciate the hook as part of its total being but not when it's being murdered.

We keep coming back, and different things do not identify with other things. You gradually get to the point, as you get back to the reel and then to the arm of the fisherman, when you realize there is no real sense of interconnectedness even though, as you pull back and you see the circuit running from the fisherman to the fish, you can see it all as one thing. That might not help you. It's a very helpful illustration, but it's not very helpful words-wise.

So you're saying that this was empty space, there was Ssjoooo, and there was a dot of light, but there was no reservoir of beings in it.

I'm trying to get you to go beyond and to dump that whole sequence. Understand that ultimately everything is everywhere all the time, and there is no way other than the way it is superimposed on that for whatever reason. That is the ultimate answer, though it is totally unsatisfying for you right now because you want to follow a trail. The trail, however, is entirely superimposed.

I see. But you came from there. Who else came from there?

Everybody is everywhere all the time. Everyone. You understand, I'm not going to stubbornly hang on to this indefinitely here. But I just want you to understand that there are times I need to say this and underline it so that you do not become attached to the theatrics, the theater of it all.

Well, it is a theater. It's a set in a theater; that's what it is. A set and setting for experience, isn't it?

Yes, it is. That's not it's nature, but that's how you experience it.

After Ssjoooo said this about the reservoir of being (I had never heard that term before), I opened up a book, and there on the page on Hinduism, it said everyone comes from the Godhood and the reservoir of being. There it is!

That tells you a little something about the people who wrote down these things. It tells you that their sources of inspiration might just stem back to exactly what we're exploring here. That's why ultimately it's necessary to understand that you can flavor the soup in many ways, including sweet, but ultimately the primary component of the soup is water in some form. The cook might not pour water into the soup, but ultimately when you distill it, the purest ingredient will come out, and after the greatest distillation process short of converting it to a gas, it is going to be water. Not counting the solids, of course.

The second interesting concept is the cosmic day. They call it the day and night of Brahma. Now does all of this, at some point, say, "Okay, we've done it all," everybody in the totality goes back into the place you are to rest and assimilate, and then we all come out to do it again? Is that how it works?

Oh, no. There isn't assimilation; everything was assimilated initially.

So everything always was and everything always will be, and they didn't come from anywhere, is what you're saying?

Oh, it came from somewhere, but it also is somewhere.

It came from somewhere?

Yes. So in any discussion we have that attempts to trace the superimposed trail back to some point of fictional beginning, I'm going to take you to the point we just visited. Regardless of your desire to grasp "it came from somewhere" was a joke on my part that you didn't get!

Chapter 17

The Constant Motion
of Totality

Zoosh

September 11, 2000

Who gave the information in Sanskrit about the reservoir of being?

All of the ancient teachings, whether they've survived until your time or not, were brought about because either someone received inspiration in a way that is being done right now — channeling — or a teacher from another planet stationed on Earth as an ET (but who looks like an Earth person) or another dimension spoke this knowledge to a selected student. Of course, you can see that the most practical method is channeling, since obviously you cannot really introduce too many, as it would be perceived, strangers into various cultures without those cultures gravitating toward creating deity-like relationships with the strangers, whereas channeling could be adapted into varied forms of culture.

Through each person in each different culture, flavored so that it was adapted to each culture, and the people in each culture could understand it?

That's right. So what is called channeling today and was called mediumship in the not-too-distant past was called by various terms as inspiration or insight and so on — various descriptors with a similar meaning — in those ancient times, and it would almost always involve a form of voice alteration, a form of energy felt, naturally, most often by those who listened to the voice but initially by the channel him- or herself. This is basically the blanket answer to your question. Now, I grant that many of these written records did not survive into your time. Certainly in Europe that was because of what you call the Dark Ages.

In other places, many of the reasons are not as dramatic as the case of what I prefer to call the dim times in Europe. It was largely because of weather. You know, you might put some kind of a record somewhere, but it doesn't last indefinitely. That's why even when wisdom is passed on from generation to generation, even if a great effort is made to preserve it in its original context, some of it gets lost. Only the most ancient cultures that are still reasonably intact in your time (reasonably meaning not perfectly intact, but close) have managed to retain some of this information but not all.

A CALL TO CHANNELS: RE-CREATE ANCIENT CULTURAL WISDOM

Generally speaking, all the information was not given to everyone, and this was done intentionally, not unlike pieces to a puzzle. This culture received this information, and there would always be overlaps to another culture. When different cultures met and eventually shared some secrets, they saw enough overlap within their sacred teachings to begin comparing notes and finding out which teaching would complement the other. It was done purposely to create that potential. Fabric can have different weaves that might look quite different from each other, but when all are stitched together like a patchwork quilt, they will perform the job of a blanket quite nicely, even though it might look a bit unusual. And in time, it could be accepted as folk art, but that's another story. In any event, so much has gone on over time to disrupt this, and as I said, when keeping a written record, someone might even put scrolls somewhere that he or she thought would be safe indefinitely only to have the scrolls totally ruined, as in the case of Lake Powell (in Arizona and Utah). You know, north of where you live now, there were some scrolls.

In caves and then they built a dam, and now it's underwater?

Yes, and it was thought that those scrolls and other means of recorded information (I'm going to leave it vague like that) would remain safe forever because the water had never reached that high, and great effort was taken to make sure that they were put somewhere the water would never reach. However, in the case of an artificial dam like this, the water not only reached that high but also inundated it. There were some people at the time who knew of this information but were unable to stop the construction of the dam. I might add that a former governor of Arizona regretted giving his approval to the building of that dam but for other reasons. Anyway, even the best attempts to preserve written information, or information encoded in some way, were not always successful. So right now the quilt has many patches missing from it, but there are still enough connections with enough cultures that those who have done this research have noticed certain definite similarities. In short, they've noticed the overlaps.

Zoosh puts Robert's fingers together with his elbows out to the side.

Yes, with the intention of really just the first joint overlapping, but not a total overlap, as in hand-over-hand. So people — scholars and so on — have noted this, and that's certainly true. I am hopeful that in time, as your cultures embrace this form of inspired communication (channeling), all that wisdom can be re-created. Of course, some people have been wiped out; their cultures have been wiped out for one reason or another. The natural tendency to explore where your ancestors came from will not be present in your time because the descendants will not be there.

It will be necessary for various channels — and I'm really putting out the call now — to re-create the cultural wisdom of various ancient peoples even if there are no descendants today and even if this cultural wisdom might seem to be at least partially a duplication of wisdom of others that is known about today. Expect an overlap. It will not overlap in every way; there will never be any more than a 25 to 35 percent overlap. So expect at least 60 to 65 percent of the information to be exclusive to those cultures. I'm calling on other channels to do that because this is not a project that we will undertake at this time. Other channels can do this and, I think, might find it interesting.

THE PRESENT IS THE POINT OF ORIGIN

There's a reservoir of being. Are these the beings that ensoul the totality? Were they there before? I know that you keep saying everything is and always was, but I need to understand how it works.

We're coming up against this as we've come up before. Your question is about time. To fully appreciate what I'm talking about here, we have to understand that the nature of what you're asking is time oriented. Let us put it this way: Can you perceive Earth throughout time having water? Then you might also ask, "When did water begin on Earth?" And I might say, well, Earth has always had water. And you might be able to accept that, you understand. This is an Earth–water question in that sense. Given that you're asking, and you must (you have no choice because of the nature of where you are living), "When did this start?" I have to say that outside of the context of time and even within the context of time (we can overlap), it was always there.

Keep in mind that the idea of a constant is easily understood if you hear a sound such as the surf on the beach. Now that's a constant. You do not expect it to suddenly go silent, all right? Let's just say that it was always present. I know you want me to say who created it, but it will not change. This is the case: The more you pursue something to its point of origin, the more you will find that point of origin in the present. The desire is to find something for which you can ultimately have absolute allegiance. You could find somebody — and it's not difficult, especially in channeling circles — to say, "I am the one who created all of this." (You know my general attitude about that has always been [makes raspberry sound], all right?) I feel dramatically that way — not to put any being down, but to put down the whole attachment human beings have to finding their leader. So this is really a "show me your leader" question. "Take me to your leader so that I can praise him, her, or it." I know you're not thinking of it that way, but that is ultimately it.

If I, Zoosh, could show you the ultimate Creator who can intellectually and emotionally prove to you that He, She, or It actually created everything from the beginning, then you would be happy. But on a personal note, if that ever occurred in life (it will, of course, occur after your death), you would be happy for twenty-four hours but you would wake up after and say, "But there must be more!" Why do you have that desire to know that there must be more? It is because in this life, the work we are doing together requires you, personally, to be sufficiently curious to want to know. Period. If you had not been curious, we would not have all these books, all right? These books are almost exclusively a result of your curiosity.

MORE IS A CONSTANT

I'm not trying to squelch your questions, but I'm saying that this question and this desire that you are involved in now is going to lead you to the same position that Ssjoooo originally found itself in when it quickly went from point A to point B, which turned out to be point A again.

But he doesn't know that; he thinks he went around ...

No, no, we're not talking about him. We're talking about you.

All right. It's the same desire.

It's the same desire; it's the desire to find your origins, regardless of what you say and how you phrase these questions: "What happened before this, and what happened before this? Who created this?" These are really the personal desire to find your origins.

This is not a criticism. You're hearing it that way, though, aren't you? It is natural for you and for anybody living in time, as you know it, to try to discover more about the present by either examining the past or discovering all the various elements of the present. Science makes a point to discover the various elements about the present, even if it incorporates past-oriented pursuits. So what I'm saying is this: We can continue ad infinitum with questions that say, "Well, who created this and who created this and who created this?" as in your original pursuit with various creations. It would be like science's exploration to create the greatest microscope that ever was to examine the smallest particle, and *whoop!* What happened? The more you examine it, the more you discover the myriad of smaller and smaller particles, which in that sense — in versus out — is the same mechanism. One finds more and more as one goes in, and one finds more and more as one goes out.

What does that suggest? It suggests that more is a constant, that more is always present, and that the desire to put things in a row (otherwise known as a time sequence) is a fallacy. You assume — and science is assuming, even today — that the best magnifying instruments can reveal that these smaller particles are part of some kind of building block that created these larger particles, but that's not the case. This is something that is in flux and in motion. It is not just a primordial soup, because "primordial" suggests past. Rather, it is something that is always present, always changing, and always in flow but not necessarily always in flux. Sometimes it is in flux and some parts of it are greater than other parts, but more specifically to the point, it is always in flow.

STRETCHING FROM THE TOTALITY AND BEYOND

Are all beings in all creations, ETs in this universe and other beings in all the other creations, aware of this reservoir of being and this place beyond it? Is it common knowledge?

It's not common knowledge because not all beings are interested nor are all cultures attached to knowing about such things.

But it's not a secret?

Correct; it's not a secret. But an individual or a group or a culture, for that matter, has to be interested to ask about that, yet there are so many other things to ask. Of course, people tend to explore their own culture first, and they might be perfectly satisfied to go no further. So what I'm saying is that it's not a secret, but it is not what I would call widely known strictly on the basis of the personal interests. Still, people might be able to ask different beings, as you do when channeling sometimes, questions that do not normally come up in the pursuit of their culture or their personal interests, and then they might obtain information that is new to them because they did not have an interest in it before. And they might pass it on. They might choose to pursue that, or they might say, "That's interesting," and get on with their lives, never pursuing it any further.

Is the space that you were residing in and that you talked to me from last time, where you had a cord out to your personality, is that what is known in our literature as Nirvana?

No. "Nirvana" is actually a word that attempts to describe a feeling through its sound. It has become quite confused in your time, and since "Nirvana" as a word does not translate very well into other languages, it has come to mean "pure thought" for many people. In fact, it represents a feeling in which sequential thought is actually not present. It also does not refer to what precedes thought, which would seem chaotic to you. Yet chaos, as they say, is always present, not in terms of its unhealthy or dramatic or unpleasant side effects but in terms of everything being present with no apparent sequence. This almost always is a precursor to any specific creation. I must say "almost always" because there is always a creator who wants to be different. But I would say that Nirvana really attempts to describe a feeling that is associated with the intellectual self because at the time this culture — now it has come to be considered a religion, but I prefer to think of it as a culture — was being formed (especially in a way in which written records were being kept), it was safer to explore, as a means of attaining inner peace, the intellect rather than the feelings. Feelings were, in those days, identified with passions, which were considered dangerous territory, and not unreasonably so, given that warriors, not lovers, were considered the most passionate beings. Therefore, the pursuit of intellect for its own sake was invariably considered much safer. That's the reason for that. But "Nirvana" describes a feeling.

All right, so you said you were in the space beyond the reservoir of being. Do other beings come and go from the totality in there and back out?

Occasionally they will come to that, and I'm calling it a space for the sake of reference, because I have to use enough terminology of your time, otherwise our discussion is entirely irrelevant not only to the reader but to you. So calling it a space, there are others who go there frequently. One might assume that beings go there to find out more about themselves or, as you have mentioned, to explore origins. But in the case of physically motivated beings or beings who are in any way engaged with the physical, most go there because they've overshot, as it were. They wanted to go somewhere, and they went a little past the point they wanted to go and had to go back; they overshot their objective. Sometimes they have a quick look around and say, "This isn't it," and then go to where they wanted to go, or they might go to this "space" because they need to remove themselves from any and all stimuli so that they can achieve an entirely clear totality of being. "Clear" in this sense means having no influences or motivations to create or pursue anything.

Why did you go there?

It's not so much that I went there; I've always been here. And I am more inclined to say that this is where I am, and when I'm in other places, I go there. But I'm stretching from this place.

Are there other beings stretching from that place?

There might be two or three others. I say "might be" because remember, "this place" and "this space" are analogies; it's not a place, and it's not a space, but those are the best terms I can use to create a sense of orientation for you. There is one that is only occasionally present, meaning the being is rooted here, but the bulk of him/her/it is almost always elsewhere. There is another who is rooted here and is present here with enough of its being to — how can we say? — make a mark at least half the time, and then there is another one who is mostly present here and only partly elsewhere.

THE TOTALITY IS CONSTANT
BUT CAN CHANGE

In the sense that everything is all one, other than that, are these beings part of you? Or are they what you would consider as separate from you?

Nothing is separate from anything else. They are a part of me, yet if you were to be able to observe within the context of space and time, you would see them as being separate. In fact, they're not. Nothing is separate from anything. That's part of the reason that everything's always in motion. Think about that. If nothing is separate from anything and you were some specific thing, wouldn't you want to explore? If kinetic motion were part of your makeup, you'd want to go somewhere. If kinetic motion were not part of your makeup, you would want to feel other things. In short, motion is natural even when there is no apparent physical motion.

Have we ever heard of those other three beings? Has anyone in the totality ever heard of them? They don't do anything that we would know about?

Oh, I wouldn't say they don't do anything, but no one in the totality of which you Earth humans exist, in this context, is likely to ever be affected by or a portion of or in any way associated with them — not likely at all — which is why they haven't come up. They're doing other things in other places. It is more likely that human beings in some form (including as you become a creator as the Explorer Race) are more likely to become aware of me in one of my many guises — not that I am some great deity but rather that I am a humble teacher.

If everything always is, even within that, then there are cycles. There was a time when there was no totality, and now there is one.

There was always the totality. Let's put it this way: Imagine there is a tree. You cut the tree down, leaving the stump, and you split the wood and stack it all around where the tree was. Granted, the tree is not a living tree anymore, although the root system is still intact and it might be able to sprout a sapling at some point and re-create itself in some form, as you've perhaps seen trees do in the forest. Yet the totality of the mass that made up the tree is still present because you've stacked the wood all around where the tree was. In short, the totality is always present even though the form might change.

OTHER EXPRESSIONS OF THE TOTALITY

All right. So can we say that there was a totality, it went back into the space where you are, and then it got bored and showed up again as this unexpressed need, sprouting again? Can you say that? Are there cycles of manifesting and unmanifesting?

No. What you can say is very much the way Ssjoooo said it: Ssjoooo and the rest of itself felt, after some consideration — "What is this? We don't recognize it," and so on — able to define it as a need. That's exactly what it was. It was like this. If the totality exists and is in constant motion, then different parts of the totality feel other parts, some parts move to other parts, some parts are simply aware of other parts, and so on. There is also the stuff that can make up, as in our analogy, a tree. In terms of personalizing the totality, one has made up many things before in the totality but has never made up the multiuniverses that you now consider as the totality. One might wish to make it up at some point and therefore might find a way to make it up. That might sound obscure to even a being such as Ssjoooo. This is, from Ssjoooo's point of view, an obscure means to prompt a totality, for it was not Ssjoooo's intention to create a totality at all but rather to create something other than itself that could deal with this need. That's all. It wasn't to say, "Well, let's begin something." It was, "Well, I don't really know what to do with this, so let's create this, and then it can do it." [Chuckles.] And that was really it. So it was more the totality's desire to express itself in a way that it had not done before. It was not really a cycle so much as the ongoing interest of definition and redefinition designed to produce something that had heretofore been an unknown expression, similar to when a baby is born. In the beginning, the parent sees only fixed expressions, but then one day the parent comes in and is talking to the baby, and the baby breaks into that first sparkling-eyed smile, which just lights up the whole room not only for the baby but for the parents as well. It's something new for the baby, this feeling of smiling.

I wish I had a camera for that one.

This feeling of smiling is scintillating in its full experience: The baby enjoys the experience, and the parents, of course, are ecstatic. So it is not unlike that. It was an expression heretofore not experienced or not defined in just that way. Maybe there had been universes before but not that way. So it really prompts a question, doesn't it? If there had been universes before, what was the point in creating universes again?

Let's talk about the totality as if it were thinking, "How can we create universes in a way that's more fun?" Then someone contributes, "Why don't we do it as a mystery? What is created will not surprise us, but the portions of us that are involved in the creation will have the joy of surprise or will experience things in some way that can increase the amplitude of joy (joy is omnipresent)." But how can we make joy *more*? We can make joy more by having some level of ignorance, even in so-called advanced societies (as you might call ET cultures). From the totality's point of view, to create joy that would be more wonderful, we have to create either the lack of joy — and the totality says, "No, no, no, can't do that" — or we must add mystery and enigma so that joy can be discovered. In the moment of the discovery of joy, such as the baby's first smile in our example, that joy is powerful and is experienced again but never quite with that same scintillating, fascinating, first-time experience. However, it will be experienced that way by other personalized beings. "Oh, yes, yes," says the totality, "let's do that!" So even in so-called advanced cultures (from your perspective), beings would still have that joy as a potential in other creations or in this creation or on other planets. Not all of them choose to have that, but many of them do because it's a way of experiencing joy — at least one time as a personalized being — that they can, in those societies, remember forever and ask each other, "Do you remember?"

"Do you remember the first time you had that wonderful feeling of joy?"

"Oh, fantastic! Oh yes, I've had joy since, but never anything quite so fabulous as that!"

Okay, but those are different expressions of the self; as you say, there's only one, so there's only one in the totality and where you are and in the reservoir of being. Could you say that ultimately we are all part of some one thing?

Granted, it's a poor way of saying it. You understand that what prompts you, especially in the past, to pursue something is when I or any of many beings talk to you, saying that you're all one (because your society uses digits), the natural assumption, especially in mathematics, is that something must precede one, and that "something" must be the parts that make up the one. Or when you do the mathematics, you might say, "Well, there's negative one, then there's zero, and then there's one, and certainly, there's two and three." So it is a bit awkward to say you are all this, meaning essentially of the circle of life; you are all part of the bowl of soup and so on. "One" has been used and perhaps overused. You are all complete and individual, just as every particle that makes up your body is part of you and also has its own personality and its own unique being. To honor science here for a moment, I'm including the particles that make up the particles.

Yes. All right, so you, as who you are, have seen other expressions of the one?

Yes. Other than what you now understand as the totality.

Many, many, many?

Many, many, many. You have to think about it: In the totality I'm talking about, it would probably explore billions, trillions, and even more ways of expressing itself. Then only after all of that has been done (at least to the point of looking strikingly similar every time) would the idea of mystery look attractive because it would introduce the element of ignorance, which would be entirely foreign to the totality in any other way than as a portion of its makeup.

You might say that in the totality there is one particle of ignorance (because everything exists), but the totality does not choose to express itself as ignorance except in one time when it chose to express that one thing. Then everyone quickly discovered that it was completely impractical, but one says ("one" meaning the totality, and they don't really think. But for the sake of the analogy, we'll discuss it that way), "Well, even though it didn't work out as a complete expression, it might be worth trying as a spice or as a small portion. If it doesn't work out in a vast way, let's try it in a small way." And one will have gone through many other expressions, not just ignorance; one might have gone through insight or joy or rapture and happiness, and so on, and create a totality from each.

You now find yourself in the expression of the totality in which ignorance is being used, homeopathically speaking, in that small portion of itself to see whether anything new can be created and whether any new alignment (new to the totality) of one portion of itself with another portion of itself can be created. Now, I have to tell you that through experience (can't really say "over time") with all of these different expressions of the totality, there have been things that struck the totality as being new and different. Therefore, it would tend to pursue expressions of variations of that, and the totality's motivation in the current totality expression that you are experiencing is largely to see whether some new alignment between the portions of itself and the other portions of itself can be created. That's the motivation. But it is not an obsessive motivation. It is not, "Well, this is what we want, and this is what we're going for." That's not it. You might want to bake cakes, and one time, you add three teaspoons — make a big cake — of vanilla. The next time, you add two-and-a-half teaspoons. The cake is still vanilla flavored, but it's not quite as significant. Or maybe you shave a little ginger into it.

Are you saying the variations in the expressions of the totality can be that minute?

Yes. And the totality is not looking to change things for the sake of change but to enjoy change if the change is enjoyable. Again, there's that full circle of expression, but it is natural, when speaking about the totality, to express it in spherical terminology when using the intellectual space-time sequence.

Well! That's very good. You got all frustrated trying to do it, but now you just did it magnificently!

Thank you.

Is there any possibility that you and the other three beings and the totality are like the All That Is, and that this is all that you are aware of?

Well, there are always possibilities. We can never say absolutely not, although I've done that, from time to time, just to send your curiosity in different directions. But I would be — how can we say? — turning a blind eye to possibilities with intent if I were to say that this is all there is. But from my perception …

Eternally, forever, a billion expressions of the totality, and you've looked, right?

Yes, to the seventh power and beyond, and I have not noticed anything else. This does not mean that it doesn't exist, but I have not noticed anything else, nor am I aware of anything else.

Then you said Ssjoooo had always been, as all beings have always been, but he had always been in that place, so he must have seen other totalities come and go?

Oh, yes.

Oh, but this is the first one he inadvertently started?

Yes, this is the first one that Ssjoooo was instrumental in actually setting off. It would be like rolling a snowball down the hill, and the moment you push it, you turn your back and go on to do something else, not really noticing that the snowball gets larger and larger and more complex on the way down.

I understand. What am I trying to imply? Some kind of a personal relationship, but not really, because everybody in the totality has known everybody forever.

Yes. Think about it as your brain. Think about all the neurons in your brain working together so marvelously to allow the brain to function. You can assume that these neurons know each other very well. What a marvelous team they are! To work so well, each must intimately know what all the others are doing so that it doesn't have to do those things, but all are bonded together as a team to pursue and express and apply themselves as a human brain so that it can do all that it must do for that human and beyond. And of course, there are the particles that make it up and the synapses and all that business. So you might, as part of the totality of being, be very happy that some other portion of the totality is doing something that you do not find personally attractive but that they do because they're doing it. As Robert likes to say in his standard joke (he has incorporated this whole thing into his personality), "Well, I'm glad you're doing that because then I don't have to." It's very much the same, which is intended to be a joke but is also intended to prompt the idea that each person does not have to do everything even though he or she might have the capacity to do it. He or she might not have a personal interest in doing that other thing.

MOVING OUTSIDE THE TOTALITY

Ssjoooo must have known you in past times, or is this the first time? He said he only became aware of you when you left.

Yes, and that is not surprising. Think about it. It is not normal for any portion of the totality to leave, all right?

Where would they go? [Laughs.]

That's right. Where would you go? But in moving outside of the totality, one is not usually entirely outside; one would normally have a cord to the totality so that the totality does not become disrupted by the loss of a portion of itself. It wouldn't create pain for the totality to lose a portion of itself. However, when you bump or scrape yourself, you have pain if a piece of you is lost, even a piece of skin, and it would bring your attention to it. But even after the pain is no longer present, you might wish to have that piece of skin back, because even though your body grows scar tissue, it's never quite the same. There would be a sense of at least temporary loss. In my case, I am actually reaching into the totality from outside of it.

Nevertheless, from the totality's point of view, I had been involved with the totality from its point of awareness of itself. In short, the totality was always present, but (this is really the answer to your initial question) it wasn't conscious of its presence before it experienced personality. Remember, the totality was constantly experiencing different ways to express itself not just because that's natural for any being to express itself in different ways but also because it was looking for — not searching, but looking for — things that it might enjoy.

A baby sucks its toes, which is not something an adult can do, but it is something you've all done as babies (well, most of you). The baby goes through different things until it discovers certain things it likes. It likes to smile, it likes to be held, and so on. The totality discovered an expression of itself that it really enjoyed, and that was the expression of itself as personality, meaning that each portion of itself had its own, unique personality. The totality loved that and said, "Oh, let's embrace that!" The totality could, at some point (if it chose to), drop that because it wasn't always that way. So before the totality began to experience itself as personality and then, very quickly, as different portions of itself or different facets of that personality, I was — how can you say? — not connected all the time to the totality. Shortly before it started expressing itself in personality, I made my connection. So when the totality in some form or facet has communicated with you in the past (meaning in your time sequence, in this life), it has done so from the point of view of being able to say with equanimity and absolute truth that Zoosh has always been present. But you were speaking to the totality in your time, and it was in a faceted personality state. If you were speaking to the totality before it was that, it would probably have said, "Zoosh who? We don't know who you're talking about; we're not familiar with this being."

Is this a recent happening, or is this many, many, many expressions ago?

[Laughs.] That's a time question, even though it was carefully constructed. I don't know how to describe this; probably song is the best way to do it. See whether you can feel this. This is a song, and the answer is a song. You won't hear it completely, but you might get it. [Long pause.] Hmm, that was when [chuckles] … that will be lost on the reader, but …

It felt wonderful; it felt very joyous.

You are doing very well, given the difficulties and, yes, the limitations of being able to question under these circumstances. You are doing very well.

Oh, my goodness, such sweet words.

DISCOMFORT AND TOTALITY

When you said the Explorer Race karma was over, the loop of time was over. The Explorer Race had done at least once everything that could be done.

Yes, just that. That's correct, in the loop only. Everything that needed to be done in order to be thorough but just within the context of the loop.

To be able to become a creator?

Yes, to do everything that would be necessary to fulfill the required learning so that as a creator, all the parts would be present.

Now, look at the extraordinary effort! You must care incredibly deeply; you have put so much effort into the Explorer Race! You started with the Creator, and you've been here all this time. You care deeply about the possibility that there will be an expansion of potential for all beings.

Yes. I felt it warranted a pursuit — not unlike the question you asked before, and I had to tell you that I could not swear that there wasn't anything beyond myself. I felt, as you feel, that if there might be more, it would be worth pursuing by any means necessary, as long as care was taken not to create the totality into something for which suffering became a predominant issue. If some sense of suffering was experienced as a focus or a motivator, it's a learning experience. For example, when you stub your toe, it hurts for a while, and then you might say, "I had better put my shoes on, and that won't happen." If suffering can be used that way and the souls are cleansed at some point later on so that the suffering does not permanently impact their personalities, it might be worth exploring, even though it would be an extreme attempt to find out whether more is possible. So I'm not saying that I created suffering but rather that, from my point of view, it could be allowed as long as there was that built-in safety mechanism.

So did this idea originate from you, then? Or from a need for the totality to become more?

Not a need so much as an exploration. You might say that because the totality could say, "Well, we have explored these different things, and look how much happier we are now that we have personality," it could also say, "Maybe there's something else that will cause us to be happier yet!" In short, once you've discovered that you're better off by something that you do, at least in your own understanding of yourself, you might be inclined to continue that process even to the point of flirting with discomfort. I'm calling it "flirtation" because it's localized, meaning the vast majority of beings in your universe do not experience discomfort.

Discomfort is localized in a small area where it can be isolated and kept from spreading. Souls who choose to be born in that area go in to experience that with full knowledge and permission before life. Of course, in deep sleep during life, all of that suffering will be expunged at some point, and the soul will feel better so that it does not have to cart the dregs of that suffering around indefinitely. A soul goes in knowing that, so from the soul's perspective before life, it sees the suffering has a purpose even though there is some concern about experiencing it. For instance, in a train or car or plane accident, or something like that, the first beings on the scene are the angelic beings. They bring not only the means to help the souls get to where they're going when they are at the end of their cycles but also the energy of their being to help those who survive. Say a plane crashes. There are a few survivors, and those survivors are suffering terribly. The victims' suffering is somewhat soothed, even though they may not know that, by the profound omnipresence of the angelic beings, meaning the pain might have been significantly worse were the angelic beings not present. This is not to suggest that they are not suffering terribly but that the angelic beings are expressing greater energy than is necessary to escort souls beyond the Earth plane they know.

This is a very small aside: Are there angelic beings in every creation?

Yes, but you might not experience them as angelic beings. They might just seem like other beings that you're totally used to.

Do we experience them because of our need here on Earth?

Well, you experience them because you are cut off from what everybody else is connected to, as you must have ignorance in order to do what you're doing here, and you must be isolated because of the discomfort that is here.

But there are times — not only at the point of death but also at the point of birth and even at times during life — when a person might experience angelic beings out of necessity. On another planet where there is no discomfort, you might not see angelic beings glowing with gold and white light. You might not see that at all. You might just experience them as another being: "Nice to see you. How are you? Looking forward to seeing you again." On Earth, they are seen emanating that light because they are bringing with them that which is typical in other places. They are bringing it almost like bringing a light into a dark room. Humans see that and experience the effect of it because of where you are, not because of what angelic beings are.

Okay, that's very good.

THE TOTALITY AND GROWTH
You touched on something that has sparked a thought. Is the totality itself growing? It was not aware of itself and now it is?

No, no. It was aware of itself and has always been aware of itself, but you have to stretch a bit. You can be aware of yourself and not have personality. It was the expression, the embrace of personality as part of one's being on the total level and then experiencing it as different facets, as feeling people or feeling a sense of individuality. So two things have been embraced so far, and I might mention other things at some point, but we can isolate two things: The first is individuality, and the second is personality. The totality was once strictly amorphous. Then it discovered individuality so that it could be all one being and individuals. Then it discovered personality, which was a way to define individuality further and still be part of a total being. So this is why the totality is inclined to experience itself in different ways: It has discovered things that it is enjoying. So it continues to move and to express itself in different ways. Another way to say that is to be in motion.

That also implies that there might be other implicit aspects that it hasn't discovered yet?

That's right! That's right, and that's why it's inclined to be in motion, just like the scientist who is attempting to look at the atom and discovers to his or her joy and shock and disappointment, all in the same moment, that particles make up the atom. It's exciting and wonderful, but the scientist is also disappointed because he or she doesn't have an instrument to examine those particles. Yet if the scientist could examine those particles, he or she would notice that they are coming and going and are not a fixed portion of that atom. You can identify the idea that atoms come and go in things.

Well, they go into physicality and out ...

That's right, into a specific expression of physicality and then on through, and then they are gone. And at the same moment, the particles that make up that atomic structure and, infinitely, the particles that make up those particles and so on are also in motion, not fixed portions of anything. In short, nothing is a fixed portion of anything else; it is always in motion all the time not because it's looking for something but because the joy of being is always in motion. Joy isn't motion, but being is motion.

That's good. I made an incredible insight recently. I realized that I never learned the joy of motion. To me, motion was work and to be resented. It was an amazing insight. I learned, and I started moving.

Well done. It's quite startling when you are raised a certain way, and the motion of play is taken away, and you no longer experience the joy of being a child. The recollection is more of a moment of loss; and then the identification, of course, as you realized yourself, is that motion represents work, which really represents pain and suffering. And you discover that motion can also be fun.

Chapter 18

The Dynamics of the Totality

Zoosh

September 12, 2000

All right, Zoosh speaking. Greetings.

Welcome! Let's discuss the dynamics of the totality. Do the citizens of the totality harvest the experience and use it in the next round of manifestation? Do they learn from each experience?

I would say yes. It isn't always learning, though, in the sense of "Aha!" It's more of what I would call reflection: You know many things, but you've never put certain things together in the same way. So it would be like a subtle change in the flavor of a soup, for instance. This basic soup would be the same, but now you've added a new subtle, not distinct, flavor, and perhaps it makes for a more complete package. That's the way I'd prefer to define it rather than saying that it's something entirely new.

Do individual immortal personalities remember what they did from the time before?

From all times. There is no blocked memory whatsoever.

So the totality manifests and it flows back into the unmanifest, and then it manifests again. Like that?

That's too sequential. I recognize you're giving an example, but it's always present. It's a constant.

FEELING IS OMNIPRESENT

Is consciousness always present whether or not you're expressing a form?

Consciousness and feeling. Understand that consciousness does not precede feeling. First there is feeling, and consciousness might or might not follow. This is a general rule, in my understanding, that consciousness as you understand consciousness to be is not a given; it is a choice. First there is feeling, meaning feeling is at the foundation, and consciousness can be built on that, but that is not always the case. Certain beings do not have consciousness as you understand it. The reason I'm splitting hairs here is that consciousness in your civilization and culture, at your time, is really a discussion or a definition, depending on one's communication at that moment, that has to do with whether the mental is aware of itself or even unaware of itself. Mental is always built on feeling, and it is always that portion of one's total individual being or, for that matter, one's total mass being, of all beings. It is always, in the case of the mental self, searching for something new.

This is a hint, but I will go on to explain it without you having to reach for it. This tells you that one of the ways — not the only way, but one of the ways — that the totality of being would reach for something new would be through the use of mentality because mentality is exclusive. This is why over the years, psychologists and psychological researchers have chosen to break mentality down into facets (conscious, subconscious, and so on): They recognize clearly that not all mental things are readily available all the time.

So the difference between feeling and mentality is that foundational feelings, such as love (which is a feeling that you can identify in your physical body right now), are constant, whereas thought ebbs and flows. You think about "this," and you think about "that." Furthermore, there are things going on in your thought process that you're not aware of all the time, though you might become aware of them at different times. This tells you that consciousness on the mental level is exclusive. You know it, or you don't know it. You're aware of it, or you're not aware of it. You encounter all those possibilities and more, whereas feeling is a constant. You might have different feelings that come and go, but you always have at least one feeling. You might be in a different feeling; maybe you'll have anger in one moment or joy or love or combinations of feelings, but one thing you always have as a human being is at least one feeling at all times. You don't have that in the mental self; you don't always have one thought all the time.

Does that extrapolate to the immortal beings that we are when we're not human?

Insofar as extrapolation, it is going the other way: from the totality to the human being. The feeling is omnipresent; it's always there. They don't utilize thought as a means of being; they utilize thought only as a means of finding something that might be new and different to them. I will give you an example of that.

You speak the English language, which in your time has a vast number of words. I'd say at least half, maybe more, of the words in the English language in your time are, in their root forms, culled either from other languages or from technologies or specific applications of different mental pursuits. But suppose you learn another language — perhaps French or German, to speak of European languages, or perhaps Afrikaans or some other language. As you begin to learn that language, you would say the words and think about the English translations, but eventually, when you become more fluent in that language, you think in it and sing in it, and all of this. When you do that, you not only have words that are equivalent to words in your first language but also that cover feeling. When you examine languages that are more ancient than English, you very often find that those languages are meshed more with feeling than with thought. English, being a modern compilation of other languages, is one of the few languages that makes every effort to disenfranchise itself from feeling. The older languages are completely engaged with feeling.

He has his hands, fingers, completely overlapped.

Yes. So if you had to learn one of the older languages, you would find that the way you think/feel — in short, experience life — through that language would be different. There would be different nuances. There might be more heart and feeling involved in the way you think. You would be in somebody else's shoes entirely, and as a result, you would probably find that some things that are difficult to do now would be easy, and some things that are easy to do now would be hard. This is part of the reason that when people from different countries get together, there is not always a language difficulty or a cultural challenge (which sometimes adds spice that is good and fun), but there is an entire way of being that is so foreign from one to another. So what I'm suggesting here, using your contemporary cultures as an analogy, is that the totality will use something foreign to its normal way of being because it is in the use of something foreign that something new might be found or understood in a different way.

THE RIBBON WITH GAPS

So in that sense, the Explorer Race is something foreign?

It is foreign in the sense that the cycle of souls are not traveling on the usual route where one might reach out and explore a series of lives on a given theme or two. This is something with an agenda that is not typical of the cycle of lives. It's different entirely in that the agenda is specific. You mix certain ingredients to create an effect and a creator who will create more effects. You normally find that you might start out in some ways as a creator, have certain creator potentials and possibilities and even applications, and then might try a cycle of lives through a creator's definition, meaning you come into a universe, and that creator forms you, in the case of the seeds and so on that come in, with

the original Explorer Race seeds. But it is not usual to then re-form within that universe to become a creator, especially to take over somebody else's creation. In short, the Explorer Race was founded through the means of the *foreign* application. It was thought based on feeling with gaps. Remember, I said when the Creator of this universe was moseying about, It saw this ribbon, but there were gaps in the ribbon. Some of the gaps were for the Creator to fill in, but some of the gaps were there simply because those who had the original vision of the totality didn't have it all. And all the beings who put bits and pieces into it didn't have it all. Much was left, and that was part of the appeal to the Creator.
He could make it in his own vision.

That's right. The Creator could say, "Well, let's do it like this." In short, it wasn't a fait accompli. It wasn't saying, "Here it is; reproduce it." It was, "Here are some of the parts. What do you want to do with them?"
What were some of the gaps?

One of the main gaps was the way things would look, meaning what form they would take. That was a huge gap; that wasn't in there at all.
Everything? The universe, the beings, Earth?

That's right. None of that was in there. Instead, there was the potential, the intent, and the basic mechanics, as you understand them: sensory, physical, mental (meaning the idea of including mental), and spirit of course.
And the ignorance?

No, I think the ignorance was only there in a nucleus, meaning that it would be considered a possibility, as in, "Here's something for your consideration, but it's not a requirement." So the Creator had to choose to do that or not.
You've always been with the Creator; you've been with It since Its inception.

Yes.
You went through the tube with Him, so you have been sort of forming Him to your ... you've been putting your stamp ...

No, I'm not putting my stamp of influence on the Creator.
No, but you've been sort of feeding Him things that you thought would work, you and the other friends of the creators, right?

Yes, I like to think of myself as being more of a pal of the Creator rather than trying to mold the Creator.
Yes, but you were there to make sure He didn't go back also?

Well, I was there to help sustain the Explorer Race agenda — not to make it happen in a given timeline, but to sustain it as something worth doing when Creator felt like this was the time or this was the moment.

THE CANVAS OF CREATION
All right. The shutting down, the going into rest, the going into unmanifestation, when

there isn't anything out there active, physical, what triggers that? Everybody says, "Well, I've had enough. I'm tired. I've learned all I can." When Ssjoooo looked out there and there wasn't anything, he just felt a need — the unexpressed need from what had been manifest before, I'm assuming. So sometimes you can see out there the totality that's all creation and then sometimes you rest? Sometimes everybody rests, right?

No. There is never what you call rest; there is always motion.

Okay, but motion without form? Motion without manifestation?

There is no such thing as no form and no manifestation. Just because you can't see it where you are doesn't mean that it isn't tangible or seeable somewhere else.

Right now, if you look, there's this big throbbing everything, billions and billions of creations, trillions, whatever ...

Beyond your capacity to count and perhaps that's just as well.

Okay, and before, when you said that Ssjoooo inadvertently started another round, there wasn't anything there. So we were all still feeling and moving, but not ... not what?

I can't say there wasn't anything there. There wasn't anything there that Ssjoooo perceived. This doesn't make Ssjoooo a lesser being; Ssjoooo is a profound being. Yet if feeling was there being radiated, the feeling represented a need for that space within certain parameters. Space is a canvas, as the artist might say. You cannot have space without something being there; the space itself is there.

Okay, the space itself is the canvas, but at that moment, there was nothing painted on it, right?

There was nothing other than feeling. The constant feeling of love is the embroidery and also the material, the fabric. From love, Ssjoooo then felt something else, and that was need. And that suggests love may have motivations of its own. Love felt that it would like to experience variety, meaning more. It wasn't missing it; it just wanted to do that.

Ssjoooo felt the love that was in that space radiating that need, but it wasn't an urgent need. Still, the feeling that Ssjoooo felt was, over experience or over time, cumulative. By the time Ssjoooo did something, the feeling had built up so that Ssjoooo felt it more prominently than was actually being stimulated by love. Let's say you were pulling KP [kitchen patrol] duty, and you're peeling potatoes. You had an inexhaustible amount of energy, and the potatoes would never rot. As you peeled each potato, you dropped it into a bin. After a while, the potatoes overflowed. Even though you were only peeling one potato every five minutes, after a while there would be potatoes everywhere. This doesn't mean that you'd have a physical energy of those potatoes pushing on something. Ssjoooo didn't feel like he was being buried under potatoes. But the cumulative effect of that gentle need affected Ssjoooo so that Ssjoooo could not ignore it.

Because there was no one else to do anything, Ssjoooo was it. It was up to Ssjoooo to do something in hopes of altering that feeling — either to bring that feeling back to its original constant of love or just to see what would happen —

and specifically note whether Ssjoooo felt the need anymore, or it didn't go back to feeling that constant of love anymore. But Ssjoooo no longer felt the need; therefore, Ssjoooo felt that it had done the right thing. It could feel the love; the love didn't go away. The love was a constant of everything else, but the need went away.

When it came time to create creators, he knew exactly how to create creators, because he had seen creators out there a million times, right?

Sometimes you do something that you don't know that you know how to do.

He had a model for creators.

He had a model, yes, but he didn't ever think of himself as a maker of creators. He'd never done it before, nor had he been motivated to do it. "He," in this sense, is just for a means of vernacular. There's no "he" or "she." It's used for the sake of cultural language denomination. Ssjoooo did this because it was, as you might say, worth a try. If from Ssjoooo's point of view, it didn't immediately change the feeling of need to being less (or at least significantly less pressing), Ssjoooo probably would have said, "That's not it," uncreated the Creator, and tried something else. But it did have the effect of immediately dropping the need to almost nothing, and the love was there with just a slight taste of need. Probably what Ssjoooo felt in that slight spice of need was the need message directed then to that Creator.

NEED PROMPTS CHANGE

Is it relevant to ask who those creators are, or does that matter?

I don't think it's really important at this stage.

But what I'm getting at is in that space out there composed of love, certainly he had turned around and seen the totality manifest before or creating before or out there before, right?

You'd have to ask Ssjoooo that.

You had seen that out there before, right?

From my perspective, I'd seen it. Remember, I'm outside of it. I can extend to it.

Right. What I'm trying to get at is that the totality had many, many, many, many, many lives before, right?

Expressions of itself. We don't want to put it into the reincarnation cycle, because it isn't that.

I'm trying to get at the manifest/unmanifest. Sometimes it manifests as something other than love and sometimes is experiencing an expression of love without form. You said there's always form, but without ...

There's always love.

Yes. But sometimes there is drama or activity, and sometimes there's not. How would you say it?

There's never drama. Drama appeals to the human being because it is a means to exert the influence of change when the human being is either bored or needs to change something for some value purpose. Drama in its own right does not appeal off to this school.

I'm looking for words that say sometimes there's a thing, and sometimes there's not. There's manifest and unmanifest; there's expression in form that we could see or not. There's rounds of experience and then not.

Picture a crystal that is slowly turning; there are different lights in the room, and as the crystal turns very slowly, one sees the lights reflected in the crystal in slightly different ways. That's an analogy.

What causes the change from one state to the other?

Need! If you were some massive thing, and you could continue to experience what you were indefinitely because that was wonderful, you would never need to change it. Of course, being this massive thing, there would be parts of you that would like to experience more, if more were *benevolently* available.

Because those parts were loved by the other parts — just as those parts loved all the other parts and everybody loved each other — those parts would, from time to time, be indulged and would exude need. If the need became sufficiently recognized in the totality, then the totality would say, "Okay." Obviously it doesn't think like that, but for the sake of human analogy, it would say, "Okay, let's do something along those lines."

The "let's do" of this totality is variety and more, which is …

Of the expression here in this universe? There isn't any "this totality"; there's the totality, period.

I'm probing because I can't get a clear picture of it, you know. My mind wants to see something. There's a house there, and then it's not there [chuckles]; there's something here, and then it's not.

Say you're in Oak Creek Canyon [near Sedona, Arizona], and you're sitting on a rock looking at the creek. If the creek is clear, you might see the rocks below the surface of the water, some fish swimming around, little bits of debris floating downstream, and reflections on the surface — not only the fixed reflection of what is there in the area, but also reflections of birds and butterflies and other people as they go by. In short, you see a constant change, to say nothing of the way the light glitters off the water. All of these different things are going on at the same time. Now, say a butterfly flies by but you don't look up at the butterfly; you see only the butterfly's reflection in the water. Once the butterfly has gone by and you do not see the butterfly's reflection in the water anymore, does the water have a memory of that butterfly's reflection? Yes, it does. This gives you a better idea of what it is for the totality: Just because you don't see it, doesn't mean it isn't there.

SSJOOOo WAS CHOSEN TO ACT

Why wasn't Ssjoooo allowed to go into the reservoir of being? Why was he, in your words, "spit back out"? Why is he out there and you're in there?

Ssjoooo was intended to do something. Let's say that it wasn't Ssjoooo; it was somebody else in that position. Another being might have felt that need and simply accepted it as some thing: "Oh, well, this is another thing that happens to exist here." Another being might have simply been able to accept the love (naturally) and the feeling of need, and say, "Oh, well, that's a different feeling. That's nice." Ssjoooo was picked to be there because it was understood, as one understands the parts of one's self, that Ssjoooo would act. It wouldn't just say, "Oh, there's need; what is it?" Or, "Oh, there's need; that's interesting." Ssjoooo would do something, especially as the feeling accumulated. The feeling wouldn't have accumulated with everybody, but it did with Ssjoooo.

So it was understood that Ssjoooo would do something about it; it wouldn't just be there and do nothing or accept it. Ssjoooo would react. Ssjoooo is the sort of being who, after an accumulation of stimulation, let's say, will react in one way or another to serve the stimulation according to Ssjoooo's best understanding of how it can be served. In short, Ssjoooo will respond and is more likely to respond in that manner, meaning it will not have a knee-jerk response the moment it feels something. It will, after an accumulation of stimulation when you might say it is certain that the message is directed toward itself, react. So Ssjoooo was specifically chosen because it would react, and the reaction would be in some benevolent and creative way.

All right, there's more, but we'll ask Ssjoooo at some point.

Well, you know the good thing about exploring this kind of issue in bits and pieces, not all at once, is that over time and life experience, for you as well as anybody else, you grow and change. You don't just ask the questions in a different way, but you assimilate the answers in a different way. So it's good not to go on and on and on about the same subject exhaustively.

HOW THE EXPLORER RACE ENTERED THE LOOP OF TIME

I want to switch topics and get it back down to the Explorer Race now. When you told us of the loop of time, you were into enigmas and said you couldn't tell us too much and things like that. If we're a million years back from the Zetas, then we either came here a million years ago, or we were inserted a million years back in time.

Inserted.

Inserted. You have only talked about the past 5,000 years.

Well, that's what's relevant to you. You could explore in detail things that happened, say, 10,000 or 15,000 years ago, but it would do a couple things. One

I consider as not good. The main hazard is that the chances of it's distracting you are profoundly high, about a 90 percent chance. And I don't mean just you, the questioner, but also the reader, the mass audience. I think that would be a mistake because distraction, while it might be interesting and fascinating, almost invariably leads you back to where you were, albeit either more enlightened or more cynical. Then when you continue on from where you were, it can be to your advantage if you're more enlightened; however, if you are more cynical, you might not continue on at all — you'd just stop. In short, I feel the risk of stopping is too great. That's why I haven't paid much attention to what went on before your readily available and useful written history. Even though you can go back further than 5,000 years with usable written history, it is generally accepted that approximately 5,000 years' worth of written history is plenty.

All right. Then Earth was moved here from Sirius 65 million years ago, plus or minus a couple …

Plus or minus a couple of billion years. It doesn't really make any difference. That whole time chart, which I was loathe, I figure that it's just meaningless because you cannot measure the measurement of time when measurement has changed. An inch is this big today; what happens if an inch was larger in times gone by?

What I'm saying is that the measurement of time is relative to the culture's acceptance of how time can be utilized in its present. Time, then, can either collapse or expand, depending on what you're doing with it. This is why nowadays people say (and you've heard and experienced this), "You can do so much more in so much less time these days." What does that suggest? That time is collapsing. You can say something that happened 65 million years ago might have only happened a few million years ago if you measured the experiences, 65 million years' worth of experiences, by a previous form of measurement of time. Four hundred twenty years ago, time may have been measured differently in terms of experience. What could you do 420 years ago, when Speaks of Many Truths walked and talked, versus what you can do today in the same amount of time? That's why I'm trying to rend you away from any actual mental attachment.

Okay, but here's what I'm getting at. We have that in a book, 65 million years …

That's acceptable for the book. We need to (editorially speaking, here), bring the reader along bit by bit. We don't have to give the reader a fact, and then take the fact away promptly. But later on, not unlike mathematics, you learn algebra and calculus in high school so that when you learn quantum physics later, which might fly in the face of algebra or geometry, you are prepared to experience a more philosophical relationship to angles, measurements, and figures. That's what we're doing here with the reader, preparation.

This should be left in, left for the reader, not taken out.

No, don't leave it in. You can leave it in. All right, if this, whatever we're talking about, goes into a book of some sort, but in the far-flung future. I don't want it to come out for a minimum of five years, this statement.

Okay, deal. I don't understand the loop of time. I don't know when we got here, and I don't even know if we were sent here. For instance, maybe all of the Orion and Mars and all these experiences were on the way to the Zetas, and they're part of our history, but not when we came back to do it over again. In my mind, there was a sequence that led along here horizontally, to the Zetas. Then there was a step back, and there was a circle that went up and around and under and is coming back right before the Zetas. I don't know which of all the history, of the experiences that we've talked about, are in the horizontal line that led to the Zetas or in the circle of the loop of time in which we're trying to do it right, and I'd like to get clear about that.

I don't think it's too important (not to treat your question lightly); I don't think the Zetas are that much of a factor. The Zetas as they exist, insofar as they've interacted with your culture in the present, are in flux not just because they're changing in to their gold light bodies, and all this business, but they might change their past, which is a million years into your future in experiential time. From their point of view, it's a million years into their past, roughly, but actually, if we measured time using the formula I spoke of before, from their perspective it wouldn't be a million years. It would be fewer.

Now, I grant that in the initial contact between the Zetas and your culture in relatively recent times — we'll target it in 1947, even though they've been in and out of your culture lots before then, because it's a date of conscious contacts and people can remember that they were here, what they looked like, and how interesting they were — it would also have been a million Zeta years from the Zetas back to your time. But now Zetas know more about you after watching your civilization since then and about themselves, based on what they've been taught and what they are prepared to assimilate. Teachers were teaching them things that they just weren't prepared to assimilate. As you know, you have been taught things in these conversations that you weren't prepared to assimilate either, and the assimilation process works in a similar way between your two cultures.

Now they've assimilated that, so it's still a million years (give or take a year or two) from your time to their time, but what was once a million Zeta years coming back has changed entirely. It's no longer a million years. It is closer to — this may not sound like much of a difference, but it is a difference — 970,000 Zeta years. When you use time as a means for understanding the evolution in consciousness, understand that time is not the causal factor but a line on the side of the beaker, as in chemistry, that measures change.

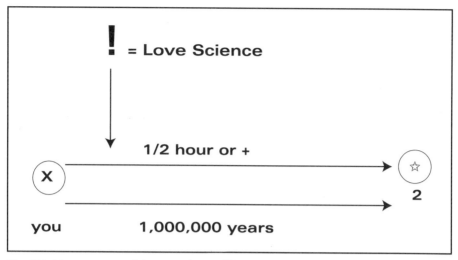

Fig. 17.1. Measurements of time can change. This image shows how Zeta years have changed over time as their assimilation of knowledge changed.

So the Zetas have assimilated enough understanding about their relationship between their culture and yours to be able to reduce the time from their perspective of connection in not only its measurement but also how it is experienced. Remember, for both cultures, this represents experiential years. Therefore, what might we suggest and extrapolate if they've changed their quantification? You're standing outside as the scientist, and you're looking at the way they are. They're now 970,000 years into the past, and they find you. Now there's a 30,000-year difference. While you're still a million years into the future, you find them. You might suggest or extrapolate from that, that this is going to build some kind of tension between your civilizations for you to be at both 970,000 years and 1 million years into the future. What's happening with those 30,000 years?

Is it like pulling us, then?

Yes. You might wonder whether this will create some bending or tension in time. Not necessarily. What might be a million years of experiential time for your culture to travel to some point might take no more than a half-hour for another culture. It depends on how they utilize time and how they apply it.

This isn't just a matter of quantification, such as instead of 365 days equaling a year, one day equals a year or 365,000 days equal a year. We're not talking about that. We're talking about the usage and application of time. Remember that this is a civilization that can travel in time; they are not rigidly attached to a timeline. A vehicle can travel in time based on the cooperative effort of every particle in the ship and the people on the ship. They don't go out to the mountains, dig the rock out, and build the ship regardless of what the rock says; everything cooperates. If that can happen at that level in their civilization and in their time, why couldn't it work for their whole planet? Why not for their solar system? Why not for their star system? Why not for their portion of their universe? If they can build a ship to do that, why can't their portion of the universe travel back in time as well? It can. Therefore, what could be a half-hour into the past for them because they are not living in fixed time might easily be a million years for you. But what happens when you have that heart technology? We need to change the concept of technology. It isn't just dreaming up new and fancier electronic instruments, because as you can see, electronics are now proceeding into organics.

MOVE TOWARD HEART SCIENCE

At some point the organics say, "No, thank you, I don't want to participate in this any more," and then the scientists say, "What's going on? Our machines aren't working." At some point the scientists have to go beyond head science to heart science and begin saying, "Would you like to participate, for your own reasons, in this mechanism that we're creating? We're not asking just so that you can perform a service for us. Would you like to do this for yourself? Would you enjoy it?" That's the key, not, "Would you like to help us out, here, buddy?" [Chuckles.]

So when this occurs, you'll find something very interesting: All science will begin to move over to heart science. This is also an explanation of why things are happening that you're not comfortable with, such as the use of fetal tissue for medical purposes, and it's easy to stand at a distance and say, "This is an outrage!" You do not say this because the fetal tissue might have become a baby; perhaps there was a natural miscarriage or something. But you say it is outrageous because you, as a citizen in good standing, are worried that women could be used as breeders for fetal tissue, as it were.

Animals too.

That's right. So you worry that such a thing could take place morally and under the value structure of honoring all life. Yet the reason that this is going on is not only to resolve the unresolved Atlantean lessons but that you all must move beyond the glamour of technology into the heart-centered space. In short, you must choose the heart-centered space for your own well-being and for the purposeful desire that others experience well-being too. One of the steps on the way is to discover, of course, that the well-being of others benevolently affects your own well-being. You have to think about that. So you have to go through all these steps. Some people won't like them, and I fully appreciate that, but it is intended to produce a desirable result. The main thing I want you to understand is that love science is what the Zetas are using to travel in time in their machines. When you discover love science, you will discover that what appears to be the same matter suddenly changes. When love science happens, bingo! The 1 million years can suddenly be anywhere from a half-hour to anything greater than that in time.

That's when we pop back up out of the loop of time?

Not necessarily. But it's important to understand that in science, love is the foundation. If you build science on love, then science is going to work for you and everybody else, including every particle of everything having to do with the application of love's uncountable facets in the application of a scientific project. That includes everything from a doorknob to the most complex computer. Let's keep it simple. If all the particles in that doorknob are happy being that doorknob, that doorknob will exist as that doorknob for as long as it's needed to be a doorknob. That means you could build a structure that could potentially last forever, and regardless of what it's exposed to, never be altered in the slightest measurable micron of its being unless alteration is desired by those who helped to bring about the shape of the doorknob in the first place.

PREPARING MOTHER EARTH FOR HUMANKIND

When we hear that the Native Americans and the indigenous tribes were brought here to prepare Mother Earth to receive humans, was that to receive the humans in this time loop?

No, it was really to prepare Mother Earth to receive humans at any time, meaning that Mother Earth would need to know how to respond to the needs of the human form, the human body, what it would need. This suggests that the first peoples brought here came with sufficient supplies to carry them over until Mother Earth could respond and readily assimilate the various things that a human being might require to survive. Of course, in the early days there was no consumption of meat or fish or anything — that evolved when the need arose — because Mother Earth was, by then, trained. Mother Earth does not have to be trained to know how to create. A parent gives birth to a child and doesn't need to learn how to give birth to the child, but she needs to know what to do and needs instructions to know what that child might need. So the midwife, uncles, and aunties, everybody tells her, "Oh, you have to do 'this,' you have to do 'that.'" In short, Mother Earth needed to know what to make available. And that's why Native Americans were there first.

I know, but I don't know whether they've been here that long. Did humans cycle through Earth on the first sequence of time to the point where they came back in time, or only the coming back in time?

I cannot now give you quantification in terms of years for what you're asking in that question, even though it may not be obvious to you, any more than I could give it to you before in any other way than as an arbitrary number. The problem with arbitrary numbers is that you inevitably become attached to them as facts when they are not facts now and never were.

Okay, ignore the years. Did we live an existence on Earth moving toward that point in, I don't know, the sixth dimension or something when we made the wrong choice and we went on the loop, the circular loop of time?

No, you didn't live on Earth.

So Earth has only received those in the time loop?

That's right. Earth is a school for you to learn within the time loop, but before that, Earth was not involved in your education or your life at all.

So the school is only the time loop? The time loop is the school? Before that we were just flowing along in the sequence and discovered we made the wrong choice? As Zetas — to focus on the mental and eliminate feelings?

Well, the time loop is almost exclusively taking place for the Explorer Race on Earth; the only exception in terms of what is part of your physical reality, as you know it, is that some of you had some life sequences on Mars. Once you get to explore Mars and it becomes widely known, you'll discover that civilization under the surface of Mars is still accessible. It'll be an anthropologist's dream! And it will be so accessible that in some places you'll feel as if you walked into somebody's culture and habitation a minute after they walked out. You'll think, "Oh, they'll be right back!" And there will be a significant amount of writings that suggest these people are around somewhere. "Maybe we better back out of this space and give them a chance to come back."

Okay, so it's not that the Martians came to Earth; it's that the souls were on Mars, and later the same souls came to Earth.

That's right.

Thank you, thank you.

THE DANGERS OF CAUTIONARY TALES AND CLINGING TO PAIN

If Maldek, as several of you beings have said, is a myth, then what is the asteroid belt? The remnants of the previous Earth?

I still do not want to talk about that.

Well, there are a bunch of rocks out there, and they came from somewhere. Is Maldek a story that we were told?

It was a cautionary tale, It could still happen, even though it's in the past, which is why I'm not going into it too much. These books are largely historical. The more you all become attached to something as having happened — you know how human beings are. Because you are somewhat at loose ends here (not having the usual connection to your total self that you have other places), the human being often becomes rigidly attached to something that might not be true at all. If you become rigidly attached to it being true, you can make it happen. Because the times you're coming into now, especially from the past ten years to this point and beyond, continue to expand at an increasing rate and have to do with your generating and reassimilating your creative capacities, the chances of my elaborating about potential past disasters diminish at an increasing rate.

Okay, but there are rocks out there. We can't say where they're from?

Certainly I can say where they're from.

Where?

It's a past disaster that could still happen. When it was originally discussed by various other beings, it was always intended to be a cautionary tale: Don't repeat the mistakes of the past. I think that it has performed very well in that purpose. Whole educational departments are set up to dwell on the unhappiness of the past for various academic reasons; nevertheless, the tendency is to perpetuate that unhappiness in the present and perhaps, even worse, to screw down, as it were, into the foundations of those disasters as having happened. Yes, they happened in their own timeline, but as you change your timeline, as you change your consciousness, and as you embrace love's applications in all ways (including being a creator), why become attached to something that happened in the past when you can use your skills and abilities as a creator to uncreate it? If you become attached to it as a pain from the past, even as a cautionary tale, you can practically not avoid re-creating some echo of it in your present or future. Any responsible creator knows that discomforts of the past must be rooted only in the past, when they happened, not rerouted by the present. Otherwise, you will continue to cycle around that to resolve it. You've asked before, "How are pains of the past going to be resolved?" I, as well as other beings, am giving different ways over time, and one of the ways the resolution takes place is for you to cease embracing it as part of your now.

THE NEED FOR PATIENCE

What's one of the first experiences any child has here on Earth in any culture? One of the first experiences you have is you're thrilled to be alive in a physical body. It's a celebration, for the most part, in the early days. Then it gradually dawns on you that what you had taken to be a given — meaning a standard communication everywhere else — doesn't work here. You have to essentially not just give up what you've been doing, but you have to learn how to talk.

So there's this exultancy to be alive, and then you sort of shrink back and realize you have to plod through learning every word to communicate, to say nothing of the cultural mores and values and so on. I'm using this as an analogy. First you experience the celebration of your expression of life with the assumption that you are going to be able to be all that you are with all of your usual communication skills, all your capacity to see the usual beings around you regardless of their dimension, and so on, and you think, "I'm going to be able to have this life here! Isn't it wonderful!" But then much to your shock, you discover that that's not true, and over time as you become more assimilated into the culture, you basically forget how to communicate in that usual way, how to see these beings, and so on.

As for your question, first picture yourself in that way, in the exultancy of life. "Oh, this is wonderful! It's fabulous!" Then a teacher comes along and says, "By all means, enjoy that, and apply yourself to it."

Learning the new skills.

Learning anything. On this level, though, it's different. You can still have the exultancy of life, and you can still have what is normal and natural to you, but you must also put some of your energy into learning these new skills. "What?" says you, "Why can't I put 100 percent of my energy all the time into expanding ever further out, experiencing assimilating, discovering, and enjoying?" And the teacher says, "You can do that, but you need to put 3 percent of your energy into learning these specific things, which you might need to do at some point." So it's not what you learn; it's the inability to put 100 percent of yourself into what it is that you wanted to do. The lesson is not what you were being taught to learn; that wasn't it at all. You were being taught patience.

Lessons for patience come in the guise of many faces; they are not very often what they appear to be. Look beneath the face. One of the very first lessons any being or any personality that becomes a being in its own right, meaning a focused expression of personality, is something that's a given when it is in the totality. The given in the totality is patience, because it is there and part of everything else. You move out on your own (though you are still connected and still in the totality) to explore creating some understanding of individuality, since you are an individual in this life (or so you seem to be). Once you begin expressing yourself as an individual, you know you are love, but one of the very first things you must learn is patience. Otherwise, you will expect what you experience when you are fully engaged in the totality, which is to have everything you want and need in the same moment. So of course, when you're taught patience, you're being prepared for sequence.

Imagine yourself in the totality and a part of this mass thing. It's wonderful. Patience, love, joy, and everything else are givens, all right? And then you become focused on your individual personality. You don't actually spatially leave the totality, but I am saying that you leave it. When you come out, you don't experience what you experienced in the totality in the same way. Being focused in individuality requires you to apply what you experience in the totality on an individual basis. Even though you come out as love, which is the foundation, you need to experience what you know to be true, not mentally but as a practical reality. You need to experience it as an individual so that you don't blunder into some ghastly error. In short, you're taught the basics all over again but as an individual.

You're taught patience, and because you are focused in an individual expression, patience prepares you for sequence, whether your sequence is only a split second or beyond billions of years. Where there is sequence, there is the potential for time and space, among other things, and in time and space, if you don't have some patience, you're going to be miserable. Of course, sequence will teach you more time and space and patience on the basis of its expression, meaning as you live. So you must learn patience, and you must learn about time and space. You must learn whatever the chosen sequence is. Without patience, it can be wretched, and love really won't allow you to experience that. If you're having a wretched experience because you've chosen to run past patience, it'll jerk you right back into the totality. It won't allow that.

So here you are on Earth, part of the Explorer Race, wanting to put 100 percent of your total being into the exultancy of expanding as an individual and into discovering things, meaning you might paint the canvas, as compared to what's underneath and is the foundation of things in the totality, which can also know about things and experience things. As you emerge as an individual, you experience things in a different way, that is, from the individual perspective. It's not the way the totality might experience a painting, but the way you as your individual personality experiences that painting. You must have certain qualities, certain tools in the bag. If you don't have them, you'll be uncomfortable, and you'll be unhappy. There will be unhappiness for which, by the time you get around to learning patience, you would have already suffered unnecessarily from the perspective of the totality. So you snap back to the totality, and you either consider that for a while or start over again from the beginning, this time saying, "Oh, gee, I want to experience my joy of discovery at 100 percent, but, thank you very much, I will learn patience with 3 percent of my being."

Chapter 19

The Constant

Ssjoooo #2

September 14, 2000

Ssjoooo.

Ssjoooo, welcome!

You have not heard from me before. I am one of the other facets.

Oh, I'm delighted! I thought you said you were Ssjoooo.

That name is adequate for the entire being. You have assumed that the facet of personality that spoke to you named that facet only, but the name was intended to be a description of all thirteen facets, and it is a description that fits me as well. Though you will find similarities, I am not the same facet.

Well, I'm delighted that you're here. Are you open to questions?

Yes. To me, the totality is an ongoing thing. If you were to see a stone dropped in a pond, you would see the many ripples fan out and, after a while, fan back. You would associate the cause of the ripples and the ripples themselves as the same event: the dropping of the stone. For me, what I see, regardless of the ebb and flow, is the way the totality changes; I do not see it as something that is repetitive or recycling but rather one constant that changes its form.

How many times have you seen it change its form?

I cannot count that high. An analogy in human terms is this: If you could see the process, how many times would you have seen one skin cell drop off the surface of your body? You know that they do — science tells you that — and you know that it is a very high number indeed in a given life. Yet you are intact, meaning your life has been physically constant. You are reasonably intact. [Chuckles.] Cells are dropping away all the time, and you are changing, yet you see the totality of you as fairly constant. It is like that for me. The totality changes, but I do not consider the ebb and flow of the change to be something that is a complete cycle. In short, I do not see things in cycles but rather in a single action.

Let's assume there's been a lot of ebb and flow. You have always been there?

Yes. The reason I know this is that I do not have memory as you understand it. For you, memory at this point in your focus is something that has a linear cast to it even though when you do deeper recollections, they are recollections of actual events, and the references in those recollections have to do with things that have occurred, meaning they are in the past or beyond this life. So from my perspective, the constant of my memory is such that I cannot say when I began because I do not have any recollection of a point of origin.

When you can imagine your own being, you will discover something very similar. At one point, where you came from might have been described to you. It's true that you came from there, but we can trace that place that was there, that thing that you were a portion of before you emerged to experience individuality.

I cannot say where I'm from, and I cannot say when I became aware of myself. Rather, I can only say I have always been aware, and I am not aware of any point of origin other than everywhere I've been.

When the first Ssjoooo wanted to look for his creator, did all of you go through that point of light looking for your Creator?

We didn't go physically. You assume "going" means, "I need a glass of water, so I have to *go* to the sink to get one," but it isn't like that. We focused; we did not have to go anywhere. That term might have been used by the other facet to allow you to identity with it. If we use the terms constantly (that would be closer to what we actually do), it would be very difficult for you to feel any sense of affinity.

So we can say your focus shifted. But did you hear what Zoosh said, how wonderful it was that you weren't allowed to go in there, because your mission was to start this round of creation in the totality?

Yes, that is personally very adequate. It wasn't my desire to explore that particular focus, but it was acceptable to me that it was explored.

Well, I think that what Zoosh said was very complimentary. They knew they could trust you to do something.

Yes, it is in our nature to take action if we assume on the basis of having tried other things that that is the next reasonable step. But "reasonable" is a factor here. It is necessary to move toward what is reasonable on the basis of the exploration of all other things first, but that's a small point.

How did you feel when you created your real creator? You didn't know you could do that, right?

It would be as if you, as a child, bumped your hand on something and heard a sound. In short, it was simple, but it was a simple thing that we had never done before.

So it felt good?

It was adequate. You will have to accept that I may not wax enthusiastic; it is not my nature to do so.

What is your nature?

What you perceive so far.

What are your joys?

Existence.

You said it's your nature to take action. What actions do you take as you are there?

It is not unlike you. If you are sitting quietly doing something and it stimulates you, you might react in some way. We are the same.

What stimulates you?

We are stimulated by that feeling.

You're an unlimited being out there in infinite time. How do you feel about the need to look for your creator? Were you attached to that?

No. The facet you heard from was interested in doing that, several other facets accepted it, and the rest of us went along with the experience. But I am not motivated. Motivation requires an agenda. I might be more reactive, meaning I might be inclined to take action, whereas other facets might be more inclined to observe. In short, I can speak for the entirety to a point, but being my own facet, I (this will be difficult for you to discern the difference) might at times say that we are inclined to take action, whereas all the facets would not say that.

Well, say "I," then. Go ahead; there's no problem with saying "I."

It is not in my nature to say "I." I will, perhaps, be able to say it at some point, but it is not comfortable at the moment.

You've never done this before, talked through a channel?

Never.

I'm so glad that you did this.

BEYOND DISENTANGLEMENT

All right. You're part of the totality, yet you seem to be able to be separate from it.

I am a portion of it, of course, and I do not go about my business while the totality goes about its business. Imagine for a moment that you could attach a cord consciously from yourself to your point of physical origin or even your pleasant memories. Think of the pleasant memories that come to mind (there are others you cannot immediately access). If you could attach a cord to every one of those pleasant memories and could still go about your life, it would tend to sustain you, meaning that sustenance comes about through the constant that connects all life.

You might build on the individual experience. You might live your life day-to-day, but if you had these cords connected to good things, it would be a constant. You wouldn't necessarily remember it in every moment nor would you have to, but the constant connection of those happy or loving times would sustain you. You would then be less inclined to generate unhappy times (I'll explain the value of this analogy in a moment) because your sustenance, our constant, is of this benevolent thing. For me, there is the benevolent thing of the totality, and building on that foundation (meaning whatever I do on my own) tends to be supported by the constant.

Now, this is indirectly associated with disentanglement. You could attach a cord to only the good times and not to the bad times, but people tend to attach cords, consciously or unconsciously, to the bad times because there is almost always something unresolved in the bad times. As a result, the cords are there so that should you ever learn disentanglement or should someone who is a practitioner of it (or your guides or teachers or angels) work on you, they would see what you are attached to. It's literally like looking at the ropes that connect you to other things so that when the end of your natural cycle comes, your guides and angels can escort you by slipping you out of these ropes.

When you do disentanglement, you might discover that even if the cords are attached to good times, there might be something uncomfortable as well. So you ask that disentanglement allow you to disentangle from all your discomforts, and you could extend that to include the causes of those discomforts. But for a short disentanglement — perhaps you are on a plane or in a bus or in the office, and other people are around, so you are not able to do your normal disentanglement — you might say out loud, "I am asking to be disentangled from all my discomforts." If you do that and just be quiet for five minutes or so, the process will complete itself. You could also request that this happen in an expedient way at the highest level that is comfortable for you. The highest level has nothing to do with those who work on you; it has to do with speed. You might also ask for gold-light beings and Earth gold-light beings and all these. You've been told about that, so I won't go over it. That's your disentanglement from my point of view.

Now, the connection to disentanglement here is intended, because I want you to recognize that I gave you an analogy that compares to incidents in your life to explain a constant. Remember that you not only attach the cords to that which is unresolved but also to that which is wonderful, to moments of great happiness. At some point when you have done enough disentanglement as described earlier, with all the names and instances you can remember plus some time beyond that (you don't stop; you continue to do the disentanglement indefinitely), you also ask to be connected to joyous sources of total support, love, nurturance, endurance, strength, and so on, whatever the words are that describe what you feel you might need that will support you in what you need to do (of course, you're saying, "I") in the immediate future, for instance. You, specifically, work very hard all the time, and then on top of that, you have to come over here. If it were a matter of driving five miles, it would be nothing, but even though there are many pleasant aspects over here (which is intended; as you know, much of the idea of getting you over here was to force pleasantness into your life), the difficult and exhausting aspect is the trip itself, both coming and going. So if you requested endurance and strength and so on before you started this trip — and you can also say, "And let it be a pleasant experience" — then the drive down, the transfers, the flight, the people that you meet, and so on, could be pleasant experiences. Perhaps you would sit next to somebody on the plane who would be fun to talk with, and perhaps some fun things might occur.

LOVE HAS PHYSICAL SUBSTANCE

Time is something that one experiences here on such an entrenched level, as far as the school goes, that it is not always easy to grasp the connection of the constant. The constant is pervasive. [Draws.] The individual lives that you live are all connected to the constant, but it is more detailed than that. The drawing does not represent a graph so much as an illustration of variations of momentary experience (see fig. 18.1). This is not just a life; this is all coming up from the constant, all right? This would represent, for the sake of our discussion, experiences associated within one-quarter of one millisecond.

Everything comes up from the constant. The constant is in no way attached to time or any other means of expression or communion, such as color and sound. Color and sound are equal to time, meaning that you can understand color. You might be in color and experience no time, or you might be in sound and experience no time, or you might be in time and experience color and sound. In short, they are all means of experience. I'm giving it to you in that form of example because within it, you can clearly see the constant, which has been described as love. Love sometimes feels vague to the mind (perhaps I should say "thinks vague to the mind"), but love is the material — if you were able to rub it between your fingers, you'd feel that it has a slightly viscous

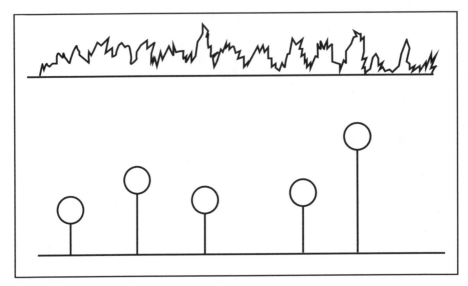

Fig. 19.1. The variations of momentary experience.

quality to it — that, utilizing its own character, is the glue that binds together that which wishes to come together on the smallest level to the largest level, from most important to the seemingly least significant. Love is this glue, the constant that I referred to, and it has an actual substance. It is not just a feeling that we take for granted; it's an actual thing.

I've heard that love is the glue that holds it all together, but I understood it as an energy of attraction, not something that has substance.

It has actual substance in the physical expression of itself. It would be hard for me to say, "Here's how you can feel it," but there have been times, usually in your deep-sleep state, when you tangibly feel it, but it's very easy to rationalize that the viscous thing you woke up feeling is your skin or your skin oils or what have you. In fact, it is possible to feel the viscous nature of love.

I think there's some here now! I think you're radiating it.

Yes, and you can feel it. When people are looking for God in the space-time place you are now, they often look for a personality. Religions in your time are very slowly moving toward the idea that God is love. To me, God is not separate. Within me, there is this constant that is also within you and within all beings, from the largest to the smallest. Beyond Earth in your time, it is understood that God is not something external, but when extraterrestrials have explained that to people on Earth in the past, humans have leapt to the wrong conclusion. They have leapt to the conclusion that extraterrestrials are somehow associated with God, meaning they are either godlike or egocentric. But that's not it. Just as you are prepared now to personalize your own worth in your process of spiritual, physical, and complete growth, so too would an extraterrestrial say, "God is a portion of me; I am God." When they say that, they do not disenfranchise themselves from the constant; they are portions of the constant. The constant is God, but God is not external. Beings on the other side of the universe and everything else close to them are also portions of God, and they feel that constant love feeling or heat, as you feel it here.

This was an attempt to remind you that it is true for you as well, but extraterrestrials were not able to communicate that in a way that people on Earth could understand at that time. However, they were able to show it to them. People who had benevolent meetings with them would say, "I felt this wonderful energy in their presence," which was a reporting of the facts, but they misinterpreted what the extraterrestrials were trying to show them — not that they are godlike, but that they could expose people to what they truly are. But as you can see in your personal development, the steps need to be taken one by one. If you jump forward, misunderstandings can result.

We do not see a disconnection; we still feel you are a portion of ourselves, even if you had never come through us. We would have felt that, as we do with all beings. We are enriched by the existence of all beings, even though from your understanding, we might never have met any of them. We have met them in the constant. The constant unites us all, and as you can clearly see, when a being is engaged consciously, meaning it is aware that it is engaged with the constant, then the knowledge that is required about another being is available. We do not choose to access knowledge that isn't required. Some beings do. Some beings might access every nuance of your life's experience, every experience, everything. They might choose to know everything about you even though they might not be communicating with you about all those things. For me and the others, we do not choose to know more than what we need to.

JOYFUL LIFE IS IN CONSTANT MOTION AROUND US

At different times in the different books, we would talk to the Council of Creators or various beings throughout what we now call the totality. They would say something similar to what you're saying: We know what we need to know when we need to know it. So it's this love, this constant ... it's not like there are lines of communication or grids or something but a substrata of this love energy that connects and allows them to know instantly anything for someone, "What about this?" or whatever, right?

"Substrata" is a good word. It is the same way a cat sees something that might not be part of your physical world. An insightful cat (not all cats see everything) might look up and see something in motion that, if you could see it, might look like a blob of light or protoplasm or something. The cat would not be frightened and run away but would acknowledge it

I've seen cats do that, and then they look at me like, "Why don't you see that?"

They look at you to see whether you see it, and they can see whether or not you do. If you do not see it, then they immediately look away not because you are unable to see it but because you are not engaged with what they are seeing, and they wish to remain engaged with it.

If another cat is around, the cat that saw something might look at the other cat or might be aware that the other cat sees it, and they both look at it for as long as it is there. Sometimes when it is there for a long time, they will just go on about their lives. But they know what it is because they are conscious of the constant.

They know through the constant what it is, and they are not alarmed. Until now, human beings have not been consciously connected. You are beginning to reach and strive for that again, but in times past, when human beings were not consciously connected, if they were to see something like that, they would run in terror. Not all would, but most. In general, cats see things. Beings are always in motion. Life is always in motion, and cats will see things. Sometimes a cat will be sleeping and suddenly open a single eye and look at something, acknowledge it, and go back to sleep. It's something cats notice because their instincts tell them something is present. And as wise beings, they open their eyes to discern whether it is something that will eat them or something that is just passing.

I had this picture when you were talking of billions of beings that we don't see floating in and out of the space. Is that how it works?

Yes, but you cannot limit it to that number. Life is always in motion. If you understand that, you will recognize that even the air that you move your hand through or [blows gently] the very breath that you blow out contains substance that is always within motion. This is startling to consider, yet it is also factual.

Even if you sat very still and focused long enough in an area that was not disturbed or affected by your breath (meaning focused in a space, not looking at an object but looking at something between your eyes and the object), you would begin to see things moving around in there. That is but one layer you are allowed to see. Another time, you might, after more time, begin to see things twinkling in there as well. That's another layer. There is always joyful life in motion around you. This is why you find yourself in physical bodies that are vehicles, in their own right, of constant motion, which your science has shown you. It is important for you to experience the microcosm of life as a personal day-to-day vehicle. If you are going to be a creator dealing with a macrocosm, you must live cut off for a time from your conscious knowledge of the constant in this microcosm so that you can feel the evidence and consequences of all your actions and so that you never, as a creator, lose sight of any individual's experience. When one is not at a creator level or higher and loses sight of the constant, it is the beginning of being disenfranchised, meaning either one is in a school, as you are in now, or theoretically, one is separating from the constant (which is, from my perspective, not possible). Separation from the constant is not real, all right? If we were able to take the conscious mind out of your body's experience, you would feel the constant all the time; even with the subconscious and an unconscious, you would feel it. But it is the conscious mind and the will it can foster that allow you to not notice the constant.

FOCUS IN THE HEAT TO GENERATE MATERIAL MANIFESTATION

So you're like the library of all the experiences of the totality plus your own experiences?

It is one of the things that we do, but it is not our job. In my experience beings do not require jobs, but if I were to say I had one, then I would say my job is to foster that creator. People tend to think of their jobs on Earth — your school — even in spiritual terms (meaning they wonder, "Why am I here? What is my purpose?") because their conscious minds are cut off from the constant unless they strive for a connection. When you feel the heat in your body, you know it is the physical evidence of the constant, which is love.

As a result, your experience of connecting to the constant that way is something that your conscious mind participates in with choice. You might say that this allows the conscious mind to begin to dispose of its attachment to will, because will, as you know, is a means of accomplishing something, but it is often the hard way. Once you are connected consciously — and physically, yes, but you are aware of the physical constant in your body with this heat — you can simply say what you need. For instance, you might say, while feeling the heat (it is required that you feel the heat all the time you say this, though, you understand), "I need now for my books that I'm publishing to sell in great quantities and be in great demand by readers all over the world, and I need that in my calendar now." You want to say "now" first and again later, as in "my calendar now." When you say that, you will find that circumstances begin to generate the ability for that to happen, and they are beyond your conscious will — the will in your mind — to make it happen.

It is a way to generate material manifestation. So you see that the heat is the constant, the disentanglement is the tool, and the spoken word is the union of the consciousness, the constant, and the acceptance that you are a worthy being who deserves good things simply because you exist, not because you've qualified through your job. When you say a living prayer while staying in the heat in yourself, being in the constant, it is more likely to come to pass. Say it once, and that's all. You will find that when you focus in the heat and then speak, you might not be able to say the exact words, but you will be pretty close. It will be simple and short. That's enough. The reason you say "now" is that the constant recognizes "now" as being a constant, a thread of all consistency. But when you later add, "in my calendar now," the constant recognizes that that means "immediately" for this request to be engendered, not just in the now of your total, always being. It refines "now."

We are not worried that someone might try to use this heat experience to inflict harm on another. It simply won't happen; it has a fail-safe. One cannot use this constant of love to inflict harm. Even if a loving couple were to fight and become violent with each other, they would not be using the constant, which keeps that violence insulated. Loving couples, or couples that used to be loving, are fighting all over the world, now — not everywhere, not everyone — but you do not personally feel affected by it because while they are always connected to the constant, their actions are kept more insulated to their own immediate places. The constant feels it, though. And this is why civilizations on Earth have risen and fallen in the past. The level of suffering for humans (and others) on Earth gets to be too much. Humans sometimes spray chemicals because they don't like to have certain little beings around. I can see that they might not like it, but there are more benevolent ways to ask those beings to go elsewhere.

THE RENEWAL OF EARTH LIFE

Recognize that should the level of suffering achieve too great an effect, sometimes some beings who have lived on Earth and who are more connected to the constant will ask for a removal and a recycling of human life. Some specimens of human beings will always survive because it is not intended that human life be wiped out but rather that things start over again. You will find reference to this in different religious books and in the wisdom stories associated with different cultures, some of which are still with you. If you look closely, you can find physical evidence. For example, scientists in your time have noted clear high-water marks that are way up on cliff walls and have said, "How is that possible?" The assumption is that the mountains are upthrusting and that in times gone by, the mountains were lower and waters were higher, and this is where those high-water marks came from. But the mountains upthrust very slowly, and the physical evidence of the high-water marks is usually caused by actual high water. Earth has the capacity (remember, she is a material master, among other things) to create water — not just to retain it within her, but also to create it.

Sometimes various beings (some of whom you'd recognize and would say, "I cannot imagine that they could do this"; others you would think, "Oh, these are from another star system; they are not from here") request that human life be re-created. They know that all beings are connected to the constant and request that death come in a quick way with, say, an inundation of water instead of something slow and miserable, such as a disease. They would never request that. It would always be something instantaneous or as close to instantaneous as possible so that the spike in suffering might be tolerable. They would also die and be re-created because that way they would know they are connected to the constant. There is a type of being, a creature, who is alive on Earth today that caused that to occur once before as a representative of the constant, meaning that the suffering level was so great on Earth that it was beginning to move beyond Earth even with all efforts to contain it. Therefore, there needed to be a cessation and a re-creation of the vast amount of life on Earth.

This is not likely to happen again because you are now all beginning to be consciously aware. Many of you are now consciously aware, but all people on Earth are beginning to be consciously aware. Examples of conscious awareness are your reference to feeling that energy, people's dreams, and people noticing how time has changed and what they can do with it. In short, even people who are not pursuing the union between the constant and their daily lives are noticing that things are changing.

Embracing this is bringing about a means by which the level of suffering, even as it exists in your time, will not be so excessive that such a renewal must take place. Renewal is just that: Since all life is connected to the constant, the type of beings who called for that and who are still alive on your planet and among you did not feel as if they were doing a violent thing but rather that they were protecting not only all beings beyond Earth but also the beings who were on it, including themselves. If enough beings are suffering greatly on Earth, it affects every being. In a benevolent society, if one being is suffering even slightly, it affects them all.

On your world where you are somewhat insulated from that, if the level of suffering gets to a certain point, you might find yourself having nightmares that sometimes are not in any way associated with your life but are simply an effect of that excessive suffering. So when all beings were frequently having nightmarish sleep, that representative or that being said, "We must do this now." So you don't know whether that being is the smallest or the largest, the most complex or the simplest, and you will never know. You cannot say, "Let's kill them all, and then they can't kill us." [Chuckles.] You will never know. There will always be beings among you who are aware of the constant so that you can be protected. It is not the case for you now, but if you were affected by the same level of suffering that occurred before, you would feel that such an instantaneous death would be a blessing. But I do not expect this to happen for you. It is very unlikely, since you are moving into a conscious awareness and are embracing the loving you, the constant you, the forever you.

Can you say when that was?

It's not necessary. Look at the myths and stories.

There was only one?

Oh no, more than one. Look at the myths and stories. Your Judeo-Christian book refers to the great flood, but there have been more renewals.

But only one within a time that would be in our history?

Only one is relevant to the Explorer Race.

Well, they just found a building 300 feet below the shores of the Black Sea, and they are dating it to 7,500 years ago, which means the Black Sea rose 300 feet 7,500 years ago.1

When Earth originally arrived in this position in this solar system, she had much more water on her surface than she does now. But she brought a lot of that down inside her body and changed some into other things. And over her "time" here in this solar system, she has at various times had greater or lesser amounts of water on the surface. Sometimes this was brought about because of these needs for renewal, and at other times, it was brought about simply because of the needs of the surface beings. When there are more fishes — water beings, you understand — then beings will experience more water, and the fewer water beings, the less water, and so on.

As your friend Zoosh likes to say, it is not an accident that you as human beings are both water breathers and air breathers. Think about all the beings on Earth that you can relate to. You might not relate to an ant the same way you would relate to another human being, but it has a body, it walks, and it breathes. In short, you share some common functions. You may not relate to a fish as you would relate to another human being, but it moves, and even

---

1.   In September 2000, American explorer Robert Ballard claimed to have found the remains of a structure 311 feet below the Black Sea. See http://news.nationalgeographic.com/news/2000/12/122800blacksea.html.

though it breathes underwater, it breathes. And when you were living inside your mothers, you breathed underwater as well. In short, you are exposed to the two types of breathing that you are likely to identify in other creatures, and include yourself as a creature. This is not an accident. The birth system would not necessarily require that you be in water. It is required so that you at least eventually say, "Water creatures are beautiful, they have consciousness, and they are important and spiritual," similar to the recent movement that focuses on whales and dolphins and sea turtles. Now, with some Earth beings — human beings, you understand — there is recognition that all beings on Earth are sacred. Of course, many human beings have known that for a time, but in the technological era in which you live, it has been an exploration of separation rather than an acknowledgment of union.

This is the first time for a long time that Robert has turned into golden light. It's like he fades away, and I just see light there. Well, listen, you are welcome anytime that you want to come in! [Chuckles.]

Well, perhaps we will continue tomorrow, then.

Excellent. Your explanation of the heart-heat as the constant has just changed my understanding of everything.

Good.

It's amazing! Thank you so much!

Good night.

Good night.

Chapter 20

Body and Soul Connections

Ssjoooo 2

September 15, 2000

I know you don't have a job, but is there any way you can say in a way that we can understand what it is you do that occupies you, that you enjoy, that interests you?

I realize that this is a typical question, but it's very important to establish the fact that I cannot speak for the vast majority of beings who are not like you but are beings who can be in many places at once. Speaking for myself, I cannot say that I do anything. I exist and, if necessary, respond. But moments of response, in terms of what's relevant to you, would have already been revealed to you. I cannot describe my personality on the basis of what I do, for that is not my focus. So the usual defining characteristics that you might use as a human being — "Oh, I'm a publisher. I'm a writer. I'm a printer" — are not relevant, and you understand that.

I recognize you are trying to find a way to make some kind of differentiation between me and the first variation you spoke with, so if you like, you can just use digits. We don't use them — I would not say I am the second variation — but for the sake of clarity, you can use them if you like. Let's not use "facet" because it suggests not only a crystalline structure but also that this is something fixed. "Variation" sounds more modulated, to my point of view, and not fixed.

THE MORE IS AVAILABLE TO ALL

Well, let's ask it this way: Do you often choose to focus your attention in the totality on someone, something, or some event?

I focus on nothing specific and everything in general.

Can you feel it all at the same time?

I don't usually choose to feel it; rather, I am aware of it. It is not always good to feel it. I do not feel you to know you, but I am aware of you without sampling your feelings.

I was going in a certain direction. The point of the Explorer Race is to become a catalyst for more in the whole totality and, I assume, your group. So I wonder what was and what would be more. That's what I'm getting at.

From our point of view, this is an experiment. It is something that, if it affects us, Ssjoooo, we will note the effect. If it is pleasing or advantageous in any way, we will try it on for a while, you might say. If it is something that is not pleasing, we will simply disregard it and remain what we are. When the more is made available, it is made available for all beings, but there is no requirement that all beings participate. This is important. It's going to be something that is available, not something that is going to demand change, which, in my way of perceiving, is a great advantage because if people are suddenly forced from one thing to another (in the case of vast population that you would understand), they would not welcome that. But they might welcome an option to be more that they could try and then see how they like it.

THE COLOR OF NEED

I'm going to try something again, and if it doesn't work, I'll give up. Robert said that through your eyes, he saw the totality as a vast glowing, moving mass. Did it look like that when there was the need? It didn't look the same way, did it?

You mean before there was the need or during the need or after?

Before there was a need, when you looked out there, did you see what you see now? Does it look the same?

It has changed.

How many times in your experience has there been that kind of a change?

Once. You understand, I'm using your terms. I noted it one way before I did what I did.

The group?

The group, us, we. And after, over experience, as the totality began to change and define itself in different ways, I noted a change. But I cannot state that I noted a change at any other time. I would say that the change, to put a feeling on it (since that might help), became happier. It was there, but it was less defined in terms of its appearance, feeling, and the general sensation you might get from looking at it. I'm using your terminology. It has changed in its appearance. It moves no more or less than it ever did, and it tends to exude a different pulse that you would perceive as gold with underlying colors, some of which are in your current visual spectrum while others are not. The most noticeable colors for you would be some reds, but that's an underlying color, meaning it is not as prominent as the gold.

Oh, that's interesting, because I saw Robert turn into golden light last night, and there was a red aura against the chair that was like a little red slice. That was neat.

Yes. Red, I would say, has to do with its expression in substance. Substance in general, or the physical definition in all of the expressions of physicality, might be most easily defined on your world and elsewhere as having a substrata of red associated with it. Do not understand that as a fixed thing, as "Where there's physical, there's red." By substrata, I mean the color often identified, along with other colors, with some form of physical expression. Red is sometimes defined in your world in other ways, and it can be viewed as associated with different feelings and needs, as well as messages to physicality beyond Earth as to need. For example, if a mountain on Earth needed more physical energy from its surroundings or from, say, another planet or even from a distant solar system (which is less likely but possible) to the degree that you could perceive such a message, you might notice, when you look at the mountain with subtle vision, the color red — not throughout the whole mountain — as the color of a request for supplemental physical energy to sustain the mountain.

Sometimes those who can perceive such things misunderstand this color. They might assume that it is a broadcast color of the mountain: The mountain is broadcasting red as its personality. However, they might look at the mountain another time and not see the red.

If you, as a human being, are connected to various spiritual aspects, the mountain might respond as you energetically (or however you do it) address it. It might respond to you in red, signaling to either you or various spirit realms that you are connected to that, and it would like something. Most often, it will not expect anything from you personally but from what you are connected to. Other times, you will be at the same mountain for pleasure or ceremonial purposes or many other possibilities, and you will not see the red. In the past when some people who have had this experience or these perceptions did not see the red, they thought it meant the mountain did not have enough energy. That is usually not the case; the red is usually a broadcast signal. At other times, the mountain might simply be seen, in its auric field or even within the mountain (to the degree the person can see it), as broadcasting or glowing in other colors. If you know the red represents a need that is being transmitted to either you (the viewer) alone or you and others (which is usually the case), then you will know that the mountain trusts you sufficiently to allow you to see this broadcast need.

Now, if I were to look at that, I would see colors that are not in your visual spectrum. Even beings who can see colors that might appear for either an observer or ceremonial purposes (some people interact with mountains this way) will still see colors that they are familiar with, colors that they can see. Someone who has made a lifelong study of color might notice other things happening in the spectrum of color transmission. If you do not see what that is and just see motion or things happening in there, you might be perceiving a color outside of the range of your capacity to define, meaning it is outside the range of your spectrum, or you might be perceiving a color you have no need to understand, meaning the message of that color is not in any way directed toward you. I mention that because some of you have made a specific study of such things and might wonder what it means when you see an overlay or even an underlay coming through, and you see a blank area or something that is moving, for which you have a sense of borders or boundaries of that moving thing. Sometimes you will assume that this is a being, and occasionally it might be. More often, it is a color that the communication aspect of or the action-oriented nature of is not meant for you.

Ah, thank you.

THE NATURE OF ORIGIN

Did you see my origin for some reason? Last night, I asked a question, and you said, "Do you mean where you originated, your origin?"

Oh, yes, that had to do with the original story I believe you received from Zoosh about beginning in this place of light and so on. You began there in terms of relevance to your current life, which Zoosh did say at the time, but you began before there. Even though Zoosh did not bring that to your attention, he eluded to it. From my point of view, you began long before then, but it's not relevant to your current life. I agree with that.

Well, can I know anyway?

You can know, but it would probably only serve to distract you. You feel I'm withholding something from you. I will give it to you like this, from the point of all understanding that you can grasp: About 600 levels of understanding have proceeded before that. When you go back to the first level of understanding, there is no term in any Earth language that can describe that beginning. This is why sometimes your friend Zoosh will talk in terms of relevance, meaning that if something is so irrelevant to you in your current form, it is pointless to go into it.

I can see it, but it is hard to describe it to you in any terms that would benefit you. Remember what I said: If it cannot be described in any language on Earth now or even by radiated feeling that I might give to you, then how could it help you? I will give you some idea. If I radiated something that you could perceive, it would have a profoundly negative (as you use the term) effect on you because it would require a personality split. When you are at the levels of understanding at the beginning, you are more than one.

In other words, to understand your origin, you would have to be more than one. This is why sometimes when people have inadvertently, in searching for code keys to understand the life (usually in an attempt to manipulate it in some way), slipped into other dimensions or even the chaos that precedes dimensions, they are later — if they survive it and manage to maintain some grip on the dimension in which they reside — perceived by others as totally insane because such people would be unable to express themselves in recognizable forms of personality. They might have anywhere from 800 to 1,200 or more personalities and would be considered insane; in fact, they have had to become multiples of themselves to assimilate the information. In that sense, one personality is not enough. So I would be unkind in the extreme if I were to reveal your point of origin to you. It would not only destroy your life but also require another snapback. This one would kill you in your current body. So know that there are some things that are better not to know in your current form. When you move beyond this form, you can have that knowledge again, but it is not safe for you to have it now.

In this form. That's a very gentle way to explain it. Thank you. And it leaves some things to look forward to, doesn't it?

Well, when you are aware of it again, it will just seem like, "Oh, yes, of course." It seems more desirable to know at this time because it is unattainable. Still, you might say it is also unattainable to live to tell about drinking nitric acid, but would you want to do that? Not likely. Those who have the experience would have preferred otherwise, and while they could tell you about it after their death, they would most likely say ...

"I wish I hadn't done that."

Yes, or they might say, "I do not recommend this experience."

THE RIBBON OF TIME

How did they keep my body alive during the snapback? Well, if I was only gone a second in this reality, then ...

That fraction given to you by your friend was more intended to give you an example of the very tenuous — necessarily tenuous — grasp that everybody has here in your place and time. When I say "grasp," I do not mean mental; I mean the actual connection that runs on the physical level right about here.

Put your hand on your belly button, come up about an inch, and hold the side of your hand. Move it across horizontally just a little bit one way and then a little bit back to the other. It is that location in your body where you connect to time. You and others are moving through a change of time. One cannot move flexibly within a dimension, even within the dimension, as it's called in your culture, without moving through a change in time. That is why it is essential that your physical grasp on time be tenuous like this. You might have two fingers hanging on the edge of something (but not dangling from it), just a slight grasp so that the ribbon of time can slip through your fingers as one might allow a rope to loosely pass through a couple of fingers, not held tightly enough to give you injury but allowing it to travel loosely. Your grasp on time is physically tenuous on purpose.

This allows you all, as beings, to move within the dimension and time to your benefit. This kind of ability is usually not granted to physical beings, but it is granted to you physical human beings here and now because of your status as Explorer Race creators-in-training. The animals can do it. You know this about cats and other animals too. Not all cats can do it, but some in their ranks have the capacity. One often identifies cats as spiritual beings because they will sometimes reveal their spirituality to you. Have you ever gone in a room, looked around very carefully for a cat friend, and not seen it and then, after looking away for a moment and back again, seen the cat in a position where it could not possibly have jumped to and landed? You see the cat curled up, but you had not perceived it there before because that cat either in that moment or in general has the capacity to let the ribbon of time run loosely through it, and it is there in that space but in a different time.

This is something that, if a cat likes you or trusts you or knows that it's part of your training (and a few other qualities as well), it might reveal to you. Not everyone sees it. Generally speaking, if you've lived with cats long enough and you like them — and the cat must like you — then it is more likely that they will reveal this to you. But if you engage a scientific study of cats, it is very unlikely that they will choose to reveal this to you, even in a way that a machine can perceive, because often the cat is being kept in a way that is inhumane or that does not allow the observer to engage on a personal level with the cat being. I mention this for those who are engaged in such studies: Do not expect to have positive results. You are much more likely to have a positive result with a cat with whom you live because you like that cat, and the cat likes you. Those who have lived with cats long enough know this. If the cat does not like you, well, that cat will be elsewhere. I mention this about cats because so many people have the opportunity to be around these beings, and they are more likely to catch your attention and reveal such traits. Although you will be around others that can do this as well, you are more inclined to notice it with cats in your particular culture.

Some of those beings that are free are little, and some are big. When you go for a hike in the forest, such beings might be nearby. For example, how many of you, even hunters, have ever seen a deer sleeping in the forest? They sleep in the forest, but most of them do not allow themselves to be seen when they sleep not only to be safe, which is a primary concern, but also because their out-of-body cycles take them to a different color vibration, and those color vibrations are not in the perceived color spectrum of the human being. Some of you have seen deer sleeping, which can mean only a few things: You can see an extended range of color that is beyond the normal person's ability to see, you are being gifted with this vision, or the deer trusts you. But if you are a hunter and you understand the soul and heart of hunting, even if you are hungry, you would never kill a sleeping deer. It is a gift when you see such a being asleep.

THE SOUL AND BODY CONNECTION

It's my understanding from Ssjoooo 1 that all thirteen of you have projections on Earth in the Explorer Race right now, which you've never done before, because of the importance of this particular time.

I agree with my cohort, but do you understand alternating current? That it pulses? We have projections there, but as in the pulse of alternating current (that's just an analogy, you understand), it is like that. We are not always connected to them in every moment, but we are connected sometimes. In this way, we do not interfere with their lives.

Because you're connected to everything, are you any more connected to them than everyone else?

We do not understand, in your term, any better by having that, but it is a means by which we can compassionately appreciate, should we connect with that life, your situation.

Ah. Was that the purpose of it?

On the feeling level, yes, it is a safe way for us to connect compassionately with your circumstances of life without engaging in that more than is comfortable for us. This is typical; your soul does something similar. Let's create an arbitrary number that is not fixed, and let's say, for the sake of the example, that your soul's connection functions similarly to alternating current in the comparison of pulses per second; it's not like that, but this is a good analogy. Your soul is not connected to you all the time, but it is connected enough to keep your body intact. However, your soul has other jobs. Now, figure 20.1 represents the soul, the body, and the pulse connections at approximately one-quarter of one-one-thousandth of a millisecond in terms of the connections that the soul makes with the body, which is sufficient for the body to know that it is still engaged in the physical life but also allows the soul to do other things.

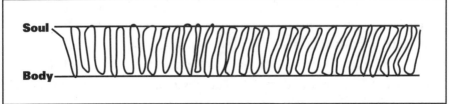

Fig. 20.1. The shape of the pulse that connects the body and soul.

What do these shapes mean, the difference in each pulse?

It is the shape of the pulse in that moment; sometimes the pulse is doing different things. The pulse might be engaged in supporting and sustaining a feeling, or it might be engaged in providing inspiration. It might be acting as an avenue of connection for guides and teachers, or it might be bringing the body support (though not necessarily in words) of spiritual past lives. In short, it does everything to sustain the body from a spiritual perspective and from moment to moment, even though your mind and your physical body (which is made up of Mother Earth) might not be conscious of it so that your physical body can be in the form of a human being and a receptacle for what you must do as an Explorer Race being, as a human being. Given the parameters of your creator training, your soul must provide a variety of pulses and impulses to support even the tiniest cell in your body, which might not be readily available to your conscious mind, though it will be available to the unconscious, which is actually associated with the function of the body.

What is the method of connection? Does the soul connect into every cell? Or what does the soul connect to?

The soul can connect to the body in the auric field through light. The auric field can also be measured in sound, by the way, for those of you experimenting with auric-field measurements, but I do not recommend stimulating the auric field in sound because it can harm the auric field of the person who is being tested, and that person's reaction can also harm the tester, who might not be aware of the damage. It has a cumulative effect. I won't talk about that at any length right now because I'd prefer you don't do it, but I will say that the capacity of the soul to connect would go from the tiniest, impossible-to-perceive particle in your current time to the full range of expressed bodies, meaning from how your body looks in inception within your mother to how it looks at the point of death. Your soul is not fixed in time nor attached to time. It wasn't intended to be attached to time. It is intended to have significantly greater freedom than that, which is another reason that you can dream the way you do. This figure also represents, in a general way, a graph of dreaming at the deepest level, and even at the level available to recollection, at least in the first few moments of waking, in that the dream comes in bits and pieces, not all of which you're intended to remember.

The soul must be free to travel, to get instruction, and to pass the instruction on to the body, but the body has a different response. That is the soul's connection to the body. This is an example of how you might think of the body's connection to the soul at any given moment. It's a wave that moves toward the soul but does not directly engage it. It is the soul's job to engage the body, not the other way around, because the body is actually Earth, and Earth does not require a full engagement with the external spiritual concerns or functions of other beings. Earth can respond on her own. In short, the body does not have to be so precise because it has a greater level of mastery than the soul. Because the soul does not have as great a level of mastery (and you can identify with this), it tends to be more precise.

Now, when you are learning how to do something that involves some complexity, you tend to follow the directions to the letter because you are not a master of that task. Once you become a master, you can perhaps be a little more liberal with its methodology. At the very least, you won't have to think about it; it will just be something that you naturally do. Or maybe you can improvise other steps. So this is a comparison. The body has the capacity to improvise and constantly be creative, whereas the soul is the student and must be precise.

I'm still not clear; the soul comes in through the aura to every particle?

No, you asked how it connects, and the soul can connect with the aura. My statement was intended to show that the soul has the capacity to connect not only with the physical body but with the auric body as well. The soul does not differentiate from the auric body or the physical body; it is all part of the same personality from the soul's perception.

The first picture I drew for you shows how it connects [see fig. 20.1]. Can you not see? The line begins with the soul; it begins on the left and moves to

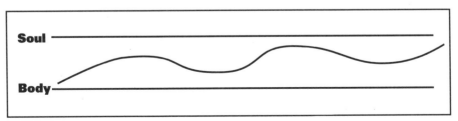

Fig. 20.2. The body's connection to the soul is a wave that moves toward the soul but does not directly engage it.

the right. That is how it does it. And remember, the soul does not differentiate between the auric field and the physical body. So the soul connects in one place or another in the auric field or the physical body just like that. It is not specific to locality in that drawing, but it does give you some idea of the frequency, meaning how often, rather than locality. It is not always the same locality. People tend to think that the soul comes in through the top of the head, but that is not always the case. It might, from time to time (you can see how often it connects), connect to your big toe, your ear, or your kneecap. It might connect to your auric field somewhere. It is not limited to a connection through the crown chakra, you might say, or to the crown chakra.

It's not limited to the chakras, to the endocrine system, which is what I thought?

It can be measured and quantified and understood through those things you mentioned, such as the chakra system, but it is not limited in its connection to those localities. Remember that the soul is a student of what's happening on Earth with the body but is constantly being instructed by its guides and teachers, and that's one reason why it cannot be with you all the time, to say nothing of things that your body is experiencing for which the soul does not have the capacity to tolerate. If the soul is guaranteed (souls need this guarantee) that it does not always have to engage you and does not always have to feel what you are feeling, it is much more likely to say, "All right, then I will do it." That is why the soul does not engage with you constantly. Of course, there is the constant of love, but the soul does not always make a direct connection with your physical body.

Where are souls from? Are they part of our immortal personality? Or are they something that we're training for the Creator? Are they projected by the Creator to give us life force in this universe? What are souls?

"Soul" is a word that describes your immortal personality, but to say "immortal personality" is a mouthful. I like that term that Zoosh used because it is much more specific, but I find that the term "soul" has a little more heart in it, and I think it's good to use because it is often considered something to cherish. One does not think of cherishing one's immortal personality.

Why does the soul need to be taught?

It needs to be instructed because it is not in its nature to be readily able to express Creator mechanics such as is required for the Explorer Race's agenda. Every moment — I've defined "moment" here with quite a bit more of a frequency than the usual understanding of "moment" — the soul requires refinement and support from a multitude of teachers and guides. I want to say, "And you would too!" but of course, you are your soul.

You see, the soul is profoundly versatile and adaptable, much more so than many forms of life that you have experienced heretofore before trying out the human being. You might say, "Oh, well, they were infinitely more capable." That might be true, but they were nowhere near as adaptable. And adaptability is what you were being trained in; therefore, your guides and teachers felt that one of the best ways to learn adaptability, and perhaps more importantly, to learn to appreciate its value, was to have one or more personal experiences of being a human. You are still learning that in your current life, but in your next life, in a few hundred years from now on Earth, you will be able to reap the rewards of your educational process. In short, have a good life as a human being, and say, "This is wonderful!"

You can see how the apparent day-to-day problems and challenges of all human beings do not in any way reveal the full quantity of what is going on. In any moment, much is going on for the soul or the immortal personality, and the body itself is interacting with many different portions of Earth. That which makes up the human body is not relieved of its Earth duties even though the material of the body is loaned to you for your purposes while you are here. It is required to do what it might have been doing in every particle of it during the different times of assimilation as a portion of your body. Each and every particle is still required to maintain its Earth function, even though you as an immortal personality, to say nothing of your conscious mind, will not be aware of that. This is why it has been said to you on previous occasions that when Earth requires something from you, such as having a dream for her or performing a task for her, you must do it. What she's really requiring is that you become consciously aware of something that your body is doing anyway. This is her contribution to your overall material mastery education.

A task for her? What other things?

Perhaps she is busy, and she cannot attend to all that she must do. You might need to help souls move on, or you might need to dream something or have a dream for her, which is another extended reality for you but might relieve a pressure for her. You might need to take over something that she provided for human beings in the past, meaning she would provide material mastery for you externally. You might need to take over, at least temporarily, some material mastery chore.

This has all been spoken of previously. But to keep your conscious mind engaged, here's an example: Mother Earth might not always be able to address your concerns with her energy body now that her body has been disrupted by some human activities, such as pollution and mining, so from time to time, she will engage your bodies to the extent that you will know or feel something is happening. Usually it will be a quick feeling, something that does not seem to be associated with your life. Sometimes it can be assumed that this is a phenomenon of some sort; other times it might take the form of a dream, which is not apparently associated with your life. And still other times, it might be a sudden, sharp intake of breath — not from fear or physical activity, but just an unexpected breath. It can be many things. It might be a sudden, unexpected movement in your body that is not associated with a physical need, such as scratching an ear or something. Don't worry about these things. It doesn't necessarily mean that you have a disease (but if you're constantly trembling, it might). You might experience a sudden, unexpected motion — it's never going to be something horrible or embarrassing — that surprises you, and you look down and say, "Oh, what was that about?" and then you'll laugh and go on with your life. That motion may be akin to something Mother Earth needs but cannot do in that moment.

I wasn't aware that we were doing unconscious things for her, so thank you for the example. I thought that there was a portion of Mother Earth that inhabited us in some way as an Earth soul, which was her connection to us.

From my perspective, which is not always the same as other beings. I do not see that Mother Earth inhabits your immortal personality. The graph I drew for you is more to the point (fig. 20.1), giving you a visual interpretation. While your soul engages the body, the body moves, as shown in the illustration, in such a way that allows it to be more engaged with your soul or less engaged with your soul, but in that sense, it is connecting. It does not reach toward you; it is simply making itself available. It would be as if someone you don't know came into the room and said, "Oh, I've heard about you. You're such a wonderful person! Thank you for what you're doing," and then walked over and hugged you. You do not necessarily hug that person back. Maybe you try to give them a polite hug because you are available for "hugability," but you're not really engaging the practice. So it is like that: You are available, but not [chuckles] initiating the action.

Souls seem to create lives without any idea about the impact on the physical and the life that's lived.

Why would they have an idea?

But why do they create lives when they don't understand what they're doing?

Oh, they don't get to create the lives. Creator creates the lives in cooperation with Mother Earth and other beings who provide the material, and then the soul inhabits the life.

I'm sorry. I meant "creates the experience of the life."

The soul does not really create the experience; it requests that it be able to learn something. For example, the soul does not care whether most beings (with the rare exception) learn to ride a bicycle. But you want to ride a bicycle, and maybe you fall down a few times and get hurt, but you are determined. Your friends are riding bicycles, and you're going to ride one too. You see, the soul did not set that up.

The soul desires to learn, from its point of view, in the easiest, most gentle, most loving way. But the soul is not the will. What causes suffering is the mental will's desire to do it "this way," and the will is largely molded by the adults who you grow up with and your peers and so on. It is the conflict that takes place within the will in response to the soul that causes suffering. The soul does not cause suffering; the soul always wants to learn in the most gentle and loving way possible.

It is the will that is the source of struggle, but the will is part of your conditioning to your culture: your immediate family culture and the culture of your community and so on. The will responds to what it perceives through life as what you must do and how you must do it, whereas the soul would not impress such manners and mores upon you. I am not saying that this will is the enemy, but it certainly is the challenge. No, the soul is very gentle. The soul is perfectly comfortable with you learning what it came to learn in, say, prebirth, when things are gently and easily done, or in, say, the later stages of dementia, where the personality enters and exits the body with greater frequency. If you ever speak to someone like this, know that his or her perceptions are not only Earth based. The soul is perfectly comfortable with doing that and does not drive a person in more physicalized times of his or her life.

As a person begins to engage with spiritual concerns, either through religion or the concerns he or she might express, then sometimes the soul's purpose is engaged a little more consciously and through other perceptive means, such as meditations or visualizations — disentanglement is an example — and then the soul can be more gently, as it chooses to be, involved with the process in a way you can consciously appreciate. From my perception, the soul never takes a firm position but is a gentle guiding light. You understand that my perception is not intended to supersede the opinions and perceptions of other beings, but it is intended to add to your overall perception. In short, it is a possibility, another way of looking at things, and it is my way of looking at them.

In the case of your — what do you call them? — expressions, projections, or lives? What's the word for the beings who are physically alive on the planet today, the Explorer Race beings? What's a word that we use to say?

For the sake of the moment, let's just say contacts.

Contacts, all right. So there is a line of energy that goes from you, the immortal personality, and then there's something separate called the soul?

Oh, I do not consider myself to be the immortal personality of these beings.

They're connected to you in some way, though, aren't they?

They have volunteered to be connected at least part-time with me, but they have their own lives. This might be another reason why the first variation of me, when it spoke to you, referred to you and Robert as direct connections, because you have volunteered from time to time to be these contacts. But no one is expected to be the contact all the time, so even though there might be thirteen variations of my personality, Ssjoooo, there are more than thirteen Earth humans who are the contacts.

Oh! But not directly projected or created by you.

Correct. It would be like an interference to do that, but volunteers [chuckles] are cheerfully appreciated. To give you a number, it is many thousands, but no one being is expected to perform what we might need all the time; it would be too much. It's one thing to make the contact occasionally, but so much is going on for the individual immortal personality that it would be a burden to expect the contact more often than that.

Say more. You said, "No one would be expected to perform what we need all the time." What is "perform what we need"?

What I said before: to understand with compassion the experience of the human being on Earth now. That's it; that's all. And it's necessary for us to keep what we need very specific so that those who have volunteered are not expected to essentially stop and perceive what it is that we need in that moment. They will know that what we need is always the same thing, which they can then adapt to, and when called on to "deliver" that experience, or a sampling of experiences, it is something they can assimilate as a potential. But to require them to do many, many different things would unnecessarily complicate their lives, so we don't do that.

All right, so at certain times, you connect with them literally as ...

For a very short moment, not unlike a singular pulse shown — not a pulse, but a singular spike on the graph (fig. 20.1), like that. It is very, very quick, and it has to be that quick. If it were, say, one millisecond, that could throw things off for you. That little jerk could cause a more profound physical response in the body, but if it is a teeny connection like that, in terms of your measured time, it will not throw anything off.

FREE YOURSELF FROM CONDITIONING

You can free yourself from conditioning with a concerted effort but not from something you bring in with you. People do not bring prejudice in with them. Prejudice is, in your time and place and culture, conditioned. It is unfortunate;

it makes your lives so much more difficult. Think how many opportunities you have missed in this life because of conditioning. You are not alone. Your cultures could have achieved many things if prejudice was not engendered through culturing to so many of you. Prejudice about appearance or religion, well, one cannot study your history without noticing prejudice as a thread from the beginning of strife to the present.

Where would you put the beginning of strife?

Perhaps to the point where separation was introduced. Inadvertently, I might add, by that being that came on the ship, Jehovah. It was inadvertent, but nevertheless, sometimes there are consequences for the most well-intended acts that are deeply regretted. Any human being, certainly any adult, can personally appreciate that. Someone might say something to you that is meant in a nice way, but because they do not know your personality, it might hurt your feelings. Or you might say something to someone else that you believe is a compliment, not realizing you are hurting that person's feelings because you do not truly know him or her. It is of value to become sensitive to your own feelings and needs because it will help you to become sensitive to the feelings and needs of others as well.

Wasn't the separation intended as part of the whole Explorer Race project?

Oh, yes, and that is why it was allowed. If it were something entirely foreign to what you would learn, it would not have happened. But it had to happen so that you could ultimately discover that it is not the path for you. People sometimes have to discover this in creator training by thoroughly exploring the false path.

But we're coming out of that now.

I believe you are. Now, I think we must stop for the day.

All right, thank you.

Chapter 21

The Journey to the End of the Rainbow

Snnn and Zoosh

November 2, 2000

I am one of the outer sons. It is my job to create from nonexistence, existence, and the potential for existence. It is a residue of that creation that light and sound happen, though that is not my direct purpose. The residue is sufficient to provide enough light and sound that other creators absorb it or utilize it for their own purposes, usually expanding it and making more. That is my purpose. If you were here and you could see, you would have a curious feeling. You would not actually be able to see, sense, or do anything. It has been said before that if a human being is deprived of his or her senses, he or she will go mad, but that's not quite true. What does happen is that they go into a state of what I call peaceful reserve. This means that you would not think, but you would essentially wait to exist again. That is the best way I can describe it. You would not see light or dark, you would not see any form of matter, and you would not taste it or sense it in any other way. Question? You wanted to speak to me.

You are one of the outer sons? How many are there?

I am aware of only one other. There is a potential, meaning a position for one more, but that one is not present.

The two of you are with Zoosh in the area beyond the reservoir of being?

Yes.

When you create, could you call yourself and the other ones the original creators?

I am disinclined to say that, since it is my job to provide essential matter and even prematter. I am disinclined to call myself a creator because I am not forming something that is experienced directly by another other than creators. So I'd prefer to say I am a precreator.

What was the first thing you saw when you became aware? And you're probably going to say you were always aware, but were you in the same place you are now?

That question is not relevant to me, so you will have to drop that format. Come up with something else. It is not to offend you that I say this, but it is not relevant.

EXISTENCE WITHOUT BOUNDARIES

All right. If I were to look out from where you are, I wouldn't see anything. As you live there, do you look out and see the thirteen and the totality, or are you totally engrossed within the space where you are?

I have a function that I have described in general terms; that is, in fact, what I do. I do not require the level of senses that you have. I am completely aware of everything in existence, as you understand it, but I am not personally involved with it. I am speaking to you at this time as a courtesy to Ssjoooo.

Well, thank you for that. How can I ask this? It's a time question. Do you feel that you were there before there was a totality or a Ssjoooo?

Oh, yes.

Oh, yes. So we have found somebody to whom we can say, "How did the creation out there start?" Who created Ssjoooo?

You mean, why did it all start? It started because my companion, the other son, felt that, considering our capacities (and one must look at this as an analogy when one is a human being on an almost daily basis as well), we were not doing anywhere near as much as we could do. Existence alone was not enough. I'm not saying we felt unfulfilled, for simply existing is fulfillment in its own right at this level. But we felt that we had all of these capacities, and we felt that — well, how can we say it? — It would be as if you had legs but had never used them. [Chuckles.] In alignment with this analogy, we decided to use our legs. In short, we began to use our capacities, and I described one of those in the beginning.

Yes.

I described the one that is relevant to your function. We will do more in time, when the third one arrives.

Where will he arrive from?

[Chuckles.] Don't you know?

No.

Think about it.

As far as Zoosh said, there was no place. It has to come from the totality, then. He said there was nothing beyond the space he was in.

That is certainly true.

But you didn't come from the totality.

No. There wasn't a totality before we began.

Is the third one going to be Zoosh?

No.

All right. How did you discover that you had the capacities you mentioned? Did you feel a need?

No. We were aware of our capacities, not unlike you might be sometimes aware of yours. Say you accomplish a physical goal that you had never done before. You become aware of your physical capabilities, you understand? But we are always aware of all our capabilities. Even though we have not used them all yet — not by far! — we decided to use one to see what would happen. For you, it would have been a calculated risk to do something like that, but we knew we weren't jumping off a cliff. We knew that what we were doing would most likely turn into something of value at some point. We had no reason to assume otherwise, and we have not been disappointed.

So how did it start? I know some beings don't like me to ask time questions, but it had to start somewhere, somehow.

Well, if a child is rolling a hoop toy down a street, when did that hoop rolling start? If it's spinning, where's the beginning of it? Do you understand that your question is not relevant? It's important to point that out to you. Imagine that you are galloping around the rings of Saturn on your spirit horse, and you've been around three or four times. Ask yourself, "Where is the beginning?"

All right, but you were in this space, and you became aware of your abilities, and at that time there was ...

No, no, you are making an error in your question. You said I "became aware" of my abilities. That's a time statement. No, we were in this space, and we knew our abilities and our capabilities. It's not that we became aware of them. I am correcting you on that because you could go off on a tangent in the wrong direction. I'm trying to keep you somewhat within the boundaries of reality here.

TRANSFORMING NONEXISTENCE INTO PREEXISTENCE AND EXISTENCE

All right, thank you. There was no Ssjoooo, and there was no totality. You created what? What prematter was the first thing that you created?

We utilized what to you would be nonexistence and transformed it into existence or preexistence. Preexistence is something that has the potential to be transformed further by other beings. Granted, there were no other beings there yet, but we saw no need to generate the totality. We had no desire or need to do that. But it occurred to us that it was something we could do, and it could do no harm, so we chose to do it and to keep doing it to see if anything would happen.

In terms of your time, we would do it for a while, and if nothing happened, then we would wait. Now, we had three waiting periods. We did it for a while, and nothing happened, so we waited. We did it again, and we did it again. The third time, something happened.

What was that?

Zoosh, followed almost immediately by Ssjoooo.

Aha! Oh, how wonderful! Could you give us a picture of it? I know that I'm trying to make it three-dimensional here, but …

That's all right; I realize you cannot help that.

Another said that where you live is separated from the totality and Ssjoooo by the reservoir of being. Do you see it that way?

No.

How do you see it? Or how is it?

I don't see any separation at all, but they see it, and that's fine. My not seeing it doesn't mean it isn't there. I simply do not recognize any separation, just as I do not recognize any separation between me and my fellow son — that's S-O-N, all right? I do not see any difference between me and my fellow son, and everything, so I do not see boundaries. While I know boundaries are comfortable for you as a means of understanding, I do not require them.

Aha. From the point of view of those of us on this side of the totality, could you say that what you created was the preexistence that became the space from which the totality and Ssjoooo emerged?

Yes, and more, meaning that although that is certainly true, there is more to it than that.

What is the "more to it"?

Remember, what you have there is existence and preexistence, and whoever acts on that must have some level of individual capacity or the ability, to say nothing of the desire, to act on it with an energy at least equal to existence and preexistence, which, if you think about it, would require some type of a creator.

But you created preexistence, which had within it the possibility of creators. Can you say that?

I can't say that, no. You could put out food for horses, but if horses don't exist, you'll be putting out food for quite a while and then waiting. It's more like we put out food, and eventually in the sake of our analogy, here, horses showed up.

Where did they come from?

I believe they showed up from the desire of existence and preexistence to express itself.

But that would still be in what you created. The existence and preexistence are what you created, so it's as if there was a piece of you in there somehow.

No, I wouldn't say that. Yes and no. I realize what you are going for, and if you want to say that, yes. But would you say that if you were to sow wheat and bundle it, and then there would be a piece of you in the wheat? You planted the wheat, grew it, and harvested it. Is there something of you in the wheat aside from your attention?

Seeds for more wheat, see? There are seeds for more wheat. The very nature of wheat says that it will grow and provide the ability to reproduce itself, so that's why I suspect there was something of you in there. If Zoosh is right, and there's nothing beyond the space where you are ...

I will not take credit for having something of me in there, but I grant that we're splitting hairs.

Yes. Why do you call yourself "son"? That's interesting. Is this S-O-N, or S-U-N?

I'm saying S-O-N so that you do not confuse us with an astronomical body. We do not look like your Sun.

But that's an odd name, because that implies you're the son of somebody.

No, only in your language.

What does it mean in yours or in some other language?

To us it relates to a sound. It doesn't connote masculine or feminine or anything like that. It's a sound. It's not the offspring of. And you know, sometimes there are sounds in other languages that you might recognize, but they haven't any similarity to the meaning you know. You find this often in words that are associated with personal names. You go to another country and someone has a last name that sounds like a word that you know in your language. Sometimes it's funny; sometimes it isn't. The converse is true as well. Sometimes you might say your name to people who speak a different language, and they laugh. You don't know why, but years later you find out, and you feel a little embarrassed.

Well, is it a word that you're using to talk to me, or is that how you think of yourself? Or is it a tone or something?

From my perspective, in terms of a tone, it would be spelled S-N-N-N, with it tapering off a little bit at the end, Snnn.

Snnn, yes, like that.

So for accuracy you could spell it that way; however, it's pronounced like "son" but with a long n.

All right. Zoosh has explored every avenue and every nook and cranny, and there is nothing beyond, on the other side, any place — up, down, sideways — that could have created you?

Not that, no. Why are you attached to that? [Chuckles.] Do you not have a myth on your Earth about finding the pot of gold at the end of the rainbow?

Yes.

Do you know that the reason it is such an everlasting myth is that finding the end of the rainbow is much more of a desire than any pot of gold?

[Laughs.]

Gold comes and goes, but do you know anyone who has found the end of the rainbow?

I've been looking for it for a long time.

This is the end of the rainbow, but it may not have all the answers you want. It might provide you with answers that, to you, sound enigmatic at times, but that is natural because the ways in which we are alike are so few in your current incarnation compared to the ways in which we are different. Now, when you are your natural self, we are a little bit more alike, but there are still a lot of differences. The main difference you would recognize immediately is in motivation. You would have to say that, no matter what form your existence takes, you have motivation. We do not see ourselves in that light.

Are you saying that you totally enjoy being, whether you're providing this material for the creators or not.

Yes, and we're at the point now where we don't have to provide very much. The creators can do it on their own. We only do it now on special request, as you say.

Are you aware of the incredible work that Zoosh and others are putting into the Explorer Race?

Oh, yes.

What is your feeling about that?

It seems a worthy gesture on Zoosh's part.

Do you feel that it could possibly affect you?

I don't see how.

UNDERSTANDING THE RESERVOIR OF BEING
Can you help me understand the reservoir of being? I see it as frothing, full-of-life force or something.

Well, that's a pretty good description. I don't think it's bubbling as one might find a pot of water bubbling on high heat. I think that it is more of a jubilant place where there is great anticipation for both what will be experienced and what could be experienced. In short, beings look forward to life and its many expressions.

Do you find that these beings have not yet had life in the totality?

They are alive and have life, but not as you know it. They are not incarnated in a form like yours, and they are not even incarnated in a form of precreation. I've seen some creators come out of there, but it takes quite a bit of cooperation.

Is that a result of the totality, or was that something you manifested?

No. Nothing in what you call the totality has anything to do with what I, or my companion, manifested. We did what I told you; everything that followed was the result of other creators.

All right. No one has quite made clear to us the difference between the reservoir of being and the totality. Where did these beings come from?

It is a source point that beings can return to after life, but they don't have to. It is a source point where beings prepare to experience some form of life, either as you know it or different. So you look where you are for hierarchies and for routes and exchanges and transfers and, in short, you look for an explainable method. But it is an optional place to come to.

So the place you're talking about is more than one thing. It's a place where beings exist before they choose to express a personality of some sort (which could take many forms), or it's a place where they've already expressed a personality and just wish to return here to enjoy the experience and then eventually go back out, because once they've experienced a personality or a form of existence as you understand it, then they usually want to continue on with that process. So part of the reason it's so jubilant is that beings who have not done it are looking forward to doing it, and other beings who have done it are interested in experiencing what these returning personalities have done.

All right. But it was not there when you first exercised your abilities.

Correct.

TAKING A NEW DIRECTION
So we found the end of the rainbow, but where do we go from there?

This might alarm you right now, but what has kept you going all this time is looking for the end of the rainbow. Ultimately, think about why that story has been changed. It used to be about the search for the end of the rainbow, and then somebody added the pot of gold. If you find the end of the rainbow and there's a pot of gold there, what good does it do you unless you take it with you and spend it? In short, take what you know, go where you are or somewhere in the totality, as you call it, and search more if you want to. This direction holds no further promise, but you can continue to look if you want to. Remember that you can be reluctant to think about giving up a journey that you have come to enjoy, but the journey isn't ending; it's taking a different direction. You have to decide whether you are going to embrace the totality or to continue looking for something greater than the totality, which has ultimately been your motivation from the beginning of this search.

If you would rather have another word than "totality," I will happily accept it.

I have no problem with that word. I think it is very accurate and useful to the reader. It may not be entirely complete, but what's the difference between saying the entirety, the All That Is, or the totality? The totality, I recognize, is your attempt to expand All That Is, and I acknowledge that.

Okay. Are many beings in the totality aware of you?

Oh, I wouldn't think so. Zoosh is, and Ssjoooo is; perhaps there are a few others but not many. They don't need to know.

You don't get a lot of visitors.

No. In the beginning there were creators from time to time, but those creators spawned other creators. The only time we do that work I mentioned before is on special request from a creator-type being. Once a creator said that it wanted to produce something with existence and preexistence that had never been produced before. That creator felt that if it came to us and received something directly from us instead of receiving some form of energy that had been used in other ways, it might accomplish that. So we said, "All right," and we provided that. From our perspective, we have not seen anything new or different; however, only that creator could tell you whether the creation is in any way different.

THE CREATION OF COLOR AND SOUND

You don't pay a lot of attention to the totality, but you are always aware of everything happening there?

No, we're not, and we don't choose to be. We are aware of everything in the totality, but that's like saying you are aware that there are other people on Earth, you understand? We don't stay in touch. [Chuckles.]

Well, I was going to ask you whether there were things out there that surprise you, but if you don't pay a lot of attention to it, then that's not a relevant question. Is there anything out in the totality that interests you?

Color. We like that.

You said that color and sound was an offshoot, a byproduct of your creating preexistence. Is that what you said?

We create existence and preexistence from nonexistence.

Right, but you said there were byproducts. Were those color and sound?

Yes.

When you did that, you would watch the colors that emerged as a byproduct, then?

Yes, that was interesting.

But the sound doesn't interest you so much?

No, that's also interesting, but we're more interested in the color.

How did the colors appear to you, as blocks or as undulating waves or rainbows? Or what?

[Chuckles.] I do not know that your language can express it but as happy color. It is a feeling. When something is color in its essence, it is profoundly joyous. It is not really a shape so much as a feeling.

Well, they say our souls are made of color and sound. Is that true?

Yes, but that's an attempt to analyze light. After all, science can tell you that when light is analyzed, color and sound are certainly two products associated with it. At least if they know their stuff, they'd say that.

But you don't say that you create light; you're not mentioning light at all.

That's right. I didn't mention that.

So you didn't mention it, or you don't create light?

I didn't say that, so you can extrapolate.

So I'm assuming that you don't create light.

I'm not disagreeing with you. Do you know why you're struggling? When you find the end of something, all of the questions you've asked to find the end cease to be relevant. So you have to find new questions or move on. That's why you're struggling.

EMBRACE THE PLACE WHERE YOU ARE

What about Zoosh? We've been working with Zoosh for a long time now. He started out as a product of what you created and has since moved into this area with you, correct?

I think that he likes being out here, but Zoosh can be more places than one, you know. He does not feel restricted by space or time.

So he came from the totality, but you don't want to talk about the third Snnn.

The third Snnn is not here yet.

Do you know who it is or where it is?

Oh, yes.

You do, oh! All right.

You tell me.

I should tell you? Oh, well, I have no idea.

Oh yes you do.

I do? Have I talked to him?

You have to rephrase that question.

In the course of trying to find the end of the rainbow, has the being talked to me who will become the third Snnn?

Well, I think I can say yes. But that answer would probably cause you to look in the wrong place.

[Chuckles.] All right, well, I won't worry about that now. What else can you tell us that we can learn from?

Almost nothing. Remember that what you are trying to learn is entirely based on something that we did not create nor had motivation to create. So if you want to learn about the place you're in, you have to put your senses in that place. You can't leave a place to learn about it. And here's a good example: If you want to know about the United States, as a citizen, you can go to a foreign country and ask people what they think or know about the United States. At least half if not three-quarters of what they say will be false, just as people in the United States have false ideas about other countries. This is not because people are embracing ignorance but because a certain nationalistic political sense exists in your time. People are not quite ready to embrace each other as equals yet, but that's coming. So if you want to know about the United States, you have to explore the United States. [Chuckles.] If you want to know about the United States, you have to be in the United States and explore it from within.

How do you and the other Snnn interact? Is there anything that we could relate to about what you do and feel or think?

If you were here, without being able to use your senses, you might notice after a while ("a while" being an uncountable amount of time) that you are relaxed, and you would realize that consciousness of us is more related to — how can we say? — a nonfeeling than to a feeling, and that tends to create this state of stasis or waiting or resting.

So you don't look forward to anything?

People who look forward to things experience time.

Oh time, yeah right.

Frustrated?

[Chuckle.] All right.

It is like the story in which a student who is searching for the truth climbs one mountain after another to find the most wise and wonderful guru. Each teacher the student encounters refers him to the next being, and on and on he goes. Eventually he reaches the last being, and it says, "To understand life, you have to live it." And that's all. The student staggers away, realizing on the one hand that he has been exposed to a profound thought, and on the other, he feels wholly dissatisfied.

[Laughs.] I see. Well, I'm pleasantly surprised. You're saying I need to go back down into 3D and explore it.

What I'm saying is that since you have chosen to live in the totality and exist there, it might be a good idea to embrace it.

I just emerged, didn't I? I didn't go there from somewhere else ... ?

Have you not been described as somebody who tends to travel, sometimes at high rates of speed?

Yes.

Beings who do that are never satisfied with where they are; they are looking for something. When you look for something, especially at a high rate of speed, it means that you're not satisfied with where you are. It might be time to consider embracing where you are as something new. You have not done that.

That is incredible advice, and I am smart enough to take it. Okay. [Chuckles.] That is beautiful. I don't have any more questions.

All right. Good. Who would you like to talk to next?

Zoosh, if he would talk to us.

Very well.

Thank you. Thank you very much.

Enjoy your explorations.

Thank you.

❋　❋　❋

THE PURPOSE OF THE THIRD SNNN

Greetings! Zoosh here. Well, well, well, well, well, how did you like that?

Oh, what a loving being! I'm going to agree to probe things closer to home, but when I get out of here, I still think there's a hole out of the back door of that place.

[Chuckles.] Well, we will welcome your probing, poking your nose at the outer boundaries, and looking for a crack. Why should that be any different from what you've been doing, eh? But at some points, I think the advice was good.

The third Snnn, can you talk about that? It sounds like a position that someone is working toward.

Well, I think that that's a perfectly reasonable statement.

Why couldn't he say who it will be?

He obviously wants you to say. He must feel that you know the answer. And I have to agree; you do know the answer.

All right. At this point I have absolutely no idea what he's talking about. Why would there even be a third one if two beings were there from the beginning or from the never-ending cycle? Why are there even arrangements for a third one?

Let's put it this way, to use our friend's way of speaking: If you have a two-legged chair, it will take considerable effort to balance when sitting on it, but a three-legged chair allows you to relax and do what you wanted to do when you sit down. In short, the third Snnn might just *start some whole new thing*.

Four legs would be even more stable! I mean, why stop at three?

Now, if that's not the quintessential definition of your personality, I don't know what else is!

All right. So that would start something else in another direction.

Chapter 22

The Mystery Solved

Snnn 2 and Zoosh

November 9, 2000

Snnn number two.

Welcome!

I can speak for a time.

Your companion said that you created precreation. How would you describe what you created?

Generated precreation.

What is the dynamic of that generation? How do you do that?

There are no words in your language; it is all feeling. I cannot describe something to you that is a feeling, you understand?

Yes. I guess the only thing I really care about is who generated you, but that seems to be something that nobody wants to talk about.

Has it ever occurred to you that life often happens spontaneously?

Do you mean that you and the other Snnn were spontaneously generated?

No, but I am using that as an analogy. If you were to study particle physics even though it's in its infancy, you would see that things seemingly appear from nowhere. Sometimes they are traveling from other places, but occasionally they are generated right there in that moment. I have a saying. If you can wrap yourself around this one …

Okay, great! You have a sense of humor!

… then I would say my origin involves generation and self-generation and inner-, outer-, and all-dimensional travel within the same space and the same moment.

All right. You have no outside agency connected whatsoever?

There is no outside agency, period — anywhere, for anything. Nothing

335

is disconnected from anything else; everything is connected. There is no authority. If there were, your religions would be right, and would you not feel uncomfortable if they were?

Oh, absolutely. So there's no chance that you came from some other totality beyond something we can ever fathom?

You cannot really fathom what we are anyway, but if you are trying to pursue some point of origin beyond our being, then no.

THE THIRD LEG

All right. The other Snnn said he took delight from the colors that came out of what you generated. Do you feel the same way, or do you consider another aspect of your life that is joyful?

I agree; I found that most entertaining.

Would you say that the colors are an offshoot of what you generated?

Oh, I do not take credit for the colors, nor does the other Snnn. That's why I mentioned spontaneity to you earlier. We created what we created, and then we noticed the colors. We did not create the colors.

Can you say that was the beginning of colors?

I can say that it was the first time I noticed colors.

Is that spontaneous generation where our colors come from?

One can only speculate. I am perhaps not an expert on the colors you experience in your world. I am not observing your creation nor have I ever.

What do you observe?

I have my own life, and I live my life. I sometimes notice lives of others who are similar or proximate, but it will be a while before I notice you as a member of the Explorer Race. That's a hint. What is your question, the question you were thinking about and were going to find out at the end of the week?

Oh, who is the third Snnn, yes!

Now pay attention to my hint.

It'll be a long time before you notice. ... The Explorer Race is going to be the third leg!

That's why it will be a long time!

The whole Explorer Race?

Yes. I knew you could get it.

[Laughs.] Somebody — I don't remember who — said the seeds and the root were going to go back to that little vein in the membrane where they came from.

They might well do that, but eventually they will re-form because when one being has joined with other beings and done something that is so magnificent, so major, and so influential, it always wants to get back together with those beings. And at that point, you will most likely decide to come here and become the third Snnn.

Tell me, what will that do?

It will change what we do.

How?

So far, our job has been to create precreation, but we don't have to do that much anymore. When the Explorer Race comes, given its origin and involvement in life — it is so much more experienced in many ways than we are — it will have a different agenda. The Explorer Race will want to create precreation that has specific orientations that we don't do now. As a result of its travels and experience, the Explorer Race will know by then what kind of orientation it wants. Therefore the precreation will most likely work more quickly and perhaps more efficiently to respond to the needs that the Explorer Race has observed. This way, the things that it perceives need altering will be fed within precreation and creation in the formats of creators who will quickly adapt and resolve what they feel needs this correction.

God, that's exciting! I knew there was some ultimate thing better than going back to the vein in the membrane.

Well, there's no place like home, as the famous line goes. But you will enjoy home for a time, and then you will become frisky.

How did that even come to be a possibility?

I believe when the original thread of the Explorer Race was sent out, it had the potential for precreator status, which does not have to (and it is better not to) be applied immediately. It's better for the Explorer Race to have a full range of experiences that explore being a creator, of course, and by doing so, it discovers more and will arrive there with an agenda that is benevolent. We feel that then the three of us will be able to do much more.

So the expansion will expand your potential?

No, but right now the other Snnn and I are not motivated to do anything else because our experience is of ourselves. But not where you are. You, the Explorer Race, will arrive with this agenda, but you will join us. And in that joining, if we feel so inclined (which is likely), we will embrace your agenda at least partially, and then we can do more.

Do you think the Creator of our system will be joining us then, when that awesome possibility comes about?

It is possible but not likely. That Creator has another destiny.

Can you say anything about him?

My understanding of that Creator's destiny is precreator training.

Ah!

What does that hint mean?

Foreplay. [Laughter.]

The fourth Snnn.

I said that we needed a fourth leg, and Zoosh made fun of me!

It will be some time (but quite a while after your Explorer Race arrives) that the Creator that you grew up with will most likely arrive to be the fourth Snnn, or as you say, the fourth leg. Zoosh can make light of things, but it is not his job to give you the answers on a silver salver. He must let you find them sometimes. If you find them, you have such pleasure.

Yes, yes. You have a totally different perspective. The other Snnn is delightful, but you're different. You're not one being.

Individuality is a reality everywhere I have observed, though I grant I have not observed that much.

COMPLETENESS

Now, the Mother of All Beings said she is totally complete within herself. It sounds as if that's what you are: You're totally complete within yourself.

Yes.

She made the statement that she could create from within herself more than she does.

That is her nature as the Mother of All Beings.

But it sounds as if you can do that too.

We are not motivated to do that, though. We are happy being what we are. It is not our job, nor do we even have an inclination to go and have an experience such as your own, so we will be what we are for some time.

But when the Explorer Race joins you, won't there be some sort of a sharing of experience? Won't you then know everything that we've gained and learned and experienced?

We might not embrace your experience that fully. We will first be interested only in your agenda. You will want to explain [chuckles] how you came to believe this, but you will find it uncomfortable at first because we will essentially say to you, "What do you want?" Then you will say, "Well," and start telling a story. Then we will wait for a polite time, and we will say, "What do you want?" And that will go on for a while until you ...

Calm down a little?

Well, yes, and then you will say what you want, and we will embrace it or not. But the stories and the justification and the rationalization and the feeling and all of this — while all of that is perfectly legitimate in the way of life where you are — is not our way. So we do not require an explanation for how you arrived at a decision. We only need to know the decision, and then we can embrace it on its own merits without requiring any persuasion.

Well, say more about what your life is.

My life is feeling. Let me say this: To the extent that you or even a shaman or mystical person has feelings (a mystical person may be able to access feelings that a person who is not of that life would unlikely be able to access), the range of feeling that I have is about to the twentieth power of that.

So what do you feel, then? You're complete, a feeling being in precreation not interested in the creation?

No, no, you've made a mistake. You said I'm in precreation. I am not. Neither is the other Snnn. We generate precreation, but we are not in it.

So what are you in?

We are in where we are, what our feeling is, and what our experience is, but I cannot put it into your words because it is not a worded thing.

So you're not motivated or curious; you're just totally satisfied with what is.

We are complete. When a being is complete, there is no need for motivation. Say you need to make some cookies, but you do not have the butter and eggs you require. Not only are you motivated to acquire them, but you need physical motivation to get you to the store. But if you do not require cookies ...

No motivation.

Yes.

Have you done anything else like this, generating precreation? Have you generated anything else?

We had an individual creator come by once who wanted us to generate a status that exists before precreation because this creator was practicing precreation (remember, your Creator was going to do that kind of training), and we showed that it wasn't viable. We exhibited the qualities of our personality that must be present to generate precreation, thus giving this creator something to say. "Well, here's something I could do." So the creator was motivated to go out and learn how to assimilate or acquire such qualities.

So there's a training school for precreators. Are there other creators who have come to the totality to do this in some fashion?

The only ones who I know are on the way are you and the creator of your now place. This being we spoke to will probably not come our way for quite a while, but working on precreation as it is, it will come our way at some point.

Was that creator the only one who ever came and asked to know how to do it?

He is the only one who came to ask to be taught from our perspective.

So what do creators have to display or do to get your teaching?

They must qualify. They must demonstrate certain traits. They must be selfless while having the capacity to be complete. So this might seem contradictory, but it really isn't. "Selfless" does not mean that they don't exist but that their existence is devoted to their creation in a uniform way, meaning that everything they create equally partakes in their energy and that there is no hierarchical energy dispersion. That is one character trait, for example.

Many beings are complete. It is not unknown for a person to be complete on Earth, but it is rare. More often, one finds this at other levels. But to be complete means that you have everything that you need and want, and you have the capacity to generate those things on your own for yourself and the openness to do so for others. One generally does not find this below the master-teacher level, but you have had, I think, one or two master teachers on your planet, maybe more.

I believe there have been a few true gurus, meaning they were complete. A true guru demonstrates no particular interest in teaching anything. He or she is not attached to the idea of anyone learning anything. A guru might share his or her life with you in some way. My idea of a guru may be a little different from your popular definition. To me, gurus (referring to human beings here) are complete and demonstrate that completeness by the way they live. The way gurus live has everything to do with it. They might very well eat, but they would honor what they eat. They probably would not cook anything, so they most likely would be vegetarian or some such thing. But that is not a requirement. They would probably have people who want to follow them but would most likely discourage that, not in an unpleasant way. But if followers were insistent, a guru might just vanish or sneak away some night, leaving the followers where they are so they could apply what they had learned to their lives. If followers are not given an opportunity to apply what they have learned, they will simply become imitators.

So why would these beings even be on this planet, as role models?

They might have been normal human beings at first but assimilated their completion while here. It is possible. It is not the usual way, but there might be a reason for it.

Most creators are not complete, are they?

If you were to ask them, they might say they were, but from my point of view, the simple fact that they are creating anything at all — in terms of planets or people or such things — suggests that they are motivated. This does not mean it is a lesser status; it's different. Without motivated beings, you would not have a creation that you understand and much less likely, for that matter, that you would be experiencing a personal life in this creation.

THE POTENTIAL FOR NEED

There must be creators or there would be no place to play. When the Explorer Race gets there, how are they going to be satisfied without exploring? They will have gone beyond all that?

They will have gotten through that; that's right. Obviously, once you are a creator, you can't go rushing off. [Chuckles.]

We've been told, however, that after this creation, the Explorer Race would go rushing off.

You [the Explorer Race] might do that, but it wouldn't be immediate.

That's incredible! Thank you for revealing this. Do you converse with Zoosh and Ssjoooo on the other side?

I have noticed they converse with each other. I have noticed they communicate. Occasionally, they will communicate in such a way that we are more likely to be aware of it. It would be as if someone in one of your buildings were to speak loudly so that others might hear them.

Does that interest you or bore you or elicit no response?

We usually have no response. If the communication interests us, we will engage Zoosh and Ssjoooo in some way so that they will come over and share.

Is the following concept correct? There is the totality of creation, and then there is this little place called the reservoir of being, and you're beyond that, but you're actually everything, right?

Yes.

But even though you are everything and in everything, you stay beyond the reservoir of being. If you're in the totality, you see the reservoir of being. The idea is that you're beyond that. Is that correct?

Beyond would be better, yes.

Now, Zoosh came, but not many other beings have an interest because they have to leave their personalities behind when they come to where you are, beyond the reservoir?

Most beings as you would know them do not come there. It's usually only creators.

Okay. Do new creators come? Do you see beings passing by?

Very rarely.

Could they come in and just enjoy the quietness without bringing any attention to themselves?

Yes.

So they might be there, but you might not even know it.

We would know it, but they might be there, just as you say, resting. But there are other places to rest.

You generated precreation, but is this a continuous thing that you do, or is it something you did once and you never have to do it again?

It is something we did once.

So you don't really do anything now?

Not as you understand "anything" to be, other than existing.

But once the other being said he discovered he could do precreation.

Well, there was a need, so we discovered we could do it, yes, but we did not have personal motivation.

What was the need that you felt?

There was a feeling that there was a need for potential, but the potential itself was not needed in that moment. Again, it's hard to define a feeling. We had a feeling, so we took action. That's the simple truth, but (you can talk [speaking to a cat who's meowing]) in trying to say more, we are making an effort to get around your language.

We learned that when Ssjoooo was out there, they responded to a need and everything was a response to a need.

From Sjoooo's point of view, that makes sense. I agree with Ssjoooo: In the world he knows and you know, that seems to be true. But for us, we did not feel a need. We felt a potential of a need, and that's why we've acted. What we created could not be turned into anything harmful; we created something that could be acted on if the need arose and was not just a potential. So when it did in fact rise, what we had created was available for utilization.

That's the beginning of everything, from our perspective. To you, it was an isolated or one-time event that was finished.

Yes.

Okay. Can we say that, because there's a need to know, you suddenly know all these things that you said you hadn't paid much attention to about the Explorer Race or the totality?

I'm responding to your need.

So in that moment of my need, you just know?

Yes. Though once that moment passes, we do not need to know it for ourselves.

It's gone.

FEELING SNNN

If I were to look at you, would I see you?

No.

If I were not in a human body but were my natural self and I came to visit you, would I see you?

No.

Would Zoosh see you?

Zoosh is aware of me. But does he see me? No.

Feel you?

Yes. I can be felt but not seen. However, I can see my fellow Snnn, and my fellow Snnn can see me.

Ah. So what does he look like? Can you tell me in words I understand?

Have you ever experienced going somewhere and feeling as if someone was present (or having that feeling without going anyplace), a sense of presence? That is the closest description I can give you that would be familiar.

Is there a sense of space there?

There is a sense of space, yes, but you could travel as fast as you could imagine, and you would not have any sensation of physical touch. So it is truly empty space.

Is it alive?

Everything is.

If the Adventurer were to travel across your space at the speed he does, would he actually move across it, or is it so big that ...

It might be that that being would not come to where we are, because we are not complex enough to draw his interest. The Adventurer pursues what is new and exciting. We might be new to some beings, but I do not recall being described by anyone as exciting.

[Laughs.] It's pretty exciting to be the catalyst for everything that is, don't you think?

If I were where you are, I might very well think that, but since I am not personally partaking in the experience, I cannot say that excitement is one of my feelings.

But you basically have all the feelings that any human has ever heard of or anything that we've read and more, more, more, more, and more.

No, we do not have discomforting feelings. If you just say benevolent feelings, yes. Yes, and as you say, more.

I truly give up. I would like to talk to you, but it's like talking to someone from not just another country but another ...

Like talking to a block of ice? Not the same language?

You're not a block of ice. You have a wonderful sense of humor.

Good night.

✳ ✳ ✳

All right, Zoosh speaking. Greetings. Well!

Ha! That was pretty fantastic!

You like my friend, eh?

I adore your friend! I am just frustrated that I don't have the words to communicate with him.

Well, all things considered, I think you did very well. The languages, if that term would apply, of the two of you are not in any way compatible.

Oh, he is great, though, and he has a sense of humor that's wonderful!

Yes.

THE ORIGIN OF THE EXPLORER RACE THREAD

So you laughed at me when I said the fourth leg, and there is going to be a fourth leg!

Is it not amusing?

Yes! It's almost unbelievable. Just think of what the potentials are! And the fact that they are interested in meeting the Explorer Race is just awesome, based on what he said about being motivated and the fact that they're interested in us. Whose idea was this?

Idea? You mean to allow the Explorer Race to become a leg and then your now Creator to become a leg?

Yes.

I think that was encoded in that thread of the Explorer Race.

But whose idea was it?

Who put out the thread?

Yes, who put out the thread? We've never exactly learned the identity of the beings involved. You were involved; you must have been.

I was involved, but I was not alone.

Who else? The Mother of All Beings?

I can tell you, but it will sound like a conundrum.

Okay.

Yourselves.

Oh, the Explorer Race! The three seeds?

The three seeds combined with the energy of the Creator that you worked with, meaning you put that out without having or retaining the knowledge that you had done so. Did you think it was an accident for that Creator that he stumbled across the thread in the vastness of all being in that exact place at the exact time?

You were leading him; you were with him.

Well, we were together, but I didn't have him by a nose ring.

[Laughs.] I think you were the daddy being.

Maybe a little bit.

A little bit, a little bit. Wow! What a way to end the totality book! How am I going to top this? [Laughs.]

It's not about topping.

I know, but we reached the end, and we have this incredibly wonderful surprise. Ssjoooo said something else, and I was so disappointed. He said the Explorer Race would just go back into the vein in the membrane at the edge of the totality and then, you know, kind of retire. [Laughs.]

But in a way, that's true.

But the Explorer Race is not going to stay retired, right?

For a time.

Yes. Ah, this is incredible. What other little surprises have you got up your sleeve?

Sometimes we need to let you guess at them so that you can have the pleasure of it.

[Laughs.] I never would have guessed. The hint he gave me was ...

You guessed after he hinted.

Oh, yes, but it took the hint to get that going.

That's what it takes sometimes for everyone.

Why are you the only one who went back into the space where the Snnns are?

You might say that one of my jobs is as the meeter and greeter.

Who are you meeting and greeting?

Well, sometimes the meeter and greeter has to prepare for that which is met and greeted, so let's just say that.

You are going to be there when the Explorer Race gets there?

Certainly.

Ah, and you're going to ...

Probably travel with you.

You're going to meet us and greet us.

Yes.

[Laughs.] You'll probably travel with us? From where to where?

From your being a creator to that place. It is rather a long way, and owing to your personality, you will see many things that you will want to stop and examine on the way. And you will do that.

Gain experience and knowledge by the time we get there.

Yes. It's not about how fast you can get there.

I don't know. Maybe I'll want to sign on.

Maybe you will at that. Now that you have seen how far you can go and considered your potentials for going farther than that, pause and consider your lives as they exist in this moment. Yes, you are great and grand and wonderful beings, but on the day-to-day basis in your lives with your families and work and places of living (your neighborhoods, yes, your planet), there is much you can do there that involves creation. You know that if you have help when you have a task or a job, the task or job often becomes easier. When you think of world peace and other noble and worthy issues, sometimes they seem so far away. Know that as you join with others — don't exclude anybody — you will experience a form of peace even if it is not in your lifetime that your world comes to it. At this time in your lives, it is more important for you to be inspired and thus motivated. It is less important, even though that might not seem true, for you to accomplish these goals than to make the effort. In the effort toward accomplishing these goals, you will discover, create, and, perhaps more importantly, re-create the means of creation.

Creation in its own right has been plodding along for some time and done in pretty much the same way. But when one is cut off from one's greater self, as you are on Earth, one has to re-create the way one does things. It is in this act of re-creation and in the sense that sometimes beings who do not look appealing can sometimes bring great wisdom or knowledge or ability to solving a given problem in any moment. With this hard-won experience, your chances of re-creating creation are greatly enhanced. Good life.

Thank you. Now, let's address where we're going from here. Snnn said something to me that caused an epiphany about focusing on life where you are, so I think we will do that from now on.

Good. That's good. Ultimately, your readers are here on Earth, so we need to give them things that they can identify with, at least sometimes, eh?

Yes. But this has been a wild a trip, you know?

Yes, but with a different result. I agree with you that it is more important to do things that are a bit more grounded for the sake of helping people resolve their daily challenges. Shamanic secrets are very helpful because they give people the means of altering their physical reality to some better way of being. The disentanglement is profoundly helpful.

All right, I'm going to say good night. Thank you, Zoosh.

Good night.

Good night.

Chapter 23

What's Beyond Is Present
Ssjoooo

Greetings.

Is this Ssjoooo?

Yes. There is a limit to how much is conceivable, even with the vertical awareness that is now happening among your population. For example, many people are tapping into a route to the greater portions of themselves. This is causing some significant confusion as people demonstrate feelings and emotions that are not their own but can be pinpointed to others around them. Those others are not to blame. The route to their greater selves, with access to their various lives and to accumulated wisdom, requires a certain amount of cooperation and benevolence in the immediate area. What this means is that normally, on other planets and in other places where benevolence is the rule, when a being makes this connection that is necessary and not an ongoing factor of life, everything in the immediate area (that is, several miles out from the exact location or the outer boundaries of the being's physical self and possibly radiating closer but at least within a half mile) has to be completely attuned, benevolent, and totally accepting.

Of course, this is not the case in your world. On Earth, everything that is not attuned to accepting you as you are bounces around inside your auric field as you begin to connect with that route. So what occurs from that beginning or that sprouting is that you need to create a synthesis within your energy self; you need to take some active participation in that creation. You cannot count on others to be compatible. You have to actively create something. Materialization? No, not that. It is more like a generated creation.

CONNECT WITH THE SUN
TO CLEANSE YOUR AURIC FIELD

I will give you the means, and then I will explain the route. The means is simple — and must be, given the destructions of your daily lives and your capacities to resolve them. What I recommend is this: If the Sun happens to be in the sky, do not look at it, but cast your vision near it so that it makes a peripheral impression. Perhaps in the past, you have glanced at the sky and didn't look at the Sun, but you noticed it out of the corner of your eye. Don't look at it for even a second. Just glance in its direction.

This is not to tell you what the Sun looks like — you all know that for the most part — but to make a personal connection between you and the Sun. The Sun needs to become a companion in that moment. The Sun is the great purifier. Yes, it nurtures, but in this case, it is the purifier. If the Sun does not happen to be in the sky, just remember or imagine what it looks like (without staring at it in your memory either). Then relax, picture the Sun, and make a connection — a rope, a cord, a reach (for those of you who can use long touch), or however you want to think of it — from your body to the Sun. Let it be a brief connection. That kind of energetic connection does not need to be long, five to ten seconds or something like that, and that's it. That's all it will take to cleanse the area around your body.

Try to do this once or twice a day. It can be done at work if the phone is not ringing, and you can step away from your desk for a moment. There should be no distractions, however. It would be ideal to go to a park or somewhere there are no distractions whatsoever. If you have a car and it is nearby, you can go sit in it for a moment. It can be before or after work or shortly after you've awoken. After you've done this exercise once or twice, it won't take more than a few seconds to do it every time. Over time, it acts in an accumulative way to cleanse not only your auric field itself but also it's capability to temporarily transform anything it is exposed to or wraps around it that is not completely compatible with you in that moment. You don't have to know all these details. The process is simple, so don't make it complicated. I'm explaining the process so you understand why it has value.

THE ROUTE TO THE HIGHER SELF

Now, to explain the route. You understand that the base is how it needs to be, but the route you are all beginning to experience is why there is so much distraction for everyone. Many of you have noticed feelings and strange occurrences. Perhaps your dreams have changed, you relate to people or objects differently, or your memory might be less accurate than it once was. Perhaps even recently, your memory was better and suddenly is not so good in a linear fashion.

What is happening is that this vertical cognizance is beginning to physically take place for all of you, and as a result, the connection that is sprouting or budding has moments when it makes brief contact with the greater you so that you have awareness of your total wisdom, your immortal wisdom. The awareness won't be that much yet, but it will be enough so that there are moments when you briefly feel disconnected from that which is around you (you'll probably notice these moments afterward, if you think about it). This will not get to the point where an entire second elapses. It might seem longer because in those split seconds when you are disconnected from what is physically around you, you are totally connected to your greater wisdom, your total being, Creator, everything. In those moments, you experience timelessness and complete balance. It is very much the way you feel before life, before conception and the egg and the sperm inside your mother, before there is any life happening on Earth. For you, this happens before life, then as you know it here, and then after life as you know it here. It doesn't happen when you're at the deepest levels of dreaming, so this is something unique and new to you as Earth's physical human beings.

Therefore, you need to do something. Fortunately, as I've said, the thing to do is not difficult. This vertical sprouting that you are experiencing will not decrease — it is not a temporary anomaly — rather, it will increase. It is really the next step, as others have said through this channel, of releasing the linear memory functions. In time, you will probably not be interested. For example, imagine computers that can tap into anything past oriented or future oriented, based on imagination or speculation, and computers that can utilize all their energy to tap into the present. Eventually, you won't want computers at all because you will do those things yourselves. I'm just mentioning that. Computer manufacturers, do not worry. This is well into the future.

The route that is forming to the connection happens only briefly and only in moments when it's safe, not when you're driving or operating a saw or any high-speed power equipment or flying a plane — nothing like that. But it does have a physical effect on machinery. This is something that is vital for your machinery designers to know. It can affect computer equipment, mechanical equipment, and even what I call liquid-functioning equipment, such as hydraulics. What happens is that the equipment might temporarily freeze. It won't seize as in a mechanical situation, but it will briefly stop. Picture it this way: There's a temporary opening in the entire reality of the physical human experiencing that moment. Imagine any photograph that suddenly has a white space, a crack, an opening, whatever you want think of it as (nothing frightening looking, just an opening) and in that white space is not anything I would call profoundly spiritual. Rather, it is the energy; the fluid of existence; or that which unites, creates, supports, and nurtures all existence everywhere.

So what you would see is a union that you experience in that microsecond or maybe a few microseconds, and that connection is taking place to build many things. First, as time goes on, this begins to happen more and more, and it is likely that people who operate equipment — drive cars, use cameras, play video games, things like that — will discover that if this equipment is not magnetically shielded (this is especially true for computer equipment), it will briefly lose contact with all of its instructions, This is not so true for mechanical equipment, which will have a moment of relaxation.

Right now, the length of time these interruptions take is short. It's not so much time that it actually creates problems in computers and computer programming, but within seven or eight years, it could be worse. Since this has to do with your immortal personalities, your connection to Creator, your connection to all life, it is not being done to cause harm to you or others but rather to revolutionize the way you live, to bring about more benevolence in your daily life, and to bring about more joy and happiness. To do that, your technology has to change over entirely. Of course, the route to the connection will fill with stimulating inspirations so those of you who create technology and who come in as a result of your inspirations will see radical changes over the next six or seven years, regardless of what is planned and what's in the planning stage.

You will see entirely new platforms that everyone will want and need because the platforms themselves will create a connection inside the human body's systems, including the nervous and endocrine systems as well as other forms of fluids in your body for which today's science either does not understand or has only a glimmer. It will create an accessibility to the body's actual functions that will revolutionize technology, and technology will not have any aspects whatsoever that are in any way harmful to anyone. Instead, this new technology will support, sustain, and nurture life of all forms. This is happening now because for the past six to seven years, there has been an influx of energy that creates a different, more benevolent future for you, which has been covered in other books.

Another reason is the entire wave of children and those who birthed them (and in this case, birthing children refers to the father as well, for the father plays a significant role, though the mother's role is more significant). So all the children who have been born, all of the parents who have been involved, and all the rest of society (because almost everyone interacts with these people) have prepared the way for what is taking place now and are not only receptive to this but are also necessary for this to happen within this timing sequence.

For most these moments of sprouting connections have been happening for about a year and a half. I want to give an example, since I feel that some of you might become a bit anxious. These moments will never occur in the cockpit of a plane for one or both pilots or other crew members in that technical area. It is not likely ever to occur for more than one crew member at a time. The reason I bring it to your attention is, as many of you who fly planes know, a great deal of the equipment (if not all of it) is magnetically shielded. But there is only so much you can do to magnetically shield equipment, as readouts and so on create some exposure. But it is possible, through the use of various prismatic devices, to create readouts that, as a result of reflections, take place away from the instruments. Now that's all I really need to say about it because people who design those things will instantly know what that means. I want to encourage that because it will make things safer. Know that none of this is happening in any way to harm anyone. Everyone's safety will be taken into consideration at all times.

CONNECTING TO CREATORS

I will provide a little more about the connection. Once the actual connection becomes more of a factor, the inspiration that you will receive will become greatly magnified. This will not eliminate guides or angels or those who support and nurture many things within you, including inspiration. Instead, it will actually increase the means by which these guides and angels (which you all have, and some of you are actually performing some guide functions while you are here in life) work. What is taking place is something that has been promised to guides and angels beyond time: their communications with you, which are vague at best right now, would become clarified, allowing them to provide you with entire sentences (in your own languages, of course), rather than the occasional word, as well as pictures, feelings, and stimulation so that you would know and recognize this as coming from your guide, from a being associated with Creator.

You will know that this is coming from an angelic being and is clearly something to pay attention to. It is meant for your greater good, as well as that of all those you will serve by acting on this inspiration. Your guides and angels have been promised that, and now it's taking place. This connection — the link, the sprouting, the root, all these words I've been using to create this connection — will make it easier for the guides and angels to inspire you and will activate the next step: Actual creator beings who work with your Creator, as well as your Creator Itself (I say "it" so that we do not say "him or her," as "it" encompasses that and more), will begin to do things for you in a similar way (in terms of the contact) as guides and angels have been doing for you until now.

You might occasionally get a word or a feeling that you know is not from one of your guides or angels (who you would have identified by that time) but is something so inspiring, so uplifting, and so magnificent that it would only remind you, if it reminds you of anything, of so-called "near-death experiences," of meeting Creator, whatever form of Creator, or God, or deity. It would be so uplifting, so magnificent, so wonderful that it would inspire and encourage you to live your life in a more benevolent way simply knowing such a thing is there and would be the beginning of the connection that most advanced beings and the most spiritually — and of course, technically, but most importantly spiritually — advanced planets and cultures in this universe experience. It will allow you to begin to express yourselves, to be your total selves, and to feel connected in such a way to creators and creatorship that it allows you to feel like you can be your natural selves while you are physical on Earth.

What a gift. How wonderful.

I mention this because this is actually happening for you now. There wasn't really any point in talking about it at much length before, but this is actually happening.

It's perfect. It ties in the third dimension to the immortal beings and the totality. I want to thank you personally for giving me energy when I was not able to attach here. They said you looked up, saw a need, and did something that saved my life.

Thank you.

I think you're very complete. I think I just felt it happen. I drifted out somewhere when you were talking. Was that what it was, or was it something else?

What is the difference?

That's complete and beautiful. You explained how it works and what to do perfectly and gave us aids. It's wonderful.

It's important to understand that what's beyond is also present.

Chapter 24

You Now Have Cords and Connections of Felt Wisdom to an Ongoing Continuity of Life

Ssjoooo

March 1, 2002

This is Ssjoooo.

Ssjoooo! Welcome!

I have been activated by events where you are. I am always activated like that. I have begun a series of connections and interconnections designed to make cords of benevolent light to connect to all things that all beings know as part of themselves. The connections will start and have started where I am, proceed swiftly to where you are, and are designed to cord all people on your planet with a cord of felt wisdom. The wisdom will not be something that will interfere with your thought process; rather, it will allow you to feel the continuity that you have individually so that this life no longer feels like it is something from somewhere — and afterward, oblivion. Not that. These connections will allow you to feel the ongoing continuity from before, in your context of time, and beyond this point.

Picture, if you would, many cords of light going back and forth and back and forth across the universes for an individual's life experiences. And when that connection is made it will not terminate with you. All these different connections to different points will not simply be something that comes down to you and stops; it will come down to you and continue on to future potentials. In terms of time, future potentials are not the same as what you've already imprinted. Future connections are possibilities that you have not yet imprinted with experience.

Such a manner of connection will allow people where you are to stop acting as if this life on Earth is all there is. Your people on this Earth are coming to the conclusion, as a fact, that certain things have to be changed. Some governments know this and have changed those things in the past. The government of the United States, being young and perhaps not idealistic at the practical, bureaucratic level, encourages that the idealism of the original founders of the government is taught even though existing facts (the way the government actually operates) are considerably different. The republican status has become decreasingly the fact, and the status of a de facto federal authority system is temporarily forming up.

I want to encourage everyone to, as your young people say, get over your cynicism. Get over it and vote. Even with the methods of cheating the voting records, as has been done many times in the past and not only just recently, if there is an overwhelming tide of votes, most of the people you vote for will get into office. So take a good look at the Congress that you have in the United States and at parliaments and other things in other countries and decide who would be the most heart centered to elect. Granted, they have to be practical and have knowledge of how things are run. Also, they have to understand legal terms. We feel that this is important, but it is also important not to allow one political party to dominate. The executive branch is one party, and the Congress ought to be something else. This forces the system to be more democratic even if the people running it do not always feel that way.

FORMATION OF THE GLOBAL GOVERNMENT

The formation of your global government is happening now, even as we speak. That is another reason that these connections that I spoke about are vital: so that the global government does not become only authoritarian. In the beginning, it will assume an authoritarian public image, not like a despot but somewhat rigid and at times bordering on the militaristic. But this will pass quickly — not just quickly in spiritual terms, but quickly in timely terms. Part of the reason it will pass is that it is spiritually a fact that everyone is waking up to a greater consciousness, and by "consciousness" I mean what you feel, what you know based on your feelings, and then what you think. That is happening and cannot be stopped, regardless of various individuals or groups attempting to stop or corrupt it, even unconsciously. Some groups have attempted to derail it unconsciously simply because of some greedy pursuit of their own, for their own agenda's purposes. But that is because the concepts of people, groups, and (to put it in a colloquial fashion) "us versus them" have been encouraged. It will not be possible to maintain such an illusion of nationalistic, conditioned propaganda much longer.

Global government is necessary and will be helpful in the long run, even though its face, initially, will not be very pleasant for some. It might be pleasant for some people, but it will look, as I say, authoritarian on the basis of using not just the so-called terrorists as a threat but, given the broad definition of terrorist, also using the idea of all those who attempt to disrupt the system for their own gain or the gain of their group. In the larger picture, the whole purpose of a global government is to unify, not to rule. But the initial establishment of such a bureaucracy will be perceived as a ruling body, not as a body to unify. Once the bureaucracy itself rearranges its identity for itself and others and moves from the head to the heart — which is not going to take as long as you might think — then it will look much better. It's not going to be something that looks like a system you've seen before. Initially it might have a resemblance that way, but it will quickly take on a form that is designed to support and sustain the lives of all beings.

Now, this global government is in its initial stages, and that is the international business community. The business community is not the right group to run or even set up such a thing, since its universal intention at this time is to make money, survive, and thrive, no matter what the cost to the consumer. That might not be the overall body of principal, but if you pull back, you'd have to say, given different perspectives, that the self-destructive nature of business and the destructive applications that affect everyone are truly giving the appearance of being terminally self-destructive.

CONNECTIONS BRING CALMNESS

So this series of connections that will allow you all to feel much more significantly connected to not the greater you but rather the continuous you, or if I might say, the continuum you, will be very helpful. A great deal of the sense of urgency that you all feel right now, since you are on the physical level feeling the general nervousness of the whole population, will fade. You won't be able to put a logical reason to that relaxation within, but you will all have the feeling that things are better than they appear. This will affect all beings, including animals and plants. It will affect all people: terrorists, prisoners, prison administrators, bureaucrats, politicians, homemakers, mothers, fathers, policemen, doctors, candlestick makers. This series of connections will affect everyone the same. So I want you to know that.

Now, let's give you some timing: When might you expect this to happen? Will it be sudden, or will it slowly phase in? You can expect it to begin to happen in March, and it will slowly phase in so that by the time September gets here, it will have increased to the level that everyone will have feelings they cannot identify. And some will be more aware than others, being sensitive, and the feeling, if you speak to each other, will be identifiable. You yourself might not be able to identify it, but the feeling is calm. Even if your life is frantic, there will be an underlying calm that has not been there before, which, when you look at your life and the environment you live in or have created, you cannot explain. But it is there, and you will find that you'll be able to relax into it if you care to.

YOU TEACH ONE ANOTHER

It will ease your sleep time. Many of you have noticed that your dreams have been vivid and sometimes uncomfortable, because you're being taught, and not always by identifiable guides or teachers, not always by faces you know. What began recently, because of this interconnectedness going on, is that you are now teaching one another. Sometimes you will recognize somebody in your dream who has been teaching you, not consciously or mentally, but that person might even have had thoughts — "If only I could explain this to my friend in a way she (or he) could understand that will contribute to the cooperation of her (or his) soul and immortal personality" — that interact with your soul or immortal personality in the dream state, and not just at the deep-dream state. Sometimes, and this is more often the case, it will occur in that dream state you have just before you wake up.

So when you wake up, you will very often have a dream impression, meaning something you see clearly — and in color, by the way. This black and white dreaming is not true. You will clearly see the individual, maybe from the back, maybe from the side, or maybe face-on. Most often, it will be from the back or side. Nevertheless, you know the individual well enough to say, "That is my friend! I recognize him (or her), and he (or she) was instructing me, about something she (or he) knows I'm working on, and she (or he) was encouraging me. I can feel it." You can tell them if you wish; it will at least amuse them and, in some cases, intrigue them. Know that no one will be teaching anybody else anything without his or her permission on both sides, you see.

But the important thing about your teaching each other is that you are living in the world that you live in now, and what you teach one another will be practical things of the world and of the culture in which you live that you, as the students, are actually trying to learn for your own benefit. You won't be taught something esoteric that you have no interest in or that would harm you in any way. For instance, you want more money or more abundance, so people you know who have that will teach you. They might not know they are teaching you, but they are; and it is their immortal spirits who are doing this. Yes, sometimes that immortal spirit is inspired, and inspiration at the level you experience in a dream is more easily attained or accessed, either one. Nevertheless, what inspires that teacher, that physical human teacher, at that level of the dream state for you both (well, not exactly for you both; the dreamer, the person who is sleeping, is at that stage, but the other person might very well be awake) is going on for him or her at the unconscious and subconscious levels.

How would you know whether you are actually working with people in their sleep states while they are dreaming when you are awake? You might or might not know. Most of the time you will not know, but from time to time, someone's familiar face might be there. As I said before, you think, "If only I could explain to my friend, in words that he (or she) could understand, this thing he (or she) is trying to learn, it would be so much better for him (or her). But I don't know how to explain it, or I don't have the opportunity." (You don't think like that, but that is the circumstance, you see?) That might pop into your head. If it does, it is either setting up a condition for a dream that person will have — so don't tell your friend that you had this thought; you don't want to interfere with the dreams — or the person is having the dream at that time. Again, don't tell him or her; you don't want to interfere. But if he or she happens to tell you about a dream that you were in and to the best of that person's recollection, you were teaching him or her something of interest and you feel some sense of truth or recollection or even déjà vu, then know that this is one of those circumstances.

BE AVAILABLE AT MULTIPLE LEVELS TO SERVE THE NEEDS OF ALL BEINGS

This is also part of your creator training, when one must be available at multiple levels to serve the needs of all beings all the time, even if one is asleep. You do not necessarily need to drop everything if you are awake; just simply be available. Sometimes people ask you for help while you are awake and doing other things, and it's not convenient. Then you have to say, "I'd be happy to help you, but not right now; wait till I'm done, and then I will help you," or "I am doing something else right now, and I can't help you; please ask someone else," or any number of other things you might say or do. This new level does not require you to physically stop what you are doing, but it might tap on your unconscious and subconscious self, and if it does, you might suddenly have a feeling that is not prompted by your surroundings.

The feeling — let me tell you what it is so that you don't wonder. It will feel exactly like the feeling you get when you are distracted. You can experience this feeling while you are doing something that requires your total concentration, perhaps even something that is dangerous, such as performing surgery. However, it is extremely unlikely that an individual such as a surgeon, for instance, would have this experience while doing an operation, because that would not be in the flow of benevolent life and could create a hazard. But if you are, say, an average citizen driving your car and you feel the distraction is too much, then this is what to do first: If there are other people in the car who are chatting to you or among themselves, ask for a moment of silence or that they talk more quietly, even whisper for a minute or two. That doesn't mean a second or two; it means an actual minute or two. If you are alone and the radio is on or you are playing something on the machine, turn it off. Granted, there will be noise from the exterior, since you are driving, or even from the car itself, but you want to reduce the quantity of your distractions, and then you can drive safely.

When that feeling of distraction within you passes, wait about one or two minutes and then tell the other people in the car they can resume their conversation as they like, or if you are alone, you can turn the radio back on. But since you will be a little more sensitive then, when you turn the radio or the music back on, it would be better for you if you turn it on quietly and play music that is gentle. Or if there is someone talking, don't turn it on for a half-hour, maybe. You need to allow your body to become calm within and center itself, which it will do on its own. That's what I recommend.

CREATOR TRAINING INSTEAD OF RE-CREATION
What catalyzed your idea? What caused you to do something unprecedented?

Well, the same thing that prompted me to do something before: the felt need coming from somewhere else. That is how I function. If the need is strong enough, I respond to the need as you would: instinctually. Because I have not responded to such a need before, there isn't a pattern of behavior that covers that. Whatever my immediate reaction is would be comparable to your instinct, which is why I use that term.

Okay. So there's a cord of light to every human and to his or her benevolent potential?

Picture all these things: An individual is born, meaning his or her personality starts somewhere, breaks off of some other mass being, perhaps a portion of a personality, and becomes its own to pursue its own individual interests. Think how many lives and existences might happen before you might show up here, for example: maybe hundreds, maybe thousands, maybe less.

But where you are now in this now school, you don't have recollections of those lives, nor do most people have a sense of having ever been anywhere and done anything, because you have been re-creating your total being and not doing the Creator School training but preparing for Creator School training, which means that you are not allowed to remember or even have the feeling of these previous existences. But now you have stopped re-creating your realities; no one is re-creating anything for himself or herself any more.

Karma stopped a while ago, and now this re-creation has stopped. Do you understand the difference? The difference is simply that the purpose of ignorance was to allow you to do things in a new way, but the purpose of that was to re-create your foundational makeup as an individual personality so that you could be more and do more should the need arise for you in some existence somewhere or should the need arise for others so that you could respond to them in a more flexible and broad way. That is over. You have all re-created as much as you ever will in this school; now, instead of doing pre-creator training, you are doing creator training. As a result, these kinds of connections are necessary. It is all part of the recollection process so that you will ultimately be able to recollect the manners — not table manners, but the manner of living that you have — on a cumulative basis that were acquired in lives and existences before you focused here on Earth and temporarily forgot them. You will be able to reacquire the personality based on such wisdom. You won't have total recollection of these previous lives, because that would interfere in your Explorer Race process here, but you will have the feeling, the motivations, and the capacities. Many of you will suddenly, find that you can do things you haven't been able to do before or haven't been able to do easily before or even haven't had any interest in doing before. You will suddenly be able to do things more easily or to quickly adapt to doing things that you might, for any particular reason, be called on to do.

Because of these new connections?

Because of life. Therefore, you will need to have the means to accomplish these unexpected motivations and needs of society in general. In short, you are beginning to remember who you are. It is necessary to instill such felt recollection — not thought, as that will interfere in what you are doing — to not supplant, but to *support* your instinctual body, which will allow you to instinctually do what you need to do or to do these things much more easily, to learn more quickly. This will allow you to very quickly (in some cases overnight when the need arises) accomplish things as an individual, a group, a society, or even a global community, and will be particularly helpful in solving what appears to be impossible.

Therefore, this is part of creatorism — creator training, yes — but the functional capabilities of a creator also involve what appears to be instantaneous transformation but are, in fact, re-creation. If you were able to stretch out what appears to be instantaneous transformation, it would simply be a step back in the sequence that all beings have lived, from the most minute to the most expansive, including the whole universe. It's not time; it's a step back in the precise sequence that everyone has done. Do you understand? It's precise sequence.

You step back and simply re-create it along a slightly different line so that the outcome is different. Say you were to look at an apple, and it suddenly changes to an orange. You remembered that it was an apple, and it appeared to be transformation. In fact, it is that kind of re-creation. It's just happening so fast that you don't see the re-creation. Because you are all becoming much more sensitive to your physical feelings, you would have a physical feeling that would happen simultaneously, even in an instantaneous transformation. You would instantaneously, suddenly, have a physical feeling that you would notice in your physical body and that would correspond to the change you personally went through so that this piece of fruit could change from one thing to another. So you would have instantaneously relived a particular sequence of your life so that this change could take place. That is creator-functional existence or creatism or creatorism, if you like.

THE MIND SERVES THE BODY

Such things are happening now. They are needed not so much to affect what you think; what you think will have to be conscious and your own choice, free will, as you say. But they are needed so situations that seem to be impossible to resolve will be resolvable not only on the basis of your wishes, dreams, hopes, and prayers but, more to the point, on the basis of what you need to feel physically. Your physical bodies are a much better means for creating benevolent surroundings because they are not attached to a perceived mental sequence that will, in your mind's eye, make you feel better: "If only I can do this, then I will feel so much better." How many of you have ever done something that you thought would make you feel better only to discover that, after the moment of feeling better has passed, you not only didn't feel better but also felt progressively worse? No, your mind's plan for how to cause your body to feel better is the opposite. Better to function allowing your body, your physical body, to make changes that your mind can then notice as simply the reaction, "Oh!"

Your mental capacity is not intended to control your body; it is intended to serve your body. As a servant, it functions well, but as a ruler, it is so far beyond its own depth that it *always* — not sometimes, *always* — becomes self-destructive. Put a child or even an adult in a situation that is extremely overwhelming and demanding, and give that person no relief from it. They will become self-destructive. Consider the mind, in this sense, the child; it is a good servant, an able servant. But if you require it to be a ruler, it will become self-destructive. It's one of the reasons your lives are not as long as you would like them to be: You put yourselves in circumstances, created by your societies, that are unnecessarily authoritarian or have unnecessary amounts of responsibility. Why run a company as one individual when many people working on the team can share the responsibility and move the load around, allowing all people in the company to work smoothly and easily together? That's the whole teamwork concept of running a business, which has proven to be very effective and significantly more profitable than from-the-top-down companies, where people at levels other than the highest levels of responsibility feel like pawns and tend to become angry and destructive because of those feelings. Not what you want in a business!

But that is just a minor thing; more often, these things are found in families. So to create the levels of creatorism that you need to apply — don't just think about applying them; you can't think about it and do it — it is essential that you allow your physical bodies to exert more and more responsibility. They are made up of Mother Earth, who has capacities far beyond your mind's abilities or even possibilities.

COMMUNICATING PHYSICAL ENERGY

This is your information that I am giving you now. I want to reassure you that when mental solutions are not possible, you are given, on a daily basis, proof that other things can solve them. How many times in a relationship have any of you — man and woman, father and son, mother and daughter, father and daughter, mother and son, or any other kind of relationships, such as friendships, business relationships, even sometimes relationships with a pet — noticed that talking just isn't doing it? You go over and touch the other person, and that touch communicates a physical energy from person to person that both parties find very reassuring. I'm not talking about a slap in the face; that's not reassuring for either one! I'm talking about a touch on the hand or the shoulder, and both parties can communicate better. This is not to control each other. How many times in your life can you remember a touch like that, where you knew that it was all right and everything was going to be okay, even though you didn't necessarily understand what the other person was saying? Later, as life proceeded, it became clear.

This has often been the case in the past with people who did not speak the same language. They talked to each other, and that was useless. Why would such a situation exist on a planet where different languages were present? Isn't it so obvious? It is simply because it has always been intended that feelings, meaning what you physically feel, be the ultimate and the foundational element of communication. Sign language, yes, but that is physical. "I don't understand French," says the English-speaking person, and the French-speaking person says, "I don't understand English. What can we do?" "Something urgent needs to be done," one wants to tell the other. You make a gesture that means, "Come this way." Or you touch the person on the shoulder or on the hand in a reassuring fashion, what he or she feels as reassurance. Then when you give your signal to "come this way," he or she is more likely to follow because the physical feeling bodies of both people are not hampered by different languages. The feelings function in the same way.

So you are surrounded with physical evidence to support that physical feelings have the capacity to bring about change within you, within others, and for all life. You are subject to physical realities, and you have the capacity — every one of you physical beings has the capacity — to influence physical reality as well. Now you will be helped to do so with these cords and connections, and you will also find that such cords and connections will help you to live, enjoy life, and experience beauties instead of complications.

MORE PEOPLE FEAR LIFE THAN FEAR DEATH
Won't an additional factor be that the remembering will cut down the fear of death?

You know, one thinks that the extreme fear of death is a big problem, but it is not the biggest problem. The biggest problem is the fear of life. How many people wake up in the morning and initially feel all right, but the more they wake up, the more tense they become because they are afraid about their lives? Think of all the things you are afraid of; you are much more afraid of life than you are of death.

That's why this is necessary. As you say, this ought to help that. That's why it is necessary to support, on the physically felt level, the continuity of life so that even when you are no longer in this physical body, you will feel, not know mentally but feel, that you are going to go on. And since you have been set up to trust your feelings (even though you have times in life when you do not trust them, but overall you do), it will be very reassuring to have that feeling of knowing that you, as you know yourself — not some vague you, but you as you know yourself, your personality — will go on, no matter what. That is very reassuring and will allow you to feel much more confident to live your life on a daily basis and gradually release your fear of living. Then, when you are not so afraid to live, your fear of dying, with that feeling of continuity, will fall away as well.

Great gift, Ssjoooo.

It is helpful, that, and necessary and part of my role in supporting your creator training.

RESPONDING TO A NEED
How did the need get all the way to you? It had to go through the totality and beyond to get to you.

No, no, it does not have to travel over a telegraph cable. Needs are broadcast instantaneously. Do you know that? Many of you are tense walking around among each other because you rationalize, "These are strangers; one could cause harm to me." But the real reason for the tension is that you are feeling each other's needs in every moment. And because you are not consciously, mentally responding to them and your conscious mental mind is disciplining yourself, because of your conditioning and the way you function in your societies, you stop yourself from supporting the needs of those you feel around you. Granted, those needs might not always be benevolent, but they are benevolent more often than anything else. And because you do not serve them, most of you feel tense in crowded situations or even with another person or two on an elevator or staircase or in a room. That's why that tension is present. As you feel the continuum more, you will not feel quite so tense around each other. That will take longer, but it will happen.

We're going to feel the continuum as a felt feeling?

Existence, not just in some vague sense but actually a sense of your own personality's continuum so that you will feel a personal connection to this continuum, not a vague sense of "life goes on, maybe." That's a thought; this will be a feeling, a reassuring feeling. Very helpful, meaning that you can feel, as your own personality, that not only is there a place for you in the universe but the universe and all universes are your home. You can be at home wherever you are, and you have been home in many other places. It is a wonderful feeling. It is not accompanied by those thoughts, but if you have those thoughts, the feeling will be there. It's very reassuring, and you need it now so that you can have easier access to a unified feeling among you all.

These unified feelings will be able to create transformation on the creator level, even though it will be unconscious, for the most part initially — meaning you will not recall how you did it — or subconscious — meaning you will have feelings associated with doing it, possibly dreams symbolically associated with doing it, such as dreams and dream symbols and scenarios, or even some vague thoughts that you might have somehow been involved in accomplishing some wonderful thing that you won't take personal credit. "I did it!" It won't be "I," but there will be a sense that you had something to do with it in a benevolent way, not just having contributed to the problem with everyone else. So that will help you, in that sense, to move beyond the need to be externally saved.

"When is that person coming who will save us all so that we don't have to do anything?" That is the whole purpose of that person having come in the first place: so you would do it yourselves. That person is not just one being; rather, it is the whole desire to have an external, loving God/teacher who saves you. The whole purpose of Creator God is that Creator God becomes internalized on a physically felt level, so you can walk in the footsteps of Creator and walk with Creator by being a portion of Creator — not by following Creator's orders. That was all right for a time, but you cannot follow a creator's orders and be one yourself.

Are you sort of checking in and watching?

No. I do not need to watch it. The only reason to watch it would be to make corrections; that is not my job. My job is to initiate, and then things happen from that.

So this is a whole new thing. You know, there's the Creator and the friends of the Creator and the Council of Creators and all that. This is a whole new, spontaneous response that wasn't in the plan or in the action plan?

I am not all-power, all-omniscient; I am not singularly responsible for all things. No one being is singularly responsible for all things. What I am saying is that I responded to a need, period. That need might have been in the plan, but it wasn't a plan I knew about, or it might not have been in a plan. It does not matter; I do not feel it matters.

It's needed. You've done it, and it's magnificent. It should be interesting. Maybe we can ask people to report on their experience.

Possibly, but it might not be till the end of the year that people will be able to do that. Nevertheless, if you wish to do that, that is up to you.

Zoosh said that a portion of our energy was being used to create unity on the planet, so that we would eventually feel every other being and feel their needs and be forced to help them because we would feel their pain.

That would have preceded this.

So is that ongoing, then? Is this taking the place of that, or is that continuing?

You would have to ask Zoosh that, but from my perspective, I can see how one would follow the other. Well, the intention ultimately is that you share energies. When you withhold responding to each other's needs, you are not just not doing something for somebody else, but you are also not giving them the energy. Maybe the doing, for them, might simply mean a touch; you walk over, touch them on the shoulder, and walk on, for instance. And that shared energy allows them to respond, to do something that they couldn't do before or perhaps didn't have the confidence to do before. It is not a mental thing. It might be something that functions physically and that does not require you to provide thoughts or words with the touch. But because you are conditioned to not do that in your society of today, you also do not receive energy from others. It's not just that you're not giving energy; you're not receiving energy. So part of the reason you don't have that extra energy that you need is that you need to have a means of unifying your energy that goes beyond the manners and mores of a conditioned society, all right? Yes, you need to touch each other more, but if you're not going to do it, what good does it do me or anyone to say that you need to do this? It doesn't benefit you, and it doesn't benefit me. So something else needs to be set up.

TOUCHING CREATES A TEMPORARY CONTINUUM

This continuum will allow you to feel more reassured and physically self-confident, yes. Then if somebody touches you to reassure you — not in some inappropriate way, but on the shoulder, on the hand, or in the case of a youngster, perhaps on the head, something like that — either purposely or perhaps you are jostled. It would not seem like a bad thing. If you do not fear it, it is a way to allow you to get through — not past, not over, but through — your fear of external threat. Now, this is more than what is happening right now. But what is happening right now is also preceding something else. In time, when you function, things happen that precede other things. When you look back, you can say, "I can see clearly how that helped to set up this, what we are doing." You do not always look forward and say, "What we are doing is going to help set up something else in the future," but of course, that's what it is.

In the society where people are not afraid of each other and where they are mutually nurturing and supportive, when you see someone who is downcast, the first thing you think of doing is not to say, "What's wrong?" That's a way of keeping people from touching each other, even though it might seem caring. It is an example of the caring person's method who is functioning in a *don't touch* society. That's what you can do. That's why you've transferred those duties of touching each other to the mental self. That's how the mind shows that it cares. "What's wrong? How can I help?" Like that. But in a society that does not have such conditioning, you don't even say, "What's wrong?" You walk over, and you put your hand on the person's shoulder (the reassuring gesture, yes?) or on the arm or the hand. You don't even have to say, "How can I help?" The touch alone says it, and it gives reassurance and shares your physical energy. You are intended to touch each other. You don't have to touch each other inappropriately or in ways that are not kind. The whole purpose of being physical (wouldn't you agree?) is to touch. You touch things. Why be physical if you're not going to touch or be touched? What's the advantage? To use the feelings. There are many senses that do not involve touch, but touch, is one of the most important.

When young people go to a rock concert or older people go to an opera or any place you gather together where there is a group energy formed (I hadn't thought of that before — maybe one of the attractions is that without touching there is a shared energy) there is a sense of support. Is that true?

Yes, but think back to the way people went to events in the past. The seats were not individualized; there were benches. Granted, they weren't as comfortable, even when they were padded, but in a crowded situation, what's going on? You are all touching each other. You are sitting on a bench, and whether you want to or not, you are touching the hip of the person next to you. That's why churches used to be like that, because you would physically form a unity. That was understood, at least by the minister sometimes. So this has been discouraged in recent times when people feel more nervous around each other because the idea of touching or being touched, in your society especially, has taken on other connotations, because of so much touching going on that is not fun, meaning violence, or is inappropriate because it's meant for some other occasion with some other person and so on. When you have a friend or a loved one, often the most reassuring and comforting thing is a simple touch, and that's what shares and communicates that physical energy.

That moment, from person to person, creates at least a temporary continuum. That's what's so appealing about it. But when you have the continuum on the feeling level that's going to happen now, this year, it makes it more comfortable, more easy, and more calm, and it also will allow more touching without so much fear — not immediately, but it will come, that feeling, universally, by all human beings and even for those of you who are perceptive, from animal to human or plant to human. Some of you might notice it with pets. When some of you go to an old or a new friend's or even an acquaintance's house where there is a dog, the dog might become less, as you say, territorial or, more to the point, become friendlier. Yes, smelling you and, yes, tasting you the way dogs do, to know what you're feeling, to know whether you're someone to be afraid of, to know whether you're someone to defend against, or to know whether you're a friend.

This is something humans used to do, and in some societies, they still do it: smell, taste, know physically — not just, "He's wearing the wrong color," or "She's not speaking my language," or "He looks different from me." None of that. Smell, taste, touch, and know: animals, humans, the same. I'm not saying you ought to do that; just recognize that what the animal does, you can do. The animal is licking you, tasting you: tasting your sweat, your body oils and, to some degree, the energy of your body through physical contact. The animal, then, knows how to react to you not just instinctually but through its full body of knowledge.

To put this into context, all of this that you're discussing — the separation, the not touching, the lack of connection to the continuum — was the Explorer Race training of separation and individuality, right? And now we're coming out of that?

It was the preconditions that allowed you to do the precreation training. The information can be found in the Explorer Race books, but the Explorer Race was not programmed like that. Rather, things that were naturally your own were temporarily set aside from you so that you would have to re-create and resolve. But now you do not have to nor is it desirable.

Now, the exciting thing is — you just mentioned it briefly — that this is going to lead to the lack of fear of an external threat, which is going to lead to a feeling of safety, which is what we need to expand our hearts and move to the next dimension, right?

Yes, but more appropriately, to cure the ills that are on your planet now. You don't just say, "Okay, let's get out of here because I don't like it." You create a benevolent society for all beings here first, and then you stand back and look at it and feel good about what you did. Now, on the analogy level, doesn't that sound familiar? To stand back and look at it and feel good about what you did? Where have you heard that before?

When the Creator created the creation.

That's right, because the whole point of standing back and feeling good about it and looking at what you did is to experience the full-bodied feeling of unity, meaning all of your bodies in physical union, having the sense of safety and the ability to touch each other in safe and good ways. You will know what it feels like to be a creator.

The lack of a feeling of threat is going to lead to peace?

Well, let's just say one of the results is peace. That might not be the most important part, but I could see why it is a strong motivator. Peace is good, but there is more. Creation is not always peaceful. When you are peaceful, you often are calm and sometimes motionless. As you can see, creation is sometimes other things.

I know that on other planets things get calm and stagnant, but here, coming to peace would be a step toward helping to clean up the planet and solve the other problems we have created.

Peace is good, but it's not everything. It's one of the good things, but there are many things that are good and are not, in the moment, peaceful. Romance, love — it's not always peaceful, but that doesn't mean it isn't good.

CHILDREN ARE YOUR MOST IMPORTANT INVESTMENTS

What I did is a very small thing, and it is no bigger than what any one of you as individual beings can do. Say, you see a child on the street (in your society, it needs to be someone you know) who's downcast. Maybe the other children have made fun of him. You go over, you touch him lightly on his shoulder, and you say, "What's wrong, Johnny?" And maybe, if he knows you, he tells you. Maybe he doesn't know you, but he still tells you. Then you give him a pep talk. If you know him, you tell him the good things he can do based on what you know about him: "Ah, but you're really good at this! And I've seen you; you're really good at that!" And he says, "Oh, yeah, but anybody can do that." And then you remind him, with your knowledge as an adult simply from living life, "No, you think everyone can do that because you can do it easily, but it's not true!

There are things you can do easily and you will get better at because they are part of your talent, and other people struggle with these things. Someday you will contribute what you have to offer to the world in a way that the world will appreciate and recognize. So don't worry about what the other kids say. I see the good things in you, the talents and the abilities in you," and you name a couple of them, if you know the youngster. "And someday others will see this and admire it too. Just like you see things in your friends or acquaintances or even people you don't know, you see things the other kids can do that you wish you could do — maybe they will become well-known for those things too. But since you have things you can do, you don't need to do the things they do. You can all help each other, doing what you do best." You don't have to add that, but you will know it. You don't have to lecture children; you just need to encourage them. Children need to be encouraged. You can't say, "I love you" to a child once, and that's it. You have to encourage them. Say "I love you" more than once. Some children need to be told more than once in a day. If they need it, you'll know. So don't be shy.

I mention this because what you might do in that situation, to tell that child that, is no less than what I did. It's exactly the same. You do something that, for all you know, will alter the life of this child forever. And it might make him feel better about himself, and who knows the good he will do someday? You might never know, but something good could come of it. You don't know, but it is a good investment. Children are your most important investments because they will not only inherit what you leave them but also create someday in ways that affect all your people that will come, and they might even be creating, someday, when you are old and need younger people to look out for you. Won't you want the Johnnies and the Janes and the Melindas and all of the children of this world reassured and confident about themselves so that they can provide what they can do well? If not one thing, then another? Children are your most important investments.

I think that is enough for today. Good night.

ABOUT THE AUTHOR

ROBERT SHAPIRO is largely known as a professional trance channel, who has channeled several series of published books. But, as he is now, he is a mystical man with shamanic capabilities well and thoroughly infused into him. He also has many unusual skills that he teaches through blogs, the *Sedona Journal of Emergence!*, and books. It is his intention to bring about the most benevolent change available on the planet now through sharing his personal inspirations as well as his channeling.

His great contributions to a better understanding of the history, purpose, and future of humanity on Earth are his epochal works:

- *The Explorer Race* Series
- *The Shining the Light* Series
- *The Shamanic Secrets* Series
- *The Ultimate UFO* Series
- *The Secrets of Feminine Science* Series

THE EXPLORER RACE SERIES

ZOOSH AND OTHERS THROUGH ROBERT SHAPIRO

Superchannel Robert Shapiro can communicate with any personality anywhere and any-when. He has been a professional channel for over twenty-five years and channels with an exceptionally clear and profound connection.

The Origin... The Purpose...The Future...of Humanity

If you have ever questioned about **who you really are, why you are here** as part of humanity on this miraculous planet, and **what it all means**, these books in the Explorer Race series can begin to supply the answers — the answers to these and other questions about the mystery and enigma of physical life on Earth.

These answers come from beings who speak through superchannel Robert Shapiro, beings who range from particle personalities to the Mother of All Beings and the thirteen Ssjooo, from advisors to the Creator of our universe to the generators of precreation energies. **The scope, the immensity, the mind-boggling infinitude of these chronicles by beings who live in realms beyond our imagination, will hold you enthralled.** Nothing even close to the magnitude of the depth and power of this all-encompassing, expanded picture of reality has ever been published.

This amazing story of the greatest adventure of all time and creation is the story of the Explorer Race, all of humanity on Earth and those who came before us who are waiting for us. The Explorer Race is a group of souls whose journeys resulted in incarnations in this loop of time on planet Earth, where, bereft of any memory of their immortal selves and most of their heart energy, they came to learn compassion, to learn to take responsibility for the consequences of their actions, and to solve creation's previously unsolvable dilemma of negativity. We humans have found a use for negativity: We use it for lust for life and adventure, curiosity and creativity, and doing the undoable. And in a few years, we will go out to the stars with our insatiable drive and ability to respond to change and begin to inspire the benign but stagnant civilizations out there to expand and change and grow, which will eventually result in the change and expansion of all creation.

Once you understand the saga of the Explorer Race and what the success of the Explorer Race Experiment means to the totality of creation, **you will be proud to be a human and to know that you are a vital component of the greatest story ever told** — a continuing drama whose adventure continues far into the future.

☥ *Light Technology* PUBLISHING *Presents*

THROUGH ROBERT SHAPIRO

ORIGINS and the NEXT 50 YEARS
Book 3

This volume has so much information about who we are and where we came from — the source of male and female beings, the war of the sexes, the beginning of the linear mind, feelings, the origin of souls — it is a treasure trove. In addition there is a section that relates to our near future — how the rise of global corporations and politics affects our future, how to use benevolent magic as a force of creation, and then how we will go out to the stars and affect other civilizations. Astounding information!

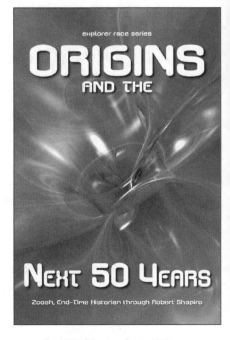

explorer race series

ORIGINS
AND THE
NEXT 50 YEARS
Zoosh, End-Time Historian through Robert Shapiro

$14.95 • Softcover • 384 PP.
978-0-929385-95-2

CHAPTERS INCLUDE
- Our Creator and Its Creation
- The White Race and the Andromedan Linear Mind
- The Asian Race, the Keepers of Zeta Vertical Thought
- The African Race and Its Sirius/Orion Heritage
- The Fairy Race and the Native Peoples of the North
- The Australian Aborigines, Advisors of the Sirius System
- The Return of the Lost Tribe of Israel The Body of the Child, a Pleiadian Heritage
- Creating Sexual Balance for Growth
- The Origin of Souls
- The Next 50 Years

- The New Corporate Model
- The Practice of Feeling
- Benevolent Magic
- Future Politics
- A Visit to the Creator of All Creators
- Approaching the One

THROUGH ROBERT SHAPIRO

PARTICLE PERSONALITIES
Book 5

All around you in every moment you are surrounded by the most magical and mystical beings. They are too small for you to see as single individuals. But in groups, they form all of your physical life as you know it.

Particles — who might be considered either atoms or portions of atoms — consciously view the vast spectrum of reality yet also have a sense of personal memory like your own linear memory. Unlike your linear memory, where you remember the order of events you have lived, these particles remember where they have been and what they have done in their long, long lives and can access the higher strains associated with their experiences as well.

For instance, perhaps at one time a particle might have been a portion of a tree, when it had access to all the tree's higher wisdom and knowledge, what it had been before or might be in the future. Or perhaps it might have been in the ocean. The knowledge of anything swimming past it or growing or simply existing nearby would also be available to it. So a particle has not only its own personal wisdom but anything or anyone it has ever passed through.

Particles, then, have a unique and unusual perspective. In reading this book, understand that some of them will have similar points of view. But others will have quite extraordinary and unexpected points of view. Expect the unexpected!

$14.95 • Softcover • 256 PP.
978-0-929385-97-6

CHAPTERS INCLUDE

- A Particle of Gold
- The Model Maker: the Clerk
- The Clerk, a Mountain Lion Particle, a Particle of Liquid Light, and an Ice Particle
- A Particle of Rose Quartz from a Floating Crystal City
- A Particle of Uranium, Earth's Mind
- A Particle of the Great Pyramid's Capstone
- A Particle of the Dimensional Boundary between Orbs
- A Particle of Healing Energy

THROUGH ROBERT SHAPIRO

EXPLORER RACE and BEYOND
Book 6

In our continuing exploration of how creation works, we talk to Creator of Pure Feelings and Thoughts, the Liquid Domain, the Double-Diamond Portal, and the other 93 percent of the Explorer Race. We revisit the Friends of the Creator to discuss their origin and how they see the beyond. We finally reach the roots of the Explorer Race (us!) and find we are from a source different from our Creator and have a different goal. We end up talking to All That Is!

$14.95 • Softcover • 384 PP.
978-1-891824-06-7

CHAPTERS INCLUDE

- Creator of Pure Feelings and Thoughts, One Circle of Creation
- The Liquid Domain
- The Double-Diamond Portal
- About the Other 93% of the Explorer Race
- Synchronizer of Physical Reality and Dimensions
- The Master of Maybe
- Master of Frequencies and Octaves
- Spirit of Youthful Enthusiasm (Junior) and Master of Imagination
- Zoosh
- The Master of Feeling
- The Master of Plasmic Energy
- The Master of Discomfort
- The Story-Gathering Root Being from the Library of Light/Knowledge
- The Root Who Fragmented from a Living Temple
- The First Root Returns
- Root Three, Companion of the Second Root
- The Temple of Knowledge & the Giver of Inspiration
- The Voice Historian, Who Provided the First Root
- Creator of All That Is

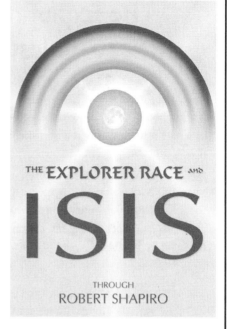

THROUGH ROBERT SHAPIRO

The Explorer Race and Jesus Book 9

In this book, I will make an effort to speak of who I really am, where I'm from, what I'm doing now, why I went to Earth, what I hoped to accomplish, what I really did accomplish and perhaps other things. I want to try to explain why things happened, why people did "this" or "that" during my lifetime. I will try to fill in details.

— Jesus

The immortal personality who lived the life we know as Jesus, along with his students and friends, describes with clarity and love his life and teaching on Earth 2,000 years ago.

These beings lovingly offer their experiences of the events that happened then and of Jesus's time-traveling adventures, especially to other planets and to the nineteenth and twentieth centuries, which he called the time of the machines — the time of troubles.

It is so heartwarming and interesting that you won't want to put it down.

$16.95 • Softcover • 352 PP.
978-1-891824-14-2

- The Teachings and Travels
- A Student's Time with Jesus and His Tales of Jesus's Time Travels
- The Shamanic Use of the Senses
- Many Journeys, Many Disguises
- The Child Student Who Became a Traveling Singer-Healer
- Learning to Invite Matter to Transform Itself
- Inviting Water, Singing Colors
- Learning about Different Cultures and People
- The Role of Mary Magdalene, a Romany
- Jesus's Autonomous Parts, His Bloodline, and His Plans

CHAPTERS INCLUDE

- Jesus's Core Being, His People, and the Interest of Four of Them in the Earth
- Jesus's Home World, Their Love Creations, and the Four Who Visited Earth
- The "Facts" of Jesus's Life Here, His Future Return

THROUGH ROBERT SHAPIRO

Earth History and Lost Civilizations Explained
Book 10

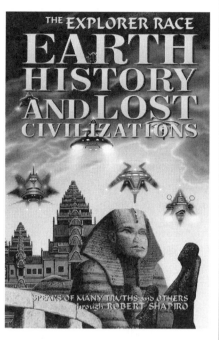

THE EXPLORER RACE

EARTH HISTORY AND LOST CIVILIZATIONS

SPEAKS OF MANY TRUTHS and OTHERS
through ROBERT SHAPIRO

Speaks of Many Truths and Zoosh, through Robert Shapiro, explain that planet Earth, the only water planet in this solar system, is on loan from Sirius as a home and school for humanity, the Explorer Race.

Earth's recorded history goes back only a few thousand years, its archaelogical history a few thousand more. Now this book opens up the past as if a light is turned on in the darkness, and we see the incredible panorama of brave souls coming from other planets to settle on different parts of Earth. We watch the origins of tribal groups and the rise and fall of civilizations, and we can begin to understand the source of the wonderous diversity of plants, animals, and humans that we enjoy here on beautiful Mother Earth.

$14.95 • Softcover • 320 PP.
978-1-891824-20-3

CHAPTERS INCLUDE

- When Earth was Sirius
- Ancient Artifacts Explained
- Fire and Ice People and Multidimensional Lightbeings
- Early Civilizations on Earth: Mongollians and Desert People
- The Long Journey of Jehovah's Ship, from Orion to Sirius to Earth
- Andazi Teach Jehovah How to Create Human Beings
- The Academy of All Peoples: Cave Paintings, Symbols, and Crop Circles
- Sumer, an Art Colony from Sirius
- Nazca Lines Radiate Enthusiasm for Life
- Easter Island Statues: a Gift for the Future
- Lucy and her Laetoli Footprints
- Egypt and Cats as Teachers of Humans
- The Electrical Beings
- The Andromedan Origins of Stone Medicine Wheels
- Carnac in Brittany
- Egypt
- China
- Tibet and Japan
- Siberia

Light Technology PUBLISHING Presents

THROUGH ROBERT SHAPIRO

ET Visitors Speak,
Volume 1 • Book 11

Even as you are searching the sky for extra-terrestrials and their spaceships, ETs are here on planet Earth. They are stranded, visiting, exploring, studying culture, healing Earth of trauma brought on by irresponsible mining, or reasearching the history of Christianity over the past 2000 years.

Some are in human guise. Some are in spirit form. Some look like what we call animals as they come from the species home planet and interact with those of their fellow beings that we have labeled cats or cows or elephants.

Some are brilliant cosmic mathematicians with a sense of humor presently living here as penguins; some are fledgling diplomats training for future postings on Earth when we have ET embassies here. In this book, these fascinating beings share their thoughts, origins, and purposes for being here.

CHAPTERS INCLUDE

- Stranded Sirian Lightbeing Observes Earth for 800 Years
- An Orion Being Talks about Life on Earth As a Human
- A Sentient Redwood
- Qua Comes to View Origin and Evolution of Christianity
- Qua's Experiences Studying Religion on Earth
- Qua on Mormonism
- Observer Helps Cats Accomplish Their Purpose: Initiating Humans

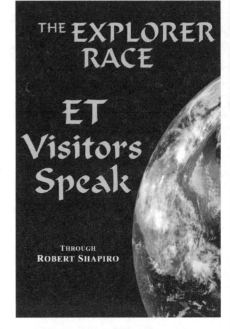

THE EXPLORER RACE

ET Visitors Speak

THROUGH
ROBERT SHAPIRO

$14.95 • Softcover • 352 PP.
978-1-891824-28-9

- A Warrior of Light, the Ultimate Ally
- Penguins: Humorous Mathematicians
- Xri from the Ninth Dimension
- Nurturing the Birth Cord
- Sixth-Dimensional Cha-Cha Dances with Humans
- Starlight for Regeneration of Earth's Crystal Veins
- ET Resource Specialist Maps and Heals Planetary Bodies
- The Creation and Preparation of the Resource Specialists' Ships: Part 3
- Future Zeta Diplomat Learns to Communicate with Humans
- Sirius Water-Being: a Bridge between ETs and Humans
- The Rock Being Here to Experience Movement

THROUGH ROBERT SHAPIRO

Techniques for Generating Safety Book 12

EXPLORER RACE
Techniques for GENERATING SAFETY

CREATE A SAFE LIFE AND A SAFE WORLD

THROUGH ROBERT SHAPIRO

The opportunity to change the way you live is not only close at hand but also with you right now. Some of you have felt a change in the air, as you say, the winds of change. Sometimes you can almost taste it or smell it or feel it. And other times it is ephemeral, hard to grasp. It is the ephemeral quality that can help you to know that the good thing that is out of your reach has to do with the future timeline. The future timeline is also an experience line. It is a sensation line. It is associated with the way your physical body communicates to you and others. It is a way of increasing your sensitivity to your own needs and the needs of others in a completely safe and protected way so that you can respond more quickly and accurately to those needs and appreciate the quality of life around you, much of which you miss because the old timeline discourages you from observing. It encourages you to study and understand, but it discourages you from feeling. And it is feeling that is the ultimate answer to your discomforts as well as the pathway to true benevolent insight and fulfillment. When you read this book, know that it is intended to give you the gift of ease that comes with the simpler path, the less complicated path — the path without attachments.

$9.95 • Softcover • 208 PP.
978-1-891824-26-5

CHAPTERS INCLUDE

- Zero Four
- The Traveler
- The Fluid of Time
- Ordinator of Souls
- The Energy Three
- The Mother of All Beings
- Benevolent Magic to Move the Future to You
- The Love-Heat Exercise
- Creating Safety in Your Life
- A Lesson in Benevolent Magic
- Claiming the Good Life

THROUGH ROBERT SHAPIRO

Astrology
Book 14

The planets and signs of astrology speak to us through superchannel Robert Shapiro — sharing not only **LONG-LOST INFORMATION** but also **NEW WAYS OF BEING** for an awakening humanity.

Astrology and astronomy are one. The heart is astrology; the mind is astronomy. But you would not, in your own personality, separate your heart from your mind, would you?

This book honors that pursuit of the lost heart. It demonstrates the personality of the planets, the Sun, the Moon, the signs. This is what has been missing in astrology ever since the heart was set aside in favor of the mind. Over time, such knowledge and wisdom was lost. This book brings all that back. It allows astrologers to feel the planets, to feel the Sun, the Moon, and the signs. This is not to abandon the knowledge and wisdom they have now but to truly include, to show, to demonstrate, to provide to those seeking astrological knowledge and wisdom, to provide the heart elements of personality.

As the planets and signs speak through Robert, their personality traits and interests, (many of which have been unknown since ancient times) can be clearly heard and felt. In addition, you — humanity — have made such progress that other new energies and traits of the planets and signs are expressed through their words. These energies, traits, and characteristics were only potential in earlier times but now are becoming available to you to become aware of and to express within your life on Earth as you awaken to your natural self.

$29.95 • Softcover • 704 PP.
978-1-891824-81-4

CHAPTERS INCLUDE
- Isis and the sun
- The Sun
- The Moon
- Chon-deh, Sun Helper
- Saturn
- Jupiter
- Pluto
- Neptune
- Astrology Expert
- Venus
- Mercury
- Mars
- Mars and Grandfather
- Unknown Planet to Stabilize Earth's Orbit
- Planet Axis
- Isis
- Uranus
- Seeker—Milky Way Galaxy
- Astrological Historian
- Mother Earth
- Virgo
- Gemini
- Etcheta
- Pisces
- Taurus
- Aquarius
- Leo
- Sagittarius
- Aries
- Libra
- The 13th Sign
- Capricorn
- Cancer
- Scorpio
- The 10th Planet
- The 11th Planet
- The 12th Planet
- Teacher of Astrology
- Reveals the Mysteries

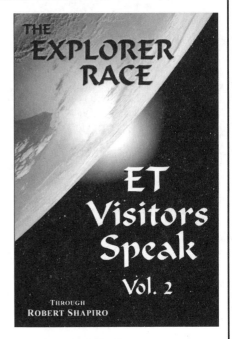

THROUGH ROBERT SHAPIRO

Plant Souls Speak
Book 16

Planet Energies Available to You:
Live Plant 100% • Dead Plant 10%

"What we intend to speak about — if I may speak in general for all plants — is how you can interact with plants in a more benevolent way for you as the human species. For a long time, you have been clear on medicinal uses of leaves and stems and seeds and flower petals and so on, but you are only getting about one-tenth of the energy available to you that way. It is always better to interact with the plant and its energies in its live form, but you need to know how.

"The intention of this book is to reveal that formula so that you can stop searching, as a human race, for the magical cures to diseases by exhausting the supply of life forms around you when a much simpler process is available. The beings in this book will not just comment on things you know about but show you what you are missing in your interaction with plants."

— Dandelion

In this book, the plant world will speak through elders. This has certain advantages, allowing them to include knowledge and wisdom about their home planets. In this way, you will learn some of the old wisdom again, shared so that you can discover how to interact with the plants while they are alive, while they are a portion of the Creator of All Things.

With this, you will learn the beginnings, the reminders, and for many of you, the fulfillment of the transformation of that which does not work in your body, in your life, in your community, and in your world: the transformation of what you call dis-ease or disharmony into harmony and ease.

—Zoosh, Isis, and Grandfather

Each plant brings a wondrous gift to share with humanity—enjoy it!

$24.95 • Softcover • 576 PP.
978-1-891824-74-6

CHAPTERS INCLUDE
- Cherry Tree
- Maple Tree
- Palm Tree
- Peach Tree
- Pine Tree
- Redwood
- Walnut Tree
- Brown Rice
- Crabgrass
- Oat Grass
- Wetland Grass
- Angelica
- Bamboo
- Corn
- Daffodil
- Dandelion
- Hibiscus
- Holly
- Ivy
- Kelp
- Marijuana
- Orchid
- Rose
- Sage
- Soy Bean
- White Rose

THROUGH ROBERT SHAPIRO

ETs on Earth, Volume 1 Book 18

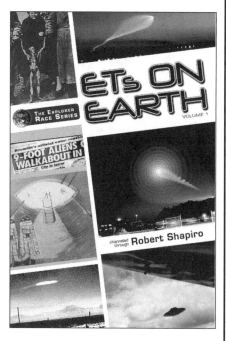

Greetings. This is Zoosh.

In the beginning of the Explorer Race adventure — that means you, all humans on Earth — way back, ETs on Earth were a normal thing. In fact, you were ETs who came from many different planets those thousands of years ago, and you felt that Earth was a wonderful place where you could thrive.

I want you to keep that in mind when you read about these ETs that happen to be still visiting Earth. In this book, as well as in other books that have material like this, if you can keep that in mind, it will not be too surprising or shocking. In fact, for most of you, you will be ETs again in another life and your youngsters just might be ETs from Earth visiting other planets in the future.

This should be a fun read and a gentle reminder that ETs are just friends from some place — you might say from another neighborhood.

Good life.

$16.95 • Softcover • 352 PP.
978-1-891824-91-3

Chapters Include
- ET Beings Use Green Light to Support Earth Beings
- Humans Are Going through Rapid Changes on Earth
- Update on ETs and UFOs
- Blue Spiral Light over Norway
- A Glimpse Beyond the Explorer Race
- Will There Be a Phony ET Invasion on Earth? Orbs Are Lightbeings Visiting Benevolent Spaces
- You Traverse to Your Home Planet in Deep Sleep
- The "Little People" Are Humans from Alpha Centauri
- Beware of a Staged ET Invasion
- Crop Circles: Origins, Purposes, and Mysteries

THROUGH ROBERT SHAPIRO

ETs on Earth, Volume 2 Book 21

You've noticed lately — haven't you? — that for the past few years, UFOs and phenomena in the skies are all over the place. Well, hold on to your hats! You can be pretty sure this is only going to increase in its frequency in the skies. In this book, you'll be able to read a little bit about who the beings in the UFOs are, where they're from, why they're here, and so on.

In the future, it won't just be airplane pilots reporting on these things. You'll be talking about it among yourselves because regular folks just like you will be seeing these ships. This time, don't keep it quiet. Just talk about it with your neighbors or your friends online. It gives other people permission to believe what they saw. People have been taught, you know, not to believe what they see. So you can believe it.

$16.95 • Softcover • 416 PP.
978-1-62233-003-4

Chapters Include

- Dolphins: Creators of Time Bridges
- Physical Feelings Are the Language of Physicality
- ET Sightings Will Increase as Earth Becomes More Benevolent
- Pleiadians Request ETs' Help in Project to Help Humans Awaken
- The Mountain Energies Are a Gift to Amplify Your Consciousness
- ETs Disarmed Nuclear Missiles
- ET Colonizers of Chinese See Promising Signs
- Fake ET Invasion — Why?
- On 1–11–11, a New Stable Pathway to the Next Dimension Was Created

⚜ *Light Technology* PUBLISHING *Presents*

SHINING THE LIGHT
BOOK SERIES
THROUGH ROBERT SHAPIRO ·

A CLOSER LOOK AT THE SERIES

The most significant events in Earth's history are happening in secret. Despite official denial and tactics of derision, inquiring minds are demanding the truth. This truth is stranger than all the fictions about ETs, alien bases, and the secret government. World-renowned authors Robert Shapiro, Tom Dongo, Dorothy Roeder, Arthur Fanning, Lyssa Royal Holt, and Lee Carroll shed some light on these controversial and misunderstood topics. The battle in the heavens has begun. Become aware of the truth, and don't get lost in the drama. Be the light that you are, and you will be forever free.

THE BATTLE BEGINS!

This courageous book shines the light to expose truths that will change forever how we view our lives on this planet. It asks the reader to join in the investigations, ask the questions, and think the unthinkable. Explore the truth about the controllers of Earth and their alien allies. Discover the updated news about what is happening on the third dimension and what it means from the higher dimensions' perspective.

$12.95, 224 PP. • Softcover
ISBN 978-0-929385-66-2

THE BATTLE CONTINUES

This book continues the story of the secret government and alien involvement and provides information about the photon belt, cosmic holograms photographed in the sky, a new vortex forming near Sedona, and nefarious mining on sacred Hopi land. Learn the current status of the secret government and those who want to usurp its power. Discover actual cosmic photographs of hidden crafts, beings, and events. The truth becomes even stranger as the story of alien involvement in Earth history continues.

$14.95, 432 PP. • Softcover
ISBN 978-0-929385-70-9

HUMANITY GETS A SECOND CHANCE

The focus shifts from the dastardly deeds of the secret government to humanity's role in creation. Earth receives unprecedented aid from Creator and cosmic councils, who recently lifted us beyond the third dimension to avert a great catastrophe. Humanity begins to learn to render the sinister secret government powerless by being the light that it is.

$14.95, 480 PP. • Softcover
ISBN 978-0-929385-71-6

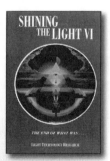

ANDROMEDA

The Andromedans and Zoosh through Robert Shapiro

The Andromedans who originally contacted the Professor speak through superchannel Robert Shapiro and again give instructions that will allow trained scientists to construct a shield around existing Earth planes so that Earth astronauts can fly to Mars or to the stars.

The Andromedans also tell what really happened on their journeys and on Earth, and they clear up questions one would have after reading the English or Spanish version of the previous book — the text of which follows the channeling in this book.

In addition, they supply a lively account of their lives on their home planet in the Andromedan constellation of our galaxy.

Ultimate UFO Series:
ANDROMEDA
Channeled Commentary by
ANDROMEDANS & ZOOSH THROUGH
Robert Shapiro

Andromedan Ship - Passaic - New Jersey

Includes the Text of UFO CONTACT FROM ANDROMEDA
EXTRATERRESTRIAL PROPHECY
UFO Books: Rodriguez • Hernandez • Stevens

⚜ LIGHT

The eight-foot-tall, highly mental crew members of the ship who speak include:

- Leia, the beautiful cultural specialist and social diplomat who so intrigued the Professor
- Cheswa, the cultural liason
- G-dansa, Leia's daughter, equivalent to an eight-year-old ET Eloise
- Duszan, the Junior Scientist
- Onzo, the Senior Scientist and Crew Leader, the youngest yet genetically modified to be the most brilliant of the crew
- Playmate, a two-foot-tall, roly-poly Andromedan who teaches communion of heart and mind

Chapters Include:

- Our Ancestors Came from Space
- Extraterrestrial Concepts of Energy
- Reviewing the Past and Feelings
- Early Visits to Earth
- Antimatter
- Our Explosive Atmosphere
- On Space Travel
- ET View of Our Religion
- Life and Death of Planets
- Changes Overcome Me
- The Extraterrestrial Photographed

$16⁹⁵
464 PP. • SOFTCOVER
ISBN 978-1-891824-35-7

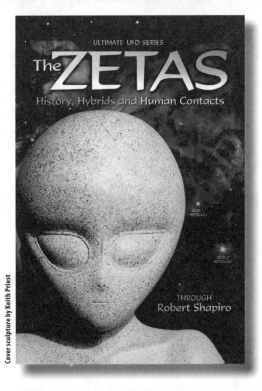